International Institute for Educational Planning

THE PROCESS OF *Educational* INNOVATION
An international perspective

Raymond S Adams with David Chen

Kogan Page/The Unesco Press

**The Process of Educational Innovation:
An International Perspective**

International Institute for Educational Planning

The Process of Educational Innovation: An International Perspective

*Raymond S Adams
with David Chen*

Kogan Page Ltd, London/The Unesco Press, Paris

LB
1027
·A255

First published 1981 by the
United Nations Educational, Scientific
and Cultural Organization,
7, place de Fontenoy, 75700 Paris
and Kogan Page Limited,
120 Pentonville Road, London N1 9JN

© Unesco 1981

ISBN 0 85038 511 3 (Kogan Page)
ISBN 92-803-1096-8 (Unesco)

Printed in the United Kingdom by The Anchor Press Ltd
and bound by Wm Brendon & Son Ltd,
both of Tiptree, Essex

British Library Cataloguing in Publication Data

Adams, Raymond S.
   The process of educational innovation.
   1. Educational innovations
   I. Title   II. Chen, David
   370   LB1027

   ISBN 0-85038-511-3

Acknowledgement

This book owes its existence to the particular efforts of seventeen people from seven different countries – and to the spirit of cooperation and consideration that characterized their work together.

N O Anim	Ghana
Abdul Hamid bin Ayob	Malaysia
P W Boag	New Zealand
Georgiana R Hedd	Sierra Leone
C G N Hill	New Zealand
J Hoffman	Federal Republic of Germany
K Bassa Kwansa	Ghana
R Ibrahim	Indonesia
A F Labor	Sierra Leone
Syed Omar bin Syed Ahmad	Malaysia
B P F Smith	New Zealand
Haji Ahmad bin Haji Salleh	Malaysia
I Schacham	Israel
B Soeprapto	Indonesia
W Spies	Federal Republic of Germany
D Chen	Israel
R S Adams	New Zealand

Contents

Foreword	ix
Introduction	1
Chapter 1. Point of Departure	7
Chapter 2. Indonesia: Quality in Quantity	31
Chapter 3. The Federal Republic of Germany: Successive Approximations	57
Chapter 4. Sierra Leone: Creating a Context	81
Chapter 5. Israel: A Total Approach	107
Chapter 6. Malaysia: An Experiment in Systematic Adaptation	140
Chapter 7. New Zealand: Institutional Inertia	169
Chapter 8. Ghana: Implementation by Osmosis	199
Chapter 9. Findings	223
Chapter 10. Conclusions	256
Bibliography	283

Foreword

The International Institute for Educational Planning takes great pleasure in presenting to readers this major work on the process of innovation in education, written by Professor Raymond Adams, of Massey University (New Zealand) and David Chen. Seven national research teams have contributed to this book. The project, which sprang from a first seminar on teaching-learning strategies (held early in 1976), took three years to complete, starting in May 1977 and lasting through to 1980. Its purpose was to satisfy the need for a fuller understanding of the mechanisms and procedures that govern the preparation and implementation of innovative policies in education, especially those aimed at raising teaching standards, and experimented with in pilot-project form prior to wide-scale introduction. An important feature of the 1970s was the unprecedented effort brought to bear on innovation and reform in the educational systems of virtually every country in the world. It is for this reason that the Institute has paid especial attention to research into the processes that underlie the planning and the implementation of these changes. Naturally, the IIEP has given due weight to the work of Unesco and the IBE in the field of educational innovations, in particular the bibliographies published by the IBE[1] and the series of case studies presented under the series title 'Experiments and innovations in education'.

Attention has also been given to the OECD's programmes (Centre for Educational Research and Innovation), and to its studies published in the series 'Case studies of educational innovation'.[2]

One original feature of the research programme directed by R Adams is that national researchers were consulted on the interpretation of facts, this method being known as 'participatory research'. This involves self-evaluation combined with IIEP-supplied technical assistance, as well as permanent consultation among the seven research teams. Another feature of this book is that instead of restricting itself to a description of an innovation in its final stage, it traces each of the seven case studies from its genesis through every stage in its evolution, examining the forces and events that fostered or hampered it, measures taken as a result, and their effects.

1 See *Educational Documentation and Information*, Nos 190 and 195.
2 (i) Case studies of educational innovation: at central level; (ii) Case studies of educational innovation: at regional level; (iii) Case studies of educational innovation: at school level; (iv) Case studies of educational innovation: strategies of innovation in education.

In concluding this study, the authors propose a model, or rather a matrix, for the analysis of processes connected with innovation.

The authors have frequent recourse to a phenomenological approach when attempting to observe events from within. The highly personal style reflects this methodological preference, and contrasts with most research in the social sciences. However, after a narrative account describing each of the innovations studied, they try, in the last two chapters, to draw a certain number of conclusions capable of acting as guidelines for subsequent innovations. The authors attach particular importance to the attitudes of the different groups and agents involved in innovation, and suggest an information system capable of monitoring the evolution of these attitudes on a permanent basis.

One important conclusion to emerge from this research is that innovation, just like a living being, evolves not as a closed system but as a sub-system subject to the influence of its socio-political environment. It is pointed out that none of the innovations studied achieved the objectives initially assigned to it. In fact, each one tended to adopt what one might call a realistic, pragmatic approach, adjusting to unforeseen circumstances – mostly unfavourable. It follows, therefore, that if all these innovations were subjected to 'evaluation in terms of objectives', their overall results would presumably be regarded as unsatisfactory. Consequently, it would be advisable not to limit ourselves to evaluative methods designed to measure how far objectives have or have not been achieved, and to employ methods designed also to measure an innovation's ability to adapt to external changes.

Other conclusions may be formulated in the following manner. To begin with, it does indeed look as if an innovation is liable to be compromised in the absence of a supporting infrastructure at each corresponding layer of the system. This support is necessary down to the level of the individual school, and perhaps even in the classroom itself. It is equally plain that until now, planners have rarely paid much attention to or spent much time on creating any such infrastructure, and that this impedes the process of reform.

Secondly, since all reforms inevitably clash with certain entrenched attitudes (whose logic has developed out of the previous situation), planners ought to envisage direct or indirect measures designed to sway mentalities in favour of reform – or at least to prepare opinion in its favour. Nothing, surely, can replace this work of information and persuasion to incite the agents concerned (teachers, administrators) to take the reform in hand.

Thirdly, a certain number of examples bear witness to the inertia of institutions and show how educational systems have a considerable capacity for withstanding the initial élan of an innovation, still more so a reform. The processes whereby institutions adjust to innovation or reform belong in a continuum whose two extremes are radicalism and conservatism. The problem facing people whose job it is to administrate and direct innovations is to adopt a sufficiently flexible strategy to arrive at a dynamic equilibrium between these two pitfalls.

Foreword

Fourthly, these studies also show that there is no single satisfactory explanation for the success of an innovation. It seems, rather, as though a complex set of external conditions needs to exist in order to offer the innovation a chance of survival and development. In particular, these conditions are apparently bound up with the degree of economic, social and, above all, educational development of the country in question. Several such descriptions are given in the seven case studies.

This book's conclusions were discussed with the national teams on numerous occasions. First, at a meeting in Dortmund, in 1979, and later during Professor Adams' journeys to Indonesia and Malaysia; lastly, at a workshop held in Paris in December 1980 to examine the administrative dimensions of the generalization of an innovation as a national education reform.

In our opinion, this book will shed fresh light on a great many questions of concern to educational planners and administrators, especially as regards the practical mechanisms and procedures required in order to set in motion an educational reform: job analysis, procedures to be used, personnel, buildings, contextual analysis, coordination and management, cost analysis, evaluation and, in particular, the logistics and phasing of the operation.

We hope that this book will be welcomed by all those who take an interest in the nature of the processes of change in educational systems. We should be happy to receive their comments, and in particular accounts of their own experiences where these might further enrich the content of this book.

Finally, IIEP gratefully acknowledges the moral and financial support of the Cooperative agencies from Germany (Ministry of Co-operation), Sweden (SIDA) and Norway (NORAD), who gave a decisive contribution to the various phases of the project.

Michel Debeauvais
Director, IIEP

Introduction

This book is about the vexed problem of introducing changes into education systems – a topic that in its fluctuating popularity over the last 20 years has brought fire to the eyes of radicals and conservatives alike, although for vastly different reasons. But the book speaks neither for radicals nor conservatives. It does not set out to exhort others to change their ways or to condemn those who are trying to do so. Its principal purpose is to study the *process* of planned innovation in education systems, firstly to try to understand that process better, and secondly to consider how changes in the system, once desired, might be achieved less painfully than is customary. The book tends to look at the problem of change mainly from the inside of the system, although it does not do so exclusively. What the inspection reveals, however, is that the 'Establishment' is neither the rigid, inflexible, stupid, bumbling, impersonal bureaucracy that its critics would have us believe it to be, nor is it the infallible, all-seeing, all-knowing, enlightened and benign organization its supporters are sometimes prone to assert it is. Whether the truth even lies somewhere in between is debatable. What does seem to be the case is that the education system comprises, as we all know but are sometimes unwilling to admit, human beings who mostly go about their business conscientiously and responsibly, acting with good intentions and as best they can under often very difficult circumstances.

Why then is the history of innovation such a doleful one? Why, according to the literature, is failure its companion so frequently? Why, given the burning enthusiasm of the advocates of reform, do teachers remain unimpressed, even glum, and administrators shudder? There are good reasons, and the following pages will attempt to surface some of them.

We have chosen as our vehicle in studying educational change seven educational reforms that have yet to complete their allotted span. So far they have neither succeeded nor failed. At the moment of writing, all are alive and well, but if they run true to what is reported to be education's past form, at least five of the seven are destined to die before they have achieved their stated purpose. But in the book we are also concerned with some of the attempts that have been made and are continuing to be made to avoid such a dismal destiny. So we set out to track the innovations from their beginnings to the present day, observing their trials, tribulations and triumphs, dispassionately but sympathetically. And sympathy is needed because the road to educational reform is indeed rough and the costs of travelling it usually very high.

The book also, perhaps with more courage than discretion, attempts to forecast the future of these reforms and, in the final chapter, to point up lessons learned that might be relevant to others contemplating reform and to those who are students of it.

These seven reforms are being undertaken in seven different countries, all of which have agreed to participate in a task of separate and mutual self-examination. Because of their cultural and economic differences and the nature of the reforms that they are undertaking, they constitute a rich environment for study. For example, both Ghana and the Federal Republic of Germany are devising educational reforms directed in particular at school leavers who are unlikely to find employment. The Indonesian and Malaysian innovations both focus on curricular change, with one anticipating a relatively rapid and systematically planned implementation and the other a longer-term process of continuing adaptation. The Sierra Leonean approach to educational and social change is direct, through a teacher training programme that foresees its 'new breed' of teachers helping in rural community development as well as undertaking teaching tasks. Israel, for its part, is attempting to construct a highly individualized 'system' of instruction designed to cater for the disadvantaged pupil in particular. By contrast, the New Zealand attempt to change teaching practices is an oblique one, in which a new school building design is used to, as it were, 'environmentally coerce' teachers into new ways.

We hope to render a fair account of the innovations chosen for study, but it is not our purpose to act as advocates of any, promoting them as lesser or greater panaceas. In fact, we will try deliberately to subdue the considerable enthusiasm we have for the specific innovations themselves, in the interest of our main objective: to understand how reform can be made to work. Some description of each innovation will of course be given and some interpretations of their effects undertaken. But the main task is to focus on educational innovation and reform as a *process*. To this end, when we take each innovation step by step (side-steps and slides included) through the events that occurred, we will attempt to provide explanations of why things happened the way they did, and we will try to indicate what some of the consequences were and what others might well be. We hope in this way to alert ourselves and others to some of the difficulties that tend to stand in the way of successful innovation.

So much for a first, general and rather self-conscious explanation of what the book is about. But we need to crave the reader's indulgence and describe the book a little further — for good reason. Unless we can manage at the beginning to generate realistic expectations about what is to be found in the text, and the issues we have in mind, then the likelihood of later disappointment increases. The additional information that is to be provided, then, is to set the scene, so that the reader may better decide whether or not to see the rest of the play.

Introduction

The book had its beginning in a general problem that is of international proportions, affecting literally millions of people, and, whatever the currency, the equivalent of millions of dollars. Viewed in its grandest perspective, it is the problem of reforming a whole society. Viewed in its tiniest, it is the problem of having a person change his ways. In a nutshell, it is the problem of social reform.

There are, however, and not altogether surprisingly, several complications. The reforms found in the book are to be undertaken through education and that means that the problem of social reform will be seen in one of its most difficult guises. By convention and conviction educational institutions tend towards conservatism and their conservatism generates a distinctive kind of self-protecting and often justifiable inertia.

Again, the task of accomplishing reform through education is also not made any easier because of the fact that attempting to innovate in education has so far been a hazardous business. Time and time again, innovations that are intended to grow into reforms are begun with high hopes, only to falter and fade. The record of educational innovations is not a cheerful one – a matter that neither deters innovators from keeping on trying, nor, it seems, results in a reduction in the proportion of failures.

'Many of the educational innovations in developing countries involve a "major system transformation". They are typically ambitious both in the amount of time, energy and material resources invested and in the degree of rapid and massive changes expected. In spite of such large-scale investments and expectations, few of these innovations appear to make a major dent at the *national level* in the educational or training problem which they were designed to solve. They appear in many respects to be giant pilot projects...

'Given the ambition of the project in relation to the country's own resources and in particular, its capacity to process a great number and variety of information and decisions concerning ongoing and new programmes, these innovations run into many unexpected problems and often have unexpected outcomes which take them far from their original objectives.'
(Havelock and Huberman, 1977)

There is behind such a state of affairs a certain kind of tragedy. In many countries reform is desperately needed. Sometimes the reasons are practical and pragmatic, for example, so that children (and adults) can learn to read or acquire skills that they can turn to good use for their own benefit and for society's development. Sometimes it is a matter of social justice and basic human rights, for example, when access to educational opportunity is less available to some than others. When reforms fail then, resources have been wasted and there is a reckoning that has to be paid. There are the obvious resource costs of money, people, time and equipment. More importantly, there are social costs. When innovations begin, hopes are raised, enthusiasms engendered and actions motivated. But then if failure follows, the major products become disappointment, disillusionment, suspicion and despondency. The original problem still remains unsolved but additional new ones have been created as well.

Under such circumstances there is a margin of inefficiency that cannot be tolerated even in education. At a time when economic conditions are becoming more and more difficult, that margin is ever shrinking. Increasing investment in education is thus unlikely and extravagant expenditure in its name will become a thing of the past. It follows, then, that education has to find ways of doing its job better and more economically. One of these ways clearly involves being able to increase the likelihood of success of any educational reform.

That was our root problem. And it translated into practical terms for us as: 'How can ways be found to *avoid* the conditions that cause innovations to falter and fail? Better still, how can ways be found to improve the progress of a reform once innovation has started?' Some of the answers to these two perhaps naïvely optimistic questions lie, we think, in having a more intimate knowledge about the life-history of innovations. We think there are useful lessons to be learned from experience – but not when the event is too long gone. We think there are particular weaknesses in retrospective accounts, primarily because they tend to fall victim to imperfectly kept records and losses of (perhaps conveniently) forgotten detail. At the other end of the continuum, prospective accounts fall victim to their own rhetoric – the vision and the dream tend to detach us from reality. For our part, our dream (our rhetoric) is to preserve a little more 'reality' by trying to trap events as they occur, by trying to explain their causes and by trying to predict (or forecast) their consequences. In future years we also hope to return to examine the folly or the wisdom of such an approach.

Our search for the realities of educational innovation has led us into various exotic parts of the world: Nordrhein-Westfalen in Western Europe; Bunumbu and Kumasi in tropical Africa; the island nations of Indonesia and Malaysia to Israel and even the 'down-under' side of the globe, New Zealand.

We have invaded the realms of educational planners and administrators, the decision makers whose appointed task is to make a good system and run it well.

We have intruded on politicians and statesmen responsible for the big business of education and the delicate craft of policy making. And we have become aware of their awareness that the consequences of adroit or clumsy policy making are both personal and national. Political survival and the public good are both at stake.

We have talked with teachers because it is through them that educational quality is achieved and sustained, and because much of the research evidence indicates that teachers are the rock on which educational reforms founder – and for very understandable reasons.

We have attempted to gain a measure of insight into the perspectives of the diverse publics on which the innovations impinge, primarily because of education's undoubted, though not always crystal-clear, effect on society.

Introduction

Today's educational investment or lack of it may be tomorrow's social profit – or loss.

We have also tried to recognize that education is becoming less and less a 'closed shop'. There are many one-time strangers to be found within today's educational walls. Parents are there, lay helpers are there and experts from non-educational fields are there. Psychologists, social workers and medical officers are there to provide their specialized forms of aid and comfort to complement the educational task. But in the broader education system are to be found other kinds of professionals: economists, sociologists, architects, statisticians, to name a few. But the educational world into which they have entered is an exotic one. In it peculiar customs are observed, peculiar beliefs are held and reality is perceived in its own peculiarly indigenous way. Any stranger, however erudite, invariably runs the risk of misinterpreting it and misunderstanding it.

Finally, we must admit to a hidden agenda that has partly served to inform our purpose. It arises out of the fact that the collaborators who mutually gave birth to the book comprised an unusual mixture. About half of them were senior administrators in their respective countries and the remainder were senior researchers. In contriving the book, we were repeatedly brought face to face with the different interests and concerns of the two factions and the fact that they both needed, perhaps even depended on, each other. So we have tried to accommodate both, addressing the problems of planning and decision making on the one hand and the acquisition of relevant and useful information on the other. This enforced dialogue has alerted us to two facts: first, that much research on innovation tends to look back, analysing events now buried in the past, and thus failing to address the 'here and now' needs of the decision makers, and second, that there appear to be unfortunate gaps existing in education between research and policy making and educational practice. This has led us uncomfortably close to the conclusion that present paradigms and procedures are inadequate for addressing today's problems in 'live' social systems and that the time may well be ripe for innovatory approaches to educational planning.

Chapter 1
Point of Departure

The problem that the book starts with, then,[1] is the problem of launching an educational innovation and ensuring its safe flight to reach its target.

That problem was surfaced by a group of senior public administrators responsible for educational decision making in 12 countries, who assembled at Unesco's International Institute for Educational Planning in Paris in September 1976. There, when addressing the issue of the link between educational research and the management of education systems, they indicated that the matter of greatest concern to them was to be able to make sure that policies once chosen could be carried out effectively.

They were not too kindly disposed towards much existing educational research. They were contemptuous (that's not too strong a word) of case studies and reports that did no more than give descriptions of events (mostly provided by those for whom the report was destined). They were intolerant of research that told them, after an attempted educational reform, that it had failed or succeeded – that, they already knew. They were even impatient with research that attempted to explain the reasons for success or failure of specific innovations. They discounted these as seldom relevant for other issues or other periods in time. Their need, they urged, was for a means of knowing as early as possible what was happening to their existing attempts at reform and, in particular, learning what might be likely to create unwanted effects, direct effects or side effects, in the near or distant future.

There were also a similar number of researchers at the same meeting. While they might have joined issue with the administrators and made points about the 'importance of pure research' and 'intellectual freedom', they chose instead to highlight two matters that were in sympathy with the concerns of the administrators. The first was that research on the processes of educational innovation was rather limited and that consequently any scientific basis for *understanding* that process was not yet to hand. The second was that the process of educational reform was clearly a very complicated one. Not only did it have many obviously educational aspects – so that aims, methods, effects and evaluation were important – but also, because education was just one part of a much larger social system, it had important

---

[1] If the reader has followed the general practice of omitting to read the Introduction, may we earnestly suggest that the omission be rectified. At least it has the virtue of being relatively short.

political aspects, economic aspects, territorial aspects, religious, moral and occupational aspects as well. This larger context, they argued, both affects education and is affected by it in turn so that diagnosing the condition of an innovation requires taking account of many of such influences. They argued further that even within the educational system itself the situation was complicated. As an example worth considering, take an educational reform which requires teachers to teach arithmetic a new way. In the first place, the teachers would have to learn it. Not unreasonably they would be likely to ask 'Why?' 'Is it' they might reasonably wonder 'because some administrator in a remote government office says so?', 'and if so, what does he know about the real problems of teaching?' Besides, the teachers having become reasonably competent at an existing method would tend to have confidence that the one they knew, at least, worked. (Novelty does not always guarantee success and it is not a characteristic of human nature to welcome change with open arms, particularly when imposed from the outside.) But despite such objections, even if the means were found for 'converting' the teachers – if in-service training courses were run, if new equipment were provided, if the materials required were produced and distributed, etc – these would all require money, time and organizational competency. But even given that these too were available and were employed wisely, other problems would remain. It would be likely, for example, that parents would not initially approve of such a change, partly because it implies that the arithmetic they learned was inadequate (and therefore that they were too), and partly because the new method would be likely to drive deeper the wedges that separate (professional) teachers from the (lay) public, and (knowledgeable) children from (ignorant) parents. Furthermore, even the children themselves could be influential, especially if their expectations about 'proper' education had been brushed unceremoniously aside.

While such aspects of what has unreasonably been called 'resistance to change' are very significant in the process of attempting to make changes work, it is still only one side of a many-sided question. To continue the illustration: the new method, because it would take time to spread throughout the education system, would mean that those teachers who used it would be seen as advanced or up-to-date and those who did not would be seen as backward and old-fashioned. Because of this, *new* rules for the status game would evolve and new candidates would come to be marked for advancement. Those unexpectedly passed by in the rush of the 'new wave' might at best reconcile themselves to disappointment or at worst might resort to active subversion of the system. At the same time, to the extent that principals might fear that they were likely to be 'upstaged' by teachers who knew something they did not know, they too would be under a measure of threat. Similarly, throughout the educational system, others in positions of lesser or greater authority might unexpectedly fall victim to their own 'new' ignorance, or might be able to profit from their 'new' expertise.

Such arguments mounted by the researchers became more and more complicated. They did not even ignore the point that, despite expectations to the contrary, educational reforms designed to improve educational quality have an unhappy knack of consolidating the privilege of the already privileged and in fact of maintaining, rather than changing, the status quo (Levin, 1975).

The debate, or rather the exchange, between administrators and researchers left both camps with a guarded respect for each other, but also with a number of lingering doubts about bridging the formidable gap between research on the one hand and practice on the other. In particular, two large question marks seemed to have been left hanging over the following issues:

1. Would it *ever* be possible to find ways of putting relevant research-based information easily and quickly into the hands of decision makers at a time and in a way that they might be able to use it constructively?
2. In the light of the complexity of the educational operation as the researchers had detailed it, would researchers *ever* be able to find paths through the apparent wilderness?

Although everybody was too polite to say so, there was nonetheless an underlying suspicion that what the researchers' message to the administrators had been was: 'There is little, if any, *scientific* justification for many of the decisions you take daily'.

At the same time, the implicit message from the administrators had been 'You are very good at telling us that we *should not* have done what we did – now help us appreciate better what we *should* do'.

So the researchers left to go home secure in the knowledge that they would not have to take responsibility for what was being done daily in the education systems. The administrators left knowing that they would continue to have to do so – unless, of course, education systems could be put into lengthy suspended animation while the researchers came up with all the necessary answers.

However, before they left, the researchers and administrators did reach agreement on the following points:

(i) Any education system needs to be in a position to plan and monitor the progress of its educational reforms.
(ii) In view of the lack of information about the *process* of implementing reforms, relevant (research-based) information is needed.
(iii) To this end there is a serious need for collaboration between researchers and administrators, particularly over the planning implications of attempting to improve education.
(iv) Although each country is in some substantial ways unlike any other country, it is also *like* every other country. Each country, though having its unique characteristics, will hold a number of things in common with others.
(v) Thus in all countries important interrelationships are to be found between school, community, the education system and society at

large; and these are likely to affect and be affected by changes in education.
(vi) Given the points above: that countries are unique, that school, community and society have effects on each other, and that research into education systems is relatively primitive; the most important issue to be solved first is to understand the optimum conditions for: initiating changes, implementing them, evaluating them and rationalizing the whole qualitative change process.

A plan for the route

There the matter might have ended had not the host organization, the International Institute for Educational Planning, perhaps having caught the unspoken messages, decided to pursue the matter further by setting up a research project that would take into account the administrators' needs and the researchers' caveats. Subsequently, following initiatives taken by the IIEP, six countries that took part in the original seminar (the Federal Republic of Germany, Ghana, Indonesia, Israel, Malaysia and New Zealand), plus one new one (Sierra Leone), agreed to work together on the general problem of educational innovation.

The purposes of this new collaborative study were formulated in a research proposal. They are quoted below not *pro forma*, but because at the finish we intend to look back and assess in the light of events that occurred whether such objectives still hold the aura of respectability they seemed to have at the time.

(i) To study in different countries a selected qualitative reform (a reform designed to improve pupil learning through the modification of teaching practices as distinct from structural or organizational reforms that are concerned with quantitative aspects). In particular, to trace the whole process from the initial idea through its introduction (and trial) and up to its broader application. To monitor what happens throughout and to measure its educational and societal effects.

(ii) By gathering information from teachers, pupils, parents, the community and the education system, to provide a basis for forecasting outcomes of each reform and what effects it might have.

(iii) By providing regular feedback of information to the administrators who are managing the reform and are responsible for it, and the teachers who are implementing it, give them the means for making better-informed decisions. In the process, to help develop an acceptable monitoring or 'quality control' mechanism for each of the countries.

(iv) By synthesizing the results from the different countries, attempt to arrive at 'general principles' of planning for qualitative change that can be used in future planning and in the training of planners.

Point of Departure

The focus of the research in each country was to be placed on a single specific qualitative change or reform. One of the two *necessary* conditions for inclusion was that the reform should be aimed at improving the pupils' education and it should require teachers (directly or indirectly) to adopt new practices. The other was that initial steps had already been taken to start to bring it about.

Given those conditions, the research issues became:

(i) To discover the circumstances that led to the acceptance of the idea for reform.
(ii) To demonstrate the way in which the whole evolutionary process of the reform developed and progressed, its easy and difficult aspects, the sources of concern, the modifications found necessary and why.
(iii) To show the effects of the process on:
   (a) the pupils: their learning and attitudes, etc
   (b) the teachers: the new job specifications, satisfactions, career prospects, etc
   (c) the school: changes in the organizational (and social) structure of the school, interrelationships between teachers, pupils, other staff and parents, etc
   (d) the education system: costs of implementation, materials and equipment, logistics of expansion, teacher training, supervision, plant, etc
   (e) the nation: contribution to national goals.

From the outset, the project was to be a collaborative one in two important and significant senses. The first was that the project required the development of a common research framework that was supposed to be flexible enough to adapt to the needs of the different countries. The second was that as a condition for participation in the project, administrators and researchers were both to be freed to participate. The purpose was to ensure that the gap between practical reality and educational research stayed as small as possible so that the research would be relevant and realistic, and its import would become readily available to the administrators.

While commendably optimistic, the proposal perhaps reflected more confidence than circumstances warranted at the time. It also suffered from the misplaced illusion that most if not all events during the life-time of the study could be anticipated at the beginning. Subsequent events were to dent that illusion, but how that happened and what the consequences were are best revealed later, when at the end of the project it is disinterred for a post mortem.

Hazards ahead

What happened next back in the real world was a series of negotiations that ultimately saw the coming together of representatives from the seven participating countries to start to develop a plan of attack. Immediately it became clear that the project was faced with a number of prospective and possibly major difficulties – or opportunities. At the time, we were not quite sure which.

The first of these stemmed from the varying nature of the participating countries themselves. There were vast differences in geographical size. The 13,000 islands of Indonesia contain nearly 2,000,000 square kilometres of land and stretch for over 5000 km from latitude 5° North to 11° South. By contrast, Sierra Leone covers a compact 71,700 square kilometres.

There were notable differences in population size. Indonesia and Sierra Leone again provide the greatest contrast: 132 million versus nearly three million. Israel, with 3¾ million and New Zealand with just over three million line up with Sierra Leone as somewhat miniscule alongside Indonesia. Malaysia and Ghana, with 12⅓ and 9⅔ million each, are not exactly massive either. The Federal Republic of Germany, with its 62 million, appears to be more sizeable, but because of the decentralized nature of the Federal Republic, the project in fact involves only one *Land* (Nordrhein-Westfalen) and its population is only (sic) 17 million.

Population growth rates do not demonstrate quite so much difference, that is, as long as they are regarded in relative terms. The growth rates of Malaysia, Ghana, Sierra Leone and Israel range between 2.7 per cent and 2.1 per cent. New Zealand's is 1.8 per cent and the Federal Republic of Germany's, an exceptional 0.2 per cent. However, Indonesia's rate, 2.4 per cent, means in absolute terms an annual population increase of approximately three million per year, or more than either New Zealand's or Sierra Leone's total population!

Table 1: *Population and growth rates of the seven countries*

	Population	Growth rate % 1970-75
Indonesia	132,112,000	2.4
Federal Republic of Germany	61,830,000	0.2
Malaysia	12,308,000	2.7
Ghana	9,870,000	2.7
Israel	3,732,000	2.1
New Zealand	3,070,000	1.8
Sierra Leone	2,982,000	2.5

Again, in the terminology that is currently fashionable (and, not surprisingly, misleading), there were three 'developed' countries in the project and four 'developing' ones. In so far as gross national product (GNP) can be regarded as an index of development, there were noteworthy differences to be found in the group. The GNP range was from an estimated US$610 million to US$457,540 million. More dramatically, the per capita rate of the richest country (Federal Republic of Germany) was nearly twice that of the second country (New Zealand), and 37 times that of the seventh (Sierra Leone) – see Table 2.

However, GNP tells only a fraction of the story. If to it is added information on the *rate* of economic development, a different picture emerges. When figures from the last few years are used as a (somewhat fallible) basis for estimating trends, it becomes apparent that in some cases the economic gap between developed and developing nations is being reduced while in others it is not. Given also the relative rate of population increase and the unlikely event that all other conditions remain the same, the prospect of an escalating *economic development* seems in many cases rather remote. Perhaps the New World Economic Order, or, as it has been renamed, the New World Order, will upset those predictions.

Table 2: *GNP at market prices*

	GNP **US$ millions**	**Per capita** **US$**
Federal Republic of Germany	457,540	7,380
New Zealand	13,120	4,250
Israel	13,980	3,920
Malaysia	10,900	860
Ghana	5,920	580
Indonesia	32,440	240
Sierra Leone	610	200

Source: World Bank Atlas, World Bank, 1977. 32pp.

Although this chapter is no place for an extended discourse on geography, it must at least be noted in passing that the physical characteristics of the countries were vastly different on a number of counts. Ghana and Sierra Leone are continental and equatorial. The Federal Republic of Germany, though continental too, freezes in the winter, while continental Israel experiences a much hotter climate. Malaysia and Indonesia are equatorial but insular. New Zealand is insular, but its climate is temperate. Water, so precious in Israel and parts of Ghana, is plentiful in the other countries. Raw materials are not known to be possessed in abundance in New Zealand, Ghana, Sierra Leone or Israel. This is not the case in the Federal Republic of Germany, Indonesia and Malaysia, but the extent to which means have been developed to make use of these materials in the three countries is dramatically different.

Three countries – Ghana, New Zealand and Sierra Leone – as producers of primary products (though of different kinds) are most vulnerable to protectionist trade practices overseas. Malaysia's primary product vulnerability is somewhat reduced by the importance of rubber and by the compensatory effects of its well-developed tin and oil industries.

The divergent features of the seven environments are, it would seem, almost infinite. However, it is their implications for the practice of educational reform that are of significance to the present study. To what extent can it be expected that they will substantially affect the process of innovation and the implementation of reform? Do they raise problems that can only be solved uniquely?

However, at the risk of sounding like the researchers at the original IIEP seminar that started it all, so far we have but touched the tip of the iceberg of national differences. Furthermore, only some obvious geographical ones that are likely to have an effect on the availability of resources and their distribution and supply have been mentioned. At the beginning of the project, these and many other aspects excited interest, concern and speculation over the viability of the project. Did the different political circumstances in which the countries find themselves constitute a significant influence that has a unique effect on the route that any reform will or can take? We had no doubt that politics were important. We appreciated that political circumstances differed in our seven countries. We were also conscious that the road to independence, and beyond it, had in some cases been travelled very recently and under difficult circumstances. What we did not know was whether or not, and if so how, educational innovations were effected in the difficult circumstances.

Again, the various educational systems reflected different stances and rested on different assumptions. Some were highly centralized, others quite highly decentralized. In some the significance of the public examination system loomed much larger than in others. Pedagogical orientations differed. Most owed their origins to either Europe, England or to a lesser extent the United States of America. But indigenous components were starting to appear with increasing force. We imagined too that views on planning differed – there were, we suspected, the dedicated and the dubious.

Such a catalogue could be extended but there is no point in raising further views in this abstract manner. No attempt will be made to catalogue them exhaustively at this point. Later, when each of the countries reports on its activities, the ones thought most relevant to each will be surfaced.

However, there are several social features of the different societies that are both distinctive and shared and that, because of their social importance, need some acknowledgement if the scene for the rest of the book is to be set properly. These are important not only intrinsically but also because they pervade the whole of society providing, it is believed, a strong motivational force. They are not easily confined within any of the convenient academic categories above. Furthermore, while their own influence is pervasive, they are subject to influence by geographical, economic, political, agricultural and other factors themselves. In seeking out these features, an attempt will be made to look just a little below the surface, necessarily setting aside the more obvious features such as, for example, the fact that three great ethnic stocks – African, Asian and European – are involved.

Some common concerns

National identity

There was not one country where the question of national identity was not a vexed one. Every country, including even New Zealand whose severance of the umbilical cord with the United Kingdom had been a painful consequence of the latter's entry into the European Economic Community, was concerned to build for itself a new identity that would be nationally, regionally and internationally acceptable.

Two of the most notable features of this general concern were: first, the extent to which the matter of national identity was being treated as one of urgency calling for self-conscious and deliberate action, and second, the extent to which the new directions being taken towards identity were bound up with the rejection or acceptance of those forces that had previously been preventing the development of that identity. Both should be discussed briefly.

It is probably true to say that in the two South-East Asian countries the issue of national identity is being regarded as more immediately insistent than in the other countries. Malaysia, with the necessity to accommodate to the interests of three main ethnic groups (Malay, Chinese and Indian) has decided on a policy that should lead to the reduction of discrepancies, particularly economic discrepancies, and at the same time should emphasize what is unique to the nation. For example, in primary school the three languages feature as the medium of instruction, but the course contents are identical for all. At lower secondary level, Tamil and Chinese speakers who wish to continue their education in the national schools must at the moment take an extra year's tuition (in the 'remove class') to acquire fluency in Bahasa Malaysia. Final examinations at this level and at upper and post-secondary level are in Bahasa Malaysia or, at the moment, in English. It is the Government's policy to convert all schools to Bahasa Malaysia so that by 1983 it will become the main medium of instruction for all courses at tertiary level.

If it were a matter of competition, which it is not, the Israelis would be unlikely to concede that any other country was more passionately devoted to preserving its identity than they. With their population having come from the four corners of the globe, and those of European descent no longer constituting the majority, more and more faith is being placed on education as the means of capitalizing on the advantages of cultural diversity and minimizing the disadvantages. Hebrew, of course, provides the medium but education is the message.

The Federal Republic of Germany, having risen as an economic phoenix from the ashes of the Second World War, is no less concerned with gaining international acknowledgement in other fields also (as her very substantial support of 'aid' programmes testifies). In West German education, however, there has been a silent though slow revolution to the extent that older 'imperial' images are being gradually replaced by democratic ones that are increasingly reflected in the curricula, structures and practices found throughout the education system. It is significant, for example, that because the 11 *Länder* have considerable autonomy, independence and freedom of choice, negotiations for the participation of a West German team in the project were conducted with and through one *Land* only.

In one sense the Ghanian situation has something in common with the West German and Indonesian ones in that Ghana too is adopting a 'unity in diversity' philosophy. There, because there are many tribally defined regions whose complex and varied social structures and practices have developed over history, these valued differences are being cherished and in fact are being used to form the basis for building national unity. Local languages thus feature during the first three years of primary school. Thereafter, however, English (adopted as the official language in 1957, the year of Independence) becomes the principal medium.

While Sierra Leone also has a well developed and cherished tribal structure, the situation is not as complex as in Ghana. In Sierra Leone there are some 18 different groups of which the Mende and Temne tribes account for 60 per cent. Because of inter-marriage there is an indication that tribal identifications are being supplemented and complemented by a growing appreciation of a national Sierra Leonean identity too. Whether or not the acceptance of English as the official language will help or hinder the growth of identity is a noteworthy issue. In so many other countries, language has been seized on as a critical component in the quest for identity. The possibility of a resurgence of local language cannot therefore be ruled out. Meantime, in compensation perhaps, Sierra Leoneans have the advantage that goes with mastery of one of the major international languages.

New Zealand's identity problem, if it is a problem, straddles the two identity issues originally raised; namely, the immediacy of concern and the influence of historical factors. Having come peacefully on independence in 1852 and attained Dominion Status in 1909, links with the mother-country Britain had remained rock steady through two world wars and up to the European Common Market. Since then, with market security vanishing, New Zealand has sought to re-gear its production with the requirements of other countries in mind. The customary myopic definition of the world in British terms has given way to a much more eclectic view which has brought the concerns and interests of other nations more into focus. It will be some time before New Zealand's identity becomes Oceanic and Asian, but there are more than a few straws in the wind indicating that it will do so. In schools, Maori (the indigenous Polynesian language) has been given an impetus and Japanese features in the secondary school curriculum. Outside the domain of education, industry and commerce now look towards South-East Asia for trade. Meantime the importance of the British connection, though still strong, diminishes and attitudes change accordingly.

It may or may not be significant that the two other British Commonwealth countries that gained their independence peacefully have retained the language of the colonizers. Ghana's membership of the British Commonwealth dates from 1957, some five years after Nkrumah brought his Convention People's Party to power. Sierra Leone's independence came in 1961, again through a process of peaceful evolution that saw a gradual transfer of control from British to African hands. But in both countries the legacy of Britain is far from gone. It is reflected in institutional structures and in the attitudes and values of the people. Most relevant among them for the case in point is an educational frame of reference that, having been exported uncritically in the first instance, is now being seen as not altogether appropriate for the African milieu. The academic aura peculiar to Oxbridge and no doubt valuable in England is to some extent out of place in Freetown or Accra or, for that matter, Wellington or Kuala Lumpur. In recent years not only has university education been brought into closer affinity with indigenous needs, but also the universities' dominance over secondary curricula has been diminished. Secondary education has become somewhat more practical, utilitarian and relevant to national development and individual vocational opportunities – or it is in the process of becoming so.

Although Malaysia, the other British Commonwealth country in the project, does share a number of features with its next-door neighbour, Indonesia, both are distinctively different. Both are of course to be found in the same corner of the world. Both hold some ethnic ground in common and both, while colonized by the British and the Dutch respectively, were also occupied by the Japanese in the Second World War. Independence for both followed shortly afterwards. In 1945 Indonesia declared independence and fought the Dutch to sustain it. Malaysia came into being later, in 1963 when the then independent Federation of Malaya (Peninsular Malaysia) and the British territories of Sabah, Sarawak and Singapore became the Federation of Malaysia, with its 13 states. Singapore separated from the Federation in 1965.

But it is at this point that two of the many differences between the countries assert themselves. The routes to independence and the links between colonizers and colonized were far from similar. The British withdrew, having in large measure helped preserve Malay society, its structures and its belief systems. Thus the period of British 'protection' is looked upon with a certain amount of favour and British practices and attitudes of mind are still to be found in the country – none stronger than those prevailing in education. It is only in recent years that the British preservation of Malay culture has been criticized for having the effect of delaying the economic development of the indigenous peoples.[1]

In Indonesia, the return after the Second World War of the erstwhile Dutch colonizers was resisted fiercely and successfully. As a consequence, links with the Netherlands are now rather tenuous, English has replaced

---

1 It is perhaps noteworthy that in New Zealand the British are criticized by Maoris for *not* having preserved their culture.

Dutch as the favoured second language and the vestiges of the (particularly limited) colonial Dutch education system are remarkably few.

To return to the main theme, these two general preoccupations of the countries – identity and acceptance or rejection of the immediate colonial past – seemed to have two effects in particular. In the first place they seemed to play an important part in determining what educational issues should take priority. In a similar vein, as social 'givens', they provided a justification for action that would seldom be called into question.

Educational development

The issues surfaced above by no means exhaust the range and array of matters that might threaten the feasibility of the kind of comparative study we originally had in mind. There were in fact two others lurking in the background which, although not initially taken too much into account, may prove to be even more critical. These were: (i) what might be called the 'developmental condition' of the respective education systems and (ii) the philosophy of planning prevailing in the separate countries. Both of these will be dealt with more fully in the final chapter but at least some small comment is necessary here.

No one has yet come up with a universally acceptable proposition setting out what an ideal education system should look like – though there are many, from Plato, Bacon and Rousseau to Huxley, Orwell and Illich, who have tried in one way or another. So it is only proper to assert that this discussion of the developmental condition of education systems starts with few preconceived ideas about the best or worst of all possible educational worlds. Nor does it assume that educational development is the same thing as economic development and therefore that the education systems of 'developed' countries are necessarily better or worse than those of the 'less developed' countries. Nonetheless, differences between systems there are. And most systems give signs of wishing to move (develop) in a particular direction. There are many aspects that might be considered under this rubric, but there are two that are particularly relevant to the present project because of its focus on teaching and learning, viz the extent to which teachers are given the responsibility to determine how and what they shall teach, and the extent to which teachers are professionally prepared for their educating task. The last of these is best dealt with first.

The small and straightforward formula for classifying education systems that Beeby put forward in 1966 has stood the test of time. Beeby, looking as it were for an embracing but manageable basis for distinguishing groups of education systems, suggested that there were two features that seemed to provide the best indicators: (i) the extent to which teachers were 'educated' and (ii) the extent to which they were professionally trained. This led him to four 'arch-type' systems where respectively teachers were:

(i) ill-educated, untrained
(ii) ill-educated, trained

(iii) better educated, trained
(iv) well educated, well trained.

If education as it is used above is taken to mean 'exposure to schooling', then it appears that education systems tend to move from condition (i) to condition (iv), usually in that order, but with all four sometimes coexisting at the same time at different levels. It also seems apparent that, again depending on the level, different interpretations of what constitutes education, and for that matter training, prevail. For example it is rare for university teaching positions in the United States to be given to anyone without the supposed high-level *education* indicator, a PhD, although until recently no *training* was thought necessary. Recently, however, there has been an increasing trend towards providing systematic in-service training for staff once they are appointed.

In general, most education systems tend to set *minimum standards* of education *and* training for teachers which vary from level to level. It appears that few, if any, set maximum standards or even optimal ones. Perhaps this is because the usefulness of both education and training are taken for granted. But if Illich and others have valid arguments, we might well be asking how much education and training for teachers is enough and, perhaps more importantly, we might also be asking what kind of education and training is most appropriate.

Be that as it may, the Illich era is not yet on us, so it is quite appropriate to apply the Beeby model to the seven countries of the project.

There are several noteworthy implications. First, given that education is both costly and labour intensive (with much of the cost devoted to labour), most of the economically affluent countries tend to have teaching forces in which the teachers are relatively extensively trained *and* educated. As well, in them there is a closer 'fit' between primary and secondary levels where, though a distinction remains, it is not nearly as apparent as in the four 'less developed' countries.

It *should* follow, then, that unless both education and teacher training are grand illusions, the teachers in the developed countries would have skills and abilities and perhaps insights that are additional to those in the less developed countries. But it may also be that those skills, abilities and insights may be highly 'institution bound'. In other words those teachers may have done little more than become more thoroughly socialized into the system – conformist devotees of the status quo. We might like to think otherwise; we might hope, for example, that because of their more extensive exposure to education, they would be willing and able to push out the boundaries of education. But the depressing testimony from some contemporary critics is that they are not. They are, it is asserted, perceptually and conceptually confined.

On the other hand, to the extent that teachers in the 'less developed' countries are not excessively socialized into the ways of their establishment, they *may* be freer to entertain alternative teaching strategies, particularly those that are more relevant to the everyday life of their pupils. But that presumably depends on the extent to which they are not (i) uncertain of their own capabilities and (ii) under compulsion by the system. However, given the capacities of both the educated and professional members of the Establishment to surround themselves with a mystique of superiority, it may be well nigh impossible for the 'naïve' teacher to be allowed to develop such a degree of self-assurance.

Autonomy and decision making

We are thus led back to the first issue – the extent to which the teachers are given responsibility to make decisions. The range and array of possible decision making that could be left to teachers is *theoretically* considerable. Not only might it include power over teaching procedures, curriculum design, curriculum development and school management, it might also extend to security of tenure and control over appointments. Irrespective of the theoretical possibilities though, the facts are that within our particular sample the greatest autonomy is accorded to teachers in the developed countries. For example, in New Zealand, teachers are free to apply for positions where and when they like and are only removed from them under exceptional circumstances. They are subjected to minimal supervision by 'Ministry' officials who visit them occasionally by right and at other times by invitation. They are virtually free to teach in whatever manner they wish (provided public opposition does not result). Jobs are extremely secure and salary coercions relatively few. Schools also have some measure of choice. For example, though the State does supply textbooks, the schools are free to choose whatever books they wish to use. Depending on the school also, the staff may exert considerable influence on management and policy, not to say professional decisions as well. Although the details differ in Israel and the Federal Republic of Germany, the situation is roughly equivalent. In both countries a considerable measure of autonomy is given to teachers. By contrast, the situation in Malaysia, Indonesia, Ghana and Sierra Leone is such that relatively more control is exercised over teachers by the central authorities. They determine to quite an extent who teaches, what, when and how, and more often than not, where. Curricula are prescribed centrally and uniformity of content is the norm.

The reasons advanced to explain such a state of affairs are varied, and may be administratively, economically or educationally sound. But in Indonesia's case in particular they have another justification that bears on the earlier discussion about identity. In Indonesia at the present moment – 35 years into its young history as a nation – centralization is seen as a means for generating cohesion and stability. Centralization is to serve the purpose of identity by helping to ensure that all the parts of that varied country come to have a common baseline.

Whatever may be the reasons used to justify centralization or decentralization, however, there are implications for the process of reform. Fairly clearly, under a centralized system, nation-wide reform may be legislated extremely quickly – overnight even. But the nature of communication in large centralized systems is such that it is usually a long time before faithful applications of the innovation occur at grass roots level and even longer for an adequate system of surveillance or supervision to be set up. On the other hand, in decentralized systems lack of uniformity and therefore perhaps inequity seem to be the costs paid for more spontaneous adoption and voluntary diffusion.

Once again, such a brief commentary does justice to none of the countries. It neither renders fair account of the nuances or diversities of the systems, nor does it explain the very reasonable reasons that lie behind the existing conditions. Furthermore, in implying as we have that the situation might be otherwise than it is, we have taken an unjustified liberty.

Even so, the fact remains that there are two relatively distinct constellations of circumstances that tend to be characteristic in this study of the three 'developed' countries and the four 'developing' countries respectively. Their effect is that the teachers who have had the relatively greatest amount of education and professional training are given more responsibility and autonomy than those who have the least. While many factors indigenous to the different social contexts may explain why this state of affairs has come about, nonetheless, the simple logic appears to be that the right to autonomy and responsibility is a function of training and education and not vice versa. Interpreted idealistically, this could be taken to mean that education and training 'liberate'. That is, they provide a secure basis for the exercise of professional and responsible judgement. Interpreted cynically, it may be taken to mean that it is only when the players have been thoroughly indoctrinated in the conventions and rituals of the system that a 'facade' of autonomy can be erected.

However, the Indonesian case suggests that perhaps an alternative view ought also to be entertained, namely that in the absence of national cohesion, the exercise of freedom and autonomy is unlikely to be responsible. Such a thesis would seem to touch a nerve or two among some of the Western countries currently agonizing over some of the conditions of their education systems. Whether, however, such a thesis can be sustained when it is remembered that in a number of developed countries, France, Belgium and Switzerland being cases in point, teachers are conceded little autonomy and independence, is an interesting question which will be raised again in the final chapter. There too, opportunity will be taken to pursue (Levin, 1975) distinctions between types of freedom, for example, freedoms under the law, freedoms within conventions and *de facto* freedoms, freedoms, as it were, behind the classroom door.

The arguments are not quite such 'straw man' arguments as they might seem to be on face value, for the following reasons. A great deal of social psychological research in the developed countries seems to indicate that resistance to change is related strongly to the extent to which the people required to change are involved in determining what that change shall be. In other words their autonomy is respected. However, there is also an increasing amount of research on innovation in developing countries that throws up similar findings. This is documented by Havelock and Huberman (1977) for education, but the number of unsuccessful development projects masterminded from the outside or mounted by foreign 'experts' who depart prematurely testifies to it as well.

This gives rise to the point that perhaps the drive for autonomy is a general human characteristic (as Western psychology would assert), rather than a professional one. If so, there may be important implications for the planning of the innovation process and in particular the exercise of control over it. However, if the cohesiveness of the social context is also a significant, perhaps even a critical, factor, then care has to be taken in reconciling the two apparently opposing tendencies.

It is extremely difficult to imagine how countries with young education systems might move swiftly and surely towards universal, equitable and quality education *without* the exercise of strong centralized control. It is equally hard to imagine how teachers could come to exercise responsible and insightful judgements *unless* they are both educated and trained. Yet?

Maybe here is the true heart of the problem that we are addressing in the study. Time will tell – we hope.

Strategies of planning

There is another underlying dilemma that may be equally close to the heart of the issue of innovation. It is clear that two of the countries in particular are treating educational planning as especially important. Both Indonesia and Malaysia have well established planning divisions within their respective ministries and are going about the business of planning, in earnest. Both also are setting their educational planning operations within the framework of long-term national development planning. Both countries are attacking some of the problems of educational development with a degree of systematic thoroughness that is not often approached in the Western world.

By contrast, New Zealand has no separately identifiable division charged with responsibility for planning. And in Nordrhein-Westfalen, although there has been a planning division for 12 years, its activities have a character quite different from those displayed by the South-East Asian operations. In both New Zealand and the Federal Republic of Germany, planning is rather an *ad hoc* business. After all, their systems have been going on for some considerable time. Compulsory, universal and free education started in 1877 in New Zealand's case and in the Federal Republic of Germany, depending on the locality, it started at various dates during the same century. The systems in both countries have their own momentum and inertia. Problems that arose in the past were overcome reasonably well, and as new ones arise, the systems seem to be able to cope. It would not be untrue or unkind to say that both systems operate on a sort of 'day to day' basis and on the assumption that whatever might happen, the system will be able to deal with it. It is also the case that the actual planning of specific activities is dispersed throughout the various sectors of the ministry, with 'renovation' rather than innovation being the principal *modus operandi*. To this extent, both systems are somewhat conservation-minded. Radical change is not thought to be necessary and, by and large, the process of evolution is expected to take care of developmental needs. In quite a real sense the stances adopted at the moment are not particularly forward looking – nor are they backward looking. Nor do the attitudes of mind prevailing appear particularly enthusiastic about change – or resistant to it. In a very true sense, both systems are reactive – not reactionary – that is, they consider themselves ready, willing and able to move when circumstances that warrant it arise. The education systems in Malaysia and Indonesia thus make an interesting contrast to these two older systems.

If this contrast were merely a matter of the 'developing' countries versus the 'developed', then Ghana and Sierra Leone would be found in the first camp and Israel in the second. But this is only partly true. In fact Sierra Leone works within the framework of a 'national development plan' and has among its five professional divisions in the Ministry of Education a Planning and Adult Education Division headed by a senior official (a deputy chief education officer). It is probably true to say that within this formal structure, planning for the immediate future rather than the long-term future takes precedence. As in other British Commonwealth countries, the long-term view is to be found in the reports of various parliamentary and non-parliamentary committees or commissions, rather than in any detailed operational statement. On an imaginary continuum between the reactive type of planning of the Federal Republic and New Zealand and what might be called the proactive type of planning of Indonesia and Malaysia, Ghana tends to fall somewhat more towards the reactive than the proactive end, while Israel falls a little to the proactive side of centre.

Given this kind of variation among the countries, conjecture becomes inevitable. When is proactive planning best? When reactive? What preconditions are necessary for either to work? What are the consequences of employing either style? What is the relationship between 'planning style' and the embedding social environment? Does either style tend to have side effects, and if so, are they beneficial or harmful? Assuming the inevitable influence of history, what were the critical incidents, the precipitating causes that tilted the balance in one direction or another?

We did not know the answers at the time the issue surfaced, but we had more than a slight feeling that, as the English say, 'There are more ways than one of skinning a cat'. If so, once again the project was faced with a substantial problem: whether or not the diversity of the seven situations would prove unmanageable and whether common ground could ever be found.

Research legitimacy

That, however, was not the last of the issues on which the project was at risk. In the early debate between researchers and administrators at the original teaching-learning strategies seminar at IIEP, the researchers had made it clear that according to their canons, the scientific evidence necessary to justify many educational decisions was not available and getting it would entail research that not only took into account the complexity of education but also, if hoping to be legitimate, would take a long time. The administrators had even made it more clear that they could not wait for this to happen and wanted useful information now. On face value, an impasse had been reached. Someone had to give. And the fact that the world would not stop turning meant that the administrators could not be the ones. It seemed then that the only alternative left was for the researchers to try to look for new ways of researching. While the rewards were potentially great, the dangers were considerable. For years the social sciences had been trying to establish scientific legitimacy – a task that had proved immensely difficult in the face of the norms that had been established in the older physical sciences. The degree of 'exactness' possible there had served as the goal and goad of the social scientists. Strive to reach the goal they did, all the time goaded by the criticism, not to say the contempt, of the 'real' scientists, who, having made the rules of their game were determined that it should be the only game in town. While the conflict between the social and the physical scientists has subsided and perhaps the softer methods and much weaker predictions of the social scientists have become tolerated if not accepted, the ghost of the old scientific legitimacy argument seeks ever the opportunity to materialize anew.

History is repeating itself. Within the social sciences themselves, research conventions are becoming firmly established and from them have evolved criteria for determining the 'legitimacy' of one procedure or another. True, there are debates still over the relative merits of various statistical procedures – factor analysis (with varimax rotation, of course!) versus regression analysis, or 'Stake' evaluation versus 'Hamilton and Parlett's', but mostly the research *strategy* is the same, it is only the tactics that are different.

And yet the gulf between research and administration remains. Could it possibly be that the research methods that have evolved are incapable of addressing themselves to the insistent everyday problems of the 'social engineers' in the way that research methods that evolved in the physical sciences address themselves to the problems of, say, 'civil engineers'? Is there a need for a paradigm shift?

For our part, as the project started, we simply did not know. Nor did we have new paradigms. But we did think we ought to try to see if other methods could work and if perhaps a glimpse of a new paradigm might be gained. As it transpired, the 'methodology' we came to employ turned out to be hybrid and its parentage not altogether apparent and perhaps rather difficult to establish. It happened in this way.

In attempting our task, we started from a very simple question and a very simple premise. The question, which though occasionally argued among philosophers of social science does not appear to impinge on the style and practice of research much, was: 'Research for what?' The premise was: 'Given a purpose for the research, investment in the research should not be out of proportion with the kind of return expected'. In other words, if there exists a problem for which a solution is needed, then the kind of research that is warranted depends on: (i) the importance of the problem; (ii) the time available; (iii) the cost of resources; and (iv) the relative benefits to be gained from any kind of solution.

Fairly clearly, such an approach smacks strongly of cost-benefit thinking (but not solely in economic terms) *and* is strongly utilitarian, *and* strongly pragmatic. To this extent it defers to the administrators' reality much more than it does to the scholars'.

The first matter that circumscribed our activities was a harsh fact of educational life. The resources that can be commanded for research tend to be extremely limited. Few educational systems (with Sweden a possible exception) have made research and development a necessary and integral part of their operation. Thus when new research is contemplated, the definition of its scope tends to remain small. Outside education other issues are regarded as much more pressing, while inside education other educational matters take much higher priority. The limits thus imposed on educational research are considerable – little money, time or manpower is available. The consequences are that the research coat, when cut according to the cloth, often turns out to be far from elegant.

In the case of the present project, it would not have been reasonable or right to ask the countries to divert too many of their own human and material resources away from the tasks to which they were already giving priority. Few could have, anyway. Nor were the resources of the IIEP inexhaustible. Consequently, we came to agree that IIEP would take responsibility for international costs and the countries for local ones. In the latter's case, their investment would be determined by what *they* regarded as desirable, given their own needs. What this meant in practical terms was as follows.

Given the IIEP's role as facilitator and each country's right to 'call the play for itself as it saw fit', the rules of the game obviously could not be set by one party alone, least of all the Paris-based IIEP. Consequently, we became obliged to negotiate procedures amongst ourselves. Participatory planning thus became the *modus operandi*. The full story of this interesting exercise in international relations is expected to be told later, but for the moment a few brief details will suffice.

The situation at the beginning was that each of the seven countries had its own particular innovation under way. In actual fact, all also had a built-in research component of one sort or another, usually designed to fulfil some sort of evaluation function. The results from those studies were to be made available for the IIEP project. As well, in each of the countries there was a certain amount of evidence to be found relating to the advent and evolution of each specific innovation. Sometimes it was contained in official reports from government or international agencies, sometimes in 'in-house' documents, sometimes in newspaper reports, sometimes in academic articles or informal records, accounts and comments. As well, all countries produced background statistical material of their own. All of the sources above, once identified and collected, could be tapped for relevant information.

Necessarily, however, such records would sample rather than exhaust the universe of information needed. The gaps remaining were likely to be considerable. To help fill the gap three devices were employed, all of which gave form and purpose to the international characteristic of the general project.

The first device entailed the production of working papers from each of the countries. These were designed to provide (i) some descriptive detail of the innovation and (ii) relevant background information on national educational and social contexts. Subsequently, these served as a basis for discussion and debate on the three occasions the group met between September 1977 and December 1978.

The second entailed the development of a data gathering instrument we called an 'Innovation Dossier' – a strange device, half-way between a questionnaire and an interview schedule but not really pretending to be either. (To an unkind observer, sight of it might well prove the point that a camel must have been a horse designed by a committee.) What the Dossier set out to do was to provide a framework within which *further* information about each innovation could be more systematically sampled. Perhaps it should speak for itself.

Innovation Dossier

Introduction

This Dossier contains an array of questions that bear on the problems associated with planning and implementing officially selected educational innovations.

It has been designed so that the answers given to the questions can be used for diagnosing the condition of the innovation (i) relative to its socio-cultural contexts, and (ii) at particular points in time. These points correspond with what appear to be distinct phases that bear on the evolution of any innovation, viz:

Origination: The conditions that existed prior to the emergence of the innovation and the circumstances that brought it about.

Specification: The development of specifications of the innovation, either general or particular.

Operation: The first uses or applications of the innovation (whether experimental or not, and whether with evaluation or not).

Implementation: The development of procedures to permit or enable the further diffusion of the innovation throughout the system.

Consolidation: The conditions existing when the diffusion of the innovation throughout the system is complete.

In a sense, the categories above could be interpreted as the developmental stages through which innovations have to pass if they are to be put into practice extensively. However, the Dossier makes no *a priori* assumption of this kind, preferring to see if empirical evidence lends support or not. Nonetheless, the Dossier does assume, firstly, that any phase will have repercussions on the next and, secondly, that for each phase to reach culmination, certain necessary conditions will have to be met. These assumptions are reflected in the selection of items in the Dossier and more particularly the acceptance of 11 main elements as worthy of consideration in *each phase*. They are:

  (i) the nature of the *rationale* developed at that stage;
  (ii) the character of the *task* and its content;
  (iii) the working procedures or *methodology*;
  (iv) the *personnel*;
  (v) the *plant*;
  (vi) the *equipment*;
  (vii) the *links* established with relevant social contexts;
  (viii) *evaluation*;
  (ix) *coordination* and management;
  (x) *costing*;
  (xi) *scheduling* and time budgeting.

Procedures

The Dossier consists of four sections, corresponding to the first four phases. Each section contains a series of questions, each with a format that provides space for (i) check list answers; (ii) further written elaboration and comments.

Preceding each section and each question (or series of related questions) are brief 'justifications' that set the limits within which the questions are to be interpreted.

The desired procedure for completing the Dossier is to take each question in sequence and after considering *every* alternative offered:
  (i) respond in the appropriate places on the *check list* and
  (ii) add in the space provided any additional *supplementary information* and comment thought necessary to clarify the answer.

The Dossier is thus half-way between a questionnaire and an interview schedule. However, if its results are to be used effectively, much will depend on the kind of information provided as elaboration or comment.

We are no longer particularly fond of the five rather pretentious names we gave the phases and will have something to say about alternatives in the last chapter. We were also sufficiently cautious about the Dossier's use to include a health hazard warning with it at the time:

'This Dossier has been prepared expressly for the research project "Planning Qualitative Innovations in Education". It has been designed by the participants in that project to be used by them in accordance with conventions they have developed and agreed upon.

Because all of those conventions are not included in the Dossier, the way in which the items are to be employed cannot be properly deduced. Consequently, any use of the Dossier other than for the original purpose will be hazardous and may even be harmful.'

The final 172-page Dossier used was a revised version of an earlier model which, after trial in the seven countries, was subjected to ruthless and detailed criticism by the group collectively over the best part of a week.

When rewritten, it was filled in by either the country representatives themselves or by groups or individuals they regarded as being particularly knowledgeable about the information asked for.

The third device used was to make provision for the IIEP member of the group to visit all the countries, sight the innovation in practice and interview as many of the people involved as time would allow. To him, together with another member of the group, also fell the task of collating the array of information provided from the sources mentioned above and of producing draft chapters which were then subjected to critical examination at the third meeting of the group in Dortmund during the week before Christmas 1978. The subsequent rewriting was allocated to the IIEP member too.

The justification for such a division of labour is fairly straightforward. The members of the national teams, as administrators and researchers, were on the spot, knew the terrain and had access to basic data. They were agreeable to supply it and could do so without too much disruption of their normal duties. The IIEP participant, on the other hand, was well placed to serve as coordinator, collator and interpreter, taking advantage of the conditions of work provided in the Institute.

The book, then, is the result of an interesting, perhaps curious, set of agreements between people of very diverse persuasions. Perhaps this is why the strategy of presentation is rather ethnographic. In telling the story of each innovation we have been obliged to use several different perspectives, somewhat simultaneously – educational, sociological, political, economic, even at times philosophical. While this is consistent with recent (phenomenological) trends in social science, and with the multi-cultural perspective that House (1979) suggests is currently the direction in which innovation research is tending, the approach was not taken with malice aforethought. On the contrary, it seemed to evolve as appropriate for the circumstances, constituting a way in which common ground might be found.

Our search then was for practical expedients rather than profound and universal truths. We took such a stance not because we deny the importance of the latter, but simply because in the 'real world' there are immense and immediate needs that justify, even demand, expedients.

For the orthodox researcher, then, the book will contain heresies. There is much to criticize and condemn according to the established credos and dogmas of research convention. But should we succeed even only half-way in exposing the nature of the immediate existing problems, perhaps the orthodox researcher may be instead tempted to set his mind to finding new ways in which research can properly address them. Perhaps in this way the gap between research and practice can come to be lessened.

To provide the first two illustrations of attempts to change the education system we have chosen Indonesia and the Federal Republic of Germany, for one main reason and a number of subsidiary ones. The main reason is that they both employ distinctive but highly contrasting styles of planning. The subsidiary ones bear to some extent on planning and have primarily to do with how educational decisions are made, what criteria are used to justify them and what is supposed to be accomplished by undertaking them. They all give rise to the questions – whose purposes *does* the education system serve, whose purposes *should* it serve and, more poignantly, what purposes *can* it serve. The Indonesian case comes first.

Chapter 2
Indonesia: Quality in Quantity

In order to give some small indication of the conditions under which Indonesian innovation has evolved, it is worth while, though quite unfair, to start with a challenge to the reader. What would you have done: if you had inherited responsibility for Indonesian education in 1945, when independence was declared? Amongst your inheritance you will find the following:

- a country of 7000 inhabited islands and 6000 uninhabited ones;
- a total area (land and sea) which, if superimposed on Europe, would stretch all the way from the westernmost tip of Spain, across France, Italy and Greece and into Turkey – a distance greater than the breadth of continental USA or Indonesia's near neighbour to the south, Australia, and equivalent to about two-thirds of the distance across the broadest part of Africa;
- a population of 110 million, that is destined in a short 30 years to exceed 130 million;
- your culture predates Christianity by many centuries and, on the evidence of the prehistoric 'Java man' skull, it is estimated that your ancestors even go back 500,000 years;
- your known history includes three great eras – great for different reasons. Round about the year AD1 began 13 centuries of Hindu migration. The Hindus then gradually became supplanted, mostly peacefully, as Arabs, Persians and other Indians made their presence strongly felt. European intrusion (mainly though not exclusively Dutch) had its beginning in the early part of the 16th century and finished four centuries later;
- the Islamic faith introduced in the 14th century has maintained its strength over the years and 80 per cent of your people are Moslems;
- your people live now mostly in villages (approximately 60,000 of them) and sustain an agrarian existence that in some cases is only above subsistence level;
- there is much poverty, although Indonesia constituted the fabled East Indies treasure islands of early European colonial days;
- the country has considerable economic potential, but not at that moment the financial means or expertise to exploit it, now that the Dutch have left;

The Process of Educational Innovation

- a 90 per cent rate of illiteracy;
- most of your people have never been to school;
- your indigenous population includes no university graduates;
- many of the schools that did exist were damaged or destroyed during the Japanese invasion;
- your aspiration and that of your people is for economic development and social equity;
- finally, during the next five years your people will be at war to make independence secure, a war that will wreak further havoc on the material conditions of towns and schools.

Much more could be added to such a list. As it stands, it only touches on a handful of the features of a nation whose culture is richly varied, centuries deep in civilization and which was, at that time (1945), beset by many problems. But this is not the place to catalogue the problems. Instead, in order to establish the baseline on which the Indonesian innovation rests, it is more appropriate to indicate what had transpired in the years intervening between independence and the present.

Only a few brief points need to be made. The first four relate to the general condition of the country as 1978 gets under way, the last five to the educational situation.

Over the period between 1945 and 1978, despite problems and difficulties, the economy has continued to grow and it has done so to the extent that the latest recorded growth rate (1977) was seven per cent.

There is now a thriving export industry in which oil and gas feature prominently (an eighty-fold increase in the last decade). Timber, rubber, tin, palm oil and coffee are also noteworthy contributors to what is now an annual export growth rate of 20 per cent.

A substantial development programme with an annual budget (1978-1979) of approximately six billion dollars is now into the final year of a second five-year plan, prior to the development of the next plan.

A successful birth control policy has slowed the rate of population increase, to the extent that the 1977 total fell five million short of the anticipated 135 million.

School rolls have increased dramatically. Before independence 2,415,000 pupils were attending primary school. By 1960 the number was 10,000,000, but with 4,000,000 still unserved. By 1975 the number was up to 14,000,000, while by 1979 85 per cent of all school age children up to sixth grade are expected to be in school.

The annual budget for education has become (1974-1975) 557 billion rupiahs (approximately US$1.25 billion) and education features as the fifth highest investment in the second five-year development plan. Agriculture and irrigation, communication and tourism, regional and local development, and government capital participation exceed it, but education ranks highest in percentage increase since the first five-year plan.

In 1945 there existed 15,000 primary school buildings and in 1970, 66,000. A new Programme of Assistance initiated in 1973 has seen the building of another 6000 primary school units (three classrooms plus teachers' room) in the first year of operation and 10,000 in each of the next two years.

By 1978 the government textbook programme will have produced and distributed some 200 million free textbooks to primary schools. A further project to produce 138 million books over a six-year period has been planned. It will consume 23,500 tons of paper.

The general expansion of education implies that more and more teachers will be required. The estimate is some 38,000 annually.

Again, such a catalogue could be extended to considerable length, but it is hoped that this very brief selection will serve to accomplish two things. First, it will indicate in particular the sheer magnitude of the Indonesian situation. Planning an education system almost from scratch is difficult enough at any time. But to do so for so large and populous a country with such complex logistic problems stemming from such an unusual and varied geography and history is a task of Herculean proportions. Second, it will indicate that initially attention *had* to turn towards the overcoming of quantitative deficiencies that existed. At first the overriding concern was to provide enough schools and enough teachers so that an increasingly greater proportion of the population could at least gain access to schooling.

It is understandable, under the circumstances existing, that at the beginning of nationhood Indonesia gave no great amount of attention to the quality of education that was being provided. But as time went by, more and more concern came to be expressed over whether education was in fact making the contribution it should to society's development or not. Then in 1969, in response to increasing criticism, an unusual event occurred – unusual in that an exercise of this kind has rarely been undertaken anywhere and certainly never attempted in a country so large. A nation-wide assessment of education was commissioned. This comprised a careful and systematic examination of the existing status and condition of education. Given the resources available and the circumstances under which the study was done, it was a remarkable piece of work in its own right. However, more to the point of the present topic, it was subsequently to provide the basis for the devising of a reform strategy that also had unusual features.

Planning a system

The reform strategy was to constitute a continuing programme for improving the general quality of the existing system and also for adopting 'A long-range programme to re-structure the entire educational system'. It is from this latter ambition that the focus of the present chapter arises.

The Indonesian innovation under consideration is a proposed curriculum reform that, if found to be feasible, will serve as a basis for this eventual restructuring of the education system. As such it is particularly important, but it needs to be seen in perspective as but one of the many efforts currently being made, all of which are directed towards the same end: national

The Process of Educational Innovation

economic, cultural and social development. The particular curriculum development exercise falls, of course, within the formal schooling system and, at the moment, touches on only a minute portion of the system. Elsewhere in the formal system more extensive steps are being taken to meet immediate needs – for example, to reform existing curricula, improve and supply textbooks, provide in-service training, etc.

At the outset of our consideration of the curriculum development project, however, there are three features of the longer-range reform plan that are particularly worth noting: (i) the reform was to be done systematically; (ii) it was to start at classroom level – on the assumption that that is where quality is created; and (iii) it was to grow step by step, with each step justified by experimental evidence derived from extensive trials.

These three characteristics – starting at classroom level, 'growing' the reform piece by piece, and basing it on experimental evidence – make this undertaking quite singular. Basically, this is a reform to be achieved through the direct changing of the educational process. As such it contrasts with the preferred stance of most countries where it would be true to say that more often than not emphasis has tended to be placed on indirect means, structural reform or legislative reform, thus making the assumption that if the structure is put 'right', then changes in the process will happen as a consequence. To allow functional reforms to dictate the nature of structural reforms, as the Indonesians are contemplating, represents a degree of divergent thinking that is quite unique. There is, however, a great deal of logic that resides in the argument that if you want to modify the education that children receive, then the most appropriate place to start is where the children get it, in the classroom.

Nonetheless, the task was to be approached with due care and caution because of the profound implications of both undertaking and accomplishing it. This last sentence has particular significance for matters that emerge later in the chapter.

Given a project of such ambition, but as well one that *is* adopting a scientific approach to development, its fate is of particular interest. But we should start at the beginning.

It was 'the Assessment', as it is popularly known, that gave the initial impetus to the reform. The Assessment had been designed to provide an up-to-date report on the present status of education in Indonesia and to consider, *without making recommendations*, some alternative routes to improvement. A representative of the Ford Foundation described the undertaking in these terms:

> 'The objective is not to produce a Plan for education, to be carried out according to a fixed formula and time-table. It is not to make a survey of what Indonesia has. Rather the purpose is to develop a *strategy* of education which could be used for guidance over a number of years, and would fit into development plans as the action goes forward. The Assessment should be an *assessment*, not an encyclopaedia

of detailed data, statistics, cost calculations in detail; nor an inventory of schools, teachers, curricula and related subdata.'

The Assessment had many points to make, but standing out among its conclusions was the criticism that the way teaching was being done at the time was inappropriate for a modern Indonesia.

'It could not meet the challenges of this age, and in particular it was not able to meet the challenges of a developing society. There was a separating wall between the school and society.'

(Mashuri, 1969)

The Assessment thus served to pose the problem, but in this case it neither proffered specific solutions, nor did it consider the means through which reform might be achieved.

A logical place to start

To have the problem thus defined is one thing — and a very necessary one — but to know what to do about it is quite another. But at least, with the problem defined, planning could begin. And it began, in what has now become a characteristically Indonesian style — systematically. The Assessment had said that the problem was located in the classroom. Logic would dictate that remediation therefore ought to be undertaken there too. Such logic is deceptively simple, because it tends to conceal the numerous and complex implications that follow, many of which could be economically, politically and educationally troublesome. The scope and size of such problems have daunted many nations who, when faced with them, have instead sought the apparently easier, but not necessarily effective, way out through administrative and organizational restructuring.

However, with the classroom selected as the point of departure, there yet remained to determine the direction to be taken and the means to be used. Again the approach was logical and systematic. At the outset of the project, recourse was made in the first instance to the general aims of education formulated by the Assembly in 1973. These were, in summary:

'To educate a "development oriented" man with the character of Pancasila and to develop Indonesians who are healthy, mentally and physically, having knowledge and skills, being creative and responsible, democratic and tolerant, being able to develop high intellectual abilities, being conscientious and loving the nation and mankind, consistent with the values of the 1945 Constitution.'[1]

Like many statements of educational aims, the ideals are exemplary, but they leave room for considerable flexibility in interpretation. However, the particular human qualities specified could certainly not be achieved by the prevailing 'chalk and talk' style of teaching. Furthermore, those human

---

1 Each five years the Government, in order to give guidance to the administration, produces a reformulated statement of general aims.

qualities were capable of being reduced to a set of specifiable component skills which then could form the basis for developing a relevant curriculum. Accordingly, this was done and a framework for reform was laid. As a first step three general desiderata were formulated:
- It is advisable that the school become an integral part of the society around it.
- It is advisable that the school be development oriented and progress oriented so that it can equip the work force with character, knowledge and skill in order to develop the nation in different fields.
- It is advisable that the school have a curriculum and a teaching method which is pleasing, challenging, and in harmony with that aim.

Further refinements were to follow, and more later still, but before these are discussed, another policy decision taken at the same time ought to be noted. It also served to set the scene more precisely and as well to put educational reform into a true perspective.

Early in the planning, a decision had been made to set up an education system, as it were, in miniature. It was to comprise eight schools within which the new curriculum would be evolved. Even at that early stage it was recognized that hand in hand with the curriculum would have to go a new approach to teaching, a new support system of plant, equipment, supervision and training, and of course a new organizational framework both within schools and throughout the mini-system. One prospect also envisaged at the beginning was that the conventional six-year elementary, three-year junior high school and three-year senior high school pattern would give way to an eight-year elementary, four-year secondary school one.

First moves

A structure for action

The scheme got off to a quiet start in 1971, with eight duly nominated Development Schools selected primarily because all fell under the jurisdiction of relatively accessible teachers' colleges (IKIPs). For the first two years, a Committee of Eleven (appointed by the Minister of Education and Culture, and consisting of ministry officials) supervised the activities of the eight schools. By and large the schools were left to their own devices, partly because at that stage the model for the project was only expressed in general terms and partly because it was thought that if the schools retained their independence, alternative variations on the theme would emerge. This was not to be the case, and after the end of two years, when the slow rate of progress was becoming a matter of concern, a series of events transpired which gave the project a dramatic new twist.

A cabinet reshuffle saw the Minister of Education receive a new portfolio and the former rector of the University of Indonesia appointed to Education. It was because of his scientific bent of mind that greater emphasis came to

Indonesia: Quality in Quantity

be placed on both the pilot nature of the present development schools and also on experimental and evaluation aspects. Coincidentally, it was decided that the project should come under the control of the influential Badan Penelitian dan Pengembangan Pendidikan dan Kebudayaan (BP3K – the Office of Educational and Cultural Research and Development), a professional organization within the Ministry of Education and Culture deliberately set up as a mechanism for inducing change in the education system. It was given considerable latitude to search for creative solutions to existing problems and was charged with, among other things, the development of operational prototypes in accordance with policy decisions. The mandate given in the present case was to go ahead and produce a demonstrably workable plan.

There then followed a series of meetings involving all the leaders of the development schools project, senior national and regional educational officials and educational experts. The meetings yielded two important decisions. The first was that a new strategy for managing the development schools project was to be devised, and the second that there was to be *one* master design to be followed by all eight schools.

The considerable resources of BP3K, channelled through its Centre for Curriculum Development, were now thrown behind the project. Four national working groups were set up, one each for curriculum development, evaluation, guidance and counselling, and school administration. Clearly a stage of centralized master-minding was about to be initiated and, as will become apparent later, in a highly systematic way. The principle distinguishing feature of the new regime was the organizational structure that was set up to facilitate progress. Its composition and character is set out in Figure 1. Clearly the project was moving out of the earlier somewhat informally organized, tentative phase into one that had a more defined sense of direction and a more precise specification of roles.

For the purposes of the present chapter, we shall be most concerned with the curriculum development group, partly because it is their aspect of the reform that constitutes the focus of the IIEP study, and partly because in the early years most emphasis, logically enough, was put on curriculum development.[1]

In quest of a teaching-learning strategy

The curriculum development group is the biggest of the groups and has seven sub-groups, one each for science education, mathematics, social studies, Pancasila moral education, Indonesian, English, and skill development. The members came from the Curriculum Development Centre itself, from the IKIPs that control the development schools and from universities and other units of the Ministry of Education and Culture – a circumstance that proved to have some drawbacks subsequently. Provision was also made for the use of overseas experts whenever their services were thought to be

---

[1] For the information presented in this section, heavy reliance has been placed on the clear and comprehensive account given by Soedijarto (1977).

The Process of Educational Innovation

Figure 1: *Managerial organization of development school projects*

Source: Soedijarto, 1977.

* Coordinated by Centre for Curriculum Development of BP3K
** Led by a project leader under the supervision of the Rector of the Teachers College Concern

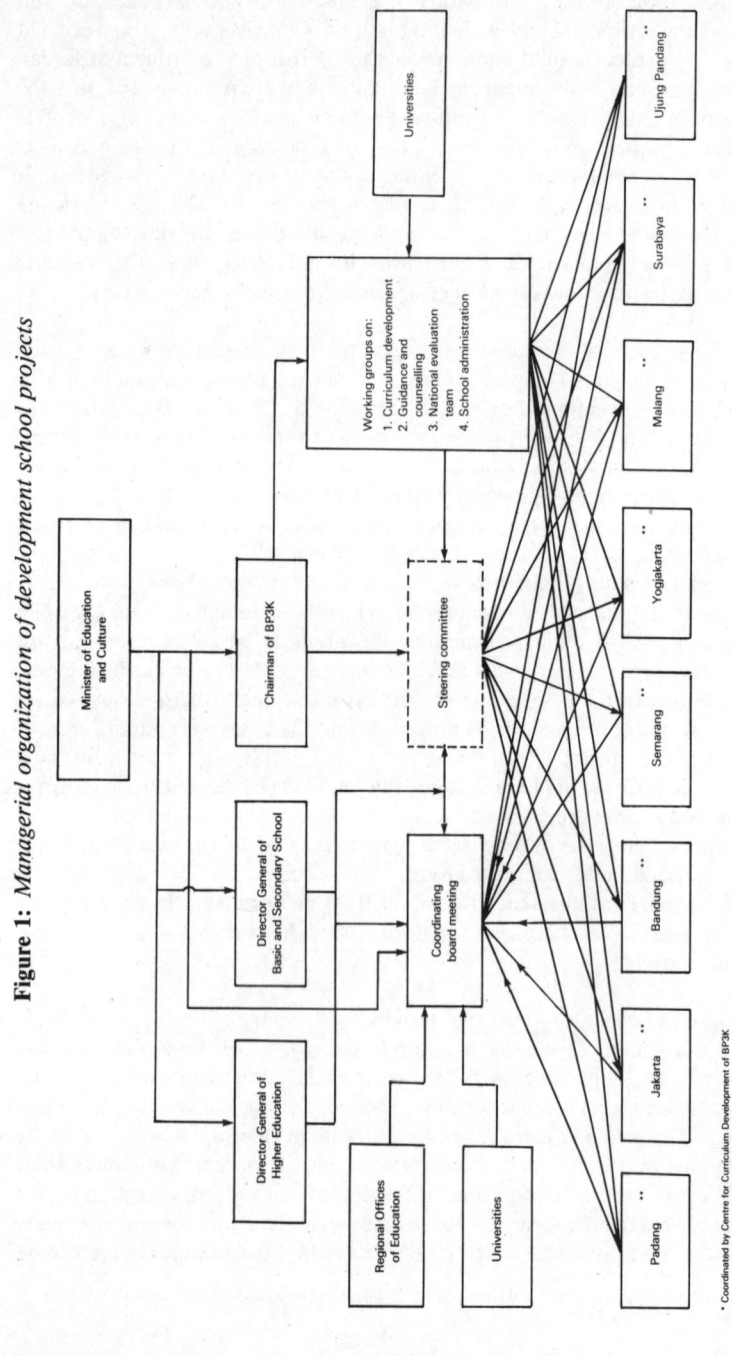

useful – another decision that was not without interesting consequences.

The first task for the curriculum development group was to come to terms with the policy decision to adopt a master plan for all the development schools. Because there are, it seems, many routes to curricular salvation, their problem was to determine which one to take. The search began, but it was a search informed by previous experience. In 1971 when the development schools were not under its control, BP3K had conducted 'a comprehensive survey to identify educational objectives relevant to national needs for development'. The results of this survey had then been used as a basis for formulating curricular and instructional objectives for all subject areas and all levels from elementary through senior high school. In this way the curriculum was expected to be closely related to the developmental needs of the country and certainly consistent with the perceptions of the community. However, it is worth noting at this stage that the specification of subject areas, while both consistent with history and serving to make curriculum development more focused, did foreclose on the prospect of a broadfield or integrated curriculum. So, to some extent, did the next development.

Any contemporary view of curriculum worth its salt includes not only the content or subject matter and the media by which it is to be conveyed, but also the system of delivery or teaching method to be used. The question in this case (which would determine how the 'syllabus' would be constructed) was: which kind of delivery system? Such a question is not, of course, merely a question of what method is currently regarded by educators as best. Clearly, it is a question that must be seen in context. At that time, in the Indonesian context, there were certain existing conditions that severely circumscribed whatever answers might be contemplated. The most insistent of these was the almost unimaginable growth of the education system. In 1945 there had been 2,500,000 children in primary school. By 1978 there were 20,000,000. The secondary school figures are even more imposing. Over the same period, the numbers went from 100,000 to 3,000,000. In effect, secondary school enrolments were doubling every six years – *a growth rate that is expected to continue over the next five years*. It needs no great imagination to recognize that the task of getting and training teachers under such circumstances is extremely difficult. As the Assessment showed, even before 1974 more than half of the existing teachers were unqualified. And since 1974 more than half of the *new* teachers for secondary schools have comprised 12th grade graduates who have been given a one-year 'crash' training programme.

It is against this background that the quest for an appropriate teaching-learning system must be seen. The quest, however, was aided by the continuing process of defining and refining educational objectives. That process had by now yielded new fruit. Ministerial Decree Number 41 (1974) had set the terms. The curriculum should be:

(a) effective and relevant to individual and societal needs as reflected in the educational programmes offered;

The Process of Educational Innovation

(b) a basis for lifelong education;
(c) efficient and realistic and consistent with the resources and capabilities of the Indonesian Government, society, and people.

Responding, BP3K produced a Project Statement that again by a process of refinement took these aims one step closer to practical realization:

1. To develop student-centred courses in all subject areas for all age levels.
2. To develop courses at the school level relevant for those proceeding to employment in rural as well as urban areas and also for those continuing their studies in colleges and universities.
3. To develop courses and a management system which are sufficiently flexible to cater for students of all interests, needs and potentials.
4. To develop courses that are sensitive to the environment of the individual and enhance national spirit and identity.
5. To develop effective means of delivering the courses, including improved buildings, facilities, materials, and teachers' education.
6. To develop a comprehensive and continuous evaluation system of students and courses so that weaknesses can be corrected and strengths exploited.
7. To develop guidance and counselling procedures so that each student can be assisted to derive the greatest benefit from the educational opportunities available.

A form was rapidly emerging, and more and more the quest was leading towards one particular solution. That solution became finally justified when some of the other circumstances existing in Indonesian education at the time were taken into account.

It will be remembered that the Assessment had made some trenchant criticisms of existing teaching practice in Indonesia. Those criticisms, however, were prospective oriented. Not concerned with allocating blame – which in the light of history would never have been justified – they did aspire to the better things. The problem was how to get from the present undesired state of affairs to the desired. Realistically, it was recognized that at the present time the teachers were faced with a number of difficulties. The teaching profession was neither held in very high regard nor well paid. To supplement their none-too-substantial incomes, many teachers also undertook out-of-school jobs that, predictably, consumed 'spare time' and exerted some toll on energy reserves. Consequently, any attempt at extensive retraining of teachers would have to start at a relatively low level and, given the size of the country, take a long time. What was needed, it was thought, was a way of avoiding such a protracted undertaking. The most promising solution appeared to reside in finding an approach that would be as 'teacher proof' as possible and would simplify rather than complicate the teacher's life. At the time too, although the Indonesian economy had been developing, there were still enough financial problems to make cost an important issue. The new system was supposed to be both educationally efficient and economically restrained.

It happened that in the quest for a better teaching-learning process, the wide-ranging search led to the idea of mastery learning, as it had initially been formulated by Bloom.

Towards modular instruction

Mastery learning as a concept has considerable appeal. It enshrines the conviction that with (i) the appropriate definition of achievable learning objectives, plus (ii) a logical exposition of the sequence of steps necessary to achieve them, plus (iii) *sufficient time*, most children (even all) can achieve mastery. The appeal lies in the essentially democratic idea that educational excellence, rather than being the sole preserve of a privileged elite, can, in fact, be shared much more equitably. In a context such as Indonesia's, where the education system was young, where much lost time had to be made up and where an educational baseline had yet to be established, the promise inherent in mastery learning was most attractive. We will have occasion later to examine mastery learning a little more closely, but for the moment it is sufficient to indicate that the basic idea of mastery learning came to be adopted in Indonesia as the general orientation first taken in search of a better teaching-learning process. However, the qualification should be made that such an orientation was taken neither lightly nor uncritically. In fact, the Indonesians, knowledgeable of writings of Piaget, Gagné and more particularly Bruner, produced their own distinctive variations on the mastery learning theme, which they then called the Indonesian Modular Instruction System.

The term *Modular Instruction* in Indonesian education refers to instruction conducted by means of a series of teaching-learning modules. In this system, a semester's curriculum in any one subject area is broken down into a set of manageable parts (called learning units) each of which is developed into a module. A module is a packet of suggestions for teachers and learning materials for students that can be used for pursuing specified learning goals for a period of time that may be as short as a week of class periods and as long as one month of class sessions. The Indonesian modular system is designed to take advantage of all sorts of teaching-learning methods and materials in the sense that it is not limited to self-learning materials.

The general structure of each module is the same. That is, every module is composed of:

'(a) a teachers' guide booklet or guide sheet;
(b) a set of learning activities students are to pursue in achieving learning objectives;
(c) a worksheet which enables the student to record his or her solutions to the problems posed in the module;

(d) a means of evaluating how well the student has achieved the learning objectives of the module.

In addition to the above-mentioned elements, a method of pre-evaluation (diagnoses), remedial activities and enrichment programmes also become the elements of a module.'

(Soeprapto and Ibrahim, 1978)

While very systematic in its approach, the Indonesian modular instruction system should not be confused with programmed learning. Soedijarto (1977) points out the differences:

Figure 2: *On the differences between the Modular Instructional System and the Programmed Instruction*

Dimensions	Module	Programmed text
Teacher's role	Important, especially in managing learning processes	Very little, almost nothing. It is purely self-instructional
Time	Flexible	Flexible
Types of objectives to be achieved	– cognitive, psychomotor, and affective – stated as well as unstated	– mostly cognitive – mostly stated objectives
Instructional approach	Informative as well as discovery	Informative
Types of media used	Multimedia	Printed materials
Student activities	Varied and lively	Mechanistic
Types of feedback	What and why**	What* (except for branching type)
Types of evaluation used	Paper and pencil as well as performance tests	Paper and pencil tests

* student knows that he is correct or incorrect.
** student knows that he is correct or incorrect and then he can ask for further explanation from the teacher.

Necessarily, of course, such a system entails quite dramatic changes in teacher role and in the role of the pupil, with, under ideal circumstances, the pupil becoming a self-motivated and independent worker and the teacher becoming an 'organizer, diagnostician, prescriber and resource person' (Soeprapto and Ibrahim) – quite a step for both teacher and pupil, given the existing state of affairs.

However, there was yet a long way to go. At the time the decision was taken to adopt modular instruction, there were virtually no means at hand to achieve it. No more than one or two people knew about modular instruction, and even fewer knew how to write modules. The decision taken in hope now had to be turned into reality.

Immediately there began a flurry of activity to provide the necessary wherewithal to proceed. A Unesco curriculum consultant was appointed, members of the curriculum development working group went overseas to take courses, and then local training workshops were run for prospective writers.

A plan for educational development

At the same time, as all this was happening, in order to keep faith with the experimental and scientific mandate, a development plan for the project was formulated. It comprised basically a programme of events, but it also set the strategy that makes the project so distinctive. Figure 3 on page 43 carries the details. If the real sense and sentiment of the Indonesian approach is to be appreciated, Figure 3 should be studied carefully.

Figure 3 lays out the rationale of the whole development schools project and indicates the basic dimensions of the task as it was conceived then. In it the systematic steps that will be taken to achieve the objectives are laid out with precision. First to come is an outline of the 'course' – that is then followed by an enunciation of the scope and sequence of content. This is to be evaluated, edited and, following discussion, sanctioned so that thereupon specific behavioural objectives for the development of *units* can be formulated. Again editing and sanctioning is to follow, this time as a forerunner to the preparation of the *modular programmes*. The latter, after initial evaluation, editing and sanctioning, would constitute the first 'package' to be put into practice in the development schools. At that stage, recognizing that without a deliberate attempt to prepare teachers, the fate of the curricular materials would be uncertain to say the least, the beginning of the first trial is to be prefaced by in-service training. Thereafter the curricula are to be applied, their effectiveness (and efficiency) evaluated, and revision undertaken. Once again editing and sanctioning by discussion and consensus is to follow before the second trial gets under way (observing the same sequence as before). Thereupon is to follow a final editing and sanctioning before the plans for the next stage are launched. This next stage is to have three components: first a teacher training component, second an administrative induction component, and third a systematically developed plan for implementation.

Finally, all of these last activities are to be undertaken with due regard for the constraints and possibilities inherent in the existing organizational and administrative structure of schools in general and the education system in particular.

There are three features about the plan that are worth noting in particular here. The first is the systematic and rational way in which events have been specified and sequenced. The second is the provision made for continuous evaluation with feedback and revision, and the third is the amount and frequency of conferring among interested parties. As a plan it must have instant appeal to many of the advocates of systematic and rational curriculum

The Process of Educational Innovation

Figure 3: *The development school project*

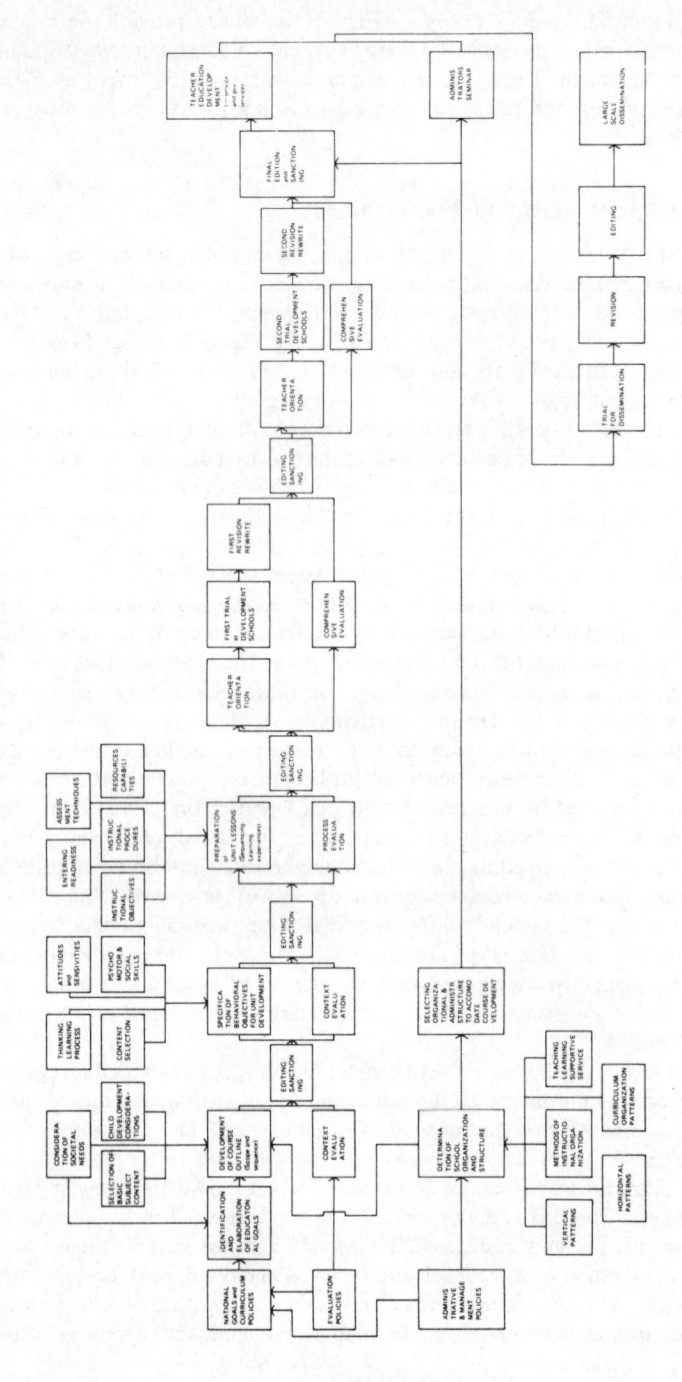

Source: Soedijarto, 1977.

development. It has an internal logic with which it is very difficult to argue, and it has as well built-in 'recovery' mechanisms, should anything go wrong.

Making the modules

However, detailed though the plan is, it by no means covers everything. So before we start to examine what happened, it is necessary to spell out one or two of the details. Perhaps the point at which to start is with the way in which the curricular materials will be constructed. The basic procedure is for teachers' college lecturers (who though now somewhat remote from teaching are subject-matter specialists) to write the initial materials. These are then to be given to teachers to put them into practice. During the teaching of a unit, a series of performance tests is to be used to identify the level of pupil achievement and what remedial steps might be necessary.

Now clearly, *any* unit of a curriculum (whether part of the modular system or a chapter in a textbook) is both selective and biased. It is selective in that some kinds of information are favoured over others, it is biased in that it must adopt a specific stance or point of view. This state of affairs may be less contentious and of less consequence in mathematics than, say, social studies,[1] but it is nonetheless a fact of life. The problem, then, is what bias should be adopted and what selection made. In the present system the *de facto* situation is that the biases – or perhaps orientations is a better word – are initially set out in the course outline and then get interpreted by the individual curriculum writers. Subsequent evaluation of the material can result in changes being made. This is how that can occur. In the process of developing performance and diagnostic tests, items are first generated. By definition they must be finite in number and cannot cover the universe. They thus also constitute a selection from among all the questions that are theoretically possible. In the trial of such tests, further selection is made among items on the basis of pupil performance. Now, because the objective of the test is to assure performance mastery, mastery itself needs definition. Initially mastery was defined as 85:75 success, that is, 85 per cent of the pupils could achieve a 75 per cent pass rate in answering the test items. In general terms, the objective was to increase the average level of mastery of the pupils and decrease the range between them. As well, there was the intention to remove disparities so that, for example, disadvantaged groups, eg girls and rural children, should not be discriminated against. Obviously, there are two ways at least to attack the problem of unsatisfactory performance on the tests. One either manipulates the *cause* of undesired performance, or the effect of it. In the present case both practices are followed to some extent. Where the prior test performances appear to have a pattern that implies the module has been inadequately written, revision occurs. On the other hand, when certain items are shown to discriminate 'unfairly', the items are changed or eliminated.

---

[1] Although Dr Soeprapto gives an interesting account of how some Indonesian teachers, having been brought up with the Van Dalen convention that specifies that in compound calculations all multiplications should be dealt with first, could only be convinced that this was 'incorrect' through demonstration on an (appropriate type of) calculator.

As part of the determination to achieve a desired level of mastery for the majority of children, another policy has been initiated. This entails: (i) the testing and retesting of materials *until* the standard has been achieved, and (ii) the accepting of the consequence that any *further* steps should be undertaken only then.

Initial progress

The newly structured, organized and planned project started making headway in effect towards the end of 1974. By the beginning of 1978 a certain amount had been accomplished and some problems had surfaced. Given that the whole plan from conception to implementation will cover many years, at this stage the project has had a relatively short life. Accordingly there is no great advantage in adopting a chronological approach in describing events. Rather, an attempt will be made to locate 'interesting' developments that have implications both for the outcome of the project and planning in general.

At the present time (1978) the eight development schools are well under way, and the project is approaching the stage nominated as the second trial period in Figure 2, when the revised materials are to be tried out again in the pilot schools and some are to be given to schools other than the original eight. By this time there have been several developments of note.

The first trial of the original draft of curricular materials did take place on schedule in 1975. While this trial served to yield much information useful for the revision of units and modules and as well some problems, it also surfaced some positive gains. Some of the gains were cognitive ones, although the most encouraging outcomes tended to be tangential to the performance issues. It was apparent that the children and the teachers, though some initially showed signs of dismay at the unfamiliar requirements of the programme, had, after further in-service training, come to be more acceptant of and even enthusiastic about it. It was apparent that the children were spending more time 'on task' than previously and, interestingly, were using the library far more extensively than before. The teachers for their part expressed their interests verbally but also tended to spend more of their time in preparation. On the other hand, the trial also revealed some problems. The high level of average performance hoped for was not yet forthcoming and the questionnaire used for gaining feedback from the teachers was inappropriate for giving the writers some of the leads they needed. This last was easily corrected; the other posed a more serious problem. The dilemma facing the developers was: should a lower than wished for performance level be accepted in the interest of keeping on schedule, or not?

After due consideration, it was decided that there was enough evidence for believing that the curricular materials and the tests could be upgraded sufficiently to yield a result not too far from the criteria originally specified. Accordingly, it was decided that after the materials were re-written, a second testing would be undertaken.

Almost concurrently there occurred another development that also indicated the capacity of the system to adapt to contingencies. Some of the problems in the modules resided understandably enough in the way teachers interpreted their roles. It was decided, therefore, to produce a teachers' instruction guide that would serve to introduce teachers to modular teaching. Reasonably enough, it was produced in modular form itself.

Public testimony

Meanwhile, outside the actual trial (which was primarily concerned with the 'educational aspects'), there were other occurrences that served to exert an influence. Provision had been made for two coordination meetings to be held every year under the direction of the Minister of Education and Culture, no less. A coordination meeting involves about 150 people and includes rectors of universities and teachers' colleges, senior Ministry of Education and Culture officials, representatives from the National Planning Board, the heads of provincial education offices, Members of Parliament and leaders of the Indonesian Teachers Association. A major purpose of the meeting is to have reports from the leaders of each development school and from the four working group leaders. Changes of programme are first discussed and then presented for approval by the coordination meeting participants. The organization of the coordination meeting is under the immediate control of the Chairman of BP3K. Preparation for it is undertaken at preliminary meetings of evaluators, writers and administrators who prepare detailed reports on the status and condition of the project.

These various meetings serve a number of purposes. In the first place they force a running evaluation of the project to be made by those who are particularly close to it. In the second place they result in the application of some 'fresh' perspectives that can be useful. In the third place they serve a very important socio-political purpose of keeping the members of the educational power elite informed of the project and committed to it. This continuing socialization is also, as the BP3K Chairman's account indicates, extended to include some of the politically powerful as well. Be it noted, however, that at this stage the consumer groups, pupils and parents, are largely on the periphery.

In a similar vein, in that it too entails the active participation of an influential network, the sanctioning meetings at all stages of curriculum development are set up to contain a mixture of professional educators and administrators. Again, several purposes are thus served. They include primarily: (i) ensuring that the administrators' perspective is accommodated to, and (ii) that the administrators do not feel excluded from a project that eventually will affect 'their' spheres of influence.

By March 1976, the sky was relatively clear, although there were one or two small clouds on the horizon. The Chairman of BP3K identified several:

1. It was proving difficult to keep to a schedule that would permit the modules to arrive in the schools on time and in the best sequence. This was due partly to the fact that competent module writers were

in relatively short supply and were only available part-time, and partly to problems encountered by the commercial printers contracted to do the job.
2. Initially too there was some difficulty in getting the most useful kind of information from teachers who were trialling the materials. It was, of course, impossible to observe every lesson and the teachers were not always aware of what kind of feedback would be most helpful to the writers.
3. Finally, there was reason for believing that the quality of some of the modules was not always of the desired standard.

Since 1976, however, progress has been steady and a number of the chinks in what was otherwise a fairly substantial suit of armour have been closed. Steps have been taken to upgrade the module writing. Not only have refresher courses been run locally, but after specific needs surfaced, overseas experts were brought in for short duration consultancies. One spin-off from the latter was the institution of a three-month module writers' course held for a team of Indonesians at one American university. Subsequently, several professional staff members in BP3K also spent time overseas in pursuit of project-relevant expertise.

The second evaluation of the modules and tests has taken place and the results were much closer to the original goal, although the ambitious objective set earlier has had to be modified. Teachers and pupils continue to express support for the project and there are two indicators of success that are particularly noteworthy, although perhaps they should at the moment be regarded with a little caution. It will be remembered that the original plan envisaged a structural change in the system with an eight-year primary school and four-year secondary school to replace the existing 6-3-3 model. Quite early in the piece that idea was abandoned and instead a hope was expressed that the work of the existing six years of primary school might be compressed into five years, so that the proposed new model became 5-3-3. Indications are that this might indeed be possible, thus in effect accelerating the progress of development school children by up to one year.

The other indicator may turn out to be transitory – but it also may not. One of the development schools is in a rural community and had not hitherto achieved any success in the public examinations held at the end of grade six for entry into secondary school. This year (1978) for the first time its students were successful – ten in all passed. And these were the first students to have had continuous exposure to modular instruction.

A look to the future

Curriculum development

At this point in the chapter it is necessary to depart from the account of events that transpired and engage in an exercise that is to become customary in each of the chapters dealing with a specific country. By the terms of the

Indonesia: Quality in Quantity

IIEP project, we are obliged to try to look into the future – to forecast what it might hold. The purpose is to try to identify potential problems and consequently to consider what might accordingly be done. Necessarily such an exercise entails that a deliberately negative stance be adopted at the beginning. We must, in order to counter difficulties, find the problems that create them first. Accordingly, the next paragraphs will attempt to probe for sensitive areas and then gauge whether the twinge is likely to develop into an ache and the ache into an ailment, or not.

Perhaps the best place to start is with the development of the curriculum. To put the comments in perspective it should be acknowledged that no perfect curriculum has ever been produced and no perfect textbook ever written. A measure of dissatisfaction with any curriculum is as inevitable as it may, at times, be divine. Predictably then, there are grounds for raising points over aspects of the curricular materials themselves and the process used in their construction.

There is a problem associated with the fact that the writers of the material now get their knowledge of the primary teaching situation second or even third hand. They do not teach children themselves and there is some reason to believe that social norms imply that they would demean themselves if they did. Consequently they derive information about the practicability of their materials from occasionally watching others put them into practice, from comments or 'hints' written on the modular materials by teachers themselves, and more often from test results. The trap in this latter case comes in making assumptions that are not warranted about what 'caused' the performance failures and therefore what ought to remedy them. Two other related occupational hazards exist because of the unavoidable necessity to employ teachers' college lecturers as module writers. In the first place the lecturers are subject-matter specialists. They may therefore be knowledgeable about the nature of their disciplines (sometimes imperfectly as the occasional module shows), but they are not always fully cognizant of either the development characteristics of children at different stages or their verbal capability. Some module writers thus make use of inappropriate language and make cognitive demands of children that are beyond them. In a similar vein the subject specializations of the writers tend to result in their not necessarily being aware of the work being done in other subject areas. This can cause complications when subjects overlap and, for example, a science activity entails calculations that are beyond the arithmetical competencies of the children.

Two other related issues bear on the matter of curriculum. It will be remembered that initially a course outline provided the organizing framework for each of the disciplines and constituted the basis on which modules would be constructed. Now the problem of defining the boundaries and territories of a discipline, then conceptually mapping it and then deciding what routes are appropriate to select through it for children at various ages, is far from an easy task. Assuming, however, that it was done satisfactorily at the outset, the techniques adopted for testing and rewriting modules have the potential for distorting the original map. In other words, the objectives originally set for a particular module *may* be lost sight of when test results are used as the criterion for prompting modification.

That said, one has to ask how important such factors are and whether or not the dissatisfaction is divine rather than realistic. To this end, it is worth commenting that there is a point in time at which a decision has to be made to accept any unit or module as adequate. Necessarily, such a decision is a function of a great many things. Not only is it affected by the magnitude and number of errors, but also by the need to have materials available in order for *any* work to be done. It is also affected by the extent of the return to be gained from a further investment of time, labour and money. Divine dissatisfaction may be commendable, but it may not be able to be afforded. Some defences could be erected against the kind of problems listed above, but whether they are worth it clearly depends on their magnitude and extent. What appears to be warranted, however, is a mechanism that attempts to gauge that magnitude and extent. But it is undoubtedly worth noting that the modular system lends itself to ready revision in that it is much easier to extract and replace a unit (or a module) than it is to replace a whole textbook.

Skill training

Of a different genre are some of the problems associated with one particular curriculum domain: skill training. Education in Indonesia has traditionally been formal and academic, excluding the practical. As well, there are strongly developed cultural values that have tended to associate educational success with white-collar occupations. Manual work is to be regarded with dismay rather than delight. But Indonesia is in need of technicians and technologists, and the majority of secondary school leavers will not continue on to further education, hence the official incorporation of skill training in the curriculum. It is here that a reforming idea clashes with established norms and beliefs. The consequences include an apparently less than dedicated attitude on the part of teachers and pupils towards skill education – neither are too enamoured of the 'dirty hands syndrome'. The consequences also include, more significantly, a certain understandable conceptual blindness on the part of the teachers. Seldom having had the inclination to engage in woodwork, metalwork, electrical wiring or general do-it-yourself activities of that ilk, they have not often had the opportunity to develop an awareness of the dimensions and scope of such domains. They have in other words no experiential rules of thumb or insights that can allow them to approach these exotic disciplines other than mechanically. Without conviction and understanding of their new craft, the teachers – who have usually been drafted into the task – have difficulty in striking a motivational spark in pupils who themselves start sharing the same less than positive attitude.

Such problems are neither surprising nor dismaying: they are precisely the kinds of problems that emerge during any attempt to induce a substantial measure of change in social systems in general and teacher behaviour in particular. They are also not insoluble.

At this point in the discussion, problems of the immediate future must give way to problems that may be looming in the further off.

Beyond the development schools

As trial phase number two approaches — and already a very limited number of modules are finding their way into the non-development schools — a further task lies ahead. Each module is, as planned, to undergo further testing. It is at this point that one of the decisions taken earlier as a matter of convenience *may* be the cause of difficulties. Originally the development schools were selected because they fell under the jurisdiction of IKIPs. One consequence of that decision was that with one exception (the rural school), the school populations were not typical of the Indonesian scene. By and large the children, a proportion of whom are sons and daughters of IKIP staff members, are above average in intelligence and come from homes whose socio-economic conditions are also above average. The school populations, then, are somewhat elite. Now, if sampling theory is correct, one would expect that with a shift to a new population (which will have been deliberately selected to have different and diverse characteristics), different performances will result. Theoretically, some of the modules *may* have to be rewritten, or their implementation may need some adjustment as children who are less bright, less experienced, less sophisticated, meet and struggle with their own particular learning problems. The most intriguing aspect of this part of the programme will be whether or not much revision or adjustment will be necessary. If it is not, then the *practical implications* of sampling theory for such activities may prove to be extremely interesting.

There is nothing original in the points made directly above. In fact, the project itself has anticipated the problem and allowed for it. What may turn out to be something of a stumbling block, however, is *if* the amount of rewriting turns out to be excessive and it becomes necessary to delay to a greater extent than was anticipated — perhaps by having a second testing, as in the first trial.

Implementation

On another tack, the project has also, since its earliest days, recognized that to develop a miniature education system was one thing, but to promulgate it widely was quite another. The issues of development and implementation are seen as separate but, of course, related. At this point, however, there are grounds for beginning to give serious consideration to this aspect for two reasons at least. The first is one of lead-time. The decision about implementation is to be taken in 1982, the date that in its turn replaced the early 1976 deadline that was set before the project came under the jurisdiction of BP3K. But 1982 is only four short years away and the mechanics of 'growing' an education system for a country of 130 million people who are (to be repetitious) as widely dispersed and culturally diverse as the Indonesians is indeed formidable. The problem, then, is the problem of having a realistic and feasible plan for implementation available at the time it is needed. The second reason is not entirely divorced from the first. Fairly clearly there are many aspects of the implementation process itself that could exert an influence on the decision whether to implement or not. To take a simple example, it may be that the cost of the implementation process itself could prove prohibitive and vitiate the whole operation. After all, the logistics problem is considerable. Presumably implementing the development schools programme entails at least the production and distribution of the new curricular materials in quantity. It may also entail additional plant and equipment to be developed specially for implementation itself, a system that manages the implementation process, a public relations task to ensure that neither public nor professional opposition arises, and so on. It will also entail a measure of teacher training – a fact that was anticipated at the outset of the project. All of these will cost money – it is *theoretically* possible then that that cost could be sufficiently high to warrant modification of the original intention. And if so, the *sooner* that happens the better.

Another factor in the implementation process itself to which the project and indeed the Ministry of Education and Culture is sensitive is the interface between older practices and the new. It will be remembered that after the Assessment, the Government decided on a two-pronged attack: one prong being the development schools project, the other a continuing upgrading of existing conditions, *including the development of a new curriculum* (called the *1975 curriculum*). It was hinted earlier that this *might* constitute a point of friction if the two curricula do not have much in common. In fact deliberate attempts are being made to use the 1975 curriculum as a forerunner for modular instruction. This is being achieved to some extent by having a measure of common content and by the introduction into the 1975 curriculum of new procedures and practices that are part of the methodology to be found in modular instruction. Also some modules from the new curriculum have already penetrated into a number of schools (other than the development schools) and a process of informal diffusion is occurring. However, here again a dilemma is surfacing. By 1982 the new 1975 curriculum will have only been in vogue for a relatively short time and there are sure to be expressions of concern over what may seem to be a premature change. Here it may be rather important to have an idea about the timing and rate of implementation. It may, for example, take many years to spread modular instruction to every corner of Indonesia's 7000 populated islands and an early start may be considered.

Beyond modular instruction
We are led by this issue to contemplate the even more distant future as well. It is entirely understandable that, given the immensity of the task of developing the new system, the development activity has demanded almost total attention. But it is not unreasonable to ask at some stage or other: what next? After modular instruction, what then? Perhaps it is premature to start yet, but there are some straws in the wind that are worth noting not only for the future, but also because of their implications for implementation.

Fairly clearly the original intention was to produce curricular materials that took into account the points at which the teaching profession might be vulnerable. This was largely to be done by providing materials and procedures that could be picked up by the teacher without much difficulty and with little in-service training. However, casual observations of the way the IKIP staff are working with teachers in the development schools seem to show two things. First, the teachers are receiving a considerable amount of help. Second, both the IKIP staff (as concerned with teacher training in general), and the teachers themselves are both seizing the opportunity to extend the professionalization of teachers. In a sense, in the interests of getting the curricular materials to come out right, the teachers are getting far more help than would be the case for teachers during the implementation.

In other words the existence of unanticipated extra attention from IKIP staff may prove to be an important influential variable in the success of the early trials. If that is so, and if the further dissemination of curricular materials to other schools is not to be accompanied by such a service, there may be disadvantages that result. There would seem to be a case then for including a certain amount of observational study of actual classroom settings. This could serve three important purposes. The first would indicate the mechanisms, devices and strategies that teachers use to attempt to accommodate the demands of the modular instruction system and the second, provided the IKIP staff are observed too, would show the extent, nature and style of their influence.

The third, however, bears on the question of 'what next?' The IKIP lecturers are currently taking advantage of the teachers' increased awareness to encourage them to undertake new activities not necessarily required by the modular instruction materials. These include devising ancillary aids, developing different kinds of presentation procedures and even in some cases writing modules themselves. Perhaps these activities represent a logical extension of the modular instruction system. In this respect it is perhaps worth noting in passing that another Indonesian reform project, the Pamong project, makes use of teachers as curriculum writers. There is scope therefore for considering the relative advantages of having teachers or IKIP lecturers as writers.

At an earlier point in the chapter it was promised that the composition of some of the groups active within the project would be referred to again. At the moment there are three networks that are of considerable importance. At the most practical level, ie the level closest to the workface, is the network involving curriculum writers, BP3K staff and to a lesser extent teachers. Next removed is the editing and sanctioning workshop which involves IKIP and BP3K staff and education officials and administrators. Next removed, or perhaps next up would be more appropriate, is the coordination committee that meets twice a year. Its complement consists of not only senior people on the project, but also Ministry officials, other prominent educationists and, importantly, others of significance from politically related fields. The groups yet to be represented include parents and the public. There is good reason for this in that until the project emerges from the experimental stage it is wise to keep a relatively low profile. On the other hand, if wider dissemination is to follow, the link between the consumers, parents and public may be of critical importance. Here is one of the reasons why. For years there has been a deliberate attempt (in nearly every country in the world) to stress the value of education. The effectiveness of that attempt is testified to by the steady increase in enrolments. But to the world in general, education is not an abstraction: it is a set of concrete, identifiable (even though idealized) components. Any suggestion that education should be different invites misgivings, mistrust and maybe opposition. Time and effort is likely to be needed to prepare the ground for public acceptance of this radically new kind of education, in which teachers 'don't really teach' and children appear to 'play' at learning.

In several previous paragraphs references have been made to costs. In general terms, the project has been directly funded, primarily from the Indonesian Government. Outside agencies, particularly Unesco/UNDP and the British Council, have made their contribution to the project through the provision of international staff, overseas training and books and equipment. At this stage the amount expended does not, however, take into account, reasonably enough, the salaries of the Indonesian staff involved, principally because that money is committed anyway. It also does not take into account the consumables that BP3K expends as part and parcel of the development process. The only possible hazard here (as with the 'concealed' incidence of IKIP 'help') is that the influence of a critical component, in this case, incidental material help, may be underestimated when evaluation (and essential cost analyses) are undertaken. Obviously, the cost issue is one of particular significance for the future of the project. There are two particularly critical aspects: the first is the actual cost of replicating in non-developmental schools the circumstances essential for the employment of the modular instruction system. For this it is essential to know what the critical components are, so that nothing of significance (like, for example, supplementary supervision and guidance) is omitted and estimates become faulty. This would entail a fairly stringent analysis of the modular instruction system in operation, its component parts, be they people, services, plant, equipment or management and administration components, and whether the costs are direct or indirect, concealed or unconcealed. The second is the cost of implementation, that is, the cost of designing and supplying the means by which the modular system circumstances *can* come to be replicated. Again there are many facets to take into consideration. To this end the Ministry has already taken some steps and a BP3K staff member is undertaking a study of relevant and appropriate techniques overseas.

The final points that have to be made in this chapter are tangential to the development schools project, but may turn out to be central to the general issue of planning qualitative innovations.

There has been a very interesting development in Indonesia. Because of the success of the Ministry in providing more access to primary schooling

Indonesia: Quality in Quantity

for more children, a corresponding growth in the demand for secondary schooling has occurred. However, at the moment it is not within the power of the existing secondary system to accommodate the demand fully. Consequently, a decision has been taken to provide, perhaps as an interim measure, perhaps not, an alternative system of 'Open' junior secondary schools. These are intended to cater for a relatively small proportion of junior secondary school attenders (five per cent at the end of the third Five-Year Development Plan) and particularly those for whom secondary schools are geographically difficult of access. Immediately a problem arises. How can children who could only come to school say once a week or fortnight be adequately served? Obviously some kind of self-instructional method is needed. Obviously too, the best and most available variant would be a modular instruction system, especially one designed for these open schools. Accordingly, it has been decided to adapt the materials as it were ahead of schedule, a decision that is as understandable as it is interesting. Much of the subsequent interest will be not in seeing *whether* the modular instruction system works or not, but rather *how* it is working or not. If a few resources can be spared to monitor the open schools' use of the modular system, some valuable insights may be gained into practical problems and, even more importantly, what short cuts might be warranted now and during general implementation.

As a final point on the Indonesian experience before it is taken up again in the final chapter, there is one structural aspect that ought to be noted. As the plan stands at the moment, the development of the development school model system is being undertaken by one particular agency, BP3K. The *plan* for implementation is also its concern at the moment. But the actual task of implementation is not. That will fall on the shoulders of the Division of General and Secondary Education. Now if BP3K runs true to form, it will engage in close and intensive dialogue with all interested parties, including the Division of General and Secondary Education. That this would be essential almost goes without saying. Clearly the Division of General and Secondary Education has not only expertise in implementation practice, but also a cognizance of the kinds of problems likely to be significant. Also, the Division has its own realities to deal with. The addition of a task of the magnitude of implementing the development school model will dramatically increase that load. Whether or not, as presently constituted, the Division has the resources to undertake the task will itself bear scrutiny. As another existing sub-system within the broader educational system, the Division of General and Secondary Education can be expected to display the kind of response to the prospect of a substantial addition to its activities that any social system would. Thus the interface between the developers (BP3K) and the implementors (the Division) is a point at which care and planning are both warranted.

With this point on the 'ripple effect' (Kounin and Gump, 1958) of change in one part of a system on other parts of the system, we must depart the Indonesian scene. When we return to it in the last chapter, one of the points to be examined for its universal relevance is precisely this one.

While the Research and Development model for educational innovation has been acclaimed as logically the most powerful, surprisingly few examples of it in practice are available. Havelock and Huberman (1977), in their survey, in fact found none. The Indonesian project with its adoption of an almost classic R & D approach then is particularly noteworthy.

The Nordrhein-Westfalen approach to be dealt with in the next chapter, however, is not so rare. In fact it constitutes a mode of operation that is the rule rather than the exception in many Western developed countries – innovation by legislation. Necessarily this approach rests on a number of assumptions quite different from those on which the Indonesian R & D approach rests. It also takes for granted that the education system has a built-in capacity to make the appropriate responses. Whether this is so or not is one of the interesting issues that only time can resolve.

Chapter 3

The Federal Republic of Germany: Successive Approximations

In the introduction to the book, passing reference was made to a universal tendency among education systems to rely on legislated fiat as a means for activating qualitative reform. That initial reference was a little less than respectful. It implied that such an approach has an incipient frailty because it runs the risk of forgetting that the reform has to be undertaken by people and that to *enable* them to do it usually requires deliberate and direct contact.

Now, the innovation selected for study in the Federal Republic of Germany is of this genre. And it is only right that it should be included here if for no other reason than to put to the test the validity of that earlier rather glib assertion. However, there *are* other reasons as well. Not the least of these is that some of the conditions in the Federal Republic of Germany stand in stark contrast with the conditions existing elsewhere. The Federal Republic's system is old and well established, and the community is spectacularly affluent. Again, in the Federal Republic, the form and style of administration is different from the form and style employed in many countries, developing and developed. There is a temptation under these circumstances for others outside the country to take one of two stances: to assume on the one hand that the differences prevent drawing any parallels with their own situation, or on the other, to see the example of the Federal Republic of Germany as an ideal type to aspire to. Either way, whether the conditions existing in the Federal Republic help or hinder, facilitate or frustrate educational innovation may invite more than passing interest.

Background

The unimaginative but obvious place to start any account of an innovation in the Federal Republic of Germany is with the economic condition of the country. That condition, however, is so well known that it need not be dwelt on. Suffice it to say that the economic revival of the Federal Republic after the terrible ravages of the Second World War has made the West German economy one of the strongest in the world. The achievements in reconstructing industry and society are almost legendary and the degree of affluence reflected in the quality and abundance of material goods and efficient and diverse services represent an epitome of 'development'. There is enough and to spare for all – and far beyond the bare necessity level, too.

Problem

Everything in the West German garden, then, ought to be lovely! But this is not quite the case. The FRG too has a problem in common with many other countries in the world. Despite its continued economic growth, despite the strength of the Deutschmark, despite the popularity of West German products, the Federal Republic has an increasing rate of unemployment. This has had severe repercussions for school leavers – especially those who are least qualified. Youth unemployment is thus the starting point for the discussion of the West German innovation, and legislation designed to provide an *educational* solution to the unemployment problem constitutes the basis of the innovation under consideration. While youth unemployment represents the 'basic' problem, as we shall see, the situation is far more complicated than this rather simple statement of the initial 'cause' would tend to indicate. However, it is to one particular *Land* or state in the Federal Republic that our attention must now turn. This is because in the decentralized West German system the separate *Länder* have a great measure of autonomy and in educational and cultural affairs are masters of their own fates. Each therefore tends to be distinctive and the federal component somewhat restricted even though there are many occasions when the federal authorities and the *Länder* administration sit together to try to harmonize their discussions – especially in vocational areas.

In the *Land* of Nordrhein-Westfalen, to which the present chapter is confined, the youth unemployability problem was felt quite acutely. Nordrhein-Westfalen is the largest of the West German *Länder* (34,069 km^2), the most populous (17 million population) and the most industrialized, encompassing as it does the famous Ruhr valley. It is also the most affluent.

In Nordrhein-Westfalen, not only was concern expressed at the personal level over the fate of disillusioned and distressed unemployed individuals, but also at social and industrial level over the consequences likely to follow. Would children become disturbed and anomic? Would delinquency and crime increase? Would industrial retrenchment follow? Furthermore, it is no secret that it is a strongly held German norm to place great value on work and to disdain indolence. It was no accident that the idea of the 'Protestant ethic' (the moral imperative for frugality and hard work) was conceived in Germany by a German. The prospect of an increasing number of unoccupied youths was therefore viewed with dismay. Finally, and perhaps most importantly, the idea that some children should be deprived of work opportunities (and hence the subsequent advantages that were supposed to follow), violated a fundamental belief in social justice and equity.

Unemployability

The facts of the matter in Nordrhein-Westfalen were as follows. The problem of unemployability had been gradually coming to a head for some years.

The Federal Republic of Germany: Successive Approximations

Vague rumblings were first heard towards the end of 1974. Then in 1975 various statements made by prominent politicians, including the Federal Chancellor and Prime Ministers of some of the *Länder*, brought the matter into sharper focus. The Ministry of Culture, responding to public concern, began to give the problem serious consideration and set about preparing plans for action. In August 1975 experimental classes for some 2300 pupils were instituted that were to provide additional education for unemployable school leavers who were willing to return to school voluntarily. By 1976, the situation had deteriorated further though the experimental classes now accommodated 11,336 pupils and the number of unemployed youths throughout the whole of the Federal Republic was (conservatively) estimated to be 100,000. The future looked grim. With the job market already saturated and the rate of production of vocationally educated school leavers exceeding the rate of attrition from the industries, it seemed obvious that each year the number of unemployed would swell more. Now too, the issue was receiving more and more publicity. In newspapers, over the radio and on television, the people were being constantly reminded of difficulties and alerted to potential problems looming. The time had come for more definitive action.

But what was the precise nature of the situation? Why had it come about? What was the cause, or more appropriately, what were the causes?

'Unemployability' when applied to adults is an accommodating term. It may refer to the unskilled or the skilled, the academic or the artisan, the practitioner or the professional. With school leavers, the term may cover those who, not having found a job appropriate for their qualifications, have not yet looked further. It may also cover those who do not even want to try to find a job. In Nordrhein-Westfalen (and also in the other *Länder*) it was all of these but to varying degrees. The causes also were various. In the first place, the output from the education system had grown as a result of a 'baby boom' of some 13-25 years earlier. In the second, the increased holding power of the system occasioned by more children staying at school longer eventually resulted in the release of more graduates annually onto the market than had been the case before. Thirdly, the decrease in the rate of economic growth saw in some cases a parallel decline in the rate at which new jobs materialized and, in other cases, even a reduction of the number existing. Fourthly, because of the increased skill and academic levels of those graduating from the system (whatever the level), there was a tendency for a top-down saturation effect to follow. With limited room in the higher status occupations and a surplus of candidates qualified to enter them, overflows resulted. Sometimes the disappointed candidates fell frustrated by the wayside. More often they spilled downwards into the level below, thus forcing out those with (hitherto adequate) lesser qualifications who in turn also overflowed in a similar manner. The whole process culminated at the bottom with a squeezing out of the least qualified, least educated and by and large least capable members of the work force. Inevitably, the poorly qualified, undereducated and less well endowed young people became the main and most apparent victims.

Admittedly, some minor attempts were made to manipulate the labour market by creating new relatively low-paid jobs in the state sector. As well, some consideration was given to the possibility of legislating for compulsory employment – a solution tried in a particular way and with unacceptable results earlier in history – and also to making apprenticeship for all compulsory. There was some justification. But the main problem fell back into education's lap rather quickly because although the problem had officially been identified as a problem of the labour market, it was seen to have an educational dimension as well.

Educational implications

Vocational education in the FRG was and is mainly organized to culminate in some form of apprenticeship. But because the number of school leavers at this time exceeded the number of apprenticeships available for some reason, not altogether apparent, the problem came to be regarded by some as a structural insufficiency in the educational system itself. Further, because the least well qualified school leavers could not get jobs, the education system was seen as having failed to educate them adequately.

Both arguments, the poor qualifications of the young school leavers and the lack of earning opportunities for them, defined the problems as an educational one. Education thus came to be regarded as the sinner. Education had been culpable in allowing this state of affairs to come about and might redeem itself if only it produced a new and effective solution. There is occasion to wonder why education is seen in such a way in so many societies. Why does education make such a convenient scapegoat? More paradoxically, though, why is the education system thereupon seen as a potential source of remediation? Often it seems that the public at large displays a touching faith in the capability of education to solve individual and social ills. Education, it seems, enhances. Not only does it improve the life chances of individuals, but it creates a sturdy foundation for society's development. Or so it used to be thought. It may also be that the education system provides a useful and perhaps valuable safety valve in times of social and political crises. After all, crises demand action and actions tend to have observable consequences – except in education. There the complexity of the institution makes it extremely difficult to disentangle the direct effects, let alone side effects, of educational actions. Furthermore, the results of educational action tend to be long delayed, partly because it takes time for any idea to penetrate and permeate the system, partly because the educational process, in extending over a number of years, nearly always defers the day of reckoning.

While this last generalization about the delayed effects of educational action is more often true than not, in the present case of Nordrhein-Westfalen it was not intended to be the case – which made the study even more interesting. Here the educational action was to be immediate and the results were expected to become visible in no more than a year hence.

The educational context

Now it is a truism that whatever occurs, occurs in context. It is also a truism that contexts often exert an influence on whatever occurs. It is furthermore a truism that sometimes there is a variety of contexts. Consequently, it is often advisable to ask which of the alternative contexts need to be taken into account. In the case of the Nordrhein-Westfalen reform, this is a tricky and important question to answer – and it will be necessary to return to it at several different points in the chapter. But one context that is clearly involved is the context of the educational system at large. And within it there seems to be an advantage in looking at both its structures, and its professed objectives, intentions and aspirations.

The structure of the system

Under normal circumstances, descriptions of the structures of education systems have limited appeal. However, in the case of the Nordrhein-Westfalen innovation, the structure of the system is particularly significant for two reasons. In the first place the structure has exerted a strong influence on how the 'solution' to the problem of unemployable school leavers is to be seen. In the second, the solution itself *may* have a profound influence on the future structure and indeed the function of the whole Nordrhein-Westfalen education system.

In Nordrhein-Westfalen education is, of course, compulsory – theoretically, for nine full-time years, but exceptionally, in the case of those who fall under the umbrella of the innovation, for ten years (or more accurately for ten years and 16 weeks).

In Nordrhein-Westfalen, as elsewhere throughout the world, the education system has come to fulfil an allocating role. Children, after they have been through the system, are labelled (sometimes formally, sometimes informally) as successes or failures and at various levels. Thus one of the principles on which the structural form of the Nordrhein-Westfalen education system is based is selection – selection in and selection out. And it is by means of the various streams or structures that the system sets up that its labelling function is carried out. Some description of the structure existing before the innovation came into being will therefore be advantageous. Necessarily, only the broad outlines can be filled in, partly because there is no space for more and partly because covering all the complexities of this very complex system will serve to generate more confusion than clarity.

Routes to success

Children enter the primary school system at six years of age. Immediately ahead for almost all of them lie four years of general education, but the system is already selective. Children who are not able to follow the normal instruction are sent to the *Sonderschule*, ie a school for special education (there are ten different types of such schools in the Federal Republic. About 84 per cent of the children in them are classified as having learning disabilities.) At the end of the first four years of general education the next selection takes place. The children, on the basis of teachers' advice and parents' decisions, are then directed into three streams in accordance with what is thought to be their future destiny. Those for whom the university is a (distant) possibility go into a predominantly academic stream at the *Gymnasium* (grammar school). Those who are anticipated to find high-level jobs in commerce and industry go to the *Realschule*, where the curriculum, though partly academic, is otherwise commercially oriented. To the third stream in the *Hauptschule* go children who hope to become skilled workers and who, accordingly, are given less theoretically oriented courses. The *Sonderschule*, however, goes on, thus constituting a fourth stream in its own right. This school, kept for those for whom a modest destiny is envisaged, is supposed to offer a remedial and 'basic' education curriculum. The original intention was to rehabilitate quite a number from this stream into the *Hauptschule*. In reality rarely more than three per cent manage it.

At the age of about ten, then, the ultimate vocational fate of most children is, to quite a considerable extent, signed and sealed. True, there is some provision for children unsuccessful in one stream to transfer to another but there is not similar opportunity to nearly the same extent for the successful in one stream to transfer to a higher.

However, though the children might be headed in a particular direction, there is no guarantee that all will get there. The next of the major selection points for most lies five years away when compulsory full-time education ceases. At that stage the two basic issues for pupils are whether or not to continue with full-time or part-time education, and if so, in what way. The system now displays a greater array of alternatives. Most of the university-bound students continue on in the *Gymnasium*. A few transfer across (downwards) to other streams. For those in the *Realschule*, there are theoretically four alternatives, viz (i) to change to the *Gymnasium*, although this chance exists only for students with good results at the *Realschule*; (ii) to continue full-time vocational education in schools run by the state; (iii) to go into what is called the 'dual system' (begun in 1919) which entails four days' apprenticed employment (with on-the-job training) *plus* one day a week at a state vocational school; (iv) to look for a job on the labour market which means *either* unskilled employment (four days a week), *or* unemployment, both coupled with one day of school per week. The children who have successfully completed the *Hauptschule* can theoretically entertain the four options above. This is also true for those who completed the *Sonderschule*, although the academic stream normally cannot be reached by these children. A final alternative is available for those who are mentally or physically handicapped, eg blind, deaf, or with impaired motor skills, etc (a definition of handicap that became particularly significant later). These children can receive *full-time courses* for one, two or three years.

There is a wide gap between theoretical chances and real possibilities. While in periods of economic and educational expansion the level of formal education plays a minor role, it becomes an important fact in a situation of scarcity. At the end of compulsory schooling in the Federal Republic children can be ranged – according to the type of school they went to and the level of achievement they reached – into at least ten different groups. The real chance of the lower group depends on what chances 'better' groups leave for them. In the present situation the chances of the lowest group (*Sonderschule*, *Hauptschule* without certificate) are about zero.

The labelling process

These various routes through the education system, then, yield different results which are sanctified by the certificates granted to the successful. By and large, these certificates indicate the stream followed (or transferred to) and that *the course has been completed*. Those who do not complete receive no certificate. The certificate was then, and still is, of course, the official label that may be used for admission to (a) specific occupations and (b) specific kinds of further education. All certificates tend to open some doors and keep others closed. Some of those doors open to reveal exciting and varied prospects, but they open only to the most prestigious certificates. Others when open reveal little that is enticing although they do reveal something. To those children, however, who have no certification, nearly all doors are closed. Any that open, open grudgingly and offer little. Now whether the system was set up to undertake this allocating role is a debatable point. History would tend to indicate that the early intentions held for education had more a door opening function in mind than a door closing one. But the fact remains that to a large extent education systems and societies have together come to accept and expect that education will serve such a function. However, the fact that it has done so in the past and is expected to in the future does not mean that it necessarily *should*. And to some extent the schools' allocating role has come under attack from some members of the education fraternity. While their ideas have not been adopted as actual policy, as we shall see later, they have nonetheless played a part in influencing some policy statements and, in fact, some of the actions actually undertaken in the schools themselves. However, at this point in the account some of the parts of the jigsaw puzzle described above can be assembled.

There was at the beginning the problem that had come to be given the general name of 'youth unemployment'. This encompassed the facts that an increasing number of young people, just having completed their compulsory nine years of schooling, were ineligible to continue their full-time education further, could not get admission where they wished or simply wanted no more education. However, a law (enacted in 1919 originally to protect children from industrial exploitation) stipulated that between the ages of 15 and 18 those not in full-time education must attend school one day a week. Up until 1967 that provided few problems although it had given rise to some pedagogical objections and to the argument that it would be better either converted to full-time compulsory education (one to three years) or abandoned. Even so, conditions up to that time had been such that the labour market was not too unwilling to take on young people on terms that meant that their services were only available four days a week and that the industry would support their education. But by 1974 the situation was different. A combination of events, the increased supply of school leavers, the surplus of 'over-educateds', and a measure of retrenchment in industry not only eliminated such job opportunities but limited apprenticeship ones too. The net effect was that to the ranks of the unemployed over 18 were added newcomers between the ages of 15 and 18. The latter, however, were still obliged to attend school once a week, an obligation that some thought was the reason they could not get employment.

The innovation

Legislation

The Nordrhein-Westfalen innovation with which this chapter is concerned is a structural change that represents a response to that situation and is called the *Berufsvorbereitungsjahr* (BVJ for short). In its first form (that lasted less than a year), it was a relatively simple and straightforward ministerial order that provided unemployed school leavers with the opportunity to return to school for a further year should they so wish. The regulations indicated that there they would be grouped into select classes and would follow selected vocationally oriented courses adapted from those offered by the school. Schools were given very general, rather brief and, it must be admitted, rather vague suggestions about what they might do. The suggestions included making use of existing facilities, 'borrowing' teachers from other schools and employing part-time pedagogically unqualified but technically competent outsiders. The whole operation was clearly not a high cost one and relied heavily on the schools' initiative, enterprise, imagination and, presumably, humanitarianism.

Time had been bought but to some extent at the schools' expense. The situation as the schools inherited it was that they were to receive back some children who, while at least sufficiently motivated (or pressured) to return, had previously left school as relative failures. The schools were required to accommodate the returners within existing facilities as best they could and with whatever teacher resources they were lucky enough to tap. They also had to decide quickly what to do with the new group and presumably why they would do it.

The shadow of substance

Now at this point the first of two further educational contexts comes into contention. The BVJ was to operate in the existing large (between 2000 and 6000 pupils) vocational schools. And the purpose of vocational schools is, by and large, relatively straightforward: to prepare pupils for entry into the world of work. The *major* orientation of the vocational schools thus was and is towards skill training. This was what the teachers were trained for, knew best and were most practised at. Furthermore, the vocational schools themselves are administratively, organizationally and materially 'geared up' for such an orientation. It is difficult to imagine then how, in the short time available to the schools, the provisions that they could make for this new special group would be anything other than vocationally oriented. Indeed, if one of the main reasons for introducing the BVJ was to reduce unemployability, it is also difficult to imagine what else might have been contemplated. On the other hand, it is even more difficult to understand how, at a time when jobs were fewer, and job seekers greater in number and better qualified, giving the least educated further training but *without the promise of a certificate* (initially), could do much, if anything, to remedy the overall youth unemployment situation. It is true that time had been bought – but with what in store?

At this stage it becomes necessary to introduce a different point of view into the discussion. Earlier it was stated that not everyone enthusiastically supported the selective bases on which education proceeded, or the labelling function of the schools or for that matter the dominance of the vocational orientation. In fact, within West German society there were several 'counter' viewpoints that from time to time came into conflict with each other. On the one hand there was to be found 'industry', in this case industrial management and ownership. Somewhat sensitive to their economic well-being as they themselves defined it, they looked with suspicion, if not hostility, at the effects that educational legislation might have on their enterprises. There was thus a measure of resistance to be found within the industry to educational activities that seemed likely to impinge on their interests. 'Over'-educating prospective workers was one such, so was the removal of workers from the job to attend school and so was the demand from government that the industry should in some cases provide and in others subsidize the education of these, their least useful workers. On another hand were to be found the trade unions. For their part, they were active in the interests of their members. Anything that would safeguard and enhance their circumstances was supported. Educational programmes were thus largely viewed with favour. But, and the but is important, most of the active and influential trade unions were unions of skilled (and often specialized) workers. Whatever concern they had for the unskilled and unemployed tended to be muted by matters more directly influencing their own people. However, it is a third hand that is most directly relevant to the BVJ case. It also constitutes the third educational context within which the innovation operates and *may* ultimately prove to be the most significant.

Among the educationists themselves, notably those in universities and teachers' colleges, are to be found advocates of a different approach to education. They have their allies in other walks of life and even within the ranks of politicians. Their viewpoint, which runs somewhat counter to the mainstream of public and political opinion about education, would want education to be seen in less vocational terms and to have a diminished allocational role. While their motivations are no doubt diverse, they do seem influenced by sympathy for the 'underdog' and a belief that the education system could be more socially just.

Now it happens that in Nordrhein-Westfalen, education constantly attracts a certain amount of public concern and interest. Educational matters are publicized in the media and debated with fervour and intensity. Some of the debates have been concerned with reforms or innovations that would serve to some extent to de-emphasize vocationalism and selection and to promote (though modestly) general education. The prospect of developing comprehensive schools has featured in that debate with, of course, the 'non-conventional' educationists lining up with those in favour. In taking such a position they were acting consistently with a line of thought that in fact can trace its history back to the turn of the 20th century and to the legislation at the end of the First World War that specified compulsory, at least part-time, education for all up to the age of 18. Then the argument was that children should not be committed to the world of work too hastily and should be entitled to the benefits that an enlarged education might bring.

In the baldest of interpretations, then, there is a basic conflict of ideas. The liberal-idealists see (i) education as the means for the all-round social, emotional, intellectual, moral and vocational development of individuals, and (ii) the system as obliged to provide equality of educational opportunity by making special provisions for the less fortunate. They stand in opposition to the pragmatic-realists who, taking a societal rather than individualistic view, argue that the present conditions in society and the circumstances prevailing in the labour market should determine what kind of education is needed and therefore should be provided. The latter orientation admits of the idea of over-education as well as under-education, both of which are regarded as bad. As well, it puts its faith in the idea that incentives motivate and the motivated are the meritorious.

Either viewpoint, if applied to the BVJ, would have results to which the opposing side would take exception. Consequently, what is likely to determine the route the BVJ takes will be the actual power that either side can marshall and, it should be emphasized, the relevance of the context within which that power is exercised. There is a nice conundrum lying in wait. If the pragmatic-realists exert greatest political power (as they appear to do at the moment) and legislation is framed according to their viewpoint, *but* if at the same time the liberal-idealists come to control the educating process (as they may do), which viewpoint will tend to prevail *in effect*? Which, in other words, will be the facade and which the foundation? The point implicit here is worth elaborating.

Before the reality, the rhetoric

It seems reasonably apparent that all social systems create around themselves their own rationale. Usually more than just a justification, that rationale also tends to contain an idealized view of the ultimate character of that social system and the conditions it will bring about. Religions provide an obvious example with political ideologies and educational doctrines not far behind. But the same applies even at the micro-system level with clubs, associations and even family groups having an idealized view of their present and future. Of most relevance to the present chapter, though, is the apparent fact that social systems, in order to verbalize their idealized views, develop rhetorical forms that serve to proclaim or perhaps advertise their (virtuous) objectives. The United Nations with its Declaration of Human Rights provides an excellent example but all such organizations large or small, formal or informal, tend, it should be repeated, to do the same thing. The issue that then becomes particularly interesting is the distance between the rhetoric and the reality and what difference the distance makes. It seems reasonable to believe that the rhetoric serves a necessary function: to support and reinforce the faithful and (try to) persuade the non-believers. It also seems reasonable to believe that the greater the gap between rhetoric and reality or, as it were, between promise and performance, the less the organization will be seen as credible. Furthermore, the less it is seen to be credible by its *own* members, the greater the possibility of its own self-destruction while the less it is seen to be credible by others, the less influence it will tend to have on them and the greater the opposition that may be raised.

The issue of rhetoric and reality as it applies to innovations in general will be returned to in the final chapter, but in the meantime, if the reasoning above is valid, there are some implications for the two major forces that are coming to impinge on the BVJ. If the BVJ continues with its vocational training emphasis *and* proves to be no answer to the youth unemployment problem, whose credibility will be at stake? Similarly, if the liberal-idealistic viewpoint comes to permeate the practice of the BVJ programme – and it appears as if it might – *and* still the youth unemployment problem is unanswered, whose credibility will this time be at risk? Finally, if the liberal-idealistic orientation does prevail and the BVJ is recognized as having succeeded (according to a publicly acceptable criterion), will there be a chain reaction throughout the system? These questions, at the moment admittedly hypothetical, are being considered very seriously by influential sectors within the education system. Because of this, it is necessary for us to pursue any further leads that can be found. The developments that occurred in the early short history of the BVJ can provide some.

The first noteworthy historical straw in the wind came in 1969 when the Federal Government made an uncharacteristic intervention in education and produced national regulations that made stipulations about the *quality* of vocational education to be provided within industries. This, it might be added, attracted the inevitable opposition of employers. There then followed in 1972 an event that time may show to be rhetoric, although when it occurred it was fully intended to become reality. It consisted of a document providing a perspective on future educational development and was produced by a commission comprising Federal-level and State-level representatives. It was a document to which all parties, therefore all *Länder*, were in theory committed and therefore in theory obliged to implement in practice. The *Bildungs Gesamtplan* (as it was called) covered many aspects of education but also provided some clues on policies that could have had bearing on the youth unemployment issue, had they been carried out. The Plan produced some projections of the numbers of youths who would leave the education system *without* certification. Starting from 1970 when the proportion had been 9.1 per cent of all school leavers, the figure envisaged for 1975 was eight per cent, for 1980 it was five per cent and 1985 but two per cent. Clearly, this implied that steps would be taken to change the labelling system to the extent that erstwhile 'failures' would now come to be regarded only as the least successful – a not completely insignificant change of attitude. Another change of attitude was also evidenced in some projections made on the state and condition of the *Sonderschule*. It will be remembered that the *Sonderschule* caters for the least educated and presumably least able, and does so by providing a basic general education programme that is supposed to be remedial. The actual enrolment trends over the last years had indicated a steady increase in numbers. In 1960 the total for the whole of the Federal Republic of Germany was 142,900. By 1965 the number was up to 192,300, by 1970 it was 322,000 and by 1974 (after the commission's report) it was to be 385,000. The *Bildungs Gesamtplan* anticipated that in 1975 the figure would be 40,000 higher than it actually was, but foresaw as well a slight decrease over the next ten years with the 1985 figure back to 355,000. Given that the *Sonderschule* produced the greatest number of un-certificated school leavers, it is hard to imagine how the overall proportion of un-certificated could be reduced to any great extent. However, other improvements to the lot of the *Sonderschule* were envisaged that might have played a part. For example, the teacher-pupil ratio was to change gradually from 1:15.6 to 1:11, the per pupil square metrage was to increase from 6.3 to 8.4 and investment in books was to nearly double. While 'liberal' sentiments were not to the fore, the kinds of actions to be taken were quite consistent with them. So was another significant but not too radical development that was supposed to occur within the field of vocational education itself. It too indicated a tendency away from specialization. The curriculum in the schools offering three years of special vocational education was to be modified. Under the new scheme, the first year would be devoted to a broad vocational field – of which there were 11 (later 13) to choose from. The final two years would be years of specialization. (Nordrhein-Westfalen ratified the agreement, duly passing appropriate legislation in 1974.) At the same time that this was to occur, the proportion of pupils receiving part-time (rather than full-time) education in the dual system was to be gradually decreased, from 63 per cent in 1970 to 48 per cent in 1985.

In a system like the one in Nordrhein-Westfalen, where most conditions that have come to exist have been sanctified by time, changes tend to be slight rather than dramatic. Because the system is highly complex, however, such small changes are often quite plentiful. It is difficult under such circumstances to discriminate among them, in order to identify those that are of most significance. The changes mentioned above are not spectacular, but they can nonetheless be taken as indicating a trend, however tentative, to soften the selective and discriminating effects of the system. If they are so, in their context they are indeed quite significant.

Towards reality

Then in 1974 occurred another event which on face value also appeared to be relatively insignificant – at the time. By then the youth unemployment numbers were growing and more and more youths were applying to the labour exchange for what turned out to be non-existent jobs and apprenticeships. Embarrassed by the big demand and small supply, the labour exchange began, on its own initiative, to send more and more 'unemployables' to full-time education at schools *for the handicapped* that were usually run by private welfare agencies. By 1975 there were 38,000 children in such schools all over West Germany and the definition of 'handicapped' had suddenly taken a new twist.

1975 was also the year when the first deliberate move was made in Nordrhein-Westfalen to try to counter the youth unemployment problem. The scheme for permitting school leavers who could not find jobs or apprenticeships to return to school for a further year was introduced. This, the first version of the BVJ, brings us into closer contact with this chapter's innovation. And it did not start too auspiciously. The response was disappointing. Whether the prospective clients were either ignorant of the opportunity offered or somewhat antagonistic to it is now an academic question, because events moved too fast. In the middle of the '70s the number of unemployed school leavers continued to grow (at an estimated rate of 15,000 per year) and the BVJ in its existing form was succeeding only in taking a few off the streets. Further action was necessary, and quickly. Then on 18th March 1976, the BVJ was made compulsory. All children having completed the nine compulsory years of schooling and not finding employment (in effect apprenticeships) and not already taking full-time education were *required* to return to a vocational school for a further full-time year. In this way, a new element was inserted into the structure of the system. It consisted of a one-year special course, as it were, tacked on to what had always been previously regarded as a self-contained course structure with a well-defined terminal point and its own pedagogical integrity. What would be the consequences? What would happen next?

The major preoccupation in the earliest days was to decide what to do with the new-old pupils. There had been some developments that gave something of a lead. On the introduction of the first version of the BVJ (the voluntary one), the Ministry had sought to arrive at some curriculum guidelines. The device it used was time-honoured. An invitation was extended to some selected principals and practising teachers to cooperate with the Ministry's experts to produce the required curriculum. Now, it transpired that there were few teachers who had had experience with the kind of students the BVJ students would be. Those selected came from the *Boutsschule* and the *Hauptschule*, but they came with certain preconceptions about the likely nature of the BVJ students and therefore about what they would need. Subsequent events tended to indicate that their thinking was somewhat influenced by (i) the noteworthy increase in the number of *Sonderschule* entrants; (ii) the somewhat looser definition of handicap that had followed the labour exchange's channelling of unemployed school leavers into schools for the handicapped and (iii) perhaps the belief that the latter were not so much victims of circumstances as victims of their own inadequacy.

Towards a curriculum

The curriculum as it was forming up then tended to reflect the idea that the BVJ students would profit most from basic education, both in the vocational subjects and the general subjects already available. The curriculum guidelines in setting out the subject matter alternatives were consistent with the earlier prescriptions of the one-year full-time course provided for those who voluntarily returned to special vocational education schools. They too allowed for the study of a broad vocational field rather than narrow specialized ones. However, in the case of the BVJ, there were nine rather than 11 options. However, the *Richtlinien* (the publication containing the guidelines) had also a broader vision. Its statement of aims included some sentiments that were, given the general orientation of vocational education at the time, both liberal and contentious. Spies (1978) summarizes them as follows:

'The BVJ is supposed to help adolescents in their personal and social development. They are to be given assistance to face conflicts, to solve problems, to face quickly changing situations, to use the talents they have got. Their ability to communicate with other persons is to be furthered. They are to get help in developing cooperative attitudes and at the same time in learning to articulate and stand for their own interests in society and (later on) in their factories. The school is to provide them with enough information and career guidance to enable them to take a reasonable choice as for their future job. They are to be trained to realize chances of further study and information to continually better their competencies.

'Such aims we do not normally find on the first page of Richtlinien for a German school. These are intentions psychologists or social workers could have for their patients. German vocational schools normally teach, give information, train skills, and lead up to examinations. In all normal German schools testable knowledge plays a dominant, an almost all-important role. Here the Richtlinien order the teachers: "Der Unterricht muss so gestaltet werden, dass er bei den Jugendlichen zu Erfolgslebnissen führt" (KM-NW 1976, p 13): "Teachers have to teach in such a way that the youths may experience success". This sentence is almost a revolutionary innovation for German vocational schools. The subjects to be learned are not so very important, the aim is to lead the pupil to the experience of being able to master something.

'The government intends the BVJ as a time and place of psychological assistance. There is the necessity for society to somehow stabilize that part of the young generation especially endangered by the economic situation.'

The Federal Republic of Germany: Successive Approximations

All these aims are quite consistent with what the *Richtlinien* saw as the reason for the existence of BVJ students. Noting that they had been unable to find job opportunities, the *Richtlinien* considered this to be due to: gaps in their learning, social maladjustment, retardation, lack of decision or unrealistic hopes. Obviously, the guidelines constituted an attempt to remedy the situation by providing the BVJ pupils with both better (and basic) skills and with an improved capacity to adjust to life's exigencies.

There is, however, an implicit assumption behind both the diagnosis and the prescribed treatment. It is that somehow or other the main cause of joblessness lay somehow in the students themselves. They were in a sense 'inadequate'. It might not be their fault that this should be the case, but nonetheless control of the situation would follow if the inadequacy were remedied.

We will have occasion later on to return to this issue. At the time attention is given to the conditions that would seem necessary if the BVJ is to be successful and the terms in which success might be legitimately expressed. For the moment, however, a brief recapitulation is in order.

The reality

As things stand at the present day, the BVJ has been in operation as a compulsory programme for less than two years. During those two years the *Richtlinien* have provided the basic guidelines for the approach to be followed. They specify course prescriptions in some detail, but in effect require teaching methods and teacher attitudes to undergo some change. The direction of that change is specified, but the means for achieving it are not. Since the inception of the BVJ, 217 schools have been operating under its umbrella. In October 1976 the BVJ student population numbered 11,366; in 1977 it totalled 11,087 and by October 1978 it was *estimated* to be up to 35,300, a figure equivalent to a little less than eight per cent of the total school population. Initially the BVJ pupils were treated as an undifferentiated group, but in 1978 a reorganization of the BVJ course structure occurred. A three-track system was introduced with one course, the A stream, tailored for those youths who, having *completed* the requirements of nine years' compulsory schooling, had earned the appropriate certificate (*Hauptschulabschluss*). The B stream course was provided to give a second chance at the *Hauptschulabschluss* to uncertificated school leavers who were nonetheless thought to have the capacity to achieve it. The C stream course was for those who were both uncertificated and were thought to be incapable of meeting the requirements of the final examination. Successful graduates from the A and B streams could then re-enter the vocational education system, ie go to a full-time school or begin an apprenticeship, if they could find a place. For them the effect of the BVJ was to prolong their progress through the vocational system for one year and to (theoretically) increase their chances to find an apprenticeship. Those who were not awarded the certificate because they were in stream C or had failed in streams A or B could not re-enter the education system and had to find presumably unskilled work as best they could.

It would not be altogether surprising if a reader with pedagogical inclinations protested, at this stage in the account, that so far nothing has been said about what the schools actually do and what actually happens to the children in them. The objection is valid but it cannot be met. Our innovation is in fact an edict requiring that certain provisions be made within certain guidelines. But what is done about it is entirely another thing and at this stage it is simply not known how schools in general have responded. It is true some isolated pieces of information have found their way into the public domain. For example, it is known that one school has its BVJ pupils working part of their time on a public service project by designing and building the equipment for a young children's traffic instruction area. Quite complicated technical and electronic skills are involved in making the small cars, the traffic signs and traffic lights (but at a sub-certification standard) and the children who participate appear to like the work although it is not altogether clear where such activity leads.

From the point of view of the analysis of the process of innovation, the BVJ constitutes a very interesting case for a number of reasons. In the first place the initial move was politically motivated and backed. The Government formulated the problem *and* the solution. The Ministry of Education prepared the specifications that were then finally brought into legislation by the parliament. In the second place, although the initial deliberations over how the problem might be solved involved three Ministries: Finance, Labour and Education, the major responsibility fell on the shoulders of the educationists. In the third, when they attempted to draw the interested parties together, ie employers, trade unions, teachers and sections of the public, to get a clear lead, consensus was not forthcoming. Consequently, and in the fourth place, when their solution was introduced, it ran into opposition, sometimes sharp, from a number of quarters. While the desire to have youth unemployment eliminated was said to be almost unanimous the practical consequences of the solutions proposed were not so readily acceptable. Employers objected that specialized vocational training was underemphasized. Some teachers sharing their view objected in principle while others, perhaps uncertain of their own capacity to meet the new demand or unwilling to try, added their opposition. The trade unions, while agreeing in principle with the plan, claimed it did not go far enough and more was needed. Many school leavers themselves were unenthusiastic about the project, as the subsequent rate of truancy came to testify. In the fourth place the Ministry provided guidelines, which were the result of a collaborative effort that involved ministry officials, principals and teachers, but which were based on a hypothetical reality. Finally, in the fifth place, despite their structural specificity, the guidelines left quite a lot of room for experimentation. Schools were thus expected to exercise their initiative and to develop their own variants, taking into account the nature of their BVJ population and their local conditions.

Basically this was a process of innovation by legislation. But it occurred in a system that has a particular style of administration and planning. Basically that style appears to rest on the assumption that during the years the education system has evolved, a structure has been formed and procedures have been worked out that are, by and large, functional and even successful. While voices have been raised in criticism of aspects of the system both inside and outside it, these no more than represent the exercise of a right that citizens have to air their opinions publicly (as they do frequently, and in areas other than education too). But whatever the criticism, the general stance taken by the Ministry and Government is that the system is sound at heart and there is no need for radical reform. Further, there is a certain measure of flexibility built into the system with schools having the power and responsibility to make their own adjustments according to local conditions as they see fit. In addition the system is well endowed. By and large, buildings are more than adequate, equipment is excellent, teachers are well trained professionals, and the organizational structure of the system is such that action can be taken quickly and efficiently whenever the situation warrants it. The system thus has a built-in capacity to adapt to whatever problem arises — partly because it has the means and the mechanisms to do so and partly because the problems that may arise are unlikely to be too big for the capability of the system. If a name were needed to describe this implicit stance, perhaps reactive-adaptive, though clumsy, might do. The stance is basically reactive in that the system waits for the problems to emerge, rather than devotes excessive attention to anticipating them. It is adaptive in that when the problems do arise, the system can take the necessary moves to accommodate itself to them. The reactive-adaptive stance, of course, does not exclude perspectives for the future (eg the *Bildungs Gesamtplan*), but in reality the adaptation to developing situations and problems proves to be more important than formulated long-term plans.

In the present situation, then, it is expected that the schools will prove equal to the task put upon them. If that turns out not to be the case, then even so it is within the power of the system to react adaptively, finding within its substantial resources means for resolving the new problems. It seems inevitable that in this kind of regulated innovation, it will take a while for the actual practices in schools to become known. While such a state of affairs means that any inventive and adaptive responses schools might make do not attract the consideration they deserve, it may also mean that schools showing few or inadequate responses do not attract consideration either. Presumably if the matter does not excite the public interest too much, the resulting 'silence' is convenient to the administration and the schools alike.

While such an account constitutes an undoubted over-simplification of the highly complex Nordrhein-Westfalen system, the general interpretation of administrative stance is sound enough. The stance, then, stands in marked contrast with other systems where forward planning for continuing change is the *modus operandi*. What the distinction means, however, *may* in part be gleaned if some speculation on the future of the BVJ is attempted. The meaning of the distinction will also be considered in the final chapter.

The future

Given what we have called the reactive-adaptive stance of the education system, speculation about the future at this stage is somewhat hazardous. We can anticipate that as events occur there will be a reaction but because that reaction will tend to be sensitive to contextual conditions existing at the time and because times change, it is rather difficult to guess what directions those reactions might take. So the guesses that follow are made with all recognition of their potential fallibility. They are also based on certain assumptions about (i) the relative significance or potency of events, and (ii) the power (probably political) of those caught up in them.

First, then, to the problem with which this paper began: youth unemployment. Is it likely that the BVJ will contribute to its reduction? So long as one assumes that it is the quantum of jobs available that determines the degree of unemployment, and as long as that quantum will not increase, the answer must be no. The cause does not lie within the students – others better trained and qualified than they are also unemployed. True, there may be some progress by individuals in the queue for jobs so that what in effect happens is that entry into work is delayed rather than denied totally. However, this will not reduce the total amount of unemployment.

Is there then any prospect that the job market conditions will ease? In the short term it seems not. In the medium term, perhaps, perhaps not. In the long term, probably yes. Here in oversimplified terms is why. Assuming that no radical restructuring of West German society and its capitalist ethos occurs, because of the distribution of age groups in society and the now existing zero population growth rate, there will be a gradual decrease in the number of children coming into the work force and a relative increase in the number of retirees leaving at the other end. Assuming too that the state will want to maintain the aged in the condition to which they have become accustomed, there will eventually be an increasing demand for skilled labour to provide the necessary production power. At that point somewhere in the distant future, the BVJ graduates may well come into their own.

In the immediate future the situation is likely to get worse rather than better if the education system continues to pass its human products out into the market place and the job market continues to contract. What, then, will be the consequences? The BVJ scheme may at that point come in for (unjustifiable) criticism, but if the Government and for that matter the education system runs true to form, the reactive-adaptive mechanisms will be put into action and another prospective solution tried. Because *proposed* solutions tend to placate the concerned at least for the moment, and while problems tend to lose their impact over time (perhaps because we become accustomed to them) any promised new solution will be likely to take precedence over recrimination. The gaps between the original rhetoric and reality, however, may not be altogether forgotten.

How the education system will fare in all this is also a moot point. While it originally acted in good faith and with the best of intentions and while it may not have had it within its power to solve the 'youth unemployability' problem, it may well come in for some criticism. Education may once again come to fulfil its role as societal scapegoat. It is less likely that it will be seen again as prospective saviour.

If that is the case, what is likely to happen in the education system itself? Here the line of argument becomes even more tenuous and rather more complicated. It also depends in large measure on what has transpired in the BVJ programme itself *and* on its embedding educational context.

At the moment not much is known about how the BVJ programme is working, as it were, on the ground. There is unsystematic evidence that some schools are tackling it with inventiveness and imagination and that some teachers are enthusiastically caught up in the programme. There is also evidence from casual observation that some teachers are antagonistic to the BVJ and some schools are somewhat less than fully committed to it. Predictably, in between fall a fairly large group of teachers and schools who, while neither overly enthusiastic nor overly antagonistic, are nonetheless making some efforts along the lines desired. There is then scope for public opinion in the teaching force to go either way – pro or con. But that again most likely depends on what happens in the BVJ programme itself.

At this point there are at least two forces that may possibly exert an influence. The first is the liberal-idealistic groundswell that is gradually gaining momentum. To some educationists the BVJ represents the vanguard of a movement towards a greater emphasis on general education and a muting of the competitive, selective, strongly vocational orientation of the normal programme. The BVJ's emphasis on social adjustment and preparation for a life defined in terms that are broader than job skills is regarded as a move in the right direction. The right direction for them implies a value shift of some significance. West Germany too has been caught up in the general concern over the 'quality of life'. Her young people are starting to assert that material well-being is not enough and even that excessive material well-being is too much. Other cultural and social goods should, they claim, be given greater prominence even at the expense of material goods. Such a value position represents quite a profound departure from the value structure that sparked and sustained West Germany's economic 'miracle'. Predictably, then, the forces likely to be mounted *against* such a swing are likely to be strong and entrenched, so that in order to prevail, the forces in favour will have to be even stronger. Now if the referendum on comprehensive schooling in Nordrhein-Westfalen is any indication, public opinion is tending back towards the conservative rather than the 'progressive' at the moment. If comprehensivation, even in the modest form proposed, could be rejected as it was, then in the public domain the force in favour of a value shift towards a less vocationally oriented curriculum is unlikely to be strong. If economic restraint continues as well, it is likely that school children and parents will believe that vocational training is *more* likely to be in their personal interests than a presumably less useful general education would be.

If this chain of reasoning is correct, then there is a certain amount of inertia that the protagonists of the liberal-idealist faction would have to overcome if their viewpoint has to be accepted widely.

And it is inertia again that might determine how the BVJ programme will turn out in practice – but this time it is institutional inertia.

When the BVJ was first instituted, it was left to the schools to decide what to do within the guidelines issued. This in fact meant that the schools were told about the legislation passed and given supplies of the 271-page *Richtlinien*. The book indicated the desirability of adopting a different, more socially and psychologically sensitive approach to teaching, but provided little indication of how this might be done. In the short time available there had also been no opportunity to provide in-service courses that might serve to prepare the teachers for a (the) new style. Further, the provisions made at first included no incentive system for schools or for that matter teachers. To the most pessimistic teachers, the scheme spelled more work and, very likely, work that would prove more difficult than their customary jobs. Add to that as well the comfort that individual teachers take from having worked out how to do their jobs to their own satisfaction, and some idea of the possible degree of institutional inertia to overcome can be gained. If it proves too powerful then the BVJ can be expected to look more and more like a watered-down version of the normal programme. So the critical question becomes to what extent motivation will be generated to tackle the BVJ in a different way so that whatever momentum is generated by the initial drive to solve the youth unemployment problem can be exploited.

One of the hazards in playing the prediction game is that because of the complexity of social systems it is impossible to anticipate all or even many of the adaptive reactions that occur. In the Nordrhein-Westfalen education system which employs a reactive-adaptation strategy deliberately, it is even more difficult. However, to be effective the reaction-adaptation strategy depends on the efficiency of its communication networks. In order to know what to react to, messages about what is occurring must come in. And in order for the reaction to be adaptive, messages must go out. This implies a series of information flow networks with feedback loops. In fact, within the Nordrhein-Westfalen education system such loops are in general established and sustained in a number of ways. Public expression is one. Those concerned about education may and do speak their minds. Similarly, university researchers are free to be constructively and destructively critical. Within the system itself there are other avenues. The most important one is that school inspectors are expected to report back regularly to the Ministry. Officials of the Ministry have regular sessions with them to become informed of the problems arising in school. There is, moreover, a rich flow of informal information from the schools to the Ministry, to Parliament. Headmasters of schools inform their local member. Headmasters telephone the Ministry. The Teachers' Unions and Teachers' Associations discuss problems locally and in their *Länder* committees etc and publish their observations or discuss them with ministerial officials and Members of Parliament. The powerful Lord Mayors, Parliaments and responsible officials especially of the large

The Federal Republic of Germany: Successive Approximations

towns in the Rhine-Ruhr-district are also well able to alert the Ministerial bureaucracies if they feel that their local schools are not quite in order. However, how intensely these networks will be used for the sake of the BVJ is an open question. It may well be, for example, that it is easier to get the telephones ringing over problems in a *Gymnasium* than for a BVJ class.

In the case of the BVJ, a further formal, though small, mechanism has been brought into play. A research team comprising some eight persons from Dortmund Teachers College and the Land-Institut for Curriculum Development and Teacher Training has been commissioned to find out what goes on in the name of the BVJ. They in turn have committed themselves to providing feedback to the Ministry. As part of a larger study that goes in depth into the origin and development of the BVJ, the research team will also find out what is happening at the pit face. They plan to collect attitudinal data from teachers and pupils, to examine performance results and also to undertake observational studies in classrooms. They may thus serve to provide a small amount of that reinforcement that is probably needed if the BVJ is to flourish and which, by and large, has been omitted from the equation. Whether these influences will be enough, however, is debatable. At the moment without any extrinsic reward system operating, greatest reliance appears to have been placed on either the obedience of teachers to the official decree or on their presumed intrinsic motivation. But how many teachers will be able to tackle successfully the difficult job of providing an appealing, interesting and relevant education for youngsters who for one reason or another constitute the most difficult and unappreciative group to teach is an open question.

This chapter cannot close without brief reference to two further issues. One is an individual one, the effect of the BVJ on individual pupils. The other is a societal one, the nature of the unemployed school leavers.

The *intentions* of the BVJ programme to provide its pupils with both basic skill training and the ability to cope psychologically with the kind of (unemployment) conditions they are likely to face is unexceptionable. However, at the moment, the odds against achieving it are not insignificant. For example, the BVJ children are likely to be the least motivated, the least hopeful and the least confident of all secondary-level pupils. As a group they will have a greater aggregate record of failure than any others and if they are realists (in that they are aware of the probability of subsequent employment), they will have no reason to believe that this new education either is in their interests or will do them much good. They were made to return to school in the first place and are retained or returned there by compulsion. Furthermore, as failures or non-succeeders, they will not be unaware of the public disapproval their condition attracts. Nor will they need to be particularly bright to realize that in comparison with the other streams, the education they are to receive ranks lowest. Given also some teachers who are unconcerned or unenthusiastic and a programme that is based on the proposition that the remedy of the children's problem resides really in themselves, and the hurdles become rather high.

Finally, there is reason to believe that the educational aim to help these children to become adept at social and psychological adjustment in the face of difficulties will be sorely tested by this target group. As a group, they must be the least well equipped to deal constructively with enforced unemployment and to adjust themselves to the social, economic and psychological consequences. If the BVJ should succeed in this aim with them it will be a memorable achievement. This, however, is not to suggest that the BVJ is not worth while. When the alternatives available to the BVJ children are taken into account, clearly the school's programme offers more than does a listless life on the streets.

Finally, the unemployment issue bears examination in its own right. There are two aspects. The earlier discussion implied that unemployment was spread somewhat universally throughout the system – it was a global phenomenon in the State. But is it the case? Some of the evidence suggests rather that it is sectional. For example, in the BVJ programme, girls far outnumber boys and the lower socio-economic groups are over-represented. As well, the proportion of bright youngsters is relatively low. If it is the case that certain kinds of children are more vulnerable to unemployment than others, then at least two strategies are applied. On the one hand, consideration might be given to tailoring the education they receive to their *actual* characteristics and presumably needs rather than to what their needs are *presumed* to be in the light of what is also presumed to be the general condition of the employment market. On the other hand, if unemployment is group- or groups-specific, there is a case for a consideration of how those groups might be able to be used to good effect in the market-place. After all, although the comparison is unfortunate and perhaps unjust, special provisions are made for the handicapped in that special occupations are provided for them under special conditions, sometimes even in sheltered workshops. The point here is *not* that the 'unemployables' should be treated like the handicapped – far from it – but that the *principle* involved in making special provisions for the handicapped (as well as for the exceptionally talented) might be extended to this group too.

There is also the point of the future of unemployment in the Federal Republic of Germany's economy. Is unemployment likely to be a long-term or short-term phenomenon? Is there any reason to believe that conditions external to the country will see German industry acting in concert?

We are brought by this argument in full circle, back to the issue of cause and cure. That this should be so is not unreasonable because whether the BVJ can provide a cure to the unemployability issue is the open question at the moment. But another causal question is involved too. It is, what consequences will the BVJ cause? Will it be the cause of a liberalization of curriculum and structures? If so, to what extent and in what way? Will it even, as some think it might, lead eventually to a gradual reformation of the whole education system? Finally, has 'youth unemployment', as a cause of concern, exhausted its potential to create concern? Will society come to accept it meantime as just an unfortunate fact of life? Is the BVJ an innovation which in reality is not designed to solve the problem, just alleviate it a little, to calm consciences? Will unemployability find its centre stage position but a fleeting one? Will another one instead steal the limelight?

The Nordrhein-Westfalen innovation required that a large number of secondary schools should make a modest (though significant) alteration to their accustomed ways of operating. By contrast, the Sierra Leone innovation about to be discussed involves only one organization, a teachers' college, but requires it to make substantial extensive and far reaching alterations. It is a radical innovation that starts from an ambitious re-definition of the role of the College. As such it entails a major personal re-orientation for both staff and students. If this itself were not enough, the re-definition also encompasses a radically different view of the relationship between the College and the community. The College, rather than just producing teachers for country schools, is to become an agent in the community development process. As such it is expected to be instrumental in bringing about tangible, practical and beneficial development results in the district under its aegis. Through this process the College is expected to produce a 'new breed of teachers' whose interests, skills and abilities will extend beyond the limits of the conventional classroom and deep into the community.

Although the extent to which the 'Bunumbu project' is to be generalized throughout the country is not yet known, within its own boundaries the undertaking is of sufficient magnitude and complexity to be regarded as an exercise in educational reform. If all goes well, the College and its community will in fact be reformed or perhaps even transfigured.

Chapter 4

Sierra Leone: Creating a Context

In a remote Sierra Leone township, located inland and not far from the border of Liberia, an intriguing and visionary teacher training project called the Bunumbu project is being carried out. It takes its name simultaneously from the township and the local Teachers College. The purpose of the project stated simply is: 'to improve rural living through education' (Labor *et al*, 1978). But one has to look behind this straightforward statement of purpose to find the real fascination of the Bunumbu project. That lies in: the way the task is being specified, the means used to carry it out and the strategic significance being placed on the clarification, refinement and regular re-emphasis of the aims of the project. This is a project in which public statements of aims are serving to generate motivation and the motivation is serving to generate momentum.

One of the most important of the public statements was made in 1973 when Dr Siaka Stevens in his Presidential Address to the nation set the seal on plans that had been developing since 1969, by making direct reference to the Bunumbu project:

> 'Emphasis will be placed on the integrated approach to social development thereby involving the rural population in a total transformation of the college into a community college and a group of primary schools, to be known as Pilot schools into the community schools.'

However, such a statement would never have been made without a considerable amount of careful prior consideration by people charged with the task of advising the President. Nor, once made, could it pass unnoticed by those responsible for carrying out national policies. It is the purpose of the present chapter here to try to (i) look back to trace the advent of the idea, (ii) look around at the immediate situation to see its present circumstance, and (iii) look into the future in an attempt to forecast its eventual form and substance.

Setting the scene

When the staff of the Bunumbu Teachers College talk about the road from nearby Kenema (the State capital) to Bunumbu, they do so with a mixture of exasperation and pride. They have good reason for both. Their exasperation stems from the fact that although the terrain is gently undulating and the distance only 60 kilometres, travelling it can take anything from 2 to 2½ hours. The reason lies in what has wryly been referred to as the 'interesting texture of the surface'. The heavy and rather frequent rains that beat on it and the vehicles that continuously navigate paths of least resistance through it have so far succeeded in defeating whatever maintenance attempts are made from time to time. The pride that tinges the staff members' reference to the road is due to the fact that in the interests of the Bunumbu project they endure its rigours with great frequency, fortitude and only moderate protest.

This rather untoward beginning to the account of Sierra Leone's very ambitious innovation that sets out to create links between education and rural development is not so irrelevant as it might seem. Not only is the Kenema-Bunumbu road, as the main supply and communications route, a critical ingredient in the project, but to some extent it symbolizes some of the kinds of conditions with which the project is confronted. Bunumbu College was chosen for this experiment in rural education mainly because of its location. As Sierra Leone's sole rural teachers' college, 400 kilometres distant from the seat of political power in Freetown, it was thought to provide both an ideal setting and a real test of the undertaking. And Bunumbu College is indeed rural.

> 'The area lies between 500-1000 feet above sea level, and is drained mainly by the river Male and its tributaries. The mean annual rainfall ranges between 100-120 inches, much of it falling between May and November. The soil is of the granite type and the vegetation consists mainly of forest and farm bush, which provides ideal conditions for the production of the two major cash crops, cocoa and coffee, in this area. As well as this the area is amply provided with inland valley swamp lands which are extensively used for the production of rice, the staple food crop of the area.'
>
> *(Labor et al, 1978)*

In 1970 when the idea of the project was beginning to germinate, Bunumbu village itself comprised no more than two hundred souls, an indeterminate number of typically rural thatched roof houses made of earth bricks, two Lebanese-owned small general stores and an open market (on Fridays). The sole electricity generator in the district was located at the College. The local water supply was less than adequate. Only the College served to set Bunumbu off from the numerous other small village communities, scattered throughout Sierra Leone. The College, which had begun as a Catechism school founded by Methodist missionaries, was ultimately taken over and became one of the five state teachers' colleges. In 1970 the student body consisted of 189 men and 36 women. Though a little smaller in size than the other four teachers' colleges, Bunumbu College in its locale was clearly of great significance. As the major illustration of government enterprise and interest, and as a corporate organization, it gave Bunumbu village a character all of its own. Later the College was to become the means through which the village and other nearby settlements gained a great deal more but the details of that had best be delayed in deference to beginning at the beginning – with the circumstances that started it all.

The basic problem

As was the case for so many developing countries in and outside Africa, when the 1970s began, the vast majority of people in Sierra Leone lived in rural areas and were involved in agriculture. Sierra Leone's rural dwellers constituted 90 per cent of the nearly three million population, and 75 per cent of the work force was employed in farming. Despite this, the country was not agriculturally self-sufficient. Agricultural exports did account for 22 per cent of total exports, but 25 per cent of all imports were also agricultural (including 20,000 tons of rice, a crop already being grown in the country). At the same time there was another matter causing concern. The rate of migration from the country areas was growing as children left the family plot to seek their fortunes in the towns. This served not only to reduce the supply of labour where it was most needed, in the country, but also to increase it where it was least needed, in the town. The consequences were that there was a decline in social and economic conditions throughout.

There were two main problems inherent in such a state of affairs: the economic development problem of the efficient use of agricultural resources to the benefit of the nation, and the social, human problem of young people displaced and disaffected with no present to speak of nor apparently much promise of a better future.

Such problems, no strangers to most nations, were in Sierra Leone parallelled by a number of other concerns about the state of education in the country. At the time only 40 per cent of primary school age children were attending school and drop-out rates were high. Most distressing was the 30 per cent rate occurring at the juncture of the first and second years of school – the point at which children knew what school held in store for them and at which parents had come to appreciate the direct and indirect cost of education. To the latter, fees and the loss of child help in the fields were both burdensome especially in the face of an apparent absence of quick educational results. As well, up to 60 per cent of the teachers were unqualified and school facilities themselves often less than ideal. Further, the curriculum, reflecting its British origins, was under criticism for being overly-academic, oriented towards the interests of higher education and not noticeably relevant to the needs of the country. A final matter inviting concern was the fact that some 90 per cent of the adults living in the rural areas were estimated to be illiterate.

If, under such circumstances then, a reform *could* be designed to address the problems of education, economic development and urban drift simultaneously, the advantage was obvious. Conveniently a new and optimistic view emerged. It considered that education could become relevant to local (particularly rural) conditions, that the school *was* capable of providing education acceptable to and appropriate for adults and that education thus could become practical and useful. The education system *could* come to cater for society's needs better, primarily by producing school leavers who were prepared for work opportunities that did exist rather than for imagined ones that did not.

This basic position came to be incorporated into government policy. A simultaneous attack on educational and economic problems might well be feasible and certainly was worth trying. The consequences for education would be profound because a radical departure from the old, bookish, examination oriented concept of education established in colonial times was implied. The Government white paper produced in 1970 gave expression to such sentiments and set new educational priorities, stressing in the process the importance of a literate work force and 'greatly increased attention' to primary education with a *rural bias*.

Towards a plan

At this point, with such a direction more or less accepted by the public at large and certainly intrinsic to government policy, the main concerns became to develop an appropriate plan and to find the means for getting under way. Accordingly, a further series of activities, some formal, some informal, were begun. They were to lead eventually to the Bunumbu project as a prospective solution for several of the current educational and economic problems. Not all of those initial activities have been chronicled and to some extent it is difficult to reconstitute that early period. This is partly because in a country of Sierra Leone's size and character, informal networks play an important and useful role. Consequently, the casual conversation here, the chance meeting there, all tend to influence the shaping and forming of opinion. The result is that when the time for official decision making comes, confirmation is sometimes a formality for which previous informal social consensus has laid the foundation. There is also a tendency, in a country whose fundamental orientation towards social relationships is sociocentric rather than egocentric, for the roles played by individuals to be harder to identify. However, reading between the lines, it does seem as if there were two forces at work that each in their own way helped to both crystallize how the policy could be put into practice and create a climate of opinion favourable to the new development. At Ministry Headquarters, the Principal Education Officer in charge of Planning continued with the task of providing a blueprint for the operation. In Bunumbu itself the Principal of the Teachers College began establishing the groundwork that would eventually see the materialization of local support in the interest of coordinating the new and increasing number of tasks involved. Regular meetings were held between the Principal of the College and officials from the two critically important Ministries of Education and Development. As we saw earlier, this activity culminated in the President's speech of 1973 which set the official seal of approval on the embryo project. It was also followed shortly afterwards by the inclusion of the Bunumbu project in Sierra Leone's proposals for its 1973-76 Country Programme put forward for support from the United Nations Development Programme (UNDP). Shortly after that Bunumbu was designated the official site for the project.

The timing was right in that not only had the problems associated with urban drift also increased, bringing with them a rise in juvenile delinquency and other social ills, but also the first draft report of a nationwide Review of Education initiated and undertaken by the University of Sierra Leone was produced in the same year. The sentiments of the first report were clearly in sympathy with the turn of events occurring at Bunumbu. (Although the final report was to make some dramatic and controversial recommendations [including changing the entry age for primary school from five to six initially, and from six to seven subsequently] that tended to steal a little of the limelight.) The next step in the Bunumbu saga followed shortly. The same year, 1973, which was a year of intense activity, also saw the arrival of a UNDP/ Unesco three-man mission to undertake a three-week feasibility study. The procedures involved: an evaluation of other rural teacher training programmes on which documentation was available at the African Regional Office in Dakar; discussions with Unesco officials and a visit to the 'Kakata' project in Liberia, which was at the time making good progress and attracting attention. The upshot of the feasibility study, and other discussions held in Sierra Leone, was that recommendations were made that subsequently saw Government officials, the UNDP Resident Representative and the mission team combining to produce the Bunumbu Project Proposal. The project was to be a five-year one and the sum involved approximately 1½ million dollars. Again, the timing of the arrival of the mission was right in that the Government was in the middle of preparing its National Development Plan for 1974/75 to 1978/79. The subsequent result of the liaison between the mission and the various authorities responsible for the Plan was that the new plan incorporated a further statement of intention:

> 'A substantial reduction of drop-outs in primary schools can only be achieved in the long run through more fundamental changes, eg by making primary education more relevant to the social and economic environment, especially the rural milieu where most of the children live.'

With little delay the Ministry of Education followed this up by producing an indication of how this was to be achieved:

> 'The Primary School Curriculum is to be revised under the Institute of Education to make it more responsive of local environment of school and to give greater emphasis to practical activities and community participation. Understanding and relatedness of subjects should be stressed.'

The Institute of Education and the Bunumbu College were to be the chief agencies to undertake the development tasks – in close cooperation with the Ministry, of course. Specifically the following concrete actions were to be undertaken:

The Process of Educational Innovation

1. Development of a new primary curriculum with a rural bias.
2. Development of a new pre-service teachers' college curriculum.
3. Development of an in-service teacher training programme and training materials.
4. Development of a basic education curriculum with special reference to adults living in the rural areas.
5. Creation of mobile inter-disciplinary terms working out of the teachers' colleges to meet in-service teacher training needs.
6. Modification of existing primary schools in the rural areas to turn them into multi-purpose community education centres.
7. Creation of inter-disciplinary teams to staff the community centres composed of representatives from Ministries having a substantive responsibility for the rural areas.

With the initial planning work well in hand, all that was wanted was the signal to go ahead. However, the green light had yet to be given. Predictably a project of this magnitude needed careful examination. While that was occurring and because the omens were good, UNDP approved an interim grant of approximately ¼ million dollars for 12 months during which preparations were to get under way.

In effect, the proposal thus constituted a kind of *educational development* plan that had been outlined complete with specified material components and provisions to meet the costs. As such it was the result of direct consultation between the local (primarily education) people and the Government, and was notably sensitive to national needs and interests.

Action

On the strength of the interim grant, one of the first moves taken was to appoint a Project Director and a Curriculum Development Officer. Their arrival led to a turn of events that once again illustrates what must almost be a universal principle in social science. Neither of these two officials had been involved in the initial planning, yet they were to be the agents through whom the plan would be put into practice. Furthermore, they came designated as Unesco 'experts' (a title that seems to be universally attracting less and less enthusiasm from just about all concerned), and with particular competencies. Predictably, their vision of the task, coloured by their own experiences, led them to have views that were not necessarily identical with those prevailing before they arrived. Predictably again, they would wish both to signal their interest and competency and indeed to invest some of their own intellectual and vocational capital in the project. In this case what happened was that after their arrival the parties concerned took the decision to sharpen the project document so that greater clarity would result. This was duly done, but not without some consequences that had some effects on the early progress of the project. These consequences will be surfaced when we return to the discussion of the delicate, difficult and demanding roles of Unesco experts vis-à-vis the community they are entrusted with both helping and serving.

For the revision of the plan, however, once again advantage was taken of the opportunity Unesco provides for collective and cooperative problem solving. At the Nairobi General Conference of Unesco, members of the Sierra Leone delegation conferred with Unesco officers, and plans were put in train for a Unesco mission to visit Freetown and Bunumbu and then hold a tripartite seminar with representatives of the Government and UNDP. This seminar was distinctive for a number of reasons. In the first place, it foreshadowed an evaluation activity that was to be repeated subsequently under the title 'Tripartite Review'. In the second, the shape that the seminar itself took was somewhat characteristic of Sierra Leone's socio-centric orientation in that representatives from both the University and the Bunumbu College made up part of the 'Ministry' team. In the third place, and also consistently with the socio-centric orientation, the paramount chiefs of the Bunumbu area and other local elders were included as well – a circumstance of great significance and importance. As a result of the seminar, the proposal was revised and all that remained was to complete official formalities – or so it was thought at the time.

The project document in its refined form was detailed and complex, and cannot be done full justice here. Nonetheless some indication of its content should be provided. First the long-range objectives of the project stipulated:

(a) the development of a new primary curriculum with a rural bias;
(b) the expansion of the present functions of the teacher training colleges to include the capability of providing in-service training and educational extension services to village community centres on a request or need basis and of serving as educational technology and information resource centres; and
(c) the development of a country-wide network of Community Education Centres providing education and training, of a both formal and non-formal nature, to young people and adults in the rural areas.

Several comments are in order at this point. The vision expressed in those long-term objectives looked further into the future than did the specific proposals for the Bunumbu College. It also carried implications for changes not only in some educational practices, but also in some of the structures that contained them. For example and firstly, at that time, responsibility for developing, testing and producing curricula was vested in the Institute of Education – a constituent part of the University of Sierra Leone. The new objectives appearing in connection with the Bunumbu project implied that people outside the Institute would at least share in the task of curriculum development and that new divisions of labour and organizational links would be needed. Secondly, for historical reasons the teachers' colleges in Sierra Leone had grown up with distinctive, special areas of emphasis, a circumstance valued because of the diversity that resulted. If one college were to, as it were, play a part in producing curricula for others, a new period of greater interdependence seemed in prospect. Thirdly, the idea of Community Education Centres, an idea reiterated in the Education Review of 1977, was at that stage far from explicitly formulated. Nonetheless it implied a whole new set of organizations plus a supporting administrative framework.

Objectives

However, at the moment we need to return to the task as the College was to face it. The project proposal itself gave an indication of the general orientation to be taken.

The immediate objectives for the College were:

'1. To collaborate with the Institute of Education in the development of a primary school curriculum having a rural-biased core, with optional components emphasizing urban learning needs to be substituted or added where appropriate.
2. To utilize the twenty Pilot schools existing within a 20 miles' radius of Bunumbu Teachers College as Community Centres in addition to their normal role of providing primary education to local children. The Primary School Programme will be based on the new curriculum referred to above. The Community Education role includes instruction and guidance in adult education, woodwork and handicrafts, nutrition, health education and agriculture. Consideration may also be given to extending the community education experiment to two non-pilot villages without the formal school system.
3. Expand the pre-service enrolment of Bunumbu Teachers College to a maximum total of 500 by 1979, including both men and women.
4. Develop a Teacher's Certificate and Higher Teacher's Certificate programme at Bunumbu Teachers College based partly on the existing curriculum as modified by the Institute of Education, and partly on the following new fields and competencies: Agriculture and Applied Rural Science, Home Economics (Nutrition, Hygiene, Childcare, etc), Woodwork and Handicrafts, Community Development and Adult Education.
5. Conduct periodic in-service training and refresher courses in the fields referred to in paragraph 4 above for the existing staff of the twenty pilot schools.
6. In collaboration with the Institute of Education, develop modular components of the work-oriented areas in the Bunumbu Teachers College curriculum to be used in in-service training, both residential (block-release) and on-site, for the pilot school staff.
7. Develop a Resource Centre at Bunumbu with production, viewing, and experimentation facilities to be made freely available to students.'

Understandably the objectives differ in the degree of specificity they display. Three which deal with quantitative or material aspects are quite straightforward and direct, viz: no. 3, expanding pre-service enrolments to 500 by 1979; no. 5, conducting periodic in-service training and refresher courses; and no. 7, developing a resources centre at Bunumbu. By contrast, the three qualitative objectives concerned with the development of new curricula are framed in a more open fashion – a circumstance no doubt the result of the complexity and difficulty of the task itself. More to the point, however, is the fact that two of the activities, no. 1, developing a rural curriculum, and no. 6, developing modular components, are at the heart of the school-based part of the reform. On them depends whatever impact the project will have on children. It should be noted that those activities were to be jointly undertaken by the Institute and Bunumbu – a matter that was to be affected by a number of factors later, including the famous or infamous Bunumbu-Kenema road. The two remaining objectives, no. 4, teachers' certificate programmes, and to a lesser extent, no. 2, community education centres, were also contingent on the advent of the primary school curriculum. But nonetheless, there remained in objective 2 enough latitude with respect to developing the 'community education role' to enable the College to take advantage of some opportunities and to minimize some difficulties that were soon to emerge.

The situation that the College found itself in as 1974 got under way is worth reviewing briefly.

First, the project was now incorporated into national policy and planning and, having also attracted the promise of substantial UNDP financial support, had assumed considerable importance as one of Sierra Leone's principal educational developments.

Second, the President's speech, as it were a symbolic 'laying on of hands', not only created a positive public attitude round the project, but emphasized the obligation of the College and the Ministry to make good.

Third, although the general direction of the project and its aspirations were clear (and ambitious), the means for achieving them had only partly been clarified – although an inspection of the catalogue of requirements of personnel, plant and equipment listed in the proposal gave some fairly strong hints of what was to be anticipated.

Fourth, Bunumbu remained remotely rural. The Bunumbu-Kenema road was still the road, and communication with Freetown was often difficult, particularly after rain had ravaged the telephone lines. Notwithstanding all the plans for the future, the demands of the present were still insistent. The College still had to continue with its day-to-day task of training teachers.

Some assumptions
Attention now turns to the plan to be followed and to some of its implications. The proposal itself had made at least four basic assumptions about how the task was to be undertaken. First, in order to go about developing the new rural oriented primary curriculum, the level of curriculum development

expertise at the College was to be raised by two methods, viz: (i) overseas 'experts' were to be recruited (some six in all), and (ii) a fellowship programme was to be employed to give Bunumbu staff members relevant experience outside the country. Second, the physical conditions of the pilot schools were to be improved by providing new buildings designed in particular for the new curriculum and for the community education activities. Third, the 'delivery' capacity of the College was to be enhanced by the acquisition of new (and sometimes sophisticated) plant and equipment, eg minibuses, woodwork machines, a printing press, videotape recorders, etc. Fourth, the general living and working conditions on campus were to be upgraded, particularly through the provision of adequate accommodation for staff and students and new electricity and water systems.

From the outset it was apparent that the complexity and magnitude of the project meant that the coordination of activities would be both difficult and important. In the last analysis, not only were many different kinds of people needed, from builders' labourers to domestic science specialists, from motor mechanics to accountants, from bus drivers to community developers, but also because *community* development was a general objective, the task could not and should not become the sole prerogative of the Ministry of Education. Accordingly, the project document made provision for a National Advisory Committee whose commission was to oversee events and give advice and guidance to the College and the Ministry on the general operation of the project. Most if not all of the official bodies that were likely to be influenced by the outcomes of the project and who in turn might be likely to influence it were represented on the Committee. The University was there, so too were the local paramount chief and community elders. The array of ministries involved was formidable: Education of course, and Agriculture, Development and Economic Planning, Health and Social Welfare. The absence of the Ministry of Public Works, however, is worth noting and, for several reasons, worth regretting. In the project document there appeared a list of issues to be considered by the Committee. They are noteworthy in particular because they directed attention beyond Bunumbu itself to some of the national implications (and complications) should the project succeed. The list gives formal recognition to the proposition that change in one part of a system (in this case the education system) is likely to have repercussions throughout. It also indicates that the Bunumbu project was being seen as a means for leading into other educational 'reforms' that although not under active consideration yet were sensed to be needed. The mandate given the Committee was to consider and 'bring into line with the project's objectives':

'(a) The certification system and the question of diploma equivalency.
(b) National certification examinations.
(c) Salaries, professional advancement, and other work incentives.
(d) Planning, development, and staff and student morale of other teacher training colleges.

(e) The attributes and methods of the school inspectors, particularly those responsible for the Bunumbu area.
(f) Coordination and regulation of new primary curriculum with secondary curriculum and with planned or on-going adult education programme.
(g) Coordination and regulation of project goals with the work of the district agricultural extension officers, the social welfare officers and health inspectorate.
(h) Coordination and standardization of general management problems relating to the pilot schools (cf. paras. 38 and 44 of the Workplan).
(i) Coordination of the work of the project's Resource Centre with the Ministry of Education's media service.
(j) Public information.'

Priorities

The initial problem however was to determine *relative* priorities. Fairly clearly it seemed as if curriculum development, while not exactly dependent on the presence of Unesco experts, would be better facilitated if they were there. It also seemed fairly apparent too that the community education component would be better accomplished if the physical conditions thought necessary for it were in place. As well, obviously, with College accommodation already stretched to its limits, the College roll could not be increased until more hostels and classroom blocks were built and housing for the new staff provided.

There were also, however, other human-social issues of considerable importance and on which the fate of the whole project depended. They were: (i) the degree and kind of support provided by the Ministry; (ii) the kind of relationship to be established between the College and the Institute; (iii) the kind of acceptance the College would gain in the community in the name of whose development the project was about to begin; and, perhaps most importantly, (iv) the kind of working and social environment sustained in the College itself. Finally, and it almost goes without saying, in order for anything to be put in train, money to meet the considerable cost entailed would have to be available. In fact, because of the cost of the whole programme, action had been taken to gain financial support from a number of agencies. As has already been noted, UNDP was to provide a considerable amount. So too was the Sierra Leone Government. But as well other specified costs were to be spread in the following way:

1. Some lecturers, books and publications – the British Council.
2. The construction and renovation of schools, partly (but not entirely) and the provision of some tools – the Catholic Relief Service.
3. Building materials – Unicef.
4. Certain equipment (eg water pump), consumables (paper, etc), vehicles and machines – Unicef.

5. In-service training programme – Unicef.

Necessarily the spreading of the cost could have logistic effects if, for any reason, funds were not made available on schedule.

With the plan articulated and the organizational framework provided, the problem really boiled down to where to start.

Now at this point events were to play an important part in the evolution of the undertaking. They were not expected and had the original plan been more explicit and correspondingly more inflexible the events might have spelled disaster. Those events, each understandable in their own way, were virtually not under the control of the College.

Problems

In the first place, difficulties were experienced (a) over getting some Unesco experts and (b) in retaining others. The causes were various: sometimes the vacancy did not attract applicants, sometimes applicants withdrew at the last minute, sometimes appointees found the situation at Bunumbu more difficult than they were prepared for, sometimes their particular talents were not appropriate to Bunumbu's needs. Expert participation in the project on which curriculum development was predicated did not initially go like clock-work.

Clearly, the curriculum development aspect was not off to the smoothest of starts. However, these were not the only problems related to curriculum. The Institute-College link proved easier in theory than in practice. Although provision was made for contact between the two organizations, and indeed one Institute staff member was specifically delegated to act in a liaison capacity, the Institute itself had many other (prior) commitments and obligations. Faced with undertaking substantial revision of the secondary curriculum, its staff, by no means numerous, were stretched to capacity. Pressed for time, they could give less attention than they would have liked to working with and helping the embryo curriculum development project at Bunumbu. The situation was further complicated by the inaccessibility of the College. The road effectively served to convert what could have otherwise been a one-day trip into two, and also created physical hardships that after a while palled for even the most hearty. Given also the difficulties of telephone communication, the opportunity for sustained and substantial cooperation between the Institute and College was somewhat restricted, to say the least. Nonetheless, the link that was established was positive, so that the Bunumbu staff were able to go about their business confident of Institute sympathy, understanding and occasionally active help and support. Testimony to the Institute's good faith was to be given in a very tangible form later when the College's own prescription for the Higher Certificate of Education was to come under review.

Now, it is possible that some meticulous readers will have noted that one rather important ingredient has so far been missing from the account – indication that official confirmation of the project had been given. It will be recalled that pending the signing of the project document, interim funds had been made available on the assumption that official approval of the full programme *and its budget* would be forthcoming. Totally unexpectedly, this was not to be the case. The liquidity crisis in Unesco was the stumbling block. The consequence of this dramatic development was a source of considerable concern in Sierra Leone at the time but in the long run turned out not to have the dire effects that were initially feared. True, the project document remained unsanctified for two years. But when it was duly signed in 1977 (on three separate occasions) in compensation for the set-back the project was extended by one year to 1980 and more funds were made available for 1977. In fact, the earlier provision of interim funding had meant that this aspect of the financial situation was less troublesome than another that came about.

In the 1970s there were few countries in the world whose economies had not been affected by what has been (unpopularly) called the oil crisis and related trade aberrations. When the impact was felt in Sierra Leone, rather than retrench on the Bunumbu project, the Government decided to seek an extensive loan from the African Development Bank to finance much of the capital cost. This was duly negotiated, but the money could not become available until 1979, much later than the original schedule provided for. Obviously, the consequential delay in building accommodation at Bunumbu would throw the plans for increased student enrolments out of gear, and it did.

The array of trials and tribulations visited on the project at the beginning might have proved fatal but for two very positive developments. In fact, there are even grounds for believing that the set-backs were a blessing in disguise in that they provided time and opportunity to give attention to certain sociological aspects that otherwise might have been neglected. These were cementing the relationships between the Ministry and Bunumbu and, perhaps more importantly, between the College and the community.

Opportunities

Following their extensive examination of relevant research, Havelock and Huberman (1977) have argued that the acceptance of reform by the people who are to be influenced by it is absolutely imperative if the reform is to succeed. Such an argument is consistent with much social, psychological and sociological research into the nature of organizations and their capacity to adapt to 'outside' influences. Havelock and Huberman also point out that this is the Achilles' heel of so many innovative projects in education, especially in developing countries. Time and time again it is the 'people' dimension that is forgotten, left to chance, or ignored.

Now the single most distinctive feature of the Bunumbu project from the point of view of the present book's interest in the process of innovation is the comprehensive and effective way in which all the appropriate networks have been contacted, palliated and incorporated into the project, sometimes with energy and enthusiasm. Of course, in this respect the project got off on the right foot – on even several right feet! In the very first place, the initial discussions between the Principal of the College and senior officials of the Ministries of Education and Development set two important precedents. First, they established that ever-important link between the 'work place' and the 'halls of power', so that both became sensitive to each other's realities and rituals. Second, because the discussions took place in a spirit of collegiality, there was little need then (or subsequently) for recourse to bureaucratic expedients. Thereafter, and once the project was incorporated into the Country Programme and the National Development Plan, these overt acknowledgements of the project's importance guaranteed official commitment. Then again the supportive statement made by Dr Siaka Stevens provided the all-important official sanction for the whole undertaking. All the right *official* protocols had been observed. Now the test was to see if the network contact principle would be extended downwards from the summit, and if so, how far.

In fact, the Ministry had no difficulty in taking the project to heart, and there began a series of contacts between Bunumbu and the staff at headquarters in general and the Division concerned with teacher training in particular, that were also to be sympathetic and supportive and from time to time tangibly helpful. Here again the difficulties experienced over the appointment of experts and funding served to help rather than hinder. Their advent called for even closer contact between the project and the Ministry. The initial links grew stronger as problem situations brought about a need (as crises often do) to tackle mutual problems together.

But it was on the local front that the most spectacular gains were made. And here again one wonders what would have happened if the funds and experts had been immediately available to attract attention towards more glamorous activities.

From the outset Bunumbu College had been community oriented, with much of its work directed towards local teachers. Because many of them had been trained at Bunumbu, contact with the College was easy. Not only did the local teachers often go to seek College help, but the College staff were given a ready welcome in the schools. There was, in other words, an educational network in the district linked through and with the College. However, perhaps the most significant feature of the local community was the role played by the Bunumbu paramount chief. Just as the Principal was a driving force in the project, so was the Paramount Chief a driving force in the community. From the outset he had been interested in the project, seeing it as a rare opportunity for community development and one to be seized. A man of vision and experience, having spent time overseas (mainly in England), he had acceded to office relatively recently. With his energy, enterprise and foresight enlisted for the project, the most essential ingredient for community support was there. His standing was such that given his attitude, the community's cooperation was assured. The fact, too, that the Bunumbu area itself was not poor and that the people were by comparison with other localities at least well enough provided for to be able to spare time from their everyday duties and obligations to help in the project, was significant.

It should not be imagined that important networks of this kind are easy to establish. Far from it. In fact, when groups and people unfamiliar to each other are thrown in close contact, mutual accommodation is a delicate and difficult business. Territorial prerogatives and vested interests, if threatened, invite formidable defences. In the present case, however, everyone stood to profit. The community would gain economic and educational advantages, the College prestige and recognition, the Ministry political approval and the funding agencies commendation for having furthered their parent organizations' (altruistic) objectives. But even with the dice as it were loaded in favour of mutual cooperation, there were many points of potential frailty. For example, if the College promoted agricultural innovations that violated conventional norms (even as apparently innocuous as prejudices against eating eggs), community resentment and hostility could eventuate. Again, if the College's intentions were misconstrued as motivated by self-interest, similar resistance could easily occur. If the College staff felt that their extra work and responsibility were not adequately recognized and rewarded, they might be inclined to seek other employment. If the Institute, finding itself unable to provide the guidance and help it had hoped to, could not approve of the curricular materials produced by the College, then friction would be almost inevitable. If the funding agencies felt the project was unlikely to realize the hopes originally held for it, their support might be withdrawn. Such 'difficulties' are not flights of fancy. Some in fact have already surfaced in the present project and the remainder elsewhere. In other words, there are not only problems in establishing networks characterized by mutual trust, support and respect, there are also problems involved in sustaining them and maintaining them against untoward developments.

In the Bunumbu case, it is somewhat unfortunate that the means by which such misfortunes have been avoided are virtually undocumented. Reading between the lines again, it seems as if a great deal of social sensitivity and political astuteness has been exhibited. Unfortunately the precise details remain unclear and the mechanisms that were used stay unknown. Actions have been taken apparently spontaneously and even perhaps intuitively. Whatever danger signals have been put up so far have been recognized quickly and responded to with alacrity. However, in order for the process of innovation to be really understood, it is precisely such insightful interpretations and responses that need to become part of the vocational capital of planners and administrators. In fact it may be that in the Bunumbu project in particular and other qualitative innovation projects in general, this aspect may be the one of greatest single importance.

But we are being ensnared by the complexity of the Bunumbu project and its many interesting facets into omitting reference to the events that came to pass. That omission needs rectifying.

Developments

As early as 1974 and shortly after the project document was first drafted, the 20 pilot schools that were to become an integral part of the project were identified. All fell within 20 miles (35 kilometres) of Bunumbu township. Without delay, a one-year orientation course for headteachers of the pilot schools began. While the course might be regarded as overly prompt in view of the facts that: curriculum development was scarcely under way, the experts were not yet in residence and the precise details of the project were not yet worked out, nonetheless there were several distinct advantages in a relatively early start. In the first place, the plans for the project were well known in Bunumbu. In the second place, it would have been unwise to allow enthusiasm to flag by taking the decision to wait until everything was ready. In the third, having the headmasters play a part in helping to create the general strategy and tactics for the project was a particularly shrewd move in that it ensured their constructive and committed involvement.

The timing of the course, to occur even before the arrival of either Unesco's Chief Technical Advisor and expert in curriculum development, is indicative of both the degree of motivation existing already and the confidence the Bunumbans had in their capability to undertake the task.

Strategies of attack
However, it is also indicative of the fact that a strategy for operationalizing the curriculum development and teacher training aspects of the project had been worked out in advance. There were in fact five mechanisms to be used, each devised to take into account the evolving condition of the project. They were respectively: (i) a pre-service training programme; (ii) an in-service programme; (iii) curriculum workshops; (iv) community education programme and (v) seminars, conferences and workshops. Reference will be made later to the form in which each of these subsequently materialized. It is sufficient for the present to note one or two things about them. The pre-service and in-service programmes, *and* the curriculum workshops, were to involve initially not only the teachers and headteachers of the pilot schools but local craftsmen and craftswomen also. The Community Education aspect, regarded as very important, was expected to cover a wide spectrum which included not only practicalities (and difficulties) of community-school and community-college interface but also the rationale and philosophy behind them. This area was to serve to clarify and crystallize the future shape of Community Education Centres and the roles of the many people involved – teachers, craftsmen, civic leaders, Paramount Chiefs, extension workers, agriculture and health officials, community developers, etc. Finally, the seminars, conferences and workshops were also regarded as an important device for disseminating the idea (and ideals) of Bunumbu.

Other developments were also to follow.

Progress

The expert in curriculum development duly arrived in October 1974 and decisions were taken on the appointment of Sierra Leoneans as 'counterparts' for the other imminent (it was thought) experts. In November the

Sierra Leone: Creating a Context

equipment from UNDP began to arrive. As momentum increased progress was made on several fronts. At the College, plans for the holding of workshops to revise the primary school curriculum were drawn up. In August 1975 the Government gave approval for pilot school teachers to attend inservice courses which were to be held once a fortnight during term time and for three weeks during the long vacation. In the community, action was under way to provide a formal structure for participation and parent-teacher associations were formed for the 20 pilot schools. Subsequently, community education councils representing various groups and interests were established in the four chiefdoms with the Paramount Chiefs as Chairmen – a development that foreshadowed the setting up of sub-committees in some chiefdoms to deal with the construction of roads, footbridges and toilet facilities. At the national level the new National Advisory Committee was appointed and thereupon revised the project document itself.

Behind this flurry of activity there was a considerable amount of groundwork put in by College staff and Ministry officials in particular. Of special importance for future events were decisions taken concerning the roles of experts and counterparts and their working relationship. Discussion is warranted.

There are many variations to be found in the way Unesco field experts deport themselves. Sometimes the situation calls for an unequivocal display of technical authority, at other times the need is for a degree of self-effacement in the interests of harmonious collaboration. Given such a range of contrast between alternatives, obviously the determination of what model to choose can become a delicate business. In Bunumbu it took a little time to arrive at what would appear to be the most satisfactory resolution of the issue. Finally, however, clarification occurred, and it occurred with due recognition of the exigencies of the moment. As the situation was developing, the College staff were faced with a considerable increase in the amount of work they would have to do. On top of their teacher training tasks would come not only more community development activities but curriculum development ones as well. The situation was not helped either by the mobility of staff and the difficulties experienced in getting (and occasionally keeping) experts. When, however, both expert and counterpart were *in situ*, the proposition was that they should complement each other. The expert would transfer his expertise, ideally becoming redundant eventually. The counterpart on the other hand would introduce the expert into local conditions, conventions and customs and thus acculturate him to the Bunumbu way of life. But this depended on there being time and opportunity for the necessary liaison and cooperation between expert and counterpart. The situation, however, conspired to make that difficult. Three factors in particular served to disturb the elegance of this arrangement. In the first place, we have seen, the movement of staff and experts complicated the situation. In the second, in order to get the many various tasks done, the services of experts and counterparts needed to be deployed separately. The experts and counterparts thus found themselves taking on (heavy) teaching loads, pursuing their community development activities in the field and working on curriculum development in their offices, often apart from each other. In the third place, the Fellowship programme that was designed to further the education of staff members (particularly counterparts) had the effect of taking counterparts out of the experts' orbit. Such circumstances, though understandable, can be, and in some cases have been, a source of frustration and disappointment. That this is so should occasion little surprise because a measure of frustration and disappointment for some is endemic in any complex social system. The main problem is to contain it within reasonable proportions and alleviate the difficulties as much as possible. In this respect Bunumbu staff and experts have achieved a measure of success and the somewhat erratic record of expert association with the project is better explained by other reasons that will be considered later.

Meanwhile it was in June 1976, when things were gathering momentum, that the President's official launching of the programme accelerated activity and even more progress. The pilot schools were designated Community Development Centres and the first inter-agency seminar was held to give attention in particular to strategies for planning an integrated approach to rural development. A second one the following year took a critical look at the achievements of the project to that date and made recommendations for improving the situation.

Then in August 1976 occurred an event that was to give considerable encouragement to College staff and students, and also recognition of the educational significance of the scheme. The Board of the Institute of Education approved the new Bunumbu teacher training course (designed with the help of the Institute itself and the Milton Margai College) as appropriate for the award of the Higher Teacher's Certificate, a qualification hitherto only applying to secondary school teacher graduates. Between that point and mid-1978, the main preoccupation of the project was with developing and expanding activities in accordance with the general objectives held. With the pending arrival of a replacement curriculum development expert (the first one had left in August 1976), and the filling of the agricultural expert vacancy (empty since April 1976) prospects looked good. The tripartite review undertaken by the Government, Unesco and UNDP tended to confirm this.

Achievements

However, now it is the time for a little stocktaking. By mid-1978, much had happened, with some of the events having particular significance for the project. The most spectacular progress was to be seen in Bunumbu itself and the pilot school communities, and it was progress precisely as desired, towards community development and educational improvement. Bunumbu township was clearly undergoing transformation. More people had come to live in the town and houses of higher quality and larger size had appeared. The Friday market had become a daily one. A bank had established a small branch office in the town and there have been two other commercial ventures in which the College has played a prominent part. An agreement has been reached with a petrol company to locate two pumps in the town provided the community houses them. The most spectacular development, however, is the cooperative general store that has been built by the College and community together. Financed initially by a shareholding system, the cooperative (which has wisely made provision for expansion) is now self-sufficient, and its pricing policy has seen a corresponding drop in the prices charged in the two other shops.

On the local educational front, community energies have been mobilized so that in most of the pilot schools the ground has been prepared for the new buildings, sand has been transported from the river and stockpiles of building blocks created. Where the Catholic Relief Service has begun the new buildings, other labour has also been forthcoming from the local citizens. In fact, intensive community involvement in this whole array of activities associated with the project is quite striking and is perhaps the most significant achievement to date.

In the short time that the College staff have been working on the project a great deal has been accomplished. Not only have all the pilot school principals been through a one-year orientation course, but many of the teachers in the pilot schools have either undergone refresher courses or further in-service training. As well, curriculum workshops have been run regularly. Initially they operated every fortnight. Subsequently the interval was increased to allow the staff a little free time because a little free time was all that was available for anyone on the project. An inventory of time spent by staff and experts alike would show not only long working days, but many evenings, weekends and much vacation time spent in the interests of the project. On balance, valour very far beyond the line of duty was the norm – a state of affairs that because of its immediate consequences and long-term implications will have to be discussed further later.

In the course of their work the staff have produced a number of curriculum 'packages' whose topics range from classroom organization to textbooks on play. These comprise printed teachers' guides, pupil work sheets and suggestions on various aspects of the new approach to teaching. As well, the College is giving particular attention to 'local language' teaching during the first three years of primary school. New materials are being developed and trialled.

Of course, it goes without saying that the regular students of the College are receiving their usual teacher training – training that now incorporates a substantial measure of community development work.

Before an attempt is made to conjecture about the future shape and scope of the Bunumbu project, there is some point in briefly cataloguing one or two points that could not be incorporated into the previous account.

They are taken chiefly from the Principal's report to the Tripartite Review Committee made in April 1978.

The aspects of the project that are on schedule include:

1. The provision of housing and other accommodation for staff and experts.
2. The conversion of some existing staff accommodation into dormitories, an expedient prior to the building of permanent buildings once ADB loan funds become available.
3. The provision of storage facilities – temporarily being used as a library.
4. The partial completion of the resources centre.
5. Revision of draft curricular materials for pre-service teacher training.
6. In-service training programmes.
7. Recruitment of students.
8. Inter-agency seminars and seminars on various topics in pilot communities.
9. Fellowship scheme.
10. Some consultant missions completed.
11. Self-evaluation of the project.

Of the matters still outstanding then the following were the most significant:

1. Buildings – both for the College and the community education centre.
2. Some fellowships.
3. Some consultant missions.
4. Some expert services.
5. Appointment of administrator.
6. Water and electricity supplies.
7. Communications.

When the original specifications of the project are taken into account, there are, it seems, three logistics problems affecting progress to varying extent. The first is the set-back to the building programme. Despite the effective remedial action taken by the Government to obtain ADB loan money, it will not be until 1979 that the money will become available and much headway can be made. The second is the coordinating of the availability of experts with the developmental needs of the project. The lack of curriculum development and agricultural experts at critical points constitute a case in point. The third is also a personnel problem in that there has been a turnover of staff at a level above the ordinary.

Given both the successes achieved and the difficulties existing, what then are the prospects for the future?

The future

The development occurring in Bunumbu and in the 20 pilot schools in the area shows every promise of continuing. There is also evidence of much greater interest in sending children to school. First-year rolls have increased radically and, more to the point, it appears as if the drop-out rate between first and second year will be dramatically reduced. As well, adult education classes already begun are likely to escalate in popularity as buildings are completed. Nor does there appear to be any lack of appropriately trained teachers for the Bunumbu area schools. In fact, the output from the College will far exceed the local demand, a state of affairs that leads to conjecture over the fate of the 'surplus' teachers.

It is predictable too that conditions at the College will improve. Notable among those that *must* improve if some quite severe difficulties are to be avoided are the water and electricity systems and the conditions of the Bunumbu-Kenema road. The water supply is the matter of greatest concern to staff. At the moment each accommodation unit has a facility for storing rainwater that is barely adequate when the rains are frequent. If dry weather persists even for a short time, recourse has to be made to an erratic supply of pumped water or more usually water carried from a nearby 'spring'. This water is brackish and impure. This state of affairs not only creates hardships for staff, students and families, it also severely handicaps much of the work of the College.

The inhabitants of the College suffer other hardships and the work of the College is also handicapped because the electrical generator can only provide power at limited periods, notably in the early morning, at lunch time and in the evening. Whatever College work depends on electricity, eg wood and metal work, craft work and anything employing teaching aids such as projectors (and, it is hoped, TV), etc, is under handicap. There is also the feeling among staff that as agents of development they lose face when the inadequacy of the College's water and electricity supplies are so obvious. By comparison, the College staff themselves are not inclined to stress the importance of the Bunumbu-Kenema road, perhaps because they have become accustomed to it. However, in addition to the consequences mentioned previously, there are others. Despite the fact that the College now has a reasonably equipped garage and trained mechanics, much difficulty is experienced in keeping vehicles roadworthy. In fact the Principal's reports indicate that several are now completely unserviceable and most of the others are unlikely to last long. The effect of this on the capacity of the College to 'deliver' its services is becoming more and more serious and it regularly plays havoc with arrangements made for refresher courses, workshops and seminars when participants have to be collected. The other roads in the area are in better condition, principally because they are not subjected to such heavy traffic. The fact that there is such heavy traffic, however, inclines one to wonder at the total cost to the community of general repairs and replacement of the various vehicles that use it. Perhaps investment in road maintenance is one way in which a further Ministry could make a positive and needed contribution to the project.

Just how important these 'impediments' are is difficult to gauge because their effects are likely to be felt indirectly. It will be virtually impossible to assess whether they have any effects on the capabilities of students as teachers. Even if curriculum production is affected, again it will be difficult to discern in what precise way and to what extent. But there is an area where the effects may become both apparent and regrettable. There has already been quite a turnover of staff. Some, finding better opportunities outside teaching, have left the profession, others have sought promotion elsewhere, while others have preferred a less active commitment. The point here is that living and working conditions in Bunumbu are demanding. Staff already do considerably more work and for little extra reward (fellowships and two steps on the salary scale) than do their contemporaries with other posts in the education system. Life at Bunumbu provides little variety and the road ensures that excursions 'outside' are infrequent. It has been said with only a little exaggeration that there is nothing to do in Bunumbu except work. But even highly dedicated and committed staff have limits to their endurance. Matters like water supply, electricity and access may turn out to be camel back-breaking straws. It is a moot point that the staff can and will sustain their efforts at the level of intensity reached so far. Already the conditions at Bunumbu have proved too much for some staff and experts alike. In fact, one of the recommendations made to the authorities has been that experts should be given a 'realistic' picture of life at Bunumbu *before* they arrive. The improvement of conditions might complement such a proposal nicely.

One of the objectives of the project is to produce a new primary school curriculum with a rural bias. Irrespective of the larger consequences of that decision, which fall on the shoulders of the NAC, meeting that objective will have its problems. At the moment the curriculum is being produced under pressure – pressure from the many-faceted nature of the Bunumbu project. For understandable reasons, the Institute cannot contribute substantially to its development at the moment. The exigencies of the situation are such that the staff with and without help from the Unesco experts are producing materials when time and opportunity permit – in all, up until the middle of 1978, some 49 substantial items. While almost any sort of curriculum with rural components would represent an improvement on established practice, there is a question of the quality of the new curriculum. So far there has been little opportunity to see the curriculum in the round, as it were. The demands of the situation have been such that individual staff members have worked on individual topics with limited opportunity to consider how they could all fit together and complement each other. In other words, there has been little scope for a conceptual mapping of the area, the specification of dimensions to be covered, the way in which the rural bias might be best manifested and the articulation of one topic with another. In this respect the curriculum will be no different from many others existing throughout the world, but it would seem that Sierra Leone's aspiration goes beyond replicating the ordinary. It is to be hoped that the recent arrival of a curriculum development expert may see more systematic coordination of the work and an extended liaison with the Institute.

Sierra Leone: Creating a Context

Diffusion

We are led by this focus on the curriculum to consider the problem with which the NAC is charged and which is of greatest concern to the Ministry: 'after Bunumbu, what?' The long-term objectives see an application of the benefits of Bunumbu throughout the nation. Presumably this objective would be met if the reformed curriculum were disseminated nationally, but reading between the lines of the proposal, it is possible to see a larger aspiration. Furthermore, if there are advantages to be gained from the Bunumbu experience, it would be unfortunate if they were left untapped. There is scope at the moment for conjecture over what those advantages might be. For one, the College is being instrumental in promoting community development in its own area. Perhaps the knowledge and skill developed could be transferred to other colleges or other agencies concerned with community development. But if so, there is need for a reasonably precise recording of those skills and that knowledge. So far there has not been opportunity to accomplish it. Also, the College is producing teachers trained to undertake community development work, but what will follow when they graduate? Unlike others in many countries, Sierra Leonean teachers have the right to apply for positions where they wish. Some will find employment in the Bunumbu area and be able to put their new skills to good effect. What of the others? First, will they choose to go to the towns perhaps to seek more variety than had been available in Bunumbu or will they seek employment in other rural districts? If the first, their community development skills will be submerged, at least temporarily, and it would be useful for the College to know what influenced their choice. If the second, then, they will have a number of difficulties to overcome in employing their new abilities. Even if they have the benefit of seniority and experience (as a number do), they will still be faced with the up-hill task of convincing others in the school and community that the new ways that they know are good ways. This means not only gaining the confidence, respect and cooperation of the community in which they are likely to be regarded initially as strangers, but also establishing their credibility with their fellow teachers. Institutional inertia, whether in a country school, rural community, or an education system, is formidable to overcome. If, then, the 'new breed' of teachers is to be able to undertake the job for which they were trained, they will need strong support from the system behind them. Already steps have been taken in this direction in that a special two-day seminar has been held for principals from various parts of Sierra Leone to familiarize them with what is happening at Bunumbu. As well, shortly afterwards the Association of Secondary School Principals decided to hold the Annual General Meeting at Bunumbu for the same purpose. These represent a beginning, but given the complicated effort it has taken to *train* the students at Bunumbu, much more than familiarization exercises will be required.

Rewards

Another facet of this question is also to come under the attention of the

NAC and the Ministry: namely, the question of reward for services. Two populations are involved: the Bunumbu College staff and the student graduates. Does the situation warrant special recognition of the extra work entailed and the more advanced skills now needed? Are higher salaries in order, or special allowances, or newly designated (and more highly rewarded) positions or for teachers, perquisites like Government-provided housing? And can the country afford it?

Cost

This chapter cannot close without reference to the cost of the Bunumbu project: it has been considerable enough to make replication of the Bunumbu project out of the question. But the replication of some parts of it would be unnecessary. Assuming that a rural-based primary curriculum is developed, unless there is a need for regional variations, that exercise should suffice for some time. To this extent, repetition of the substantial UNDP and Unesco inputs would not be needed for such a purpose. From the financial point of view, though, it is important to know what other costs are essential and for what purposes. For example, does the development of community education services depend on erecting new buildings and providing new plant and equipment? Does the training of teachers similarly depend on the kind of new (and obviously useful) machines and materials that were supplied to Bunumbu? Again, does the delivery of 'community education' also depend on the resources provided at Bunumbu, cars, minibuses, cassette players and portable TV? It is presumably advisable to establish the necessary and sufficient conditions for the undertaking of such tasks prior to considering what is entailed in the process of wider implementation of them.

A dilemma

There is a final point that also ought to be made. Many countries have travelled the road that the Bunumbu project is travelling although they did so in a much more hesitant manner, at a different time and under different conditions. However, many have now come to the conclusion that the distinction between rural education and urban education has served its purpose. The development of rural communities has led to enlarged horizons and aspirations for country people. Consequently, they come to wish that the education their children receive should provide them with as many vocational and educational opportunities as town children enjoy. If history were to repeat itself in Sierra Leone, then there is some advantage in being forewarned. On the other hand, if that particular development is to be forestalled, other means of enhancing the appeal of the country may well be needed, a point that no doubt the idea of integrated rural development would wish to take into account.

In this brief chapter it has only been possible to touch on some of the many interesting and evocative facets of the Bunumbu project and to guess at only some of the consequences. The fact that the Bunumbu project is so complex and so many-sided means that it is particularly important for the

IIEP's study of the *process* of innovation. Obtaining a clear and systematic view of its evolution poses a special kind of challenge – and one that is typically faced by administrators in any developing system. If in the final chapter a measure of this clarity can be obtained, the Bunumbu project will have added another credit to its already impressive balance sheet.

The Sierra Leone innovation, incorporated as it was into the National Development Plan, could rely on the fullest support that the Ministry of Education could muster. It was officially sanctioned at the highest level and accordingly, could almost be regarded as 'doomed to succeed'. Not so the Israeli innovation. The NILI project is basically undertaken independently of the Ministry of Education. True, the Ministry vetted the initial proposal and subsequently provided what was, for Israel, the considerable amount of money needed to mount the project. But the Ministry has never committed itself to any implementation beyond the initial experimental sample of schools. The most the Ministry has ventured so far is a word to the effect that it might consider implementing *part* of the project – a prospect regarded more with dismay than delight by the researchers who see NILI as nothing less than a complete and indivisible 'package'.

The relationship between an Education Ministry and independent research organizations is always a delicate and difficult one. It is not made any easier when one of the organizations is a university and a university that has not customarily become involved in action research for education. Interestingly, in the present case, there is a further significant component to be considered. The two Municipalities whose schools are being used for the project have become enthusiastic supporters of it. Their enthusiasm has become contagious and other Municipalities throughout Israel are mounting pressure to become involved too – with or without Ministry support. There appears to be a kind of 'grassroots' political groundswell building up that may, in the short term, see initiative for implementation taken outside the Ministry and may even in the long term change aspects of the national education structure. The contrast between the Israel situation and the Sierra Leone one, is, in this respect, most marked.

Chapter 5

Israel: A Total Approach

Without question, in giving an account of the Israeli innovation, the hardest task is to find a descriptive label for the innovation that does not lead the reader down the garden path and into a hornet's nest of false assumptions about it. To be sure, the innovation has an innocent-enough looking name. It is called the NILI project after the four Hebrew words of its title. However, the innocence begins to disappear slowly when any translation equivalents are used and even accelerates when any elaboration is attempted. The problem arises essentially because the NILI project embodies a number of more or less well-known and more or less fashionable components. For example, the project includes a curriculum development component – but the project is considerably more than just a curriculum development project. It includes a materials design and production component but that aspect too is only part of the total undertaking. Again NILI is often referred to as an experiment in individualized instruction which, though partly true, is an unfortunate label for it on two counts. First, as before, that label only tells some of the story. Second, its use has resulted in misunderstanding and misinterpretation both locally and abroad. The misunderstanding and misinterpretation follow primarily from the (understandable but false) equation of the NILI approach with other overseas variations on the individualized instruction theme that have achieved reputations for several defects, eg isolation of the learner, negative reinforcement, lack of order and structure etc. While none of these latter are features of the NILI project, nevertheless something like individualized instruction[1] is indeed an important and central aspect. But once more, however, individualized instruction is but one aspect. The project also includes organization and management components. They extend not only to the classroom but to the school as another influential and influenced setting. Also a component is the interaction between the school and community as is too a strong, continuous and somewhat different kind of in-service teacher-training.

To such a rough catalogue of components has to be added two further pieces of information about what might be called the organizing principles on which the project is based. The first is that in attempting to arrive at a

---

1 One NILI member has tried for nearly seven years to have it called 'personalized' instruction.

new interpretation of the teaching-learning process, the NILI project has committed itself to as comprehensive an approach as possible. The basic argument is that pupil performance is the result of a combination of circumstances. These circumstances include not only the innate and acquired characteristics of the learner, but also the characteristics of the teaching context which in turn include the teacher, the programme (curriculum in its narrow sense), plant and equipment, frame factors like the organizational constraints that affect the operation of classroom and school, and, of course, other general environmental conditions under which teaching and learning take place. The second is that the teacher, in operating as a 'manager' of the learning situation, needs material (pedagogical) and sociopsychological supports *but also* scope to exercise autonomous judgement. Consequently, the teacher-training component should not only provide education in the appropriate new skills and competencies but also in adaptability – the capacity to adapt, modify and develop curricula (in the broadest sense) in accordance with the existing circumstances. This latter, it must be added, is only thought to be achievable once teachers have internalized the principles on which the new approach is based.

Such a brief and breathless résumé of the NILI project has not done it justice. It may not even have succeeded in accomplishing one of its own purposes – to convey something of the NILI flavour. However, it is to be hoped that it has succeeded in warning the reader against coming to a premature conclusion about the nature of the NILI project, what it is, what it is trying to do, what are its strengths and weaknesses, and what its fate might be. By the end of the chapter those issues may be clearer. But we must start at the beginning.

The start

The origins of most innovations tend to become forgotten, lost in the mists of time. When attempts are made to retrace their early beginnings, the resulting reconstructions often reflect a degree of precision, logic and sweet reasonableness that belie our everyday experience of reality. In the case of the Israeli innovation, however, it has been possible to capture some of that early detail to a degree that our other case studies cannot equal. The story that results is an intriguing one of doubt, uncertainty, trial and error, frustration, territorial jealousies, amateurism and professionalism, good will and indifference, emotional commitment and opposition, poverty and disadvantage, political interest and disinterest, and many other facets of social interaction, usually small but occasionally large, that are the stuff of everyday institutional life. In fact the story is a recognizably universal one that had, of course, its own particular characteristics too. Accordingly one of the main tasks of this chapter is to try to identify those features of the situation that might be regarded as common to other similar situations and those that are unique. The purpose is to disentangle them – to try to assess their relative potency. It needs to be done because, to take a position that special features of the situation are either all-important or of no account, is to foreclose on the kind of lesson that may be learned.

The story really has two beginnings. One of them by nature is nebulous and ill-defined. It is the beginning that served to establish an emotional and attitudinal climate that made the time right for what eventually was to become NILI; it will be dealt with shortly. The other was the precipitating event that sparked the first action. The latter, which has a touch of the romantic about it, arose as a crisis of large dimension to the principle actors but a matter of no great significance to almost everybody else because such a thing had come to be regarded as an inevitable fact of life. The principal actors, who need not be identified, were two five-year-olds. Their (personal) crisis was – beginning at school. They started off happily enough but, as is often the case, as the days went by their school experiences became less entrancing than their expectations, their natural curiosity and their interests had led them to imagine it would be. Their gradually growing unhappiness communicated itself to their parents. In this case, their parents rather surprisingly took it upon themselves to intervene, to approach the school to at least inquire into the possibility of improving the situation.

At this point we have to ignore the plight of the principal actors for some time because now the adults – as adults are rather inclined to do – take over and the story becomes theirs.

Concerned parents are common enough, though ones that approach the school are relatively uncommon. Furthermore, those who do are not often received with open arms. Parents usually spell trouble. The fact that this was not the case here invites speculation.

There were features in the situation that were unusual. In the first place, one of the concerned parents was a university professor and a professor of education at that. This, of course, could have cut two ways. He might have been seen by the teachers as a powerful and useful ally but he might equally have been seen as an opinionated academic attempting to employ a form of intellectual coercion. The second parent also carried prestige because of her position in a research institute concerned with educational development and technology. The paths of both parents had crossed initially when the University School of Education and the Israeli Educational Technology Centre, MATACH (a privately funded research organization) combined to organize an international conference on 'Educational Technology'. Again the status and expertise of the other parent could have prompted a positive or negative response on the part of the teachers.

It is thus tempting initially to 'explain' the origin of the innovation in two ways. First, there were significant key individuals. Second, there was a coincidence (the conference). The first leads to a kind of 'great man' theory of innovation; the second to a fatalistic one – neither of which is particularly useful for educational planning.

However, and this is where the other beginning comes into account, there was an attitudinal aspect of the situation that might be considered coincidental, depending on how widespread the attitude was. The three adults involved, the teacher and the two parents, had all for a long time been independently nursing a feeling of dissatisfaction with the state of education in Israel. Their professional perspectives may have been different but they shared in common the belief that the Israeli system was neither providing the results that it could or should, and that the way teaching was being done offered few gratifications to pupils, teachers and parents alike.

Now at this time there was no such thing as NILI, nor even the hint that NILI might emerge – just three professional educationists with a shared problem – a rather vague one at that. Presumably then there were a lot of things that could occur between that moment and what turned out to be a 14 million Israeli pound[1] research and development NILI project. The first of these was the inclusion of four other similarly concerned teachers in the dialogue. Early in the piece it became apparent that the parents (and the children) were not the only ones with problems. The teachers too had theirs. Given, then, reasons for *mutual* concern, the major problem became to arrive at an accommodation – an agreement on matters of priority. Fairly clearly, such agreement could not be reached overnight. So it was decided to hold regular meetings once a week, sometimes at the school, sometimes in the homes of the participants, to thrash the problem out. While this might give the impression that the exercise was moving away from the reality of the classroom, the reason for the continuing discussion was that it was becoming clear that the real problem was to identify the real problem, that is, the one that was the root cause of the general dissatisfaction. It was not only a matter of two small disappointed children, two concerned parents and five teachers – it was also (now that the principal had joined the group) a school problem. More complexity was to come.

The group thus had a mixture of both down-to-earth practitioners and researcher-academics. While they thus had the potential to be at cross purposes, they also had the prospect of complementing each other to mutual benefit. The latter turned out to be the case. As a consequence, it became possible to take advantage of additional external resources to add more inputs. As the second year of meetings got under way, this happened in two ways in particular. First, several staff members from the University joined the group bringing further expertise in the area of curriculum development and educational psychology in particular. Second, the group was able to turn to good account the presence in Israel of two notable scholars from overseas, Benjamin Bloom and John Goodlad. Both curriculum specialists, one met the group and discussed specific and general issues of curriculum development with it. The other's association was confined to senior staff members in the University. These contacts, however, served to provide a measure of usable information and also to reinforce the group itself – to encourage it in its task and to build up self-confidence further.

[1] Equivalent to anything between $US 1.4m and $US.7m depending on the time and the fluctuating exchange rate.

Towards a definition of the problem

So much for the social and organizational evolution of what might now be called an informal planning group. However, the particular significance of the group obviously extends beyond the events that led to its existence.

The meetings as we have noted served to indicate that the basic issue to confront was the definition of *the* problem that lay at the heart of everyone's disquiet. The search for it had surfaced a great deal of information not only about education but also about conditions existing in schools and, as the perspective widened, throughout Israel's education system. This information led more and more towards the earlier feeling that all was not well with the education system, either in terms of what everyone *hoped* would be its state or in terms of what might be possible.

Now such a conclusion has been reached before in other systems and at other times. And it is probably true of all systems and will continue to be true of them for many, many years. So the issue is not so much that the conclusion was reached but what were the terms on which the judgement was made and, later on, what was to be done about it.

A quotation from Schacham and Chen (1978) serves to indicate the basis for the judgement and, at the same time, to indicate how far the group had ranged in its consideration of 'their' problem.

> 'In the massive educational system where even in as small a country as Israel, 30 per cent of the population are engaged in learning, the variability of students is expressed by the variability of achievement. If, by the criteria set by the educational system the *yearly drop-out* in the high school students is 15-20 per cent, we then face the fact that only 20 per cent of the students can cope with and survive by the existing standards of successful achievement set by the educational system.'
>
> *(Schacham and Chen, 1978)*

Clearly the criterion invoked is an exacting one. It presupposes that many more students than 20 per cent ought, after their exposure to high school, to complete the course and receive appropriate recognition. Such a criterion appears to call into question the selective function of the education system – the role that it appears to have in allocating people to various occupational levels in society. It also implies that a measure of adjustment of the selection device itself might overcome the problem. If, for example, the system decided arbitrarily (as it could, and as some have done) to pass more students, then the problem would theoretically be solved. However, such a solution would not have addressed the essence of the situation as the group saw it. At that time, the Israeli education system could not be said to have been exercising its allocative role in tandem with the needs of society. Unlike many other countries, there was in Israel a demand at all levels for qualified and competent 'workers'. Such a shortage would not have been remedied by an arbitrary adjustment of pass rates. The need was for more competent school leavers, not more labels. Consequently, the question became rather: why not better results in the system? The initial concern over the plight of two small five-year-olds who were not realizing their potential had become enlarged (to put it mildly) to include a substantial proportion of the nation's school population who were presumably not realizing their potential either. The frame of reference had become not one classroom, but the nation's education system.

Causes and effects

Historical

But this state of affairs must be seen in social perspective. If the education system was performing at less than optimal level, then there were reasons. And predictably some of those reasons would be found not only within the education system, but in society at large and in prior events whose influences still are to be felt. Elaboration is necessary.

The autonomous and independent nation-state of Israel, like several others in this volume, is among the youngest in the world. The Israelis as a nation-people, however, are among the oldest, and their influence on world civilization rivals that of the Greeks and Romans. The existence of present-day Israel, however, is so bound up with the tortuous history of the Jewish people, that some brief and palpably oversimplified reference to it must be made. As a nation-people, the Jews have had nearly 2000 years of territorial dispossession – although the Jews have been admitted with greater and lesser degrees of freedom and acceptance to many countries all over the world. Throughout their history they have preserved a fierce sense of national identity that has survived in the face of vicissitudes beyond belief. What served to sustain the Jews under such circumstances defies ready explication but one undoubted factor was their long-cherished desire and hope to return to their Holy Land home. Towards the end of the 19th century, this dream was beginning to become true for increasing numbers of Jews who were able to migrate to Turkish-occupied Palestine, as it was then called. The Turks were the residue of the Byzantine Empire that had wrested the Holy Land from the European crusaders in the 11th century after the crusaders themselves had wrested it from the Saracens, who in their turn had taken it from the Romans. It was from that Roman-named province of Palestine that the people of Israel were exiled in the year AD70. The end of the First World War, however, had produced yet another occupation, this time by the British who by 1923 were acting under a mandate from the League of Nations. During the period between that world war and the next, immigration increased (mostly from Europe) and culminated in 1948 with the United Nations' recognition of the right of the Israelis to establish (re-establish) their nation-state. After 1900 years of national homelessness, to Jews all over the world the new nation-state of Israel acted as a magnet. They immigrated in a steady stream.

Demographical

The facts are imposing. In the years following the creation of the State, there was an enormous increase in population. In 1948 the Israelis numbered but 1,174,000. By 1978 they totalled 3,650,000 – a 210 per cent increase at an annual average rate of 4 per cent. Such a figure conceals more than it reveals. For example, almost half of that increase was *not* accounted for by the birth rate (which stood at 2.1 per cent). The rest was the result of immigration. And that immigration was from the four corners of the world. The immigrants came speaking different languages, bringing different and often conflicting traditions and representing vast differences in educational and social and economic backgrounds. If America can be called the 'melting pot' so too can Israel. Religious identity there undoubtedly was – national identity in a territorial sense was yet to be created and the task was far from easy.

Not surprisingly, as elsewhere in the world, education was looked to as one of the means for achieving that national identity. In fact, in Israel education is regarded as a good, almost unquestioningly. There appears to be a nationwide consensus on the desirability of having as much education of as high a quality as possible for as many people as possible. This viewpoint is extremely consistent with age-old Jewish beliefs in the value and importance of education – witness the Israelis' reference to themselves as the 'nation of the book'. This value remains steadfast even though in other parts of the world there has been something of a retreat from that position. While other countries talk of over-education, in Israel the concept is not even admissible.

The tangible evidence of the Israeli article of faith in education is found today in the provision made for it. Early childhood education is available for 3- to 5-year-olds on a voluntary basis and compulsorily for 6-year-olds. Elementary education (6-12) and secondary education (12-15) are both free and compulsory, while post-secondary (15-18) is partially free but not compulsory. As from 1978, however, the free and compulsory aspects are to be extended downwards to 4-year-olds and upwards to 18-year-olds.

Because this attitude towards education has prevailed from the beginning of the State of Israel, there have been many difficulties for the system to overcome. Clearly, the rapid growth in population was a major one – and one that is worse than the detail produced early might lead one to expect.

If the education system had only shown the same rate of growth as the country at large, the situation would have been difficult enough for a young nation trying to establish the framework and fabric of its social system. But in fact the figures there were dramatically different. While the population of the country was growing at an annual rate of 4 per cent, the student population increased at a rate of 8 per cent overall and even reached 14 per cent between 1949 and 1960. Predictably, there was a corresponding increase in the number of people employed in education, but at an even more accelerated rate. For example, there were 6000 teaching positions in 1949 and 26,000 in 1960 (a 14 per cent annual average increase).

Within the general overall increase in numbers, particular priority was given to children of kindergarten age. The reasoning, which can find one of its justifications in Western child psychology, is that the earlier children start education, the better. It is better because of the rapid rate at which young children learn and because the effectiveness of future education depends on the soundness and breadth of the foundations laid. To defer laying the foundations is to lose irrecoverable opportunities. But in Israel there was another powerful reason, too, that arose out of the cultural diversity of its new citizens. The cultural imperative was to establish community – in both senses of the word. What better way than to provide all with a universal, shared, communal education?

There were thus two main thrusts to the Israeli education policy, to extend education as much as possible and to equalize opportunities as much as possible. To these ends the whole education system from pre-school to university underwent unprecedented expansion – quantitatively and to some extent qualitatively too. The growth of the kindergarten service has been characterized by a degree of experimentation, inventiveness and creativity that has led to what most people regard as a considerable degree of improvement. In the elementary schools it is also true that learning conditions have generally improved. Initially progress there was relatively slow, but in recent years the rate of innovation has increased with new methods, materials and teaching styles making inroads into the dominant, traditional 'frontal teaching' and 'memorization learning'. Over the period too, despite the continuous increase in the school population, the average class size has gradually reduced, while there has been a much more marked change in the ratio of pupils to labour units in the school system. In 1960 it was 1:31, in 1970 1:23, in 1975 1:21 and in 1977 1:18.

A similar but less marked trend was characteristic of secondary education too. The rate of change and modification had increased and more children stayed longer at school as the drop-out rate declined.

Why, then, under circumstances that indicated considerable educational expansion and a noteworthy amount of 'improvement', should the small group of teachers and parents with whom we started the chapter be concerned?

Disadvantage in education

The principle reason was that the broad picture failed to disclose the detail. As is often the case with aggregated data, variations and deviations become statistically liquidated. To parody an old aphorism – one cannot see the trees for the forest. The human trees in the Israeli educational forest were indeed many and varied. The educational performances of the children reflected this difference. Equal educational *provision* there undoubtedly was. Capability to profit from that provision, there was not. And the reason is not hard to find or understand.

Most of the early immigrants to Israel came from developed countries, primarily in Europe or, if outside Europe, countries that were European in character. As erstwhile citizens of mainly developed countries, the migrants had become familiar with institutionalized education and its possibilities.

(There were also other 'development' values that had been absorbed too, but there is no need to pursue them here.) However, over recent years the predominant character of the immigrants had changed with the rate of those from Asia and North Africa showing a dramatic increase.

This growth rate was reflected in the education system as well. For example, in 1965, of every 1000 students in the 14-17 age group, 291 were of African-Asian origin. By 1977 the corresponding number was 679 – an increase of 138 per cent and an average annual rate of 8 per cent. The overall picture was not quite so striking, but even so it was striking enough. In 1967 the proportion of the total population who were of African-Asian origin was 46.5 per cent, while in 1977 it had increased to 49.4 per cent. At the same time, the proportion of children of African-Asian origin in high schools had risen from 35.6 per cent to 50.9 per cent, whereas in 12th grade (the terminal year of high school) the corresponding percentages in 1967 and 1977 were 18.9 per cent and 46.6 per cent respectively.

On the whole, the background of the African-Asians was different. Their exposure to education was different, their view of education was based on different values and perceptions and their capability to meet the kind of performance demands prevailing in the Israel education system was limited. What the aggregated figures concealed, then, was the relative underachievement of certain regionally identifiable groups.

Such differences in educational performance became more noticeable partly because the education system's success in providing for universal and compulsory education brought them into the school's orbit. It also became more and more noticeable because as more children with learning 'difficulties' penetrated the various class levels, teachers, parents and pupils became more and more aware of their problems.

There was a further contributing factor. The rate at which trained teachers were being produced had not been able to keep pace with the creation of new teaching positions. Consequently there was need to employ teachers who had received intensive but short-term training and even others who were quite untrained. This, combined with the increased demand for education and the gradual reduction of class sizes, led to a dilution of the overall quality of teaching and a corresponding decline in educational standards. To put the matter in the simplest of terms, for understandable reasons, the system was not operating at an optimal level – it was not operating as well as it could or should.

This was, in effect, the tentative conclusion reached eventually by the small group of teachers and parents with whose concern this chapter began.

In search of a solution

The world does not lack for people who declare that *they* have discerned exactly what is wrong with education. Nor is the world altogether short of people who profess to know exactly what would put education right. The group was not so opinionated nor so confident. While they believed and hoped that the performance of the education system could be improved, they had two basic doubts. They were uncertain about why the system had got into its present (unsatisfactory) condition and they were even more uncertain about what would happen as a consequence of changing it. In other words, they professed to have little prior knowledge of cause and effect. Because the scientists among them, in the absence of that knowledge, regarded themselves as disqualified from proposing solutions, the task of the group again underwent re-evaluation. What was needed, they believed, was a systematic and scientific attempt to establish connections between performance and its causes – some basic research. But, and the but is very important, they would need to do it in such a way that the knowledge gained could be used to bring about improvement in the system. Their basic problem still remained the same – to identify the basic problem – but this time there was a twist in its tail. The kind of inquiry to be employed should carry with it the promise of a solution that could be used – action research, if you like.

Such an approach has an incipient weakness and an incipient strength. The weakness lies in confining the search for explanation only to aspects of education where subsequent manipulation would be possible. (One is reminded of the story of the inebriated character who one night, having dropped a coin at one end of the street, insisted on searching for it at the other end because that was where the street-light was!) The strength lies in its pragmatic realism. If one discovers a cause of a problem and no use can be made of the knowledge, what is the point of knowing? In other words, the group at the outset asked itself the question with respect to its own prospective activities – so what? Some scholars *may* be dismayed (although they should not be), but most practitioners and administrators would be delighted.

Given the group's original concern to help two children gain more from education and their subsequent one to contribute to the general educational well-being of the State, their range of possible choices was quite considerable. However, the broad orientation or strategy they had accepted gave no indication of where best to start or what to take as givens and what to take as unknowns. When the time arrived to resolve these issues, the specific interest and awareness of the group members began to assert themselves. Collectively they had come to appreciate the problem of educational disparities existing in the education system, especially as they affected certain ethnic groups. They also retained their special concern for individual children, not just the original two five-year-olds, but all children as individuals. Furthermore, the group could muster a diversity of expertise. The teachers were knowledgeable of the real world of the classroom, and the school administrators were knowledgeable of the school as an organization. Some of the educationists were experienced in the study of curriculum development and others in the study of child development. Finally, some of the researchers could call on their familiarity with technological aspects of education. These interests and experiences, coupled with the contributions made by occasional 'outsiders' (some expert, some lay), eventually crystallized to provide three basic working principles.

Working principles
Foremost among these principles was agreement with the proposition that the results that the education system produced were influenced by many factors and in many ways. There was no simple, let alone single, explanation of what caused the results to be as they were. Although not taking a doctrinaire 'systems' approach, nonetheless, the basic attitude and orientation of systems thinking was accepted. The group assumed multiplicity of causes and multiplicity of effects. As we shall see later, the ultimate $64 questions became which causes and what effects should be selected for special consideration.

The second principle accepted a position that, although now regarded almost as a truism, had for years (until the late 1950s to be precise) been literally ignored in educational, psychological and pedagogical research: within the formal education system, the classroom is *the* locus of learning. The group, no doubt strongly influenced by the teachers, were persuaded that it was through the manipulation of factors (variables) *in the classroom* that learning performances would most likely be changed (improved).

The third principle adopted had both a psychological and a philosophical justification. The group, having started with a concern for individuals, agreed that their (learning) unit of study was to be the individual. Solution to the problem of improving conditions for learning, then, should be first sought through individualized instruction methods. (There will be occasion to explain the Israeli interpretation of that evocative [and often misinterpreted] concept later.) The justification arising out of educational psychology was that individuals, because they *are* individuals, learn in different ways at different rates and for different purposes. The justification arising out of philosophy was that they were entitled to do so – provided as well that there was a basic 'common core' for all. Individualization of educational ends and means above and beyond that core would result, their argument went, in enhanced fulfilment for individuals and greater diversity of alternative capabilities in society. Both conditions, it was thought, were functional in that they made individuals and society both more adaptable.

First steps

It should not be imagined that such a position was arrived at hastily or without a considerable amount of debate, argument and accommodation. Nor should it be imagined that it was held without qualification. In fact, though there was confidence that such an approach seemed promising, no illusions were held that it could not be wrong. Evidence of this caution is contained in the first practical steps taken down the research lane. A small-scale feasibility study was undertaken jointly by the School of Education of Tel Aviv

University and the Israeli Educational Technology Centre. It set out to answer the following questions:

1. What are the aims of individualized learning projects elsewhere?
2. What are the major difficulties with respect to the handling of individual differences at Israeli schools?
3. What are the possible variables in the teaching strategies which lend themselves to experimentation?

This study neither sought nor was given official blessing or support from other than the two organizations involved which, be it noted, are largely autonomous and certainly on the outer edge of the state education system. It was thus an independent venture which, however, required (and readily got) the participation of two schools. As things turned out, however, the schools' involvement did not win the unqualified approval of some of the Ministry agencies operating in the field. Some differences of opinion resulted. Behind the small 'contretemps' implied, there is a structural explanation that has bearing on the remainder of the account.

Down an uneven path

The Israeli education system is both centralized and decentralized. There is a national Ministry that exercises certain functions, mainly forming general educational policy, allocating funds, supervising operations and providing curriculum guidelines. The responsibility for the actual educational operation falls on the 17 municipalities who, within their areas, build and maintain schools, provide supplies, hire and fire teachers, and generally administer their systems. The schools themselves have a certain degree of autonomy. Provided they work within the curriculum guidelines, they can use whatever syllabus (and teaching materials) they wish and of course whatever teaching strategies they prefer. Depending on the district, the parents may or may not exert any influence on the school's activity. Linkages between the Ministry and the municipalities are of two kinds: (i) the usual administrative downward demand-permission and upward request-report routines; (ii) the supervision-guidance routine exercised by the Ministry professionals in the field. Predictably, it is at the interface of the two systems that any delicacy in relationships tends to appear. In this instance it was not always the case that Ministry supervisors (school inspectors) were in full sympathy with what seemed to be an intrusion of something alien into their schools. Their reactions were sometimes designed to preserve the old order rather than promote the new. While this had no immediate effect on the feasibility study, there is reason to believe that it may have had an effect subsequently when, with the feasibility study completed, an overture was made to the Ministry for support.

Such expressions of territorial defence are to be expected. They are common to all social systems. As well, all social systems have their own power groups of greater and lesser potency and, of course, people who, because they know the game, can exert influence in ways other than those to which the formal system subscribes. There is, then, to use an old-fashioned term, an informal system behind the formal, and it serves a number of useful functions. Not the least of these is to enable individuals to use their discretion – a provision without which no organization can function efficiently (as work-to-rule strikes demonstrate only too clearly). However, the 'informal' system also has the potentiality for subverting the system as well. Its power, then, can be used for good or evil – the definition of either depending on one's attitude towards the system. The NILI project was no exception and as we shall see later when the project became duly finalized, the fact that four major and different organizations became closely involved in the project complicated things a little. Not only was there the issue of the internal territorial dynamics of each separate organization, but also the dynamics of the interrelationships between them. As the story continues, though, the first and least complicated example comes to hand.

For two years the University and the Institute of Technology and one municipality collaborated in undertaking a modest feasibility study. More accurately handfuls of people from the Institute, from the Education Department of the University of Tel Aviv and from two schools in the municipality worked together from time to time. Most of these people had already spent a year together worrying over and planning this undertaking. There had been ample opportunity for them to adjust to each other, develop a professional working relationship, make a congenial social climate and gain respect and affection for each other. As a small social system itself, it had managed to become creatively viable and viably creative – not, of course, without effort or for that matter moments of crisis. However, though having its own internal integrity and cohesion, the 'cooperative' did not necessarily have external credibility. In the schools themselves other teachers not involved in the project were occasionally suspicious, sometimes hostile and sometimes even obstructive – a circumstance not to be wondered at. In the University community itself there were divisions of opinion mainly occasioned by those whose view of scholastic propriety saw educational field-work as somewhat unacademic. In the Institute of Technology, too, there was, predictably, a diversity of attitudes largely the result of sectional interests.

These differences in viewpoint had no great effect on the operation of the feasibility study. True, they created minor inconveniences, some anxieties and occasional worries, but they did not, at this stage, consume either much time or energy. In fact who knows if the 'opposition' did not serve to harden the team's resolve, enlarge its own perspective and provoke it into making creative adjustments?

The first stage completed
Be that as it may, the feasibility study did finish with results that led the group to believe (i) that the lead they had been following was worth following; (ii) that it *ought* to be followed in Israel for Israelis; (iii) that to follow it would require a major long-term effort; (iv) that they could provide a plan

and design for that effort; and (v) given financial support, they could carry it out. The first task obviously was to create the design and write a proposal. Their decision to do it began what came to be called the NILI project, and provided the justification for the inclusion of Israel in the IIEP project on innovations. Construction of the proposal was undertaken with care. Subgroups were formed and allocated separate tasks and eventually the entire group isolated itself for three days in a hotel to negotiate and hammer out the last details.

The main undertaking

The plan

It is logical and deceptively simple to start any elaboration of the project with the general aim of the project, viz:

> To develop a learning-instruction strategy which will optimize learning outcomes.

If ever words conceal, they have seldom done it more effectively than that brief statement does. What lay behind them was the intention to mount a teaching-learning research-development operation that would be extremely complex and complicated. Going further than did the well-known IPI (Individualized Programme Instruction), and the IGE (Individualized Graded Education) and even the CAI (Computer Assisted Instruction) programmes, the project planned to deal as far as it could with the *total* school learning environment during the first three years of schooling.

Again a caveat ought to be made. It would be easy to jump to the conclusion that the proposal had already pre-specified the nature of its curriculum, the nature of its curricular materials, its kind of teaching style and its kind of organization-management etc. In other words, one might imagine that the writers *knew* what the answers already were and, in the proposal, were dangling them carrot-like in front of the potential funding agency. After all, there are few research proposals that get funded if they do not do so. Again, the fact of the matter was that what the proposal was offering was *not* a set of solutions to an (undefined) problem, but a means for attempting to define the problem accurately and then, if possible, arrive at practical and feasible solutions.

Reportedly Gertrude Stein, when asked on her death-bed 'Gertrude, what is the answer?', replied 'What was the question?'. In one sense the Israeli project was asking 'What is the question?', but it was planning to do so in a way that would lead to the trying out of possible answers at the same time. In other words, it proposed a kind of spiral research and development strategy. That strategy might be characterized as a continuous sequence of the same two questions, viz: if this is the problem, then what should be the answer (or that or that), but if this is the answer then that should be the next problem (or that or that) and if that is the next problem then that (or that or that) should be the next answer (or that or that) and if that ... and so on ad (almost) infinitum. But even this tortuous explanation of the project strategy misses a main point. That is, that the questions are to be asked with respect to a number of different educational components (curriculum, materials, organization, teaching-learning, etc) and, as far as possible, at the same time.

It is small wonder, then, that the proposal document gave some attention to trying to explain its comprehensive systems-like approach. It is equally not to be wondered at that, given an education system that was basically formal and traditional and in which educational cause-effect thinking was characteristically linear, the NILI point of view was not understood by quite a number of (sometimes important and influential) people, neither at first nor subsequently.

Be that as it may, the proposal, with procedures, personnel, organization and logistics specified, was submitted to the Ministry of Education with a request for financial support. Such a procedure was quite conventional. What was not conventional was the amount of money asked for (1.2 million Israeli pounds for each of three years). This represented by far the largest amount of money ever sought for educational research. Perhaps it is not surprising that approval was not immediately forthcoming. As time dragged on, the planning group found itself in a state of suspended animation – not knowing what the future held in store.

Verdict delayed

There seem to have been two reasons for the delay. In the first place the Ministry had not been 'pre-socialized' in an altogether positive way. The indirect and haphazard contact its field officers had had with the early feasibility study had not turned them into enthusiastic advocates. In the second place, the amount of money requested was frightening – to educationists. Medicine may spend enormous sums on research, the physical sciences may buy expensive research equipment, and industries may devote as much as ten per cent of their budgets to research and development, but education systems, everywhere, look very much askance (or askew) at investing more than a very modest amount indeed on research. The justification used for such caution often is that research has 'failed' to yield obvious advantages, therefore there is little point in investing in it. This 'don't-go-near-the-water-until-you-can-swim' philosophy of course guarantees that a determined and effective research attack on educational problems can rarely be made.

For a time, then, the proposal lay dormant in the Ministry. Official protocol had been followed by the proposers. The proper channels had been used, but somehow the Ministry did not respond with the degree of alacrity it customarily showed.

With no other prescribed forms of procedure open to the group, an impasse had apparently been reached.

Now, had the Ministry been a rigid bureaucracy and had Israeli society been excessively preoccupied with form and formality, perhaps this is where the story would have ended. However, by taking advantage of informal mechanisms within the system, means were found to spark the Director General's curiosity. Interestingly, it was the teachers in the schools who turned the final trick. The Director General, having read the proposal (and listened to the rhetoric), visited the two schools where the initial exploratory work had been undertaken. The evidence he saw and the testimony he heard persuaded him that the venture was worth undertaking. Within days, formal approval was given to go ahead with the project.

Action

Then began a flurry of activity because, in three years, the research-development phase was supposed to be completed so that two years of evaluation could then follow. First, staff had to be hired. The terms of the proposal had ensured the project's integrity and autonomy. There was thus no need to beg, borrow or steal the time, services and resources of people whose primary commitment (and obligation) lay elsewhere. The need was to obtain competent and professional staff who could undertake the necessary research and development job. Thus most staff were to be full-time, although others were to be released, part-time, from their university or MATACH posts. First hired were four section leader curriculum specialists in music, mathematics, science and language-arts. Their task was to begin to conceptualize an approach to curriculum development in these areas that would be consistent with the general 'individualization' aim of the project. They, with small teams of three or four, were to develop broadly conceived curriculum packages for trial, modification and evaluation. The four areas specified were selected because of their structural differences – mathematics and science falling towards the logically ordered end of the continuum, and language-arts and music falling towards the other end. Two further team leaders were to come later – a school organization team leader and an evaluation team leader. When everybody was in place, the full complement would consist of (i) 30 R & D researchers, including six section leaders, plus (ii) six part-time senior research-administrators, three each from Tel Aviv University School of Education and from MATACH, and (iii) 40 experimental teachers and four school principals to complete the contingent. Just as the budget, untypically of education, was not a shoe-string one, so was the operation, equally untypically, not a 'hole-in-the-corner' one.

If the preconditions of the project thus were closer to the ideal than those to be found in most educational projects, did everything go without a hitch? Of course not – and although some of the causes of the difficulties are easy enough to explain, others are not. Accordingly there is some point in setting out the operational scene of the project in a little more detail.

Organizational structure

It need hardly be mentioned that in mounting a project with 100 workers and involving four major institutions, some organizational structure was called for. The structure became formalized with the four institutions represented on a steering committee (together with senior project staff). The steering committee was responsible (ostensibly) for policy decisions. Beneath them came the project directory with three representatives each from the School of Education at Tel Aviv University (SE/TAU) and the Center for Educational Technology (MATACH) who were responsible for research and development planning. Next in line fell a senior staff committee consisting of supervisors (from the Ministry), the project director, school principals, the Mayor of the Yavne municipality and the Dean of TAU School of Education. They had control of and responsibility for field experiments. Then came the 30 researchers who were to do the field-work and finally the field team of teachers, principals and (Ministry) superintendents.

The structure (see Figure 4) implied a division of labour, some specification of roles and a chain of command. On face value all the necessary institutional and personnel linkages were there.

Predictably, to enable the structure to work, provision had to be made for regular meetings. The steering committee held scheduled monthly meetings. The directory met frequently and semi-regularly and as the occasion demanded. The section teams were in a relatively constant state of conferral. When not, their members were regular visitors to the schools. Most contact with the teachers occurred in their classrooms.

Both the structures and the functions as they have been described imply a kind of hierarchy, with the high officials at the top and the teacher 'workers' at the bottom. In between came the researcher 'workers' who carried out the wishes, 'orders', of their directors. Given the number of people involved in the project and the necessity for some division of labour, such a tendency towards bureaucracy (in its non-pejorative sense) is understandable. But clearly the nature of the research and development task was such that bureaucratic procedures would be harmful rather than helpful. When it is remembered that the first necessity was really to discern causes and effects in the classroom and arrive at constructive procedures for improving learning, and when it is also remembered that the approach was not based on very many *a priori* assumptions about what would work best, then the need for inter-communication between *all* levels is obvious.

Such inter-communication happened in two ways. Although the total group was big, it was not so big nor was the interaction between members so infrequent that many members stayed strangers to each other. There was therefore much opportunity to exercise the 'informal' system. Furthermore, Israeli society is not overly status-conscious and there are not many conventions that stand in the way of people communicating as equals. The distance between the 'top' and the 'bottom' then was not great.[1] As well, however, local arrangements were made for interaction between the various interested parties.

---

1 This is not to imply that within Israeli society there are not groups of people who, socialized elsewhere, still do not know how to voice and promote their own interests under such circumstances.

Figure 4: *The structure of the NILI project*

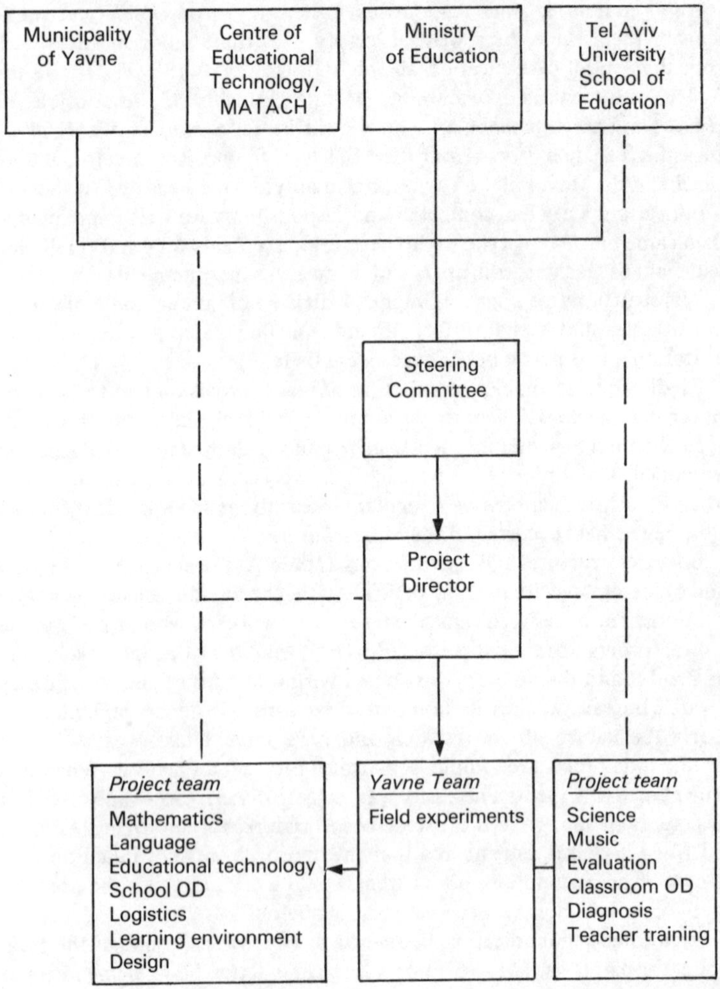

```
┌──────────────┐  ┌──────────────┐  ┌──────────────┐  ┌──────────────┐
│ Municipality │  │  Centre of   │  │   Ministry   │  │   Tel Aviv   │
│   of Yavne   │  │ Educational  │  │ of Education │  │  University  │
│              │  │  Technology, │  │              │  │   School of  │
│              │  │    MATACH    │  │              │  │  Education   │
└──────────────┘  └──────────────┘  └──────────────┘  └──────────────┘
```

┌──────────────┐
│   Steering   │
│ Committee   │
└──────────────┘

┌──────────────┐
│   Project   │
│   Director   │
└──────────────┘

Project team	*Yavne Team*	*Project team*
Mathematics	Field experiments	Science
Language		Music
Educational technology		Evaluation
School OD		Classroom OD
Logistics		Diagnosis
Learning environment		Teacher training
Design		

Schacham and Chen (1978) in reporting on the first years of the project outline the major activities accomplished in 1975. With a fine sense of understatement they list them as:

1. Setting up the project team.
2. Defining objectives and planning.
3. Beginning of organizational development in four schools.
4. Beginning of curriculum development (reading, maths, science, music).

5. Beginning of development of diagnosing instruments.
6. Establishing data base.
7. Development of research design and instruments.

First problems

Although there will be occasion later on to describe the substantive approach adopted in the NILI project, at the moment it is more appropriate to surface some of the problems experienced in the early days. They can almost all be summed up under the general heading of 'creating an organization'. Those difficulties were by no means unique. First, it was not possible to obtain a perfect match between competencies required and the capabilities of applicants for posts. Second, in some cases it proved difficult to make best use of whatever capabilities some appointees had – and impossible in one or two others. (The latter left.) Third, not only was there the difficult matter of adjusting the internal dynamics of the small sections but there was also the even more difficult one of the sections' learning to accommodate to each other. This might have been easier but for another difficulty. Language, perhaps not surprisingly but unexpectedly, constituted a fifth problem. Although most of the team were educationists they did not always comprehend each other. After a while, it became apparent that although people used the same words, they did not necessarily have the same things in mind – individualized instruction was a classic case in point. Eventually, partly in desperation, a lexicon was created in which critical and controversial terms were given a 'working' definition that then could always be invoked in time of difficulty. Sixth, the project was virtually an autonomous operation but was associated administratively with two established institutions – TAU and MATACH. As such it was new, strange and (possibly) threatening to established interests. The embedding institutional environment, then, was not always hospitable. Finally, in these early days, the Ministry input at the highest level was relatively slight. No doubt the addition of one or more tasks to the lives of already busy officials provides part of the explanation but the immediate effect was that the project did not have as much benefit from their insights and knowledge as had been hoped. There was another consequence that will come up again later on.

Further developments

Schacham and Chen have an equally laconic listing of the activities that were undertaken in 1976 and 1977:

Second year (1976)
1. Continue organizational development.
2. Design and change of physical environment.
3. Try curricula materials.
4. Test research instruments (formative evaluation).
5. Redefine objectives.

6. Planning and preparing for implementation (36 affiliated schools).

Third year (1977)

1. First year of experimenting with the work system.
2. Intensive evaluation (summative evaluation).
3. Continue organizational development.
4. Complete development of curricular materials, teacher-training schemes, physical design, testing and diagnosing instruments.
5. Continue extensive development with affiliated schools.

Further detail is needed. Perhaps the best place to start is with a brief recapitulation of what the project was trying to do.

Essential elements

The project started by noting the 'gap' existing between the educational potentiality of many (especially disadvantaged) children and their educational performance. They believed this gap was due to an inappropriate use of the 'educating' resources that were available. They also believed the gap could be reduced by using those resources in a better way – 'optimizing learning conditions' they called it.

The research team had a systematic view of learning resources that might be 'optimized'. Before that view can be presented, however, an important point has to be made. The group took a further pragmatic decision similar in style to the one that had led them to concentrate on research and development procedures that had the potential of being useful. They were only too aware of the environment-heredity debate in both its ancient and modern forms and they were also aware of the conclusions that psychologists have persuaded themselves to accept about how much educational variability can be explained in environmental terms. Now whether or not 70 per cent or 60 per cent or 30 per cent of educational potential is genetically predetermined is beside the point here. What is important, though, are the facts that (i) *some* educational potential *depends* on environmental circumstances; and (ii) *environmental conditions can be manipulated* while (presumably) genetic ones cannot. Accepting these first premises the group asked itself: what then could be regarded as constituting manipulable learning environment?

The conclusion reached (after much discussion) was that eight elements might tentatively be regarded as those most important – and, potentially manageable. They were: (i) the quantity of time spent on schooling; (ii) the cognitive level implicit in the learning tasks; (iii) the social climate in which teaching and learning occurred; (iv) the utility of learning aids and materials; (v) the supportiveness of the organizational framework in which learning-teaching took place; (vi) the physical environment; (vii) the efficiency of the way in which information flowed; and (viii) the appropriateness of the learning-instruction strategies employed.

Obviously a number of assumptions were implicit in the choice of such elements, for example that:

(i) the flow of information from various sources (teachers, learning materials, aids, etc) conveyed by various modes (verbal, visual, tactile, etc) in various forms (segmented, sequenced, etc) yield differential learning effects;
(ii) learning is a function of time spent;
(iii) learning is a function of the developmental level (cognitive, social, emotional, etc) of the learner;
(iv) social climate (interpersonal relationships, cooperation, conflict, etc) as an intervening variable affects learning;
(v) the physical environment (buildings, equipment, decor, etc) as an intervening variable between learner and information sources also affects learning, and so on.

These and other implicit assumptions come together in the concept of learning-instruction strategies. A learning-instruction strategy is basically the mechanism whereby what has to be learned is delivered. In the NILI case, it was also supposed to take into account: (i) the individual learner's receptor condition and his performance capability and potential; (ii) the alternative means available for delivering the message; and (iii) the general organizational context with its various components (pupils, teachers, other personnel and organizational 'frame factors').

This account does not exhaust either all the elements in the NILI formula nor does it perhaps convey the degree of tentativeness with which the original *position* was held. What has been described is a conceptual framework which at that stage existed in outline only. The concepts were roomy – and not necessarily discrete. They nevertheless constituted the point of departure for what was to become essentially a piece of action research. It was anticipated that later, after specification and trial (and error), these abstract terms would find a concrete form. They would, in effect, come to have an operational meaning, a meaning that would evolve through a series of successive approximations. This was the dream, and there is reason for the reader to wonder whether or not the dream became a reality and, if so, what that reality was really like.

First facts of life

The reality that resulted can be described to some extent and again in an oversimplified fashion by focusing on an imaginary classroom. Before the beginning of the project, it would be an ordinary classroom with about 40 children, one teacher and a limited amount of equipment. The pre-project classroom's work would be dovetailed in with the work of the rest of the school and the teaching would be basically authoritarian-authoritative and 'frontal' as the Israelis call it. By the end of three years that classroom would be noticeably different. In the first place, it would not be the same classroom any more. Some of its walls would have been removed to include (wasted) corridor space and to make it a learning area, or rather, a series of learning spaces. There would now be a fluctuating organizational pattern with sometimes no teacher apparent and sometimes a cluster. Also, from time to time, other adults would be seen in the setting. Some would be workers providing teaching assistance, while a sizable number would be researchers performing various tasks (including curriculum development and trial, observation and evaluation). There would be little frontal teaching – although there would be many occasions in which the children were in groups (some of them 'mother groups' expressly for socialization purposes). Most often, however, the children would be working independently (but not in isolation) and 'teachers' would be moving from one to the other, watching, helping and advising. If, as an observer, you chose to examine what the children were doing, you would find a considerable amount of variation. The standard pattern to be found in many individualized learning programmes would not be there. All the children would *not* be working merely at different places on the same material and they would not necessarily be working towards the same end. You might therefore notice that there was a considerable diversity of learning materials to be seen. If so, beware of jumping to the false conclusion that there was one of everything for every child – not so. One of the consequences of including the organization of information flow as one ingredient of individualized instruction research was that queuing strategies could be employed to maximize access to the limited resources.

Ways, means and rationale

How then had this reformed mini educational system been brought into being? A systematic strategy had been employed that was based on three principles: (i) diagnosis; (ii) follow-up; and (iii) matching. Explanation is warranted.

In the beginning, consistently with the assumption that some characteristics of the learner were more likely to be responsive to educational interventions than others, the NILI strategy chose to differentiate between two clusters of learner properties. On the one hand were to be found the 'learning styles' and 'cognitive styles' and 'personality characteristics' of individual pupils that (they assumed) would stay relatively constant – at least over a one-year period. Consequently *diagnosis* of all three could be undertaken annually once suitable means were selected or developed. This latter proved more of a problem than anticipated, primarily because the research on 'learning styles' is rather underdeveloped and because few approaches to research on cognitive style have gone beyond relatively simplistic bi-polar strategies of conceptualization. On the other hand were to be found a cluster of features that could show a measure of change over the year. It was assumed that the learners would display variations in their development of (i) mastery over (subject-matter) concepts; (ii) motor skills; (iii) attitudes; and (iv) the quantum of information acquired. Diagnosis in these cases should be continuous and regular.

So much for learner characteristics. But it will be remembered that the general learning-instruction strategy was predicated on an interaction between the learner and the educational environment. That environment also needed to be subjected to a measure of diagnosis so that the extent to which its condition corresponded to learner 'needs' could be assessed. The components thought relevant for consideration were: (i) the 'quantum' of information available in the classroom; (ii) its implicit cognitive level (relevant to the children's capacity); (iii) the amount of learning time available; (iv) the general social climate; (v) the 'level' of organizational development (of the system); and (vi) the physical condition of the environment.

The basic strategy to be used entailed a continuous *matching* of the educational condition of the environment to the educatable condition of the learner. Diagnosis of both was to be the mechanism used for gauging the present state of match or mis-match. *Follow-up* was to be the pedagogical mechanism through which learner and environment were brought to a state of equilibrium prior to extension into the next learning phase.

Again it must be remembered that in the early days everything in the system was tentative. While nothing started from scratch, each test, each testing, each diagnosis, each pedagogical practice, each piece of equipment, each curriculum element etc was negotiable. The negotiation was carried out between the teachers, the members of the MATACH field team and the University researchers. And it was carried out within a classroom and school organization structure that was itself also being subjected to continuing scrutiny, negotiation and change.

In attempting to understand the organizational constraints (and possibilities) existing in the situation, the team members undertook a certain amount of task-analysis. This in turn led to both a differential allocation of tasks (according to teacher abilities) and to a fairly continuous redefinition of old tasks and of the creation of new ones. This also in turn led to a restructuring of the classroom situation and eventually some restructuring of the school organization too.

An ordered system

Now while uncertainty characterized the initial phases of the project, the hope and intention was to reduce that degree of uncertainty considerably as time went on. This has been substantially achieved so that the way the classrooms and schools operate now has an aura of order and system about it that was certainly not to be seen in the early days.

What has resulted is basically a structured system of personalized instruction within an extremely (though unobtrusively) ordered organizational framework – although the casual observer, seeing some children working independently and others doing various things in various groups in various locations, might easily overlook the organizational frame. In most classes the system works through a simple management strategy. Each day the teacher puts the order of (differentiated) activities up on the blackboard (the timetable if you will). Children follow the timetable independently. From time to time the teacher lists on the blackboard the names of children who are to work with her at the time. Children wishing her attention also write up theirs. They receive it as soon as the opportunity offers. Everybody in the class has the obligation to work at his or her allocated tasks – most seem to do so, most of the time.

To help them, however, there is a considerable amount of curriculum material and a variety of teaching aids – some visual, some manual, some electronic, some human. The curricula materials are colour-coded according to level and type of medium for which they are designed. And thereby hangs a tale.

The NILI approach is a personalized one. That is, it attempts to tailor its learning environment to the needs of individual children within certain broad categories – by taking into account different rates of learning and also preferred styles. At the moment it settles for three rates of learning – fast, average and slower – and for three preferred styles – auditory, visual/graphic, verbal/written. Over the course of the project, curriculum materials have been produced in all of the styles (perhaps 'communications mode' would be an apt description) for each of the rates, for each of the four curriculum areas. Children are regularly allocated to a particular set of materials and aids in a particular mode and at a particular level according to the teacher's diagnosis. It should be noted in passing that each set of NILI 'modules', though differentiated in this way, focuses on the same subject-matter. The initial diet is the same for all. What differs is (i) the form in which the nourishment comes, hors d'oeuvres, soup or fish; (ii) the culinary intricacy displayed, hamburger, steak and onions, châteaubriand; *and* (iii) the size of helping. The purpose in keeping the subject-matter in common is to ensure that when group discussion follows, all have a basis for joining in.

Clearly for teachers to undertake and manage such a set of procedures requires coordination and planning – the conventional 'ad hoc' approach that is stock-in-trade for all teachers (at least sometimes) just would not do. Planning therefore became an important ingredient. Chen (1977) describes it.

'*Dynamic Planning (weekly and daily)*

This is a major element in the individualized learning strategy where teacher and students participate in a process of planning and sharing responsibility for the daily learning-instruction processes. On the part of the teacher this includes: planning structure of learning groups, contracting individuals, planning programs, allocating time for special projects, maintaining learning centers. The main role of the teacher lies within the matching process – that is the coupling of the learning diagnosis to the learning process. This role is analyzed now by linear program techniques and principles and solutions involved are studied. Children participate in the daily and weekly planning by sharing social and organizational responsibilities, taking part in the diagnosis process, choosing learning opportunities and initiating new activities.'

Implicit in such an approach is the need for a strong supporting infrastructure. In the early days this was provided by the MATACH fieldworkers and university researchers. Now as the school teams have built up their competencies and confidence, they have tended to become self-sustaining – a condition greatly dependent on: the capability of the teacher given responsibility for general supervision, and on the goodwill of the Principal and on the sympathy and understanding of the Ministry inspector. For newly interested schools (and there are now 70 affiliated or tentatively committed schools) a long and careful in-service teacher-training course is required, if the inevitable early trauma associated with the new teaching style is to be survived. The MATACH field staff have already gone considerable distance in developing such a programme and have interesting plans for converting the training programme to a personalized instructions strategy too.

There we must leave the classroom to put the project into broader perspective. According to the earlier plans, in 1975 there were to be five experimental schools that were expected to undergo a research development and change process over a period of three years. Between 1977 and 1979, 11 more municipality schools and 36 affiliated schools were to be added. Between 1979 and the prophetic 1984, 100 more affiliated schools and 200 district schools were, *subject* to the results of evaluation, expected to be incorporated. Whether or not the system would thereupon be diffused to all 1800 Israeli schools was also expected to be subject to the results of evaluation and one or two other rather critical conditions, like finance and politics.

The way ahead

However, as we start to consider the future, it is worth noting that NILI is almost at its moment of truth – within the next few months its future fate may virtually be decided. What is intriguing about the situation though is that NILI's fate may or may not hang – as the earlier plans assumed it would – on the decision of the Ministry. Already there are clear indications that NILI has generated its own groundswell. The Yavne Municipality has decided unilaterally to extend the NILI programme to its five other primary schools. As well, other municipalities throughout Israel, having heard of the project, have been seeking the opportunity to be involved. This has led to some 70 schools in various parts of the country joining the project as 'Associated Schools', ie schools intending to adopt the programme when circumstances permit. The permitting circumstances comprise (i) that materials are available in sufficient quantity, and (ii) that the lengthy teacher-training component can be provided.

Now whether such a groundswell has enough momentum by itself to carry the NILI approach with it is one of the key questions at the moment. If not, how much external help will be needed and if so, from whom? Either way, what will be the Ministry's role? Will it welcome such initiative from schools in a preserve that has customarily been its own? Will it feel the inclination to provide whatever support is necessary to sustain the momentum?

Will it alternatively feel that Israel's best interests would be served if the Ministry from its advantageous position took over full responsibility for the project or will it consider that it would be better if NILI were not continued at all? These questions provide the backdrop for the remaining discussions. But before some of their answers can be conjectured about, it is necessary to give a little attention to some of the problems that have surfaced up until now. They are not without relevance to the larger issue of continuation.

Problems past and future

Perhaps the largest and most predictable one is the problem of coordination. With so many people involved in so diversified an undertaking the project itself posed its own problems in systems design and operation. There were inevitably occasions when the right people were not at the right spot and others when the wrong ones were.[1]

Furthermore, despite the amount of systematic planning that went into the operation (even including PERT analysis), not surprisingly all possible eventualities were not anticipated in advance. Things cropped up unexpectedly to add an amount of noise to the system.

Not unrelated to this first problem was another that resulted from the unusual institutional framework within which the project was organized. The parent-child relationship has always had its difficulties. But when there are four parents (university, MATACH, municipality and the Ministry) and it is not quite clear to whom the child really belongs (or should belong) and whether, in fact, it is quite legitimate, the difficulties seem to increase. Much time was spent by a number of people in undertaking what can only be called political trouble-shooting. Such trouble-shooting was not confined solely to external relationships with the parents but a certain amount was required, understandably, within the project team itself and some even at the interface between researchers and teachers and between the research project and the test schools.

Again, and predictably, the existence of some project classes in a school had disruptive effects on the school. It was hard for the teachers in the rest of the school to proceed with business as usual while in the two or three project classes strange and disturbing things that could not but be noticed were going on. New people were constantly visiting the school, some to look, others to do what they called 'work'. New equipment materialized. The one-time respectable colleagues of the regular teachers began to do new and unorthodox things in their classrooms. Their children stopped sitting in rows and being quiet. Their classes didn't pay any attention to the school bells and were excused from fitting in with some school routines. What is more, the parents (and other strange helpers) started to come to the school. Finally, and most menacingly, the citadel of the classroom itself was breached – some privacy-protecting walls were demolished.

---

[1] One project official spoke ruefully of the time when *seven* different research specialists arrived simultaneously in the same classroom.

Within the experimental schools there were other predictable problems too. For a variety of reasons there was quite a turnover of teachers in the schools (slightly above average). This, of course, raised training and socialization problems for the research team who had then to devise 'instant education' methods for the new replacements. From a research point of view, it would have been ideal to keep the same teaching staff throughout the experiment. But it must be admitted that staff mobility is as much a fact of educational life as, say, school books are subject to wear and tear. Perhaps it too should have been incorporated as a systems variable.

The turnover of *project* staff was also an unanticipated source of inconvenience. None of the project staff other than the six part-timers from TAU and MATACH had security of tenure nor the prospect of any beyond the end of the project. Mostly young, they reasonably wished to gain more secure toe-holds on the career ladder. When opportunity knocked outside, understandably they took it.

It is too early to identify curriculum development problems. Theoretically, the evaluation should do that. However, it is worth noting in passing that the transitory character of the project meant that senior and experienced people were not attracted except to the top and permanent positions. In fields as tricky as curriculum (even if confined only to the first three years of schooling), maturity of understanding and insight have some advantages. Some of the difficulties in this respect may have been avoided by a decision taken early in the piece to specialize in four defined subject-matter areas. By deliberately deciding not to attempt to create an integrated curriculum (the group believed that to be an idea ahead of its time), its task was simplified – somewhat, at any rate.

It seems inevitable in any experimental, innovative situation where success is being felt that work seems to increase. With apologies to Parkinson, in the present project, work seemed to expand to *exceed* the time available. Many people in the project, especially the teachers, found themselves carrying heavier and heavier loads. Sometimes this was adequately compensated for by the reward system. For example, the teachers received official recognition (sometimes ceremonially), occasional gifts and certificates while some of the researchers improved their (university) qualifications. But sometimes the reward system was not strong enough, so that disappointment resulted but, to be fair, in notably few instances.

One of the project participants, when reminiscing about problems in the early years of the project, made a number of points that seem to penetrate to the heart of innovative planning and development. 'We made one rather false assumption' he said, 'we assumed we were operating in a system that was under control'. There was no cynicism in this – merely an observation that many, as it were, random events occur in schools in particular, and in the education system in general. This perhaps inevitable circumstance does not exactly simplify the lives of field researchers or the research question itself. Another point he made must also strike a chord in the heart of many an aspiring reformer: 'we underestimated the power of opposition'. This meant two things. First, opposition sometimes comes from unexpected quarters; second, when opposition did occur (which was not very often) it took more effort to overcome than was anticipated. The consequence was not that the project failed, or even faltered, just that time, which might have been better used, had to be devoted to dealing with the situation.

At the substantive level, there has been a problem that has been a little worrying to the researchers – who like other people wish to be understood. The study itself is based on several premises that are difficult to convey to those who are unfamiliar with them. One is the system's approach which to many, because of its complexity, appears to be an attempt to accomplish the impossible. Single causality is much easier to comprehend. Another is probability reasoning, a feature of social science that implies to some that conclusions reached are too fragile to trust – reasoning that might be acceptable but only if a better alternative were available.

The situation that exists as we leave the NILI project is particularly interesting. Much of the research-based development work has been completed but its worth and worthiness yet remain to be evaluated. There are many indications that give confidence and encouragement to both researchers and teachers – but they are of a casual and unsystematic kind. Teachers and children and parents appear to be enthusiastic, there are substantial observable differences in styles of teaching, and classrooms appear to be happy and busy places. However, we must wait a while for the kind of evidence that the proposal itself stated ought to be produced for effective evaluation to be made.

NILI: to be or not to be

In the meantime, what might happen? And this brings us back to the conjectural questions raised earlier.

It is predictable that one of the features of the proposal that originally helped to gain support of the Ministry was the provision made for stringent evaluation. The whole curriculum development part of the project was, of course, to be subjected to continuous checking or 'formative evaluation', as some evaluators will insist on calling it. The development of diagnostic test instruments was also to be undertaken with formative evaluation playing a critical part. By the third year, the results achieved by the learning-instruction strategy would themselves come under scrutiny – this time as summative evaluation revealed, it was hoped, what degree of educational profit had been gained. In the two last years (of the original five-year proposal) extensive work was to be done on further evaluation in particular so that whether the problem had been defined and practical and useful answers found would become clear.

At the moment, as the last of those critical two years lies ahead, it is worth asking what criteria might be likely to be employed by the Ministry in making its judgement about the future. On the information supplied in informal meetings with Ministry officials, it seems as if the evidence from the evaluation would be required to demonstrate that discernible benefit had resulted. To gain Ministry approval NILI should yield better cognitive and social results than does the standard approach and it should do so at least within a similar cost range. Nonetheless, some compromise might be acceptable if something less than the ideal were to result. However, even given acceptable educational results, the final decision will not hang on that alone. With a fine sense of realism, the point was made that whether *any* innovation is considered worth implementing on a wide scale depends on at least three factors. They are: (i) the political climate – in the national external sense and in the institutional or local sense; (ii) whether there is sufficient 'energy' in the system to sustain it – energy in the form of material and human resources; and (iii) its place in the general array of educational priorities.

Such a frame of reference obviously has relevance both for the evaluation and whatever other activities the NILI project members are prepared to contemplate in the interests of their undertaking. Clearly, an *educational* evaluation in the conventional (classical) sense need not necessarily address any of the three critical issues that are listed above. But it could do so provided it recognized that each of the criteria is legitimate, and addressed them in the interpretations of the implications of the evaluation results. Perhaps some illustrations are in order – but leaving the vexed issue of political climate till last.

Within the framework of the criterion, '"energy" in the system' one decisive issue is cost. Already Israel spends a remarkable proportion of its budget on education: seven per cent overall, or 22 per cent when defence and debt repayment are excluded. Of the amount available, some 31 per cent goes on primary education. Anything that therefore adds to the cost of education is likely to be viewed unfavourably, especially while the economic situation is showing no improvement. Now, on face value the NILI project has been expensive. And already critics, using an extrapolation to the whole system, have argued that an operation of such cost cannot be contemplated. But the extrapolation and the argument are false. The NILI budget was a research and development budget. It is quite wrong to assume that dissemination requires repetition of the research and development activities. It is equally wrong to use a pupil-unit costing as a basis for calculating eventual expenditure, as has apparently been done outside the project. In fact, as part of the project activities themselves, cost comparisons have been made between traditional education programmes and the NILI one. They have shown the two to be comparable. In some cases, the NILI package would cost less (in already affluent schools), in others (the disadvantaged) it would cost more – an expenditure that social justice might deem reasonable. Table 3 carries the details of this cost comparison between NILI teaching and traditional (frontal teaching) schools in the disadvantaged municipality of Yavne and the not-disadvantaged municipality of Rehovot. Four categories are used – Manpower (including all supporting and administrational positions), Buildings (depreciated over 30 years), Equipment and Materials. Obviously in the NILI schools equipment and materials cost proportionately more but these constitute but a small proportion of overall cost. On the other hand the major cost, labour, is reduced in Yavne and remains the same in Rehovot.

Table 3: *Cost comparisons: traditional versus experimental schools*[1]

	Yavne municipality			Rehovot municipality		
	NILI	Traditional	NILI ±	NILI	Traditional	NILI ±
Manpower	240,000	250,560	−4.2%	173,700	173,000	+.4%
Buildings	17,300	17,300	same	17,300	17,300	same
Equipment	10,250	7,300	+40%	10,250	7,300	+40%
Materials	8,650	5,720	+50%	8,650	5,720	+50%
Totals	276,000	280,900	−1.8%	210,000	203,300	+3.3%

Also as part of the 'energy' in systems there exists at the moment a means for monitoring in-service training for teachers. The MATACH field team has now had considerable experience in this difficult task and has plans for streamlining its activities considerably. That resource, though currently available, will however be dispersed if project funding ceases and MATACH is forced to turn its attention to other things. This would not only mean the loss of an asset in which there has been considerable investment but also, should the decision be taken later to extend to other schools, extra cost would be entailed in re-establishing the teacher-training programme.

If analyses of this kind are correct, it would seem reasonable enough to incorporate this into the evaluations. The 'political climate' aspect however is not so easily accommodated. The NILI project, undertaken as it is with the blessing and support of the Ministry, as an operation, is left essentially in the hands of personnel from the University of Tel Aviv and MATACH. It would be true to say of them that their preferences do not include becoming involved in the kind of political dealings that would enhance the cause of NILI in the eyes of those who have decision-making power. They prefer to do their professional jobs *and* to wait until the educational evidence is somewhat stronger. But if the political climate is significant, and if legitimate attempts to use it are neglected, then the NILI project may be lost by default. In this respect there is quite a hint that the Municipalities may wish to exert some political influence of their own. Whether they will and whether that will be significant enough to prompt Ministerial approval is quite an open question.

Should approval follow, there are several other critical issues lying in wait that may or may not determine the ultimate fate of NILI. Ostensibly, the decision to implement on a national scale will be taken in 1984, although a decision on implementation to a sizable but still limited number of new

[1] Matched by socio-economic status.

Israel: A Total Approach

schools is due in 1980. At the moment, no plans for undertaking the implementation process exist. Fairly clearly, a number of alternative strategies could be contemplated, each with its own advantages and disadvantages, costs and benefits. Without some evaluation of the relative costs and benefits of the alternative strategies, taking a decision to implement or not would be rather hazardous. What this implies is that if the evaluation results are such that the Ministry would wish to see all Israeli schools sharing in the benefits, then prior to deciding to implement, it would be desirable to give considered attention to *how* implementation might best be undertaken. This in turn implies at least implementation planning and preferably feasibility studies as well.

Perhaps less obvious among the remaining hazards that are likely to affect the future of the NILI project is the fate of the project team itself. It was set up to have a limited life. As things stand, in two years' time (or more likely before that) most of the researchers will have to find themselves other positions and the NILI project social system will start to break up. Predictably, too, the MATACH and TAU part-timers will be tempted back into their parent organizations or perhaps on to some new and interesting enterprise. Without the mental, moral and physical support that the research and field teams provided, will the NILI ideal survive – even in the schools that have adopted it whole-heartedly? After all, some teaching staff will move too. The newcomers may or may not be NILI trained. The Principals (who have played important supporting roles) may also seek and find new posts, thus leaving the schools with leaders unfamiliar with the programme, while they themselves have to face afresh all the problems associated with the initiation of innovations. Institutional inertia may yet come to prevail unless some sort of support system is set up to provide help. The Ministry's role in this may also be of critical importance.

Finally, there is one major issue which ultimately cannot be avoided. It concerns the rest of the primary school system. NILI's work stops at Grade III. Assuming that the NILI system is better than the traditional one, then the logical thing to do would be to extend it upwards throughout the primary school and ultimately into the secondary. But that implies a whole new research and development operation that would need to continue for some years. That in turn implies an organization of somewhat more permanence than the NILI team. At the moment, the Ministry could not mount an operation of that size, although its structure provides few barriers to the development of one. But whether or not such an undertaking might be better pursued by a more autonomous organization such as an officially instituted R & D centre (a possibility that no doubt would take into account the trials and tribulations of R & D centres in the USA) seems worthy of serious consideration. In the meantime, it is hoped, the NILI project will not fall victim to the re-emergence of sectional interests. For example, if the Ministry were to indicate that it might accept at least part of the package, competition could develop between those who have vested interests in curriculum materials, those who have vested interests in technology, those who have vested interests in teacher training, etc to the detriment of the integrity of the total programme.

But all this takes us a long way away from the present and even further from what began it all – our two small five-year-olds. Perhaps what happened to them is of interest. Well, their school became a NILI school and although they were too young to be part of the NILI project, they did not exactly live unhappily ever after. Rumour has it that they even rather like school – now.

At a basic conceptual level the Israeli innovation and the Malaysian innovation have much in common. Both are concerned with the first three years of primary school, both envisage new styles of teaching, both aim to reduce disadvantage and both are attempting to evolve practical solutions to their problems.

There are, however, a number of noteworthy differences. In the first place, the Malaysian experiment is being undertaken within the framework of the Education Ministry. In the second, the scale of the two operations is somewhat different. The Malaysian team is substantially smaller than the 100-strong Israeli one. In the third, though both countries are young, Malaysia remains influenced by a colonial past that has not been part of the Israeli experience. In the fourth, while the issue of identity is consistantly pressing for both countries, the diverse cultures in Malaysia are also religiously diverse in a manner that is not to be found in Israel.

Perhaps the most interesting comparison between the two though is in the strategy of approach adopted. In a very real sense the Israeli approach is strongly technocratic – not just in its use of technology but in the systemic thinking that has determined the whole design of their project. By contrast, the Malaysians are, for various reasons, adopting a much more pragmatic-realist approach that is tempered to meet contingencies and exigencies as they arise.

Chapter 6
Malaysia: An Experiment in Systematic Adaptation

A number of innovations are in the process of development and trial in Malaysia. Most fall under the jurisdiction of the Ministry of Education's well appointed Curriculum Development Unit and/or its larger godparent, the Educational Planning and Research Division. Among the innovations is a modestly scaled attempt to re-form the curriculum for the first three years of primary school – a reform that, if fully developed, will result in a change of teaching style that in the light of traditional practice will be dramatically distinctive. The fact leads one to conjecture firstly, what prompted the attempt, secondly, how it might be achieved and thirdly, what the consequences might be. Such conjecture perforce requires that the social context and historical antecedents of the innovation be clarified. Accordingly, the first pages in the chapter are devoted to setting the scene – and at some length because of forces at play – before leading into a more detailed examination of the innovation itself.

There are so many striking features of Malaysian society that it is difficult to determine which ones to focus on. It does seem, however, that four are of particular significance to the Malaysian educational innovation that is under consideration in this chapter. Two relate to the structure and condition of contemporary Malaysian society, namely the issues of national identity and economic development. Two relate to the character and thrust of its education system, namely the directions in which policies point, and the rate and state of development of the system. Because the former provide an imposing backdrop to the latter, they warrant first and more elaborate attention.

Advent of a nation

Anyone who chooses to wonder about the *raison d'être* of nations could not fail to be struck by the intriguing nature of some apparent ambiguities in Malaysia's case. For example, geographically it comprises but part of the Malay Archipelago, plus part of the island of Kalimantan (Sarawak and Sabah), but with the physically tiny, centrally located Singapore excluded. Also, much more populous Indonesia sweeps down in a large semicircle to the south, half enclosing it. Again, not all people of the Malay stock are in

Malaysia: An Experiment in Systematic Adaptation

Malaysia – far from it. And not all those in Malaysia are Malays. The Chinese nearly equal them in numbers and there is as well a smaller but substantial population of Indians. Within these ethnic groups also there are sub-cultural variations of considerable distinctiveness. The country too shows a diversity of economic, occupational and religious circumstances that compounds the complexity. Malaysia is indeed a pluralistic society with a degree of heterogeneity that rivals even the USA's.

Obviously, the explanation of Malaysia's nationhood is better sought in historical terms than in some perhaps naïvely presumed logic. There the story is inextricably bound up with a long record of the migration of peoples, conquest and occupation, but it is recent history that holds the key.

Malaysia is a *new* nation, emerging from the aftermath of the Second World War and the decline of colonialism. It consists, by mutual agreement, of a Federation of geographically adjoining territories which had in common British and Japanese occupation and some ethnic affinities which, in the years prior to 1957, had not caused much interaction between them. Malaysia owes its present-day form to two principal facts. The first was that the British, after having established a commercial presence in the area (Penang, 1786; Singapore, 1819), responded to an invitation from feuding Malay nobility and moved in to provide 'protection'. That protection eventually established the English firmly in control. The second was that the Japanese invasion during the Second World War changed that situation and opened the door to the end of European imperialism. For the present paper, however, it is not the fact of British rule that is of consequence, but rather some of the effects.

Because the British adopted a policy of preserving Malay society, as it were, intact – an orientation not difficult for them because of its distinct affinity with British society and its orientation towards nobility – there were two significant consequences. In the first instance, the predominantly rural and basically feudal character of Malay society endured with little change right throughout the British Period. At the same time, to fuel the furnaces for new industrial enterprises, to till the fields for new agricultural developments and fill the offices for new commercial ventures, the British resorted to a practice that they had found cheap and convenient elsewhere. They imported indentured labourers, many of whom stayed permanently. The populations of Chinese and Indians thus began to swell. The Chinese established dominion over shopkeeping and trading, the Indians over working in the rubber estates. The underdeveloped rural sector remained almost solely the domain of the Malays. True, some Malays succeeded in penetrating into industry and commerce, and some small provision had been made for the employment of Malays in the lower echelons of public service, but in general

> 'The pro-Malay policies . . . helped preserve the traditional patterns of Malay society and its peasant basis. At the time these policies seemed benevolent and appropriate, but they did not help the Malays to come

to terms with the modern world or adapt themselves to a competitive economic system.'

(Mean cited in Nordin, 1972)

In the second instance, over the period, Malaysia inherited from the British many institutional forms. They ranged from Parliament to polo, from jurisprudence to driving on the left. Present-day Malaysian industry bears the mark, often the trademark, of Britain. Malaysia plays British sports (sometimes spectacularly well, eg badminton), sends hundreds of her students to study in Britain every year, and her military forces have clearly been cast in the British mould. The English language is almost universal throughout the country. Malaysia belongs to the British Commonwealth. But such British features are something of an overlay, a veneer, a recent surface coating on a much older, more substantial and venerable edifice — of cultures which have roots deep in the past and associations with great religions of great antiquity.

Once the British had gone in 1957, however, and Malaysia was left, as it were, to her own resources, and once the Federation of Malaysia had become firmly established, attention could be turned to the future growth and development of the young nation.

Towards nationhood

As stock was taken of the situation, two things became apparent. First, it seemed likely that with wise use of natural resources and manpower, economic prospects were good. (They became even better with the subsequent development of the oil industry.) Second, if the concept of social justice were invoked (a concept that was integral to British ideology, but not necessarily its practice), there were obvious social inequalities existing in society.

The major problem that thus faced the young nation-state was, under such circumstances, to determine how nationhood might be achieved. Given three important ethnic groups, given the country's economic potential, given foreign influences (notably British and later Japanese), given no history of union, what road should be followed? How could it be travelled? Perhaps even more importantly, how fast might progress be made?

Now when independence comes as it did in Malaysia, constitutionally and without violence, there is always the possibility that the necessity of establishing an independent national identity might be regarded as less insistent. After all, there can often be other factors in the situation that would have dampened motivation for it. That some of the effects of colonialism were beneficial can be an incentive to preserve some, perhaps much, of the immediate past. Again, the interests of the one-time colonizers can still be extant. For reasons that may be altruistic or acquisitive, utilitarian or evangelistic, links remain that can be difficult and even undesirable to break.

Malaysia: An Experiment in Systematic Adaptation

The accumulation of such circumstances, however, does not diminish the necessity for national identity. It is not surprising, and it is obviously wise, that in Malaysia greatest priority was given to nation-building: the creation of a corporate identity. But because the idea of identity, by definition, implies both similarity with one's own kind and difference from others, the task facing Malaysia was considerable. In the early days of nationhood, there were not many existing reasons that would permit all inhabitants of Malaysia to say 'This is how others are different from us'. History had made Malaysia a 'manufactured' state. Now it was faced with the problem of manufacturing the Malaysian man. The importance of that task and the consequences of success or failure are at the heart of the survival of the country and portend much for mankind.

'If Malaysia could provide one example in Asia of a nation able to maintain democracy and tolerance in the most difficult racial situation in the whole Eastern hemisphere, it would be an achievement of historic significance.'

(Hunter, 1966)

But this dramatic task was to be attacked at the same time that another drama was unfolding – the drive for Malaysian economic development. The resources were there in abundance. The resources of raw materials were generous, power was potentially plentiful and manpower was available in quantity and, prospectively, in quality. The nation became committed to as fast a rate of development as possible.

Development planning
The challenge that resulted was the challenge to reconcile economic development with societal development and, in particular, to achieve a degree of economic equity that had not hitherto prevailed. The challenge was taken up, helped by a prevailing world-wide trend on which Malaysia capitalized as one of the consequences of coming upon nationhood in the 1960s. Her birth coincided with a period when national planning on a grand scale was enjoying considerable vogue. Malaysia, noting this, has in the course of its short history had the benefit of three national plans. In the last, the essential direction that Malaysia is following was succinctly put by the Prime Minister:

'We seek an economic order in which the well-being of Malaysians of all races, from all walks of life and in all regions of the country will be enhanced. We seek an economic order in which all Malaysians will have the fullest opportunity to utilize their individual talents to their benefit and in so doing, contribute to the national good. Above all we seek an economic order within a democratic system in which the opportunity for self-fulfillment will be guaranteed for all who are prepared to make the effort.'

(Foreword to the Third Malaysian Plan: Datuk Hussein Onn, 1976)

Abdul Hamid and Syed Ahmad (1978) summarize the situation in these terms.

'The overriding objective of Malaysia's socio-economic development as stated in the Third Malaysia Plan 1976-1980, is national unity. The Third Malaysia Plan is designed to facilitate the eventual achievement of this objective through the New Economic Policy. The latter is aimed at the reduction of poverty and the restructuring of society in order to correct racial economic imbalance within the context of an expanding economy.'

That such objectives are found to be desirable provides an indication of Malaysia's inclination towards some of the Western idioms. Material improvement is there, individual gratification within a national obligation is there and democracy is there. With less timidity than is often found in the West, however, overt recognition of 'racial' inequality is there and so is the promise of overcoming it. That deliberate attempts are already being made to deal with the latter problem and on a large scale is also a point of distinction from Western nations whose situation may only be different in degree. There are, however, circumstances in Malaysia that are conducive to such action. One of the British legacies has been a representative democratic parliamentary system. That parliamentary system of government was threatened in the 1969 elections by incidents of overt racial conflict that left all aghast at the implications. Many in the world predicted the 'death of democracy' in Malaysia. But such has not been the case.

Parliamentary government was restored less than two years later, and the leaders determined that racial divisiveness should not be part of the Malaysian society. A larger political consensus was forged when the pre-1969 ruling Alliance Party was broadened into the National Front, which, as the recent election (1978) has indicated, is the only political party that commands support from all ethnic groups in the country. The constitutional government is thus in a position to undertake the process of redress and has set out to do it with a sense of urgency tempered with caution. It is concentrating initially on access to circumstances that yield advantage. Not surprisingly, education features prominently in such a project.

And it is here that two particular features of the present education system should be noted briefly in anticipation of their relevance in later pages.

National goals and education

At the moment, Malaysian education has two particular thrusts: upgrading the quality of education, particularly through the teaching force, and giving special attention to the problems of rural education. In the first place Malaysia has invested heavily in the quality of her teaching force. Strenuous efforts are being made to increase the length and improve the quality of pre-service training. In-service training proceeds in various forms and curriculum research, development and reform is well under way. Attempts are being made to improve the teacher-pupil ratio. Some classes are still large but the allocation of staff is such that in the bigger schools, teachers can get non-teaching 'preparation' time during the school day and in most schools the headmasters and headmistresses can be spared considerable time for administration and managerial tasks. Teachers are trained as professionals, regarded as professionals and may not supplement their teaching duties with other employment.

The emphasis that is being put on rural education stems from a belief in the power of education to assist in achieving greater social equity. This has resulted in a particularly strong drive to increase and improve provisions made in rural areas. The school building and equipping programme emphasizes the priorities of the rural sector. As well, much hope is being placed on the development of new curricula and teaching methods that will accelerate the rate at which the rural-urban education gap is closed.

Administrative legacies

There is a second educational circumstance in Malaysia that creates both problems and rather unique opportunities. There have been dramatic and signal changes in the administration of education and indeed, as Nordin (1972) and Roff (1967) have pointed out, throughout the whole structure of public administration. The British had done little to prepare Malaysia for independence. Further, they had operated in the civil service with maintenance as almost the sole objective:

'The main feature of the civil service before the war was regulating ... [but after independence] the traditionally quiescent role of government gave way to the concept of dynamic government concerning itself with the active direction and operation of vast enterprises, insurance schemes, health services, transport undertakings, industrial and commercial concerns and the like'

... and, it must be added, a brand new, burgeoning education system.

Complicating the situation was the fact that the public education system the British had introduced was elitist, and primarily (but not exclusively) for the sons of the nobility. It was also extremely restricted, catering for but a scant 15 per cent or so of the population.

At the time of independence, therefore, neither was there a large pool of educated manpower for the new public administration to draw on, nor had indigenes been groomed to any appreciable degree to fulfil the tasks of running a country of some 13 million people.

Under the pressure of circumstances, the administration was forced to expand very rapidly, the number of teachers employed by the Ministry alone growing from 67,821 in 1970 to 110,000 in 1979. Inescapably, it had to look towards youth – those who had had at least some relevant experience or the potential for (rapid) training. A number of schemes were adopted that increased the competency of those chosen, one being to send many young people overseas for training – a policy that has had a particular consequence on the emerging system.

Given the circumstances of a rapidly expanding system with an expertise infrastructure as yet not fully developed, with new people constantly being acquired as new tasks materialize, it is predictable that the structure of such a system will take time to consolidate. In early years, and while expansion continues, the broad outlines of the structure may be formed, but the fine detail will continue to be in a state of modification or flux. However, flux is not always helpful to the process of organization – at any rate from a conventional bureaucratic perspective. Furthermore, while roles and functions are in the process of clarification, it becomes a matter of general concern to determine where boundaries might best be set. To avoid the dangers of trespass, there occurs a thrust towards observing formal protocol and formalized information channels almost in self-defence. But, given structural flux, not all protocol has yet been decided and, more importantly, not all channels are open or even formed.

Now if to this state of affairs is added the regular inflow of (young) graduates from overseas who, in the interest of the best use of their new skills, receive appointments that call for more seniority or experience than would normally be the case, this too has effects on the structure of the system. As the new staff now in positions of responsibility apply their newly acquired knowledge, they tend to consider what changes would be beneficial. A series of redirections, perhaps small, perhaps large, is brought about, and the state of flux continues – a condition that carries much promise but also one or two problems, as the last chapter will wish to indicate.

Educational policy
A number of events have influenced the way in which education has gone about taking up its part in the task of national development. The Razak Report published in the Federation of Malaya (now Malaysia) in 1956 during a brief period of British-supervised 'self-administration' has been the corner-stone. Awang Had Salleh (1977) summarizes its recommendations and those of the subsequent 1960 Rahman Talib Committee thus:

'...a national system of education acceptable to the people of the Federation as a whole which will satisfy their needs and promote their cultural, social, economic and political development as a nation, having regard to the intention to make Malay the National Language of the country, whilst preserving and sustaining the growth of the language and culture of other communities living in the country.'

Then in 1973 appeared the study that has since become popularly known as the 'Drop-out Study'. In a thoughtful, comprehensive and pioneering social survey submitted as two reports, one a 'study of opinion about education and society', and the other of the 'causes of educational wastage', Datuk Murad bin Mohd Noor provided some telling evidence and argument that subsequently played an important part in directing attention towards the disadvantaged. Its advent, prior to the Third Malaysia

Malaysia: An Experiment in Systematic Adaptation

Development Plan, helped determine some of the latter's educational orientation.

It is in the Third Malaysia Development Plan (1976) itself, however, that the overall mandate for education's role is given. Its chapter on education begins:

> 'The education and training system has a multi-faceted role to play in the creation of a society based on the principles of Rukun Negara and the realisation of the objectives of the New Economic Policy (NEP). *The overriding objective is national integration and unity.*' (Emphasis added)

Later, after giving an account of substantial developments achieved in education during the previous five-year plan, the document outlines briefly how the educational goal of the next five years was to be met:

> '1333. The education and training objectives under the TMP will be to:-
> (i) strengthen the educational system for promoting national integration and unity through:
>   *(a)* the continued implementation, in stages, of *Bahasa Malaysia* as the main medium of instruction at all levels;
>   *(b)* the development of personality, character and good citizenship and the promotion of moral discipline through curriculum and extra-curriculum activities;
>   *(c)* narrowing the gap in educational opportunities between the rich and poor, and among the various regions and races in the country, through a more equitable distribution of resources and facilities; and
>   *(d)* the eventual integration of the educational systems in Sabah and Sarawak into the national system;
> (ii) the orientation and expansion of the education and training system towards meeting national manpower needs, especially in science and technology;
> (iii) the improvement of the quality of education in order to reduce wastage and increase its effectiveness for nation building; and
> (iv) the expansion of the research, planning and implementation capacity to meet the above objectives.'

What is implied here is not only that education should be available, but that it should be worth having. And worth, in this case, is being defined in terms of the overall objective of national integration and unity.

Review

Because the Malaysian innovation to be treated in this present study is a qualitative one designed to produce education that *is* worth having, there will be advantage in keeping several of the points made above in mind. Perhaps this would be the time to summarize them:

1. The overriding concern of the young nation is to achieve national integration and unity.
2. The principal hurdle that is thought to stand in the way is the potential that economic differences (that in the past have had regional and ethnic correlates) have for creating divisiveness.
3. Education is seen as *one* important agency through which disadvantage may be helped to disappear and through which its disappearance may be extended into society as a whole.
4. However, Malaysia's economic and social development beyond its present state depends on more than the reallocation of opportunities within the population – as it were a shuffling of the same cards and a redeal. It also depends on obtaining a new and bigger pack and perhaps changing the name of the game. In other words, the nature and character of education must change to (a) increase the range and variety of opportunities available, and (b) improve the quality of what is provided in order to enhance the use to which the results can be put.
5. The education system itself is in the process of continuing formation and growth that leaves it open to minor (or perhaps major) changes of direction, a condition that is both inevitable and desirable if full advantage is to be taken in the interests of rapid educational and economic development. But it is likely to have attendant problems.

The innovation

Rationale

The Malaysian innovation that features in the IIEP study is a curriculum development project for the first three years of primary school.

At first glance, it might seem that the jump from the centrally significant and preoccupying problems of building a nation's identity and promoting its economic development to the first three years of primary school is rather large. But there is a logical argument about the connection between curriculum and identity and curriculum and development that is difficult to fault. As one of the important institutions that serves to promote and protect society's values, education helps play a part in the process of moulding citizens. The main mechanism it employs in the process is the curriculum – the set of experiences to which children are exposed at school. It is through the curriculum that the children come to believe in the values and norms that they do. If a new identity is required, it must therefore be taught.

Similarly, economic development depends on the level and type of education provided. Devices are needed if the schools of the future are to create in abundance technicians, technologists, professionals, scholars and administrators whose combined efforts will coalesce to precipitate economic and social progress. By implication, much of that production will hinge on the nature, scope and content of school curricula.

There are, however, one or two practical issues that at this point give cause for thought.

The first can be reasonably readily dismissed. There may be some difficulty initially in seeing that efforts directed at six-, seven- and eight-year-olds can bear very powerfully on that immediately insistent problem of nationhood. Today's children will undoubtedly be tomorrow's citizens, but the particular tomorrow when the present six-, seven- and eight-year-olds come to wield political power is a considerable distance away. In explanation, however, the new curriculum is but a first step (among others) in a programme of reform that will, it is expected, eventually penetrate the whole period of schooling.

There is a second issue to take into account. The children's eventual political viewpoints will depend on many factors other than the curriculum they had at school. No matter how enlightened that curriculum may be or how single-mindedly it exerts its influence towards national integration, it will do so within diverse social contexts, schools, homes, mosques, temples, kampongs, cities, through which ethnic and economic differences still cut a swathe. If the curriculum is designed to promote unity, it is likely to be doing it in various environments, some of which may not be fully aware of the ways the idea can be supported or, for that matter, what might tend to subvert it. The curriculum, in setting out to promote national unity, may inadvertently experience circumstances outside its sphere of influence that run counter to its aims.

There is, however, a third and more subtle point to be made. After all, it is likely that where the curriculum and the norms and values of the different communities directly and obviously clash, then the need for accommodation and adjustment will be easily appreciated and readily undertaken. The third point revolves round the issue of *unrecognized* incompatibility between the curriculum (including the 'hidden curriculum') and existing social attitudes, norms and values. It is here that some of the arguments expressed by the 'new sociologists of education', in their debate over the sources of control of knowledge, come into contention. The existing approach to schooling in Malaysia is basically formal. The syllabus is prescribed, teaching methods are essentially 'chalk and talk' methods and the class is regarded and treated as a 'collectivity'. The combination of circumstances therefore conspires to perpetuate what is (or was) the status quo. It served to perpetuate the values, norms, attitudes and beliefs of the authority which set it up. But, and importantly, that authority was not initially Malaysian and there has been little opportunity so far to inject much that is essentially Malaysian into the curriculum. Bahasa Malaysia represents one element, but even the way that it is transmitted is usually in traditional style. Now it will be remembered that the whole thrust of contemporary Malaysian society is towards identity, integration and equity. And that thrust has been taken in order to counter the kind of conditions existing first at independence. It is necessary then to have means for delivering education that are consistent with the new desired Malaysian image rather than those appropriate for the old undesired colonial one. Perhaps a concrete illustration is useful. It is undoubtedly true that traditional, expository class-teaching methods tend to favour the advantaged pupil over the disadvantaged. Those children who come from an economically, socially and educationally rich environment tend consistently to do better than those who do not. Such a 'delivery method' thus serves to perpetuate existing conditions, ensuring that advantage stays with the advantaged and disadvantage with the disadvantaged. What presumably is needed is a delivery system that does *not* have such an effect. Instead, the need is for a delivery system appropriate to the needs and aspirations of contemporary Malaysia. One that should permit *differential* treatment of pupils so that the disadvantaged obtain the kind of education that will help them to overcome their disadvantage.

Problems of compatibility

Now it is also true to say that among the conceptions of education that have emerged recently in the Western world (including England), there is one that appears to have the capacity to do this.

It places emphasis on the individualization of instruction, the tailoring of education to meet the different needs of different children and on the concept of 'compensatory education'. However, it also places value on the idea that knowledge is ever changing, that questioning and querying and discovering for oneself is the appropriate form of learning and that the teacher should, though presumably authoritative, adopt a guiding, supporting, non-directive posture. It is this kind of delivery system that is under examination in the Malaysian innovation. However, it is a delivery system that, in the Malaysian situation, may have its hazards — at least at the outset.

For example, it is reasonable to ask what might happen (in Malaysia, but not necessarily only in Malaysia) if, into the educational culture that still has colonial overtones, such a Western variant finds its way? Might it sow the seeds of dissension between school and community? Might it isolate them from each other? Might it result in a public demeaning of the educational profession in the eyes of the public? Might it incite a 'counter-culture' education? Might it subvert older values, driving a wedge between young and old? Might it, in other words, lead to social disintegration rather than the integration hoped for?

Obviously, there is no point in continuing such a line of conjecture without recourse to facts and circumstances. But in the account that follows of what was first called the 'Development of the Integrated Curriculum for the First Three Years of Primary Schools in Malaysia', these points will have to be kept in mind if, as the IIEP project intends, problems are to be anticipated in advance and possible solutions are to be devised.

Evolution

The brief history of the early stages of the 'Integrated Curriculum' project provides an exemplary illustration of rational education pre-planning and collaboration with international agencies.

First, as we have seen, came the identification of major national problems and the decision to emphasize the 'eradication of poverty' and the 'restructuring of society'. Then came the selection of education as *one* of the means for achieving this task – a decision that took into account four previous inquiries into education – the Razak Report of 1956, the Rahman Talib Report of 1966, the Aziz Salay Commission of 1971 and the 'Drop-out Study' of 1973.

With the existing condition of education thus well appreciated, attention turned towards the kind and degree of change that would next be needed in the education system and the means most likely to achieve it. It must be remembered that in the intervening years between independence and 1973, considerable strides had been made towards remedying some of the earlier quantitative deficiencies of the system. Many schools had been built, the proportion of the relevant age group at school at each level had increased steadily and near-universal primary education (to Form III) had been achieved. As well, further plans for continued quantitative development were in full swing. All this had entailed setting up and consolidating appropriate organizational structure in the Ministry and throughout the country.

With these two aspects, quantitative development and organizational restructuring, sufficiently under control, it was time to turn attention to other aspects. Recognizing that the kind of educational objectives desired could only be achieved through the actual educational experiences that children would have, emphasis shifted to qualitative aspects. First came the project to improve primary science and maths for the rural school. A year later, in 1973, came the important move of setting up a Curriculum Development Centre in the Ministry.

Curriculum development

The new Centre was charged with the responsibility of establishing and systematizing curriculum development for all levels of the school system. It was also to look into the improvement of the quality of education offered in schools and to make the school curricula more relevant and effective for achieving national educational objectives.

The Centre has the following main functions:

(i) to identify national needs and aspirations and to translate them into curriculum specifications;
(ii) to conduct curriculum research and experimentation;
(iii) to plan and develop curriculum programmes for continuous systematic and qualitative development in education;
(iv) to develop and produce curriculum materials such as syllabuses,

teachers' guidelines, pupils' learning materials, evaluation instruments, audiovisual aids and prototype science and other equipment;

(v) to set up teachers' centres for the dissemination of curriculum information and for the offering of in-service training for teachers in the use of specific curriculum programmes and materials.

The Centre began its existence at a time when, as a result of a study of curriculum development needs, a number of international agencies were offering finance for special curriculum projects. One of the projects that gained support from Unicef is the one with which this present chapter is concerned. Among the prime reasons for Unicef's stated priorities was that it was *related to national development* and within the existing *national development plan*. It was also concerned with the *economically disadvantaged*, and with the *physical, intellectual and emotional development of young children*. As well, the proposal *aimed to solve a problem*, was *innovative* and was likely to have *multiplier effects*.

At the time of its acceptance, however – and it was a committee consisting of representatives of the Ministry of Education, the National Economic Planning Unit and Unicef that gave approval to proceed – an important qualification was made. This undertaking was *not* to be authorized for immediate implementation on a national scale in the way that necessity had made customary for many earlier reforms. Because of its significance, potential impact and possible cost it was to be evaluated in such a way that by 1980, when Unicef funding would cease and Malaysia would resume full responsibility, the Ministry would be in a position to decide either to:

'1. Take no further action if the project did not produce any results in curriculum programmes and teaching practices that were significantly better than the existing curriculum and teaching practices.

or

2. To implement the proved programmes, teaching practices and materials in all primary schools in the country.'

The responsibility of both developing the new curriculum and evaluating it was to fall mainly on the shoulders of the staff of the Curriculum Development Centre, or more specifically on the newly set-up project unit within the Centre.

Initial difficulties

However, there was an initial set-back. The proposal had been put forward in good faith on the assumption that suitably trained and experienced personnel would be available to man it. But this is the point at which one of the colonial period chickens came home to roost. It will be remembered that at that time, Malaysia was no more than 16 years old. Furthermore, in the period prior to independence, it had not been British policy to prepare the indigenous people for responsible and senior administrative or professional roles. Thus in the early years of the new education system, there was a desperate shortage of staff with capability and, it must be admitted, even remotely relevant experience, to fill senior posts. Many young people were precipitated into positions of great responsibility and given tasks that in the normal course of events they might have expected to come upon much later in life. There were many consequences of this state of affairs – some strikingly successful, as the development of the system shows, but some rather less fortunate. One of the latter was the unavoidable denuding of the education service of, if you will, middle-level expertise. And it was middle-level expertise in the form of curriculum development training and experience that was needed to mount the 'Integrated Curriculum' project. The force of circumstances was such that the best available candidate was a linguist with no direct experience in curriculum development. When he came to assemble staff, similar problems confronted him and he had no option but to fall back on the recruitment of experienced teachers to aid him. Again experience and training in curriculum planning and development was a missing component.

To compound the difficulties, negotiations over the acquisition of an overseas consultant ran into problems and the arrival of the expert was delayed for a year. When, eventually, he came, he proved rich in experience in teaching and supervision in his own country (England), but somewhat unfamiliar with the Malaysian scene and also with the technicalities of curriculum development. The resulting delay in carrying out the planned activities did provide breathing space that was put to good effect. Some of the project staff were enabled to take an AMEC (Anglo-Malaysian Educational Cooperation) study to the United Kingdom to observe classes that were using integrated curriculum approaches there. As well, opportunity was taken to revise the project's schedule.

This new schedule anticipated a systematic programme involving the identification of six laboratory schools and the observation of their pre-experimental conditions, the development of curriculum guidelines and materials for the laboratory schools, the conducting of an in-service training course for teachers, then monitoring, formative evaluation and modification prior to extending the project to a further 20 pilot schools. The experimental work involving the pilot schools would also be monitored, formatively evaluated, modified and, finally, summatively evaluated for each level in turn. In 1980 the report would be presented to the Minister. It was expected to include sections on:

(i) style of teaching,
(ii) pupils' achievement in reading and other basic skills,
(iii) remedial teaching and programmes for slow learners,
(iv) furniture design and
(v) integrated curriculum content and pupil materials.

But that time was not yet come and the year of the consultant lay ahead. During it, much that was planned came about, but not without some 'moments'. Initial time was lost as the consultant wisely engaged himself in learning about the Malaysian situation. With momentum increasing, however, the selection of the six pilot schools took place. The criteria were: (i) their relative proximity to the Curriculum Development Centre, (ii) willingness to cooperate, (iii) some evidence of good work being done, and (iv) the staff's capacity to communicate in English – criteria that were understandably pragmatic if not exactly experimentally pristine. Curriculum materials began to be developed by the project staff and in August 1975 the first in-service course for project staff and cooperating teachers was held. Some of the tutoring was carried out by two more English consultants who, though unfamiliar with Malaysia, provided courses on (i) child development, (ii) teaching practices in British primary schools, and (iii) the preparation of teaching aids. Curriculum development theory and practice was not included, no doubt because of the tutors' greater familiarity with other fields.

However, by the end of the year, the six pilot schools were under way and the consultant had departed. Among his several recommendations was one that the project leader's particular talents might be better used in a domain for which he had been trained. His transfer to a language curriculum project followed shortly. The net short-term result on the 'Integrated Curriculum' project, however, was that momentum was lost again and that the staff, now reduced to two experienced teachers, were left to manage as best they could. Under difficulties they continued to produce curriculum materials, visit the schools and encourage the teachers. They also organized the second in-service seminar, calling on the services of one of the earlier tutors plus another who turned out to be a practising (English) headmaster.

It is perhaps understandable that the combination of circumstances began to prove too much for some of the schools. In effect only one school was continuing with confidence and that was due to a freak of fate that ought to be explained. By chance the headmistress had in earlier years received training in Montessori pre-school education. Subsequently, as a headmistress of a primary school, she had not had the chance to put her training to use. When the opportunity to participate in the project came, she, recognizing the common ground between its aims and her earlier training, seized on it with delight. It was due in no small measure to her enthusiasm, her support of her staff and, above all, her capacity to help them as problems arose, that her programme continued to thrive. Without the evidence of that school's success (and of the success of several other isolated teachers), who knows whether or not the post-1976 hiatus would have proved too much and the whole project would have collapsed?

Reorganization
However, at this point in time, the light began to show at the end of the

tunnel. An inquiry by the Curriculum Development Centre following Unicef's query about unexpended funds led to a reorganization that saw the advent of a new project director who, fortuitously, had been a member of the evaluation unit monitoring the project. To his familiarity with the early trials and tribulations of the project, he could add specialized training in curriculum development. But the task was formidable and decision-day lay less than four short years away.

Fairly clearly, in a curriculum innovation that is concerned to change the quality of children's education, some of the most important factors must be what the teachers do, what they do it with and what happens because of it. For this kind of information it is necessary to look more closely into the substance of the project.

The particular curriculum strategy chosen for use resulted not only from the broader objectives discussed earlier, but also from the belief, supported by reports of inspectors and a study undertaken by the University of Malaya, that current practices in schools were not conducive to the kind of education desired. For historical reasons much of educational practice in Malaysia, as in South-East Asia in general, was still 'largely bookish' (Miller, 1968). Emphasis was placed on rote learning. The accumulation of certificates rather than competencies tended to be the pupils' goal, a phenomenon by no means exclusive to that part of the world. As well, the primary curriculum then existing in Malaysia was subject-based, made up of prescribed courses of studies organized in the form of separate subject syllabuses. In many primary schools, learning, to the pupils, was almost confined to reading and writing from textbooks. To teachers in such schools, 'teaching' meant simply to cover the textbook contents.

Task definition

The project thus got under way again with the aim of making the following changes in the actual classroom practice – the patterns of behaviour that constitute the teaching-learning interaction:

(i) to change children's classroom learning from passive learning, merely receiving instructions from the teacher all the time, to active involvement in the learning process;
(ii) to change teaching from classroom instruction by the teacher to the whole class all the time, to teaching children individually or in small groups most of the time;
(iii) to change teaching from the syllabus rigidly all the time to giving children some opportunity to decide what to learn;
(iv) to develop better communication skills both in language and numerical expressions.

These general changes also resolve themselves down into more specific behaviours that in general reflect a desire for more animated activity on the part of the children and for learning to happen more spontaneously, but under circumstances that are to be, as it were, engineered by the teacher. 'Engineered' is both inappropriate and appropriate as a metaphor. It is inappropriate because some of the materials for the learning process are not manufactured to the teachers' specifications (although the teachers in the laboratory schools have been involved in their development). In fact, the materials produced by the Curriculum Development Centre are expected to play quite a large part in the reform process. They will comprise, firstly, teaching materials, handbooks, guides, tapes and slides, together with examples of pupils' work for replication – teaching-learning kits that will give substantial direction to the teacher. Secondly, they will also ultimately include an array of differentiated and remedial materials that will cater for the diversity of capabilities in the school population. Thirdly, they will consist of redesigned plant and equipment that will be more suitable for some of the newer tasks. However, 'engineered' *is* appropriate because in the last resort it is the teacher who takes the ingredients and the pupils and using his (60 per cent of Malaysian primary teachers are men) skills and insights, combines them to produce the educational project.

It is hoped that the net result will be that the procedures used will be based as far as possible upon the child's first-hand experience of the world in which he lives, and that as a consequence he will come to acquire knowledge, understanding, skills, values and attitudes in such a way that he can perceive relationships more easily. The procedures to be used are also based on the assumption that for such an approach, which entails much greater integration of content, teaching method and materials than has hitherto been the case, a new kind of teaching style is required – the management of learning situations, as it were. While such a style may be familiar to some newly trained teachers, it is likely to be unknown to the majority of teachers in the service.

There are three matters that warrant brief elaboration before any attempt is made to venture interpretations of the situation and to honour the terms of the IIEP project by conjecturing about the future. They are: (i) the process by which the curriculum will be developed, (ii) the strategy being used to develop it, and (iii) the assessment that will be made of its effectiveness.

Process
The materials are being developed by the six-man team (others being sought, so far in vain) in collaboration with the 30 teachers in the laboratory schools who try them out and provide feedback for modification. However, it is not intended that a package of diversified materials and the requisite directions for their use will be developed to the extent that they come to constitute *all* the work and *only* the work that should be undertaken – something to be 'covered' as textbooks once were. Rather, a certain amount will be produced which will serve to familiarize teachers with the *principles* behind the new operation so that (i) they come to internalize them and (ii) they can

then create additional material and activities consistent with the idea of the integrated curriculum.

In this respect it is perhaps as well to note in passing that the original title of the project has undergone change. An interesting and perhaps significant modification has been made with 'improved' being substituted for 'integrated'. The change was thought unlikely to detract from the original objectives and at the same time to avoid giving the impression that radical, and therefore threatening, change was afoot. The new title then is 'The Development of an Improved Curriculum for the First Three Years of the Malaysian Primary Schools'.

While the Curriculum Development Centre staff will work directly with the laboratory school teachers and undertake training activities for them, a different and ingenious strategy is to be used with the pilot schools – and for national implementation, should it come about. The burden of teacher training is to fall upon the principals of the schools *after* they themselves have received training in the new system. Clearly such a plan has logistic and cost advantages compared with a direct teacher training alternative. It may also prove to have several other important advantages that had better be left for later discussion.

Strategy

The second issue, the strategy of development, is the one where dreams and realities come face to face. When the new project director took over, a stock-taking of the situation was made of what the prevailing circumstances were, the resources to hand and, perhaps more importantly, what it would take to get from where they were now to where they wanted to be, but *with the resources available*.

The outcome of the stock-taking was particularly interesting on a number of counts. The first was that the teachers were to be seen as the prime means for achieving the reform. This was consistent with a habit of mind that had tended to prevail from the outset. Continuity was thus preserved. It was also consistent with the powerful logic that if teachers are agents of education, then reform should start with them. The second was that in facing up to the 'how-do-we-get-from-where-we-are-now-to-where-we-must-go' question, a sequenced model incorporating four (teacher) development stages was worked out. Each of the stages was then broken down into sub-tasks that were also put into a developmental sequence. If an academic name were desired for such an approach, 'sequenced functional prerequisites' would perhaps be suitably solemn.

Basically, the 'development' of the teachers is predicated on the belief that in order for them to master the complexities of creating and teaching an integrated curriculum, they should learn, first, how to teach a single subject well, second, how to combine two subjects, third, how to use larger blocks of time, if possible employing more than two subjects, and fourth, how to use a completely integrated approach. Within this sequence, however, it is assumed that certain skills and competencies are needed – an assumption that was strongly confirmed by the teachers' response to a survey of their needs, as they perceived them. They are: (i) classroom organization and management skills which, with the increased use of group work and individualized teaching, are vastly different from the established 'chalk and talk' methods; (ii) skill in using the new types of curriculum materials which, as multi-task packages, differ greatly from the textbooks hitherto in use; (iii) planning skills that take into account differentiated pupil performance levels, remedial work and enrichment – again tasks not hitherto regarded as necessary; and (iv) design and use of supporting materials and equipment – a task to which the skills of the Curriculum Development Centre unit itself were also turned.

All this was to be developed (and is developing) through a series of trials, evaluations and modifications undertaken in the light of results and teacher feedback.

It is also worth noting that the project staff are adopting rules that are somewhat different from those of other Ministry officials. Recognizing that the success of the endeavour depends on the good will, cooperation and commitment of the teachers themselves, the characteristically 'official mien' has given way to a more comradely one. That this role is welcomed and valued is often testified to voluntarily by the teachers and principals involved.

Evaluation
The third matter for discussion is the assessment of effectiveness of the curriculum – evaluation. Always a difficult and tricky business, in the present experiment, evaluation includes evaluation at input, process and output stages. With the six schools and 30 teachers remaining relatively constant during the initial preparation phase, the objectives are to ensure that (i) the curriculum materials are logically consistent with the idea of an integrated curriculum; (ii) their use in practice coincides with the original integrated conception; (iii) they work, in that teachers do what they are expected to and understand what they are doing; (iv) the direct cognitive effects are positive and the results show learning gains in the expected directions; (v) the side effects (or at least those thought to be important) are also positive, in that pupil and teachers like the work, and parents and the public generally approve and (vi) the teachers, having internalized the principles, can proceed to develop their own programmes giving due regard to the circumstances facing them at the time.

The prospect of change

It is appropriate to begin this final section of this chapter with three obviously self-justifying quotations from the keynote address 'Sustainability of Change in Education', given by Professor Awang Had Salleh to a Bernard van Leer Foundation Seminar on early childhood education in 1977.

'Change may be regressive or progressive, planned or unplanned, beneficial or harmful. This is true of social change in general.

'One characteristic of change in education is that its effects, be they positive or negative, are not immediately felt.

'The implication of this fact is twofold. First, it makes educational administrators and planners feel that everything is all right. There is a danger that the educationists in administration and planning will adopt an attitude of taking things for granted. Second, it makes the non-educationists in administration and planning feel that education is not a highly specialized discipline requiring special professional know-how because any mistakes in planning and change are not likely to invite dramatic public outcry since education, unlike medicine, security or economy, does not have an emergency or urgency feature in it.'

If we start with Professor Awang Had Salleh's caution about the possibility that change can be regressive or progressive, and add to it the stark fact that much of the future cannot be foretold, then it becomes apparent that any decision to act becomes an act of faith. So does a decision not to act. The question at the heart of this chapter, then, is to what extent some of the uncertainty about the future can be reduced so that the possible consequences of acting or not acting may become that much clearer. It thus addresses the fundamental dilemma to face the Ministry and the Government in 1980 when the decision will be taken.

It would be true to say that at other times and in other places, when other governments have been faced with similar problems, the decisions are usually made on other than educational grounds – usually political and/or economic. But in this case the Ministry has made what may reasonably be seen as a *political* commitment to base its decision on educational grounds. Nonetheless, it would be unreasonable to imagine that economic and political contingencies will not play a part. If the cost of the reform were to be excessive or if particular groups in society were to be alienated, then it might be unwise to base the decision on purely educational grounds.

What this implies, then, is that the educational justification for the extension of the project should itself be a politically sensitive one. That is, it should either address itself to matters that are likely to have political and economic ramifications, or the political and economic implications of the undertaking should be pointed out as far as possible.

Justification for change
Where, then, does one start? Presumably with the fundamental decision that a certain kind of curriculum change is desirable. There seem to be strong face value arguments for moving towards a curriculum that has its bases in understanding rather than the acquisition of information, in integrated knowledge rather than isolated facts, in pupil-motivated learning

rather than teacher-prompted learning. But the arguments are basically economic development arguments (and as such are politically appealing). Their implication is that this kind of view of education is more conducive to the inculcating of enterprise, initiative, ingenuity and self-reliance, which in turn will accelerate the kinds of activity that will yield an increasing economic return – individually and nationally. The implicit model is clearly a Western-Anglo-Saxon one, finding its major justification in the United States, the United Kingdom, etc. It is not quite the way that the French would make their educational interpretation, nor, one imagines, the Germans, the Japanese or the Swiss, and certainly not the Chinese or the Russians.

The point is that there is implicit in the curriculum approach being employed – as there must be in any curriculum approach – a particular view of man in society. This particular view does happen to coincide with one of the views prevailing in some Western countries. In those countries it is currently thought to be a view that as well as describing reality, does it viably *and* desirably. To this extent it has become, for them, a self-fulfilling prophecy. Its consequences are self-evident – they believe.

That such should be the case and that the Malaysian reform appears to have 'outside' overtones are neither necessarily good nor bad. The reasons for raising the point here, though, are three-fold. First, it is reasonable to expect that the search for national identity in Malaysia will lead ultimately, if it has not already done so, to a (healthy) scepticism of things foreign and to the desire for an indigenous model. Hand in hand with that will come the temptation to reject the alien simply because it is alien, thus running the risk of failing to exploit it for whatever it may be worth locally. This leads to the second point, that accepting one apparently foreign transplant does not necessarily mean that the whole plantation has to be made exotic too. The third point, and perhaps it is worth keeping to the last analogy, is that not all climates and soils constitute environments appropriate for foreign transplants. Is it the case, then, that the diverse cultures of Malaysia may not be receptive to the particular curriculum if it is seen to be too alien?

There are many implications that follow from raising these three points. They bear both on the general issue of national aims and the specific issue of educational development.

Because it is beyond the mandate of the IIEP project to do otherwise, let us accept without question the curriculum in the form that it has taken and continues to take, turning our attention to the problems of its development and absorption into the system.

There does, however, seem to be an advantage in recognizing its affinity not in content, but in strategy and character, with American-Western practice – for two reasons. First, if the curriculum is likely to attract prejudiced attack *because* it is foreign, then a logic for its defence needs to be arrived at. Second, because it *is* a transplant, due caution needs to be observed over what else is thought necessary to bring with it. The most important issue in this respect may well be what is regarded as an appropriate form of evaluation.

Evaluation: in broad perspective

Given that there are many publics to be served by this reform – pupils, teachers, principals, parents, local communities, the Ministry, the Government and the nation – the issues to be faced are which of those publics should the evaluation serve and, therefore, what terms are acceptable to *them*. This, as anyone who has but stumbled on the Anglophone literature of evaluation will appreciate, constitutes a virtual hornets' nest. There are, it seems, 'clinical models', 'agricultural models', 'anthology models', 'anthropological models', 'phenomenological models', 'ethnographic models' and 'performance models', to name a few. There are various schools of thought represented by the famous – who agree and beg to disagree strenuously – Tyler, Bloom and Popham, Connant and Kerr; Smith, Parlett and Hamilton, and Stake; Stufflebeam and Lessinger; Campbell and Stanley; Coleman, Mosteller and Moynihan; Scriven; Levin and Wolf. All have their particular advantages and disadvantages, or 'risks and payoffs' as Stake puts it.

All of which leads to the reasonable question: how much evaluation is enough in Malaysia for Malaysian purposes? And what kind of evaluation is likely to be appropriate for what purposes?

The answer to the major question of evaluation hangs in part on the extent to which the curriculum materials are to become sacrosanct. The more they are to be made 'teacher-proof', thus prescribing and defining what the teacher shall do, the more important it is to reduce the extent to which the teacher may exercise discretion and initiative. And this implies complicated testing procedures that ensure that all the ways in which misinterpretation might occur are forestalled. Such an intent, however, would be rather inconsistent with the intention held for the pupils – to increase *their* initiative and motivation.

If, then, the intention is to provide a well worked-out but illustrative framework within which teachers may exercise a certain amount of independence of action, the materials can be produced according to somewhat looser specifications, but it becomes important for teachers to appreciate the principles behind their teaching. The evaluation then ought to pay particular attention to the teachers' understanding of curriculum making, their attitudes towards the task, and whether or not the consequential demands on their time are reasonable or not.

But for teachers to become familiar with such a skill and competent in it will take time – time, it might be added, that is available to a far greater extent to the laboratory school teachers than the pilot school teachers. However, because the work and attitudes of the laboratory school teachers are likely to improve, and *because*, as part of an experiment, attention is focused on them, it would seem advisable to give the matter of pilot school teachers particular attention.

Apparently, one of the reasons for the present success of the 'Improved Curriculum' project is the degree, intensity and kind of care and attention given the teachers by the Curriculum Development Centre project staff.

Clearly, it will be extremely difficult to sustain a similar guidance system with the pilot school teachers and virtually impossible with the larger teaching force beyond, should national implementation follow.

However, it is likely that the ingenious device of using principals in the training process will show added benefits here, provided the principal is given recognition (and perhaps reward) for the extra work entailed. The use of the position and authority of the principal may have the desirable effect of making the project a school-based one. Also, by gaining the support of the most influential person in that setting, it should avoid, as reforms often do not, leaving the principal in ignorance of what his newly trained teachers are doing, and it should also take advantage of existing (power) structures to protect the innovation. This suggests that the important tasks for the principal with respect to the teachers and the curriculum are: (i) to understand the new method; (ii) to have an appreciation of how to teach it and (iii) to know what follow-up (and trouble-shooting) procedures to adopt. In addition, however, if research is correct (and not just Western research at that), the principals will need to develop (probably new) insights into how the innovations will be likely to affect their schools as institutions and the necessity to establish a network of mutually committed people *throughout* the school to act in quick support and defence of the innovation.

It would be easy, but possibly an error, to assign to principals the next task that would need to be covered, maintaining an appropriate liaison with parents and community with respect to the reform. It may be that principals can do it alone – and the evaluation might well probe to find out. But the point of greatest friction and possibly the most intricate form of 'resistance', or rather caution, will probably be found at the community-school interface when (and if) the innovation is seen to be at odds with local values, attitudes and beliefs. More than likely, principals will need much support from educational officials directly as well as indirectly (via radio and TV). If the message is reinforced further from different quarters, say other ministries, politicians, influential citizens, etc, it is much more likely to become acceptable.

To omit such a step on the assumption that communities will readily acquiesce to high level decisions made on their behalf and that teachers will concur out of professional loyalty (though one objective critic of the project unhesitatingly volunteered her own commitment to it should she be required to give it) would be to take an unnecessary risk. It would seem better to use the authority of the authorities to testify publicly to the reasons for and benefits to be derived from the new approach.

What does this add to the evaluation task? What else needs to be assessed in addition to curriculum development aspects?

(i) Can principals be 'trained' to act as in-service teacher trainers themselves and will they do it?
(ii) Can schools cope with the innovation – can the teachers in the first three standards teach it, and can the rest of the school accept and support the innovation?

(iii) Can parents become supportive of the innovation or, if not, can they nonetheless accept it without opposition or disquiet?
(iv) Can the education *system* as a whole absorb the innovation to its own advantage? In other words, are the institutional structures and systems of reward and recognition such that the new innovation can 'fit in'?

In order to generate further confidence in the ultimate success of the project, then, it would seem that the following are needed:

(i) Convincing demonstrations of the *propriety* of the curriculum. This will need to be shown in terms that are acceptable to the respective audiences. It *may* be that the innovation's propriety can be demonstrated to some audiences convincingly by statistical-experimental evaluation. It is more likely, however, that most, if they are not to be exposed to a kind of academic sleight of hand, will need a different kind of evidence. Such demonstrations, then, should be tailored in sympathy with the circumstances in which those audiences find themselves and the kind of concerns that they might have (legitimately) over the reform. For example, pupils may fear for their academic qualifications, teachers for their status or workload, principals for the displeasure of the parents, parents for their own values about education, politicians their political popularity, etc. In this respect, one of the headmasters of one of the laboratory schools has himself become convinced about the new curriculum and has succeeded in conveying his sense of excitement to parents because of some interesting evidence before his own eyes. Last year the first of the pupils who had gone through the (initially sketchy) programme (and even now the laboratory schools are only employing it two days a week), sat the end-of-school-year standard five tests. The results were dramatically better than previous years. Pupils who had transferred to other schools in order to avoid the programme showed no such improvement.

Here it is perhaps worth making the point again that the 'Improved Curriculum' project is but one of a number being undertaken by the Curriculum Development Centre. It is possible that some of these have something to contribute to each other. Cross-linking and mutual exchanges would seem to be potentially useful. For example, some of the furniture designed for the 'Improved Curriculum' project looks to be not only appropriate for other projects, but also more cost-effective than existing, less useful furniture provided.

(ii) Convincing demonstrations of the *viability* of the curriculum. This will need to be demonstrated not only in terms of educational effectiveness, but probably also in terms of the logic of the link between education and development, and education and national identity. It will clearly have to be demonstrated in economic terms. At the moment most of the costs are being borne by project funds (partly from Unicef), while some come out of the operating budget of the Curriculum Development Centre. At the time of writing, although the structure for implementation of such a reform has been established within the Ministry, the cost of it has not come into consideration. Fairly clearly, implementation costing is a complicated business. To produce the materials in quantity and on time, to distribute them to set up the in-service training schedule, to make allowances for plant, equipment, salaries, etc, and to coordinate them all into a coherent and effectively managed and supervised plan, is no small task. Some relatively simplistic estimation of implementation costs at this stage is likely to be valuable if only to confirm that the implementation of the curriculum in its present form will not prove prohibitively expensive.

(iii) Subsequently, a careful analysis of the immediate consequences of the reform might well be worth while. The effects it is having on the various publics could give valuable insights on progress and prospects pending an assessment of longer-term effects. That task will be formidable, partly because of its nature, partly because it has been attempted so rarely in education. While a comprehensive 'systems approach' to education that purports to map its complicated territory accurately and in detail is well beyond us at the moment, the systems principle nonetheless applies. The education system has various parts that, in interacting with each other, also affect each other's operation. The education system also has effects throughout society and society has effects on the operation of the education system. Sooner or later we find out about some of them, usually with dismay. In the interest of finding out more sooner and, it is hoped, without dismay, it will be useful to try to gauge the points at which the impact will occur.

Future prospects

What then is the future of the project for 'The Development of an Improved Curriculum for the First Three Years of the Malaysian Primary Schools'? As an *experiment* its fate is secure – up to 1980. As an experiment it has already produced curriculum materials that appear very satisfactory and certainly indicate that current textbooks should profit from substantial modification, if not replacement. As substitutes for those textbooks themselves, though, it is not yet clear how they will be used, whether they will be liked and indeed if they are effective. On face value it would be very hard to imagine that they would not make very good successors to their textbook ancestors. And if the decision had to be taken now, on educational grounds alone, the indications are sufficiently good to warrant their adoption as better than the existing alternative. But the decision does not have to be taken yet and there is still time to gain further evaluative information – which will, of course, turn out to be less than was desired – it always is. By then, too, some vitally important cost information should have been gained and, as well, there will be additional information available on the economic and political status of the nation. Whether or not the resulting *mélange* of circumstances will yield a 'go' or 'no-go' decision, it would be unwise to judge at the moment – although it might be possible to come to some conclusions about the consequences of either kind of decision.

Thumbs down

If the decision were taken not to proceed with implementation, at least in the meantime, the immediate consequences are likely to be relatively slight. The Ministry may, on the one hand, be criticized for being timid and perhaps reactionary, but on the other praised for being deliberate and careful. Those anxious for faster social change will be disappointed; those with a more conservative frame of mind will be pleased. Presumably, too, such a decision will result in short-term economies in educational spending. If the education profession or, for that matter, any of the groups involved with the reform were enthusiastic over its prospects, they will be dismayed and may suffer some loss of morale. Predictably, those closest to the experiment will be most affected. Such an enterprise cannot be mounted without commitment, involved effort and devotion. A measure of disillusionment is to be expected.

However, *not* to proceed might serve to delay the development of the education system itself – a consequence that would not be in the long-term interests of the country or, perhaps, the political decision makers themselves.

Clearly, the brief set of conclusions above is based on the assumption that either the curriculum reform itself would, if implemented, prove beneficial or the very act of undertaking the reform itself would be so. In Professor Awang Had Salleh's terms, the change would have been progressive and positive. Of course, if it is not implemented, no one will ever know, but the critics of that decision will be able to argue aggressively that it would have been, and the supporters will be forced to argue defensively that it would not.

Thumbs up

In the event that the decision were taken to implement the reform, there would be many more implications and, sooner or later, the evidence would accumulate to indicate some of the ways in which the decision might be considered right or wrong – a threat or a promise, depending on the kind of results achieved.

In the event of continuation, however, there would be a great number of mechanical, organizational and logistic consequences of the decision to proceed that need only be touched on briefly here. Estimates would have to be prepared, plans drawn up, logistics worked out and costs calculated for the plant, equipment, personnel and communications systems required. That undertaking would be complex, time-consuming and have its own internal logistics and cost needs.

However, there are other implications of a social and educational nature that merit consideration.

To implement such a curriculum scheme on a national scale means that the interests (perhaps vested interests) of many people are likely to be affected. It is imperative, if Havelock and Huberman's analysis of the research is valid, to undertake a very careful, systematic and persistent dialogue with the various interest groups in order to avoid opposition (perhaps even fatal opposition). Usually, it is at this point that most innovations fail. Unfortunately there are very few precedents which indicate what should be done. The one point that does come out consistently, though, is that such a process would be delicate, time-consuming and absolutely essential.

Educationally, there is another consequence of considerable importance. The reform aims at the first three years of schools. The selection of that target group would find strong psychological vindication in the literature on child development. It could also be justified on pragmatic grounds. The writing of early stage education curricula is somewhat easier than the writing of later-stage curricula. As well, as other countries have demonstrated, it is easier to induce change at that level of the education system than higher up. After a while, too, the effects gradually filter upwards.

But, given the implementation of the curriculum for the first three years of schooling, with its new approaches to teaching and learning, what then?

The long-term objective is to have the newly desired education qualities found in mature school *leavers*. How is this to happen if the rest of the system sustains its older practices? What, then, should be the interface between the new procedure and the old? Is it to be expected that new curricula will be developed to keep pace with the graduating pupils? That would be logical, but if it is needed then an early start would be desirable. After all, at the beginning of the next academic year, the Standard 3 experimental students will be back to the old style (a circumstance that would warrant researching). In other words, the long-term implications of *beginning* such a curriculum would need examination in detail if the ultimate objective of widespread implementation is to be accomplished.

In this respect there is another issue that was hinted at in the early pages of this chapter: the discussion of possible effects of the old on the new and the new on the old — whether the effects would be socially integrative or disintegrative. It is highly predictable that in one way or another, overtly or covertly, old teaching practices will find a way of prevailing, at least to some extent. Adaptations will be made in the new curricula by teachers trained in the old style so that they can utilize their past skills, economize on time and effort, and remain with activities that have brought them comfort and reward in the past. It is also predictable that some social groups will oppose a curriculum reform that requires teachers to violate their expectations for the 'proper' role of the teacher. If they combine forces it is possible that old-style teachers and 'conservative' communities can constitute formidable opposition to change. If the attempt to change is too rapid and too comprehensive, that opposition is likely to escalate.

Accordingly, there may be a good case to be made for a phased introduction of the new curriculum, not only by one level at a time, but within levels as well. This would mean the old and new roles would exist for a while side by side in the same school and, more significantly, in the same teachers, thus increasing each one's range of available alternative skills. Furthermore, this would allow for the fact that teachers differ, sometimes substantially, from one another, and will make progress at different rates. Consequently, at any one time one should expect to see quite a diversity of development stages evidenced throughout the profession.

Such a suggestion leads to a third kind of decision that might be taken: the decision for partial implementation, but with momentum accelerating as the reform takes hold and its utility and feasibility become apparent.

While these thoughts arise out of the way the 'Improved Curriculum' project has developed so far, they are put forward rather tentatively. It is not within the mandate of either the curriculum project, or for that matter the IIEP project, to presume to make recommendations. Their mandate is to raise issues that appear likely to be of significance in the evolution of the curriculum project, and, having done so, to conjecture about some of the possible consequences.

The incomplete data we have at the moment have prompted the points we have made. Some more are yet to come, but because they are general points that have something in common with the other studies in the IIEP project, they are best kept until the concluding chapter.

The New Zealand educational system is in a state of transition but, unlike the other countries in this book, a state of gradual transition largely free of the influence of any relatively recent and dramatic national events. As the system has evolved it has been toying with an ever increasing amount of decentralization – but what might be called 'guided decentralization'. The next chapter provides an illustration of what can happen under the intriguing circumstances when a central Department of Education (Ministry) engages in a somewhat democratic approach to planning and then, having given its blessing to an enterprise, leaves the initiative firmly in the hands of a specific school.

Because the New Zealand innovation as yet only involves one school, the chapter adopts a somewhat more myopic perspective than has been the case in the other chapters. It takes the reader into the school setting and, using a researcher's perspective, provides an interpretation of what transpired. This micro-perspective, however, stands in nice contrast to the more macro-perspectives of the other chapters and provides the timely reminder that, in the last resort, it is in the school itself that qualitative innovations meet with triumph – or disaster.

Chapter 7

New Zealand: Institutional Inertia

If one had a supply of shovels, a sturdy insulated suit, some fortitude and the urge to start digging a hole about a hundred kilometres north of Madrid, eventually the hole should come out in New Zealand. Probably the first thing to fall into the hole 'down under' would be a sheep, because there are 60 million of them – 20 for every person. The sheep are not irrelevant to the present study of innovation, because they contribute substantially to New Zealand's overseas earnings and their well-being and the state of the world food market does affect how much educational investment is possible.

At the time the New Zealand innovation was first under consideration, the economic situation seemed healthy and investment in education was running at an all-time high. With immediate anxieties few, the time was right to view the future a little ambitiously. While conditions in the intervening years have changed, and not for the better, the situation in 1974 was characterized by optimism rather than pessimism, and confidence and assurance rather than resignation and hesitation.

A problem

In such a climate of optimism, a relatively small (but not insignificant) practical educational problem surfaced. It had to do with the speed with which new secondary schools might be built. The reason was simple. Over the years the lead time from production of plans for a school to the completion of the building had gradually increased. That fact, coupled with inflation and the year-by-year finance-estimating procedures adopted by the New Zealand Department of Education (Ministry), meant that building costs were coming to exceed estimates – sometimes quite spectacularly. The problem then was, how can new secondary schools be built faster? Predictably, such a simply stated problem did not turn out to be quite so simple to deal with, and this was partly due to the prevailing feelings of confidence in the future and to a burgeoning hope for an even better education system. That 'small' architectural problem was turned into a quite sizeable educational opportunity. Instead of just focusing on the logistic difficulties of plant design, development and supply, the opportunity was taken to ask a much more fundamental question – what should the school of the future be like?

169

This present chapter will attempt to examine how this happened and the consequences of retranslating the problem in this way. To do so it is appropriate and necessary to describe briefly the circumstances that gave rise to the initial 'small' problem.

In New Zealand's education system, which manages at one and the same time to be both centralized and decentralized, responsibility for building and replacing state secondary schools (of which there were, at the time of the experiment, 241)[1] falls on the State. The central Department of Education has a Schools Development Section that produces plans and specifications which are then translated into reality by another ministry, the Ministry of Works, operating through its field staff and local contractors. In earlier days, when school rolls were increasing rapidly and the main problem was to provide enough classrooms to meet the demand, the Department of Education had adopted the procedure of producing prototype or master plans which were then used throughout the country with only minor local adaptations. Over the years, various prototype secondary school designs had been produced with the latest, the S68 design, appearing in 1969. This design, it should be noted, rested on the assumption that the ideal school should be based on subject specialization. In the main, rooms reflected the needs of specific subjects and specialist teachers were duly ensconced therein. The students came and went according to the dictates of the timetable.

By 1974, when building delays were becoming worrisome, what was needed, it was thought, was a new 'delivery system' that would speed up the production process and save money. The architects, in searching for a solution, were toying with the idea of using a modular construction method that would enable sections of the building to be prefabricated at one spot, and thence transported to sites for relatively easy and quick erection. The architects concerned were specialists in educational buildings, seconded from the Ministry of Works. They were domiciled in the Department of Education and worked hand in glove with the educational professionals in the Schools Development Section whose task it was to provide the 'conceptual *educational* component' for the architects to turn into bricks and mortar, or more typically, timber and corrugated iron.

For reasons that are perhaps incidental, maybe even coincidental, this organizational structure and the way it has operated has resulted in a degree of creative tension in the Section that has led to some very interesting and practical architectural solutions to educational problems. Over the years, the Schools Development Section had come to perform a number of singularly important functions. In one way or another it had become a kind of repository of educational wisdom relevant to the design and use of school buildings. Its information had been gleaned from the literature, overseas research and experimentation, and indirectly and informally from the reactions, prejudices and opinions of the teachers in the schools (and to some extent parents and even pupils). This wisdom, accumulated, digested,

---

[1] There were 109 independent schools as well.

reinterpreted and adapted to the peculiarities of the New Zealand scene, was used to provide the basis for dialogue and decision making within the Section. It should be noted in passing that although practitioner opinion found its way into the councils of the Schools Development Section, there were no *official* channels and mechanisms for it to do so. The right of consumer opinion to be represented was not officially recognized.

The problem redefined

When the building issue was being worried over by the Schools Development Section, the Director of Secondary Education seized on the original architectural problem and converted it into an educational opportunity. In violation of the traditions of the educational bureaucracy and of territorial imperatives, the unsuggestible was suggested. The idea was mooted that, before the Section made an attempt to change the design of secondary schools, they should ask other educationists what they thought the school should be like.

Perhaps because the time was right, perhaps because of the prevailing sense of optimism, the idea was found acceptable. Authorized by the Director General and sanctioned by the Minister of Education, the idea then got translated into a plan and the plan into action. A seven-day residential conference was organized and to it were invited (i) a mixture of educationists who were thought to be able to address themselves to the problem of 'tomorrow's school', and (ii) some of the architects and developers who would later have the responsibility of preparing plans.

Towards a solution

Accordingly, some 25 people duly assembled at a relatively inaccessible but very pleasant conference centre in the country. Most were, it must be admitted, unquestionably educationists, but within that narrow definition quite diverse. There were senior officials of the Department of Education (the Administrative, Curriculum and Schools Development Sections), the President of the secondary teachers union (the Post-Primary Teachers Association), a number of principals and deputy principals of secondary schools (one primary school principal), primary and secondary school inspectors (also in force) and representatives from the universities and teachers' colleges. The Director of Secondary Education presided over the meeting.

Predictably, many of the participants knew each other and had in the past been either protagonists or antagonists.

The mandate given them was straightforward: 'Produce a professional educational brief so that the architects can design a school for the (not too distant) future'. The group was asked to imagine, in the light of their own experiences, knowledge and insights, what tomorrow's school would be like.

Three constraints were put on the group. First, they had to reach consensus. Second, unless and until consensus had been reached, escape was impossible. Third, in no way, shape or form was the group to try to attempt to take architectural aspects into account. The job was to provide the *educational* blueprint. It was up to the architects to re-interpret that into architectural terms. It was they who had to take note of the constraints of materials, space, construction costs and the like, *not* the educationists.

The original problem – of how to build schools faster – in undergoing transmutation into the new problem had become infinitely more difficult and challenging – and fundamental.

It is unlikely that the full story of that conference will ever be told – although some of the incidents will be a long time in disappearing from institutional memory. Suffice it to say that the debate was long (sometimes into the small hours of the morning), sometimes heated, nearly always animated and, for those who took part in it, immensely rewarding. At the end of the seven days, consensus was reached and escape the participants did, but, though exhausted, reluctantly.

The deliberations of the conference were written up and were given to the architects. Subsequently they also appeared in refined form in a departmental publication, *Secondary Schools for Tomorrow: A new approach to design and construction*. Some of the flavour of the results may be gained from the rather free summary given below.

Educational terms of reference

Tomorrow's secondary school should:

(i) constitute an environment in which the school would become a 'caring and sharing' institution, responsive to the educational and social needs of its (various) inhabitants;

(ii) enter into a give-and-take relationship with its community, serving the community directly and indirectly, and employing the community's diverse resources in the interests of effective education;

(iii) thus provide a congenial setting in which children, teachers, parents and others can, in their mutual educational interests, cooperate;

(iv) accordingly, have an environment suitable for adults and children to undertake individual work, small group work and large group work as desired and needed;

(v) be, in so far as the environment allows, conducive to feelings of 'spontaneity and belonging – the antithesis of boredom, regimentation and alienation';

(vi) enable each pupil to 'develop insights, knowledge and experience so that he can understand himself and the people he lives and works with in both the smaller and larger community, and to make the most of what he can do personally that is unique and vital to him. Dignity and self-esteem are essential to every human being.'

Obviously, the ideas expressed above are not new. Nor are they phrased with great precision; this makes them overly vulnerable to semantic attack. They are rather excessive, but, as ideals, they were consistent with the expansive view prevailing at the time. Their advent came, be it noted, just before economic problems brought a retrenchment perspective back into fashion and just before the educational performance controversies in the United States gave rise to the 'back to basics' movement. Had the publication been written a year or so later, the 'professional brief' might have been more vocal about academic and scholastic achievement, vocational education and transition from school to work. But in those days, those things were largely taken for granted.

Clearly, the kind of generalizations listed above would have provided a quite inadequate basis for architectural decision making. And indeed the main thrust of the week-long conference had been to spell out the implications of pursuing such a philosophy to its *practical* conclusions. The architects had much more to work on. For example, one working group at the conference produced a detailed array of tasks and roles resulting from a systematic application of the question 'In the school of the future, who will do what, how, when, where, why, with what, and to and with whom?' Another, influenced by ethology, came up with statements of territorial desiderata. Another, pursuing a social-psychological line, specified conditions needed for effective (and affective) social interaction etc.

An architectural solution

Armed with the resulting piles of paper, the members of the Schools Development Section retired. Some 12 months later they produced the results of their labour: a set of preliminary plans of the new school, duly and faithfully reflecting the sentiments of the conference, but also adjusted to the constraints within which *they* had to work – space per pupil, materials, cost, etc. At a reunion of the original conference group, convened specifically to review and critique the design, the work was acclaimed, the architects were rightly congratulated on the job well and ingeniously done, and appetites whetted for the advent of the first prototype. To mark the occasion, the new-type school was given a name that sought to symbolize the togetherness of the two dominant cultures in new Zealand – those of European stock and those of Polynesian. 'Whanau House', it was called: 'whanau' meaning in its simplest interpretation 'extended family', and 'house' having something in common with the old English school house system. Despite the fact that advice had been sought from experts on Maori language and Maoritanga (Maori culture), there were times subsequently when the choice of name was regretted.

The school was to consist of several units. Howarth (1977) puts it concisely:

'The philosophy behind the new design was that, irrespective of the total roll of a school, it was desirable to group pupils in smaller numbers. A home base, called a 'Whanau House', was proposed, which would provide an environment for 250 pupils. It consisted of five rooms and two seminar rooms grouped around a common-room, together with a resource room and a staff planning area. The plan was to be as flexible as possible to allow for any type of school organization.'

A completed Whanau House school would comprise no more than five Whanau House blocks. There were to be as well two administration blocks, the first containing the offices of senior administrators and professional staff, presumably the system's 'intelligence HQ', while the other contained offices for service personnel, resource (preparation) rooms, guidance and health-care rooms, etc – presumably the system's 'operations centre'. There were to be two arts and crafts blocks, a practical block, a library, a gymnasium, auditorium, drama and dance block, and a boiler house (see Figures 5, 6 and 7).

Undoubtedly, in the New Zealand context, the most striking characteristics of the plan were:

(i) that after years of debate over the optimum size of schools, it was recognized that a maximum limit could not be set and that what was needed was an evolutionary design that would allow the school to 'grow' (and perhaps shrink) as conditions warranted;
(ii) the deliberate anticipation of *future* building needs so that sites could be developed in an orderly, systematic and *coherent* fashion, not, as conventionally, 'like Topsy';
(iii) the use of a modular construction method that looked as if it might solve the initial problem of erection delays and costs;
(iv) the incorporation of a special educational philosophy into building design – on the expectation that while the building could not dictate how good education should proceed, it should nevertheless provide a setting which would permit it.

When the original meeting was held to produce the architects' brief, the Schools Development Section was adamant that the educationists should not concern themselves with the limitations within which the architects had to work – costs, area per person and the like. Yet they themselves had to give due regard to such constraints, and in doing so had apparently succeeded in providing much more 'living' space than in the past. Their solution was ingenious. They had, in effect, eliminated corridor space – a solution that was permitted by the educational philosophy to which the planning group had subscribed. That philosophy, which favoured organizational groups of no more than 250 pupils, required the building to be a 'home' or 'house' for them. The architects' solution not only provided a

New Zealand: Institutional Inertia

Figure 5: *Whanau House school*

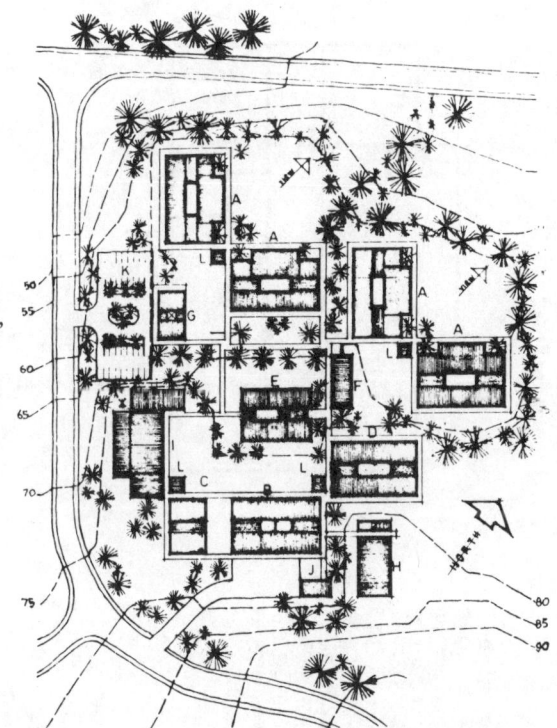

The site layout design is not intended to suggest a 'standard' form of arrangement. Its purpose is to illustrate the degree of flexibility which can be achieved with the new block forms.

KEY

A WHANAU HOUSE
B ARTS & CRAFTS I
C ARTS & CRAFTS II
D PRACTICAL BLOCK
E LIBRARY
F ADMINISTRATION I
G ADMINISTRATION II
H GYMNASIUM
I AUDITORIUM, DRAMA & MUSIC BLOCK
J BOILER HOUSE
K PARKING
L TOILET BLOCKS

175

Figure 6: *Block A – the Whanau House classroom block*

The Whanau House is entered via the Commons which is a large general-purpose room. It also acts as a main circulation area and has provision for pupils' lockers. Associated with the entrance are the property office with its small refreshment counter, the Head of Department's office and a small interview room. On either side of the Commons area are classrooms, seminar rooms and a staff room. The long side of the Commons is bounded by a classroom, activities room, resources area, preparation area and a laboratory. Between these rooms and the Commons is an internal court which permits cross ventilation and acts as an acoustic buffer while providing a visual amenity for teachers and pupils.

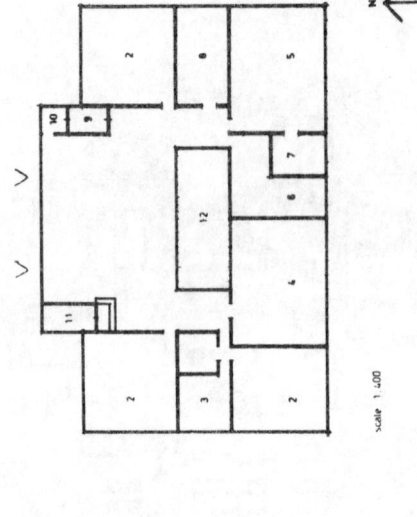

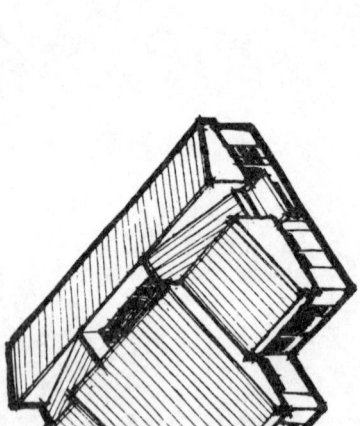

scale 1:400

Whanau House

KEY

1. Commons areas
2. Classroom
3. Seminar rooms
4. Activities room
5. Laboratory
6. Resources room
7. Preparation room
8. Staff room
9. Head of Department
10. Interview room
11. Property and snack bar
12. Internal court

Figure 7: *Whanau House sections and elevations*

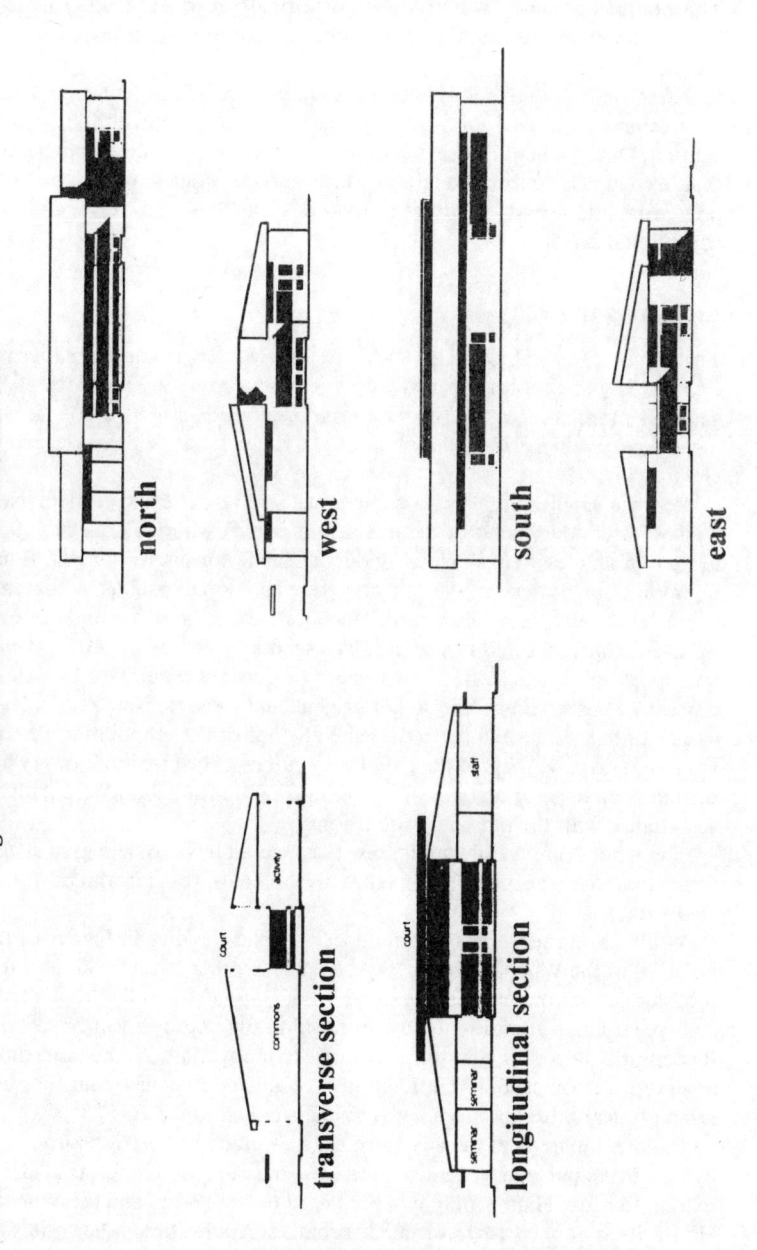

large 'commons' for students, but grouped the teaching spaces around it. This not only did away with the need for formalized traffic routes, but also helped eliminate the characteristic institutional atmosphere that corridors seem to generate.

After one or two mildly anxious moments for those concerned, the Government approved the plan in principle, but decided to proceed with caution. One Whanau House unit only was to be placed in an existing school that needed extra accommodation. This was to be done mainly in order to test production and building procedures, but also to 'evaluate' the educational effects.

From plan to reality

The first unit was to be built at Auckland[1] and located in a nearby suburb at Penrose High School. It opened with due public ceremony in March 1977, some 14 months after the first sod was turned (not exactly a sod, it was located partly on existing tennis courts, the rugby fields being too sacred to violate).

Penrose High School is to some extent more or less typical of New Zealand secondary schools in that it is a school without extremes. It is located in an area that is neither unduly affluent nor disadvantaged. It has no more nor fewer of the social and educational problems that are characteristically found elsewhere. The pupils are by general standards well behaved, courteous and responsive. The school has quite a good academic and sporting record. It has something of a cultural reputation as well (it possesses a substantial collection of original and valuable New Zealand artworks, and it is a testimony to the general ethos of the school that, though always on display, none of the paintings, sculptures or pieces of pottery has sustained damage of any kind). The ethnic mix in the school is roughly in accordance with the national proportions.

The school on several counts, however, would have to be regarded as a better-than-average school, quite attractive to go to, teach in and be associated with.

While in one sense this would appear to load the dice in favour of the 'success' of the Whanau House 'experiment', in other senses it did not. It is predictable that any reasonably good school would be willing to give fair and constructive attention to any proposition for improvement or reform. By definition also, it ought to be receptive to innovation. At the same time, however, a good school, confident in its status and achievement, has less reason to want (and perhaps need) to change than do others.

Initially the news of the advent of the new block was warmly supported by the Principal and generally created a measure of enthusiasm in the school. Penrose High School was privileged to be selected and the Whanau House itself looked to have much promise. At the time when the first

[1] New Zealand's largest city – 750,000 population.

negotiations were undertaken between the sponsoring Department of Education and the School Authorities, the prospect was exciting, and there was no reason for doubt or uncertainty.

Summary

At this point in the saga there is need to step aside from daily events and attempt a résumé, in preparation for a shift in reporting stance.

In response to an identifiable and practical problem, the Department of Education, acting with imagination, had identified a more basic problem – the problem behind the problem, as it were. And they had set out to solve it. The mechanism they used was to call in experts, mostly from the establishment itself, and entirely from the educational fraternity. It should be noted (without prejudice to future conclusions) that other interested parties were not included. There were no 'independent agents' (although the participants were certainly independent-minded and were ostensibly chosen because of it). The community (if that is definable) had no official spokesman, neither did the secondary school Boards of Governors, the parents or the pupils. There are a number of reasons why most, if not all, of these were not invited. One wonders what might have been different if they had been. But even so, there is strong enough support in the literature for at least coming back to this issue of exclusiveness if things do not turn out as well as they might. Nonetheless, the experts produced their professional brief and it was professionally converted into architectural blueprints. The process of consultation employed met with virtually unqualified approval from all involved and, initially, from those who were to be first to put the concrete realization of the plan into educational practice. The designs themselves were also greeted enthusiastically, although there was, it must be admitted, an occasional note of criticism to be heard.

Towards evaluation

Up to the point of building the first Whanau House unit, there were, however, two unresolved issues – whether the building *could* be put to the educational purpose for which it was primarily designed, and, more materialistically, whether it *could* be constructed quickly and at no more expense than its predecessor.

The means and mechanism for undertaking the evaluation of the latter were already established and would be employed as normal procedure. The means for undertaking the former were not. To provide them the Department of Education set up what turned out to be a research confederacy, asking a university to participate. Recognizing that the educational evaluation game is a difficult one (more notable for what is not and cannot be done than for what can be and is done), the terms of reference employed in the contract became 'study'. At the same time the Department agreed that one of its researchers, then on leave from a secondary teachers' college and experienced in classroom research, would be free to devote part of his time to the Whanau House study. The Department also allocated to the task a local secondary inspector of schools who, as a member of the original conference group, had subsequently provided a regular educational liaison with the architects' sector. In addition, because the Principal of the school had already acted to name staff for the new block well before it was completed, it proved possible to gain their cooperation in the research also. The overall result, then, was that a small research network with four sets of partners was set up. Their task was to map the way in which the building was used and to discern the extent to which it provided an environment that was acceptable to staff and students and conducive to effective education. A further subsidiary purpose was to trace the evolution of the Whanau House school from the initial inception of the cooperative planning idea through its trial period and adaptation (if any) to its eventual wider application in the education system (if any). This was to be achieved initially through the seven subprojects. They are:

(i) *The evolution of the Whanau House school:* a descriptive study to trace events and identify problems as they arose during: (a) the initial planning, (b) building and (c) dissemination of the educational concepts entailed.
(ii) *The school we created:* a study describing, from the inside, decisions about the way in which the school was to be organized, run and staffed.
(iii) *Teaching and learning:* an observational study of teaching and learning in the Whanau House, and an investigation of the way in which pupils and teachers 'perceive the reality' of the Whanau House operation.
(iv) *Space-use:* an observational and questionnaire study of the way in which the various locations (or territories) in the Whanau House became defined and used — patterns of access, communication, and the reactions of inhabitants to their environments.
(v) *Educational effects:* a study of the performances of Whanau House pupils compared with the performances of a matched sample in the other part of the school.
(vi) *Impact study:* a study to gauge the impact of the Whanau House on: (a) the rest of the school, (b) the parents and (c) the community.
(vii) *Denouement study:* while the above studies are operationally discrete, their findings are thought likely to be complementary. Accordingly, a final study was planned to draw the threads together and, in this way, provide a three-way 'evaluation' of the Whanau House, viz its functionality, its educational effects and its social impact.

At the time of writing none of the projects, of course, has been completed,[1]

---

[1] This is because the study is ongoing.

although a number have covered quite a lot of ground. Consequently, some of the statements that follow are, at this stage, tentative and rest on first impressions of the data that have been looked at so far.

The course of events

Now we can return to the running account, but with the focus shifting to discernible effects and possible consequences.

While the building of the modules for the school was under way, the principal actors in the drama – the ten teachers – began their work. Meeting often and regularly during their spare time (they were currently undertaking their normal teaching duties, of course), they studied the earlier documents produced on the Whanau House and its philosophy, and began to produce their own. Towards the end of the year they were given a week off to make sure the plans they were developing would be operational.

Now at this stage the point should be made very strongly that, despite the fact that New Zealand secondary schools *do*, almost without exception, gear their efforts towards the requirements of university entrance and therefore operate within a very broadly defined syllabus that specifies a mandatory amount of core and optional subject time, the schools *can* exercise a great deal of discretion over how they do their job. It is a fact that the amount of latitude possible is seldom used fully, but it is also a fact that in the final analysis a teacher teaches what he wishes and how he wishes, and it is very difficult for anyone to say him nay. So the Whanau House teachers were under no obligation to take the Whanau House philosophy from *Secondary Schools for Tomorrow*, and certainly they could not be compelled to do so.

It should also be noted that it has never been a widespread practice to provide *teachers* with very much opportunity at all to engage in concerted policy making and planning – principals, yes; teachers, no.

Educational aims

In the end, the philosophy the teachers worked out for themselves was to some extent like the conference group's. However, there were some differences. For example:

1. The teachers were more preoccupied with 'learning' issues

The teachers in the formulation of their working plans placed particular emphasis on the *individual pupil*, streaming, 'student initiative', 'self-motivation', 'individual study', and pupil 'centredness'. As a logical consequence, each student was expected to fit into the work programme at a *level* commensurate with his own capabilities, and would progress at whatever rate was appropriate to his ability. The work programme itself was to be diverse and varied (to promote interest) and entail some compulsory lectures, but independent work as well.

II. The teachers gave less overt acknowledgement to the need for community-school liaison

It is true to say that, for very understandable reasons, the teachers took their main task to be to teach their pupils. Whatever reference was made to using community resources tended to be desultory and spontaneous rather than systematic and deliberate. (It is true that a visit to a Marae – a Maori tribal meeting place – was discussed at length, but nothing came of it.) Grasping the very sticky nettle of community-school liaison was not regarded as a priority. In all truth, throughout the secondary school system in New Zealand, despite the expression of the best of intentions over a school-community romance (see, for example, the McCombs' Committee Report on Secondary Education), little that is not superficial has been achieved yet.

III. The teachers also gave less emphasis to guidance, that is, in the psychological sense

However, they did talk a great deal about the kind of social climate they would want to create in the Whanau House. This was to be a benign and friendly place with teachers freely accessible. They envisaged the Whanau House's being open earlier and later than was customary in the school. They envisaged spending much of their own 'spare' time (at intervals, lunch time and before and after school) in the public areas and with their pupils.

Some sense of the extent of the effort put into the planning task by the teachers may be gained from reading between the lines of the brief summary above. Even so, the extent of the commitment shown, the self-sacrifice exhibited and the seriousness of purpose evidenced must not be underestimated. The fact that many educational innovations start with similar dedication does not make the display of it in this case any less impressive. Furthermore, the teachers' willingness to cooperate in the research project and the work they subsequently did for it without complaint constitutes a fair indication of the kind of unselfish professionalism that was the hallmark of their whole approach.

Perhaps predictably and understandably, the differences between the *Secondary Schools for Tomorrow* philosophy and the working principles the teachers devised is only one of degree. In New Zealand's homogeneous education system, as in its homogeneous country, marked polarization is unlikely. Seldom are the divergences of opinion, conviction and viewpoint so marked as to invoke violent antagonism – with all the excitement, challenge and frustration that can often be found elsewhere. The usual result is socially bland, but relatively peaceful and predictable.

It so happened that for several months previously, the whole staff of the school had been engaged in an exercise of self-examination and had been taking a long, cool look at the school's own practices and philosophy. The result was that a new philosophy was gradually being formed. Perhaps for this reason, the position the Whanau House teachers took seemed not to be very much at odds with the general stance their colleagues were coming to accept. Indeed, there were grounds for wondering at the time whether or not a Whanau House block was a necessity for such 'reforms' at all. Subsequent events, however, were to lead us to reconsider that first estimation of compatibility and as well our assessment of the effects of the advent of the Whanau House on the rest of the school *and* the rest of the school on the development of the Whanau House.

Initiation

Construction
The contract for the development of the building modules and construction of the Whanau House was let to a local firm as a 'one-off' job — a necessary procedure, but one that could not yield the economies of scale envisaged had many more modules been required. At first, everything proceeded smoothly despite bad weather (and the necessity for a round-the-clock 24-hour 'pour' of the concrete foundation pad). It seemed as if the deadline of 1st February 1977 could be met. Alas, this was not to be. A delay in obtaining a critical building component slowed progress so that the last sub-contracting tasks fell due at the Christmas (summer) break — when virtually the whole of New Zealand closes down for vacation. Momentum slowly picked up afterwards, but nonetheless the official opening was postponed until May — the beginning of the second of the three school terms.

Two problems
The delay had some educational and social consequences. First, some disappointment and (fortunately only temporary) loss of morale occurred among the teachers and pupils selected to be the Whanau House occupants, who, since the beginning of the year, had had to make do with temporary premises. Second, there was time for two misconceptions about the function and nature of the school to surface and create tension. Both arose out of the name 'Whanau House'. On the one hand some parents (mostly Pakeha)[1] jumped to the conclusion that pupils in the Whanau House would be exposed to a new experimental, completely Polynesian education which would be suspect on a number of counts, not the least being that the academic achievement of the children would be placed in jeopardy. On the other hand, some members of the Maori community became exercised over the use of the word 'whanau', which in some of its (several) connotations has deep symbolic significance. The fact that some of this symbolic significance was not appreciated and that some Maori values were being savaged (yet again) led to firm and sometimes impassioned opposition.

> 'Literally, "whanau" means "to give birth" and in fact the Whanau was indeed the birthplace of the larger "hapu" and finally the "iwi". The thing that kept the Whanau together was the blood line. Everyone was related in some way, therefore there was a duty to help other members — this was a common obligation.

[1] The New Zealand term for white men.

'Organization or leadership within the Whanau was a simple affair. The elders took a leading role in decision making, but the most effective form of leadership was by example.

'When major decisions were to be made, a "hui" was called to let everyone take an active part in the decision making. This was not, however, a free-for-all, but there was strict control of who might speak and when. The elders – or Kaumātua – were there to guide the discussion and give counsel. Once the decision had been made – and normally the discussion would continue until some compromise was made – this would be binding on all members of the Whanau.

'Perhaps the main guiding force behind the Whanau is "aroha" – love – if you ever lost this feeling of aroha then perhaps you had reached your time to move on...

'In setting up a Whanau here at Penrose, the just thing to do would be to meet with local Maori elders to seek their permission and advice. It is no good writing a newsletter or putting an advertisement in the paper. You are seeking advice and help so you go to visit these people personally.

'Having met with the elders, the next step is to call a hui where a committee can be set up with several sub-committees to investigate and plan matters concerning the setting up of a Whanau. One of the things to be done will be to find a name for your house. "Whanau House" is meaningless as a term.

'If things are to be done properly then the buildings will be dedicated at the commencement of construction in order to involve the community right from the beginning. This places the buildings under "tapu". When the building is complete there will then be a ceremony of Whakanoa to lift the tapu and open the House officially for use. This function will generally be accompanied by entertainment and feasting...'
(Account from a local Maori)

'First of all the name. Whanau is more than a word to us, it is a concept which we as Maoris hold very dear. We feel that we have made so many concessions that we have almost given away our culture; we have listened to people mispronounce our names and place names; we have made concessions in rituals such as the tangi, to help conform to your society; we have given up our language under the misconception that it will help us to learn to speak English and all in all, when we look at the scales, we find that all the concessions have been made by us. This being so, we now say – NO! to any further concessions concerning those things we have left and hold so dear.

'Despite the prevailing fallacy, Whanau is not just a word or a term to be bandied around, it is part of our remaining culture. If the spirit of Whanau in the Maori sense is not upheld, then I for one can have no part in it and I will have to resist vigorously the morally unjust way in which it seems it will be used.'

(Extract from a paper by a specialist in Maori studies)

The cause of ethnic harmony, it seemed, had not been advanced by the attempt to create a contemporary culturally united concept by melding 'whanau' and 'house'.

The school's reaction was quick and positive – and conventional. Two meetings were called at which explanations were given of how the school was to operate. The fears over academic degeneration were (largely) allayed – certainly to the extent that only four of the 250 pupils offered a place in the Whanau House subsequently withdrew. As well, within the limits of time available to the people involved (but not to the extent that Maori tradition would have required) attempts were made to talk with Maori parents and leaders and to observe some of the conventions. A tapu *was* placed on the site and *was* lifted subsequently. There *was* a ceremonial opening at which Maori elders officiated along with the Minister of Education who observed Maori convention by singing a 'wiata' and delivering an oration in Maori. There *was* a feast – a pakeha-style afternoon tea and later a Maori hangi (and an American-style barbecue). Later again the Whanau House was given its own name, Hinau House. The omens once more were good.

The physical environment

The new block when finished was quite attractive – particularly inside, where the décor and furnishing had been thoughtfully and tastefully composed, but with utility and durability always kept in mind. There was a very nice balance between subdued and earthy browns, fawns and greens, with occasional splashes of bright reds and yellows to complement the considerable amount of wood panelling and the exposed structural beams of the ceiling. The hard-wearing dark brown carpet on the floor of the commons added an air of sumptuousness that belied its functional character. By contrast, the outside appearance of the block seemed somewhat spartan. It looked more functional than aesthetic. However, surrounded by newly planted native trees and grass and concrete courts, in comparison with the last S68 design (not unpleasant itself) the new building was quite striking. It was indeed a new and different type of school environment for New Zealand. Other people seemed to appreciate this fact too, and during the year the Whanau House was besieged by visitors, a state of affairs that soon lost its glamour for those trying to work in it.

To work

Before the school year began, in the interests of the 'experiment', a decision had been taken that the Whanau House population should consist of a 'vertical slice' of the school population:

- 90-100 first-year students selected randomly
- 90-100 second-year students selected randomly
- 50-70 third-year students chosen on the basis of a common course, ie English, maths, science, geography, history and biology.

The pupils selected were to do most of their work in the Whanau House, but nonetheless would retain a measure of contact with the rest of the school, mainly through the taking of 'outside' options, attendance once a week at school assemblies, participation in the School Council and, of course, by informal means. In general, but not exclusively, the teachers were to teach in the Whanau House and not in the rest of the school, but the Whanau House staff would be complemented from time to time by other teachers from the main school. Timetabling in the Whanau House was to be flexible within ordered constraints, and, given the different types of rooms available, the location of classes would be a matter of daily negotiation and decision. Like the building, the curriculum was to be modular – with blocks for subjects and sections of subjects. Advantage had also been taken of the situation to purchase a range and array of new individualized teaching materials appropriate for the proposed courses.

With plans ready at the beginning of the school year, the delay in building had even allowed time for consideration of some potential difficulties that might be lurking over the otherwise clear horizon. The more important ones were listed in a staff circular. They included the possibilities that:

- As a 'special' group, the Whanau House pupils might be subjected to undue pressure to out-perform their not-so-special peers.
- A sense of privilege, even elitism, might develop – both in the Whanau House itself and, more likely and more dangerously, among those on the outside.
- Staff would need to be trained for their new roles – a task to fall on the shoulders of the Coordinator (the teacher in charge of the general running of the programme).
- The assumption made that students will *want* to learn may not prove true. Accordingly, some provision for compulsory attendance and work assignments would be necessary with provision for the rehabilitation of children for when the Whanau House had not proved successful.
- Additional ancillary staff and facilities might be needed – a rider without which no commentary on conditions is ever thought complete in New Zealand!

And so the school year, or the remaining two-thirds of it, got under way. During it, the teachers taught, the pupils learned, researchers researched and the continuous stream of visitors continued. By the end of 1977 it was possible to arrive at some loosely formed conclusions about the past and some even more tentative ones about the future. But before they can be presented, the terms of reference for such an undertaking need to be clarified.

Some consequences

It will be recalled that the original architectural scheme envisaged a complete

Whanau House school. Obviously, the present situation fell far short of that. The existing Whanau House block was but one unit in a complex of some 20 buildings. Furthermore, in many respects it seemed alien, even aberrant in the total school environment. And yet the research-based 'evaluation' was supposed to address itself to the educational and architectural viability of the original scheme, to the extent it could be reflected in a single block.

As the researchers had anticipated, this could only be done within certain important limitations. For example, an indication *could* be given on how the rooms were used. Information on attitudes and beliefs about the popularity and utility of the building could also be gathered. And to some extent comparisons could be made between the performance of the Whanau House pupils and others in the school. But disentangling the influence of the Whanau House from the larger school environment would be virtually impossible, and results would inevitably be contaminated by the very context in which the Whanau House block was set. Furthermore, whatever the results would be, they would to some extent be relative to that setting, those teachers, those children, that time and other specific contextual features.

The researchers found themselves thus obliged to regard the two issues, the Whanau House complete school and the Whanau House single block at Penrose High School, as separate and distinct. The tentative report of the situation up until the end of 1977 that follows takes this distinction into account.

The research studies

Environmental preferences

Two questionnaire surveys of pupil attitudes and preferences, mostly employing five-point scale responses, were conducted – one half-way through the school year, the other at the end. The most noteworthy among the results was that student ratings were very positive and remained consistent over the period – thus disconcerting the researchers who thought that the initial euphoria would evaporate, at least after a while. In brief summary:

- The opportunities for *all* learning, relaxing and social activities were rated highly.
- The pupils found the place comfortable inside and attractive inside and out.
- There was distinct evidence of the pupils' awareness of the effects of colour schemes – with high consistency they preferred quiet colours (earthy browns, golds, autumn tones) for private study, reading, talking with friends and classroom learning. With equally high consistency they favoured very bright, vivid and contrasting colours for cultural activities (but earthy tones take second place among the five options provided).

- Natural lighting was preferred.
- Background music (available in the commons) was liked – even for studying and learning in the classrooms, but softly. Loud music was an anathema, but so was silence.

The pupils also expressed a wish that the building could have provided them with locations where they might be alone and private on occasions when they had a desire for solitude. This judgement confirmed the opinions of the 'territorialists' at the original planning conference, an opinion which in the plan itself became the victim of cost and space constraints. As well, the pupils, despite their appreciation of the attractive décor and condition of the building (designed by the Ministry of Works decorator), expressed an unequivocal wish to play a part in determining how the setting should be decorated. They gave strong indications of wanting to personalize the ('their') environment – but also to take responsibility for its condition and tidiness.

Space use

In order to check on the occupancy of the various locations in the Whanau House, a systematic programme of photography was employed. It was spread over four weeks in all, but was confined to intervals, lunch time, and before and after school. (There was no question that the classrooms were consistently occupied during class time.) The pupils took the photographs with a wide-angle lens 35mm camera and from prescribed locations and at specific times.

The results showed that the less formal settings were fully used, but that the teaching rooms, in which the furniture and equipment clearly broadcasted their educational function, attracted only the occasional occupant. The fact that 'signals' were given by the physical condition of the environment was very clearly illustrated in one series of photographs. Originally it was thought that the children would make use of the Whanau House before and after the normal school hours. In fact this proved not to be the case and the photographs provide a possible explanation. It has long been the custom in New Zealand schools for children, at the end of the last lesson of the day, to put their chairs upside down on the tables to make the cleaners' job easier. The chairs stay there, of course, until the first lesson next day. To any intruder, the bristling array of porcupine-like chair legs is a most uninviting sight that implies that the territory is not for use. Although the chairs in the commons area are not so treated, the photographs revealed another related circumstance that in its own way gave a small but unequivocal non-verbal signal that the appropriate time for vacating the room had come. Regularly at about 3.45 pm the janitor, complete with vacuum cleaner, appeared. Now janitors in New Zealand schools are forces to be reckoned with and it takes determination, charm and great diplomacy to negotiate a change in terms and conditions of their appointment. Consequently, it is not altogether surprising that children and teachers, not insensitive to workers' rights, were inclined to retire from the field rather than contest it.

Pupil performance

It would be naïve to assume that any differences in the general performance of pupils in the Whanau House block could be attributable *only* to the building in which they did most of their work. But if clear and consistent trends appear *and* they are sustained over a period, then at least coincidental 'cause' can be assumed. Time will be needed to tell – a point stressed by the planning conference group when they called for evaluation, *after* the initial euphoria had faded. From the researchers' point of view, but not necessarily the students', there are some happy circumstances that permit performance comparisons within the school. There is a ubiquitous nationwide public examination called the School Certificate examination. This examination, which comes at the end of the third year of secondary school (11th year of school), is something of an educational watershed that serves to indicate (but not determine) who are and who are not potential university material. When the mean scores of the first Whanau House candidates for the School Certificate examination were compared with other candidates from the rest of the school, the comparison did nothing to either confirm or deny the superiority of the Whanau House environment. As Table 4 shows, except in one case, the differences were not statistically significant.

Table 4: *School Certificate performance 1977*

	Whanau mean	Main school mean	Difference Whanau – main	t test
English	47.9	45.9	+2.0	NS
Mathematics	52.3	55.3	−3.0	NS
Alternative science	44.0	43.4	+0.6	NS
Biological science	51.1	47.3	+3.8	NS
Physical science	62.7	55.0	+7.7	NS
Geography	48.4	43.0	+5.4	.05
History	49.6	45.6	+4.0	NS

Such a result can bring neither delight nor dismay to either the supporters or the opponents of the Whanau House. On the other hand, there is some attitudinal evidence to be reported later that suggests that some of the side effects of Whanau House life are quite beneficial.

There is also another indicator that may be worth taking into account. In the first place, absenteeism rates can give an indication of the extent to which pupils may be voting with their feet. A spot check taken over the last six days of the second term, when temptation is high, showed that the Whanau House group, in comparison with the four other House Groups into which the school was now divided, had the lowest incidence of absenteeism – 83 pupil half-days compared with 93, 110, 121 and 145.

Teaching and learning practices

Data for this study were gathered by participant observation. Visits were paid to all class groups in the Whanau House on a systematically determined schedule to (i) tape record events that transpired and (ii) at convenient points, interview pupils and later teachers about events occurring. The intention was to record the 'perceptions of reality' of the various actors and subsequently to enable the actors themselves to compare them, and, if they saw fit, reconcile differences. The technique is used quite extensively overseas, particularly at the University of East Anglia (UK) and at Washington University (USA). Its protagonists are persuasively vocal in its support. Normally the technique is relatively open-ended, with the interviewer's intuition determining what questions are appropriate. In this case, the observer augmented his intuitions with a systematically derived set of questions that were designed to ensure that certain aspects thought important would be covered.

The resulting tape recordings, once typed, were available for analysis, either in conventional ethological ways, or on the basis of the conceptual system incorporated into the questions. This, the most complex of the research studies, requires more elaborate and time-consuming procedures. The final results are not yet available and the comments below result from first impressions. The initial interviews with the pupils seem to indicate that they liked being in the Whanau House, that they *did* see themselves as a *little* privileged, but in no way isolated from the rest of the school. They liked in particular the relaxed atmosphere, the opportunity to be a bit more autonomous, the chance to have easy access to teachers and the generally 'civilized' pupil-pupil and teacher-pupil interaction that the building seemed to facilitate.

The teachers too were initially quietly enthusiastic about the situation, finding the environment, their colleagues and their new 'personalized' approach to interaction with the pupils very gratifying. But, like people, no institution is perfect, and gradually over the year the judgements began to become qualified. This seemed to be occasioned by the spotlight effect of always being on view – if not to visitors, to some extent to each other. Preference for occasional privacy was not confined to pupils alone and teachers quietly began to find ways of retiring (escaping is too strong a word) to the school world outside from time to time.

However, gradually too, that outside world began to change. Attitudes, perhaps initially benign, perhaps latently hostile, began to harden negatively. More and more – but still not excessively – the Whanau House occupants began to be seen as somewhat apart, a little aloof, a little overprivileged. But even so, the balance was well tipped on the positive side and the euphoria pendulum had only just begun its down swing. How far further it would descend remained at the end of the year an open question – to which a return will be made shortly.

For the formalized analysis of the transcripts of interviews (*and* staff meetings *and* documents produced in the school), a system of categorization, in part original and in part relying on some rather obscurely worded theorizing by the sociologist Talcott Parsons, was used. The objective of the analysis was to find out: (i) what issues tended to predominate in the working of the Whanau House; (ii) to what extent there was compatibility between ideas expressed and action undertaken and (iii) what consequences might be deduced. At this early stage of the analysis, only one or two points are worth making and they are presented tentatively in the full recognition that further information may oblige their revision.

These early analyses tend to show that the initial planning activities, the parents' meeting and the first classes recorded were preoccupied with *organizational* matters. Parents were worried over 'discipline and educational opportunity': 'Will this innovation allow my child too much freedom and thus lessen his chances of getting a School Certificate?' Staff were concerned over workload in relation to administration, planning problems, classroom interaction and the demands of the new situation, particularly with respect to increased exposure to pupils.

Some pupils mirrored their parents' concerns to some extent: 'The teachers aren't making us work hard enough to get past our exams'. Countering their viewpoint, but within the same basic orientation, was a proportion of students who felt that 'free time provisions enable us to get more work done and thus enhance our examination chances'.

Now it will be remembered that the whole Whanau House school was based on a specified philosophy with quite obvious objectives. And indeed the strategy of presentation employed in the preceding pages of this chapter has been inclined to return to philosophical aspects from time to time. One might reasonably ask, then, has the philosophy been realized in practice? Has the type of school envisaged come about? The answer is – yes and no.

The transcripts indicate that the pupils approached the Whanau House with relatively open minds, adopting a 'wait and see' attitude. They also indicate that with the passage of time the pupils *did* perceive the situation to be more human, humane and friendly in comparison with their previous school experiences – but, be it noted, all within the subject matter and examination orientation. That, they thought, was only proper.

The teachers, despite the early expressions of their hopes for a different kind of social system, had, by the time the building was opened, retreated a little, perhaps in self-defence. There was some indication that they had been inclined to anticipate that things 'would be just like in the main school but in a different building'. Clearly, after some time in the Whanau House, they now felt this not to be the case, but were having some difficulty in adjusting to the fact.

However, as against this, when goal units, ie segments of the transcript that could be classified as reflecting objectives, were examined, they seemed to indicate that the kind of goal orientation perceived seemed to be associated with status level. The higher the status of the person concerned, the more were the goals that were operating in the Whanau House thought to be 'facilitative' rather than 'directive', 'guidance-centred' rather than 'subject-centred'. Down at the bottom of the hierarchy, among the most junior pupils, the opposite was thought to be the case.

Before we leave this topic to venture a summary of what the situation seems to portend and what implications may be drawn for the Whanau House complete school, some further events occurring early in 1978 need to be touched on – noting in passing that the information base here is even sketchier.

Recent developments

At the end of 1977, the Principal of the School was appointed elsewhere.

It is very difficult to assess the exact magnitude of the Principal's impact on Penrose High School and the Whanau House; it would also be very easy to understate it. But there are many who would attribute the school's success to his leadership. It is certainly true that his very positive reaction to the Whanau House proposal, his sensitive and thoughtful steering of the scheme through its early stages at the school and, in particular, the strong and unwavering support and encouragement he gave the teachers and the project, helped ensure that momentum was generated quickly and sustained.

At the time of writing it is not known how the new Principal views the situation and what further steps he is likely to take with respect to it. This ignorance on our part is a two-edged sword in that it makes any assessment of the future hazardous, but on the other hand it frees us to take an, as it were, impersonal approach. The points made below are in the present case very conjectural, to say the least.

However, and firstly, research evidence from elsewhere indicates very clearly that principals tend to initiate changes (often structural or organizational ones) at a faster rate at the *beginning* of their terms of office than at any other stage. Secondly, it also indicates that appointees from outside the school tend to initiate substantially more changes than do those appointed from inside. (The new Principal comes from outside.) Thirdly, it is to some extent predictable that some of the first changes made are likely to be directed at perceived anomalies. Fourthly, it would not be at all unreasonable if the new Principal, not having been party to the earlier negotiations over the Whanau House experiment, could perceive it as something of an anomaly. The Whanau House could be seen to be (and maybe is) a small bastion of (over)privilege, with certain pupils and staff receiving favoured treatment.

There are already some indications that this latter view was being taken by some members of staff outside the Whanau House and that some pupils shared it. Further, the distinction between the Whanau House team of teachers and those outside had been made sharper over an academic controversy. The teachers from the other four houses had produced a paper that drew attention to what they considered to be an overall decline in academic standards implied by the school's results in the School Certificate examinations, and suggested remedial action. A counter-paper, rebutting the somewhat restricted academic viewpoint taken and arguing for a more liberal approach, came from the Whanau House staff. The gap widened.

Finally, as 1978 got under way, several changes of policy were put into play that affected the structure and function of the Whanau House population. The conditions imposed for access to the Whanau House were changed and at the time of writing it now seems as if some 400 pupils are in one way or another associated with the building. As well, the Whanau House staff now spend a much greater proportion of their time teaching classes in other parts of the school. It goes without saying that under such circumstances the original concept of an 'educational family' will be rather difficult to sustain.

Towards the unknown

To be consistent with the mandate of the IIEP project it is now necessary to attempt to continue further in the prophetic vein that crept into the last paragraph. Some attempts at predicting future events must be undertaken. The authors do so with due hesitancy, conscious of their own temerity. The best assurance they can give is that they have attempted to exercise care and responsibility.

Will the Penrose Whanau House prove successful?
In several senses it already has. It proved able to be built, within a reasonably short space of time and at a reasonable cost. People seem to like it.

This is the answer that the architects sought and had good reason to expect. But it is not the answer to the educational question.

Will the Penrose Whanau House prove educationally successful?
That depends – not only on future events, but also on the criteria invoked. If we are tempted into a myopic evaluation by objectives, then the indications are that success may be difficult to demonstrate. There are enough straws in the wind that indicate that if the present trend to 'open up' the Whanau House to the rest of the school continues, then many of the basic objectives stressed in *Secondary Schools for Tomorrow* cannot be achieved. The 'family' has already experienced a population explosion that is likely to make it impossible to sustain the level of inter-dependence envisaged. As well, the idea of its (separate) embeddedness in the community – which never really became realized beyond the initial ceremonial – would be harder to achieve.

There also seem good reasons for believing that there are certain logistic consequences of opening up the Whanau House that will eventually result in the block's becoming integrated almost fully into the rest of the school. Clearly, the greater the number of pupils that use the block, *and* the more diverse the classes they come from, *and* the greater the number of teachers who teach in it, then the greater the necessity to include the block in the school timetable. Flexible scheduling (an initial objective and practice of the original teachers) will have to become a thing of the past. If this assessment proves correct, then what will have been evidenced is the power of institutional interests to prevail over sectional ones.

However, as well as being evaluated against 'objectives', the Whanau House may also be evaluated against the effects it is thought to have had. Indeed, the Whanau House study, when included in the IIEP project on qualitative innovations, only asserted that the advent of the Whanau House would permit change in the behaviour of the teachers to occur – not that any specific behavioural changes would necessarily follow. Here the evidence is particularly slight, partly because the 'controlled' selection of pupils was not sustained into the second year, and partly because some of the more significant effects appear to be side effects, influencing the general school environment, which unfortunately was not initially studied.

An immediate effect – perhaps good, perhaps bad – of the advent of the Whanau House block was that the school itself converted to a house system. This in turn is to result eventually in some physical modifications of existing buildings to create 'commons' for the other houses as well. However, up until now no other house has a complex that could to any extent match the Whanau House. There are, of course, pros and cons of this development in that any house system is not without its drawbacks. It *can* become divisive. It *can* develop destructive rather than constructive competitiveness and it *can* lead to chauvinistic intolerance. Of course, it need not. There are not enough indications at the moment to make an informed guess about which way the house system is going.

Another side effect of the advent of the Whanau House was, according to the teachers, the incentive they received to re-examine their own practices. They testified that this was extremely rewarding and beneficial. There is reason to believe that this was not confined to the Whanau House teachers alone. However, while the Whanau House may have contributed to this state of affairs, the existence of such a building is neither a necessary nor a sufficient condition for its coming about.

Should more Whanau House blocks be built in established schools?
Although this was not a question originally asked of the research team, it is a reasonable one because the modular construction system is likely to be more economical the more it is employed – and obviously many existing schools will need additional or replacement buildings. Furthermore, as secondary school rolls stabilize, and even drop, there will be less call for the building of entire new secondary schools and a greater call for replacement of parts of existing ones.

In so far as Whanau House blocks are supposed to yield the educational outcomes listed in *Secondary Schools for Tomorrow*, and in so far as the trends observed continue at Penrose, and in so far as they are representative of a general institutional reaction, there are reasons for giving some consideration to the way in which such 'implants' would be carried out. On the evidence of the present study the advent of this kind of 'unusual' building is likely to have ramifications for the rest of the school that could be undesirable. This implies that it would be worth while to develop procedures for introducing such a block into a school that alerted the staff, pupils and parents to what might possibly happen. Also implied is the possibility that some school-based in-service training of staff would be useful, as would the continuous monitoring of the early acclimatization phase of the new building.

Such caveats nonetheless *could* be ignored if the Whanau House were seen as a means for *provoking* institutional animation — no matter what the nature of the result might be.

Should a complete Whanau House school be built?

In part this question is redundant in that the decision has already been taken to do so. But the evidence from the present study cannot provide grounds for supporting or not supporting the decision educationally. Because institutional factors in the Penrose case look likely to prove overbearing, the case for or against a complete Whanau House school is simply not proven — yet.

What implications can be drawn about the building of a Whanau House school?

There is an additional piece of information outside the present study that does appear supportive. Independently of the official Whanau House project, another school (Hillary College) in the same city, acting on its own initiative, created a Whanau House-type complex (a much less grand one) by making some structural modifications to existing classrooms and then developing the appropriate type of curriculum and organization. The Principal of this school had been a member of the original planning conference and believed firmly, even passionately, that in his school with its large population of Polynesian children, the Whanau House concept would be viable and valuable. There is some research evidence (see Munro, 1977) and a number of word-of-mouth testimonies that indicate that while far from trouble-free or opposition-free, the Hillary College Whanau House has functioned in a manner reasonably consistent with the objectives spelled out in *Secondary Schools for Tomorrow*.

Apart from this, however, it also seems logical to assume that in a complete Whanau House school, where all pupils are equally well housed and the conditions are, theoretically at least, completely appropriate for the application of the philosophy, the situation will be considerably different from the Penrose one.

The Penrose case, however, does hint at one or two of the problems that are likely to develop — although they did not need the Penrose case to demonstrate them. For example, there will be administrative coordination problems. These are likely to be minimized if the new school grows bit by bit, as was the intention originally and if new administration practices are developed to accommodate to the situation. However, even so, institutional patterns (even very young ones) will always firm and consolidate, so that each new growth will be seen to be alien, and to some extent threatening.

There will be strong pressures towards conservatism – or, perhaps more properly, conservation. These will not only take the form of denying newcomers and their ideas house room (if the pun can be excused), but will also be likely to be manifested in, if not a retreat into older teaching practices, at least only a modest movement away from them. Fairly clearly, change seems to be something to be viewed with caution, and perhaps rightly so. In fact, it appears that the infrastructure (to use Havelock and Huberman's (1977) very useful concept) necessary to support change has to be developed carefully and reinforced repeatedly. This was not the case at Penrose, otherwise the Whanau House staff would *not* have found themselves isolated; lined up, as it were, *against* the rest of the school. Had an effective, informed and committed infrastructure developed *throughout the school*, the Whanau House 'experiment' could have been sustained longer.

And maybe here is the nub of the Penrose story. With the advantage of hindsight, it is possible to see now that Penrose's own initial problem was that the school just needed more classroom space. But they got, oddly enough, more than they asked for. It was more in that the physical plant itself, not designed for their setting, was grander and more varied than the practices prevailing in the school would have needed. It was also more in that it came complete with appendages – a 'message' that was almost a doctrine, a galaxy of senior and interested officials of the Department of Education, and a small entourage of researchers. London Bridge was indeed come to Texas – and the tourists followed too!

For the school, the seductions of the situation were powerful but transitory. The captains and the kings departed, leaving their monument – and the researchers – and what *was* basically an experiment. In order for that experiment to continue it had to be viewed *as an experiment* and perhaps protected as an experiment. Such an attitude of mind would, however, represent a rather radical departure for teachers who, reasonably enough, give priority to the educational needs of their present pupils rather than to educational 'science'. But without the protection of the experimental aura, at least for a time, the Whanau House's capacity to sustain a somewhat independent existence was severely limited. To achieve such a *general* commitment from staff, parents and pupils would have entailed not only lengthy and persuasive negotiation, but also the regular reinforcement of the idea. This in turn would imply an active network of people (and a structure) capable of sensing problems as they emerged, and trouble-shooting them. In the present case the research mechanism employed appeared to have been inadequate for this purpose. The network developed was not appropriately representative, ie with outside teachers and parents, and the structures for communication to interested parties were far too underdeveloped.

Conclusion

There are four final points to be made before ending this chapter. The first is that the account above is not in any way intended to imply guilt. There *is* no

New Zealand: Institutional Inertia

blame to apportion. The school has every right, by law, to manage its own domestic affairs. There is also no reason to believe that any of the people in the situation acted other than responsibly and in accordance with their principles. There were reasonable reasons for *all* the events that occurred – those supportive of the Whanau House, those not.

The second is that if one searched for an explanatory principle behind the events that occurred, the best one might be that equity takes precedence over educational experimentation. As a result, although events conspired to prevent the few (in the Whanau House) from making considerable profit, the many (throughout the school) may have made a little.

The third is that, in this final summation, a number of rather doubtful guesses have been made and conclusions drawn from them. It may be that the trends perceived at Penrose will change direction as new factors influence conditions (including this chapter, perhaps). The Penrose Whanau House story is by no means ended, nor is the Hillary College one, and the story of the first complete Whanau House school has barely begun. More is yet to come.

The fourth and final point is that there do appear to be some general principles hidden in the account that, when drawn out, may be useful in other cases of institutional change. Not the least of them is the issue of autonomy or, as it was put in *Alice in Wonderland*, 'It is not a question of right or wrong, merely a question of who is to be master'. Who should determine the philosophy and practice of a Whanau House school – outside experts, departmental officials, the Principal, the teachers, the parents, the pupils? However, that question and others of a similarly general nature are to be left until the last chapter of this book.

When is an innovation a success and when a failure? This perplexing question receives a measure of consideration in the next chapter on Ghana. The Ghanaian innovation is particularly interesting because it violates some of the beliefs commonly held about the need for centralized control in young education systems. True, the Ghanaian innovation had its genesis in the central offices of education. True, it initially received official (and financial) support from the Ministry of Education. But it was not left to the Ministry to keep sustaining momentum. That happened in other ways – ways that lead one to conjecture about the mechanisms by which an idea becomes contagious and about the conditions that are necessary for sustaining that contagion. Judging by the country's initial response, it seems as if the 'timing' of the innovation – at least at the outset – was perfect. But whether this occurred by accident or design is perhaps an open question. What is also an open question is whether or not the Ghanaian case is exceptional or universal.

Chapter 8

Ghana: Implementation by Osmosis

The Ghanaian innovation consists of an attempt to introduce a measure of practical work into what was, at the time, a basically traditional, examination oriented academic curriculum. Called the 'Continuation School Project', it is based on a very straightforward and uncomplicated idea. The children were to devote a proportion of the school week (up to a third, but often only one day) doing something that would yield an economic return. They were to spend time growing things, making things or providing services; practical activities that not only produced tangible (and profitable) results but also entailed the mastery of productive skills.

The Ghanaian innovation is the oldest considered in the book. In comparison with the Federal Republic of Germany's sprightly, one-and-a-half-year-old *Berufsvorbereitungsjahr*, with which Ghana's Continuation School Project has much in common, it might even be regarded as a veteran. The first classes designed for the purpose, the continuation classes came into being as long ago as 1969, following an idea mooted even earlier, in 1962. West Germany's first functionally equivalent classes, by contrast, date only from 1977.

However, anyone going to Ghana in 1980 hopeful of seeing a continuation school is likely to be disappointed. By then the continuation schools will probably be no more. Thus, as 1978 draws towards its end, so do the continuation schools appear to be approaching theirs. What does their pending disappearance mean? What has brought such a state of affairs about? Were they not successful enough? Were they too successful? These questions and others like them are to be the principal concerns of this chapter. Whatever answers are appropriate, therefore, had better then wait until some of the available evidence has been presented.

The Ghana project, however, does provide an opportunity that none of the younger innovations does. Because of its age and durability (so far), we have the advantage of being able to look at the way time has exerted its influence. We can therefore consider, at least to some extent, the manner in which conditions and circumstances have pushed and pulled at the innovation. We can also examine the way the innovation has done a little pushing and pulling on its own account.[1]

[1] Unfortunately, the record cannot be as full as we should have liked. As is often the case with retrospective studies, it has not always been possible to retrieve earlier details.

The root cause

In the beginning, the Continuation Classes Project (its initial name) emerged, as did Germany's BVJ, as a response to a matter of public concern with which many nations of the world are now only too familiar. There was a growing number of school leavers who could not continue their education further and who were not equipped to deal with their new independence because paid employment, even of an unskilled kind, was not available for them and they had no cultivated work skills. The story has a familiar ring, and behind it lies a basic dilemma arising out of the uncertainty of the relationship between education and national (particularly) economic development. At that time, the education system, built on colonial foundations, was too young to have evolved its own particular character and thus to have come into line with the existing social and economic needs of the country. But on the other hand, the economic condition of the nation, influenced by many external and internal factors, did not seem to be able to provide the means for bringing about educational reform at the rate desired. With education falling short of making the kind of economic contribution to the country that it might, but with the economic condition of the country preventing the kind of investment in education that would enable it to do so, a kind of impasse had been reached. In the light of harsh reality, what should be done? What *could* be done? It was far from clear what the wisest moves might be.

Such a state of affairs had not prevailed in Ghana in quite the same way at Independence. True, the condition of the economy's development was regarded as unsatisfactory but not only was aspiration there to improve it but also the confidence was there that it could be done. The British experience seemed to indicate that, given the circumstances existing then plus the country's potential, there was reason to hope for rapid progress. True again, the educational condition of the country was regarded as unsatisfactory. The British had created an embryo education system, initially mainly for an élite (although in the last years with a greatly accelerated provision for more and more children) but at the time they left, still 73 per cent of people above school entry age had never been to school and the illiteracy rate was estimated to be high. Even so, education had come to be perceived as a means to the development end. But, and this is the rub, for understandable reasons it was a particular view of education that was thought to hold the key, and to provide the basis for confidence. Discussion is warranted.

A legacy of history

Critics of colonialism often make the point that the colonial powers failed to prepare their colonies for independence and nationhood. The neglect was most apparent at the political, administrative, technical and educational levels. A major consequence was that decolonized countries were usually left with personnel neither trained nor experienced in the complicated task of creating and running a nation. Nor did there exist the organizational and social infrastructure that would support and provide the means. The criticism is valid enough in the sense that at the end of colonial rule such conditions often existed. But accusations of culpable neglect tend to mask a further factor in the situation that exerted a more subtle influence, that may perhaps in the long run be seen to be a more powerful one. Hand in hand with whatever economic gain the colonizers accrued to themselves also went what they, in their own eyes, saw to be a contribution to the advancement of the colonies. They brought new material goods, new techniques, new technologies, new religious 'enlightenment' and new social perspectives. They also accompanied this particular contribution with their particular view of reality. The material goods they brought were from their own shores, the techniques were theirs, so were the religions and so were the concepts of government, law, social propriety and education. But always in accompaniment came an overweaning conviction of the superiority of their own cultural perspective – an attitude of mind by no means confined to colonial powers.

When the British departed Ghana in 1957, they left an attitudinal legacy of considerable potency. The belief that the British had in the virtue of their own culture and institutions had effectively rubbed off to quite an extent on the indigenous people of that part of West Africa. Some of that belief had been acquired under difficulties. While the final withdrawal of the British was a peaceful one, the early years had seen bitter and prolonged fighting between the British and the major tribe in Ghana, the Ashanti. That conflict had succeeded in impressing on the Ashanti that education was of critical importance if the power of the whites was to be countered. It is understandable, then, that at Independence, when the first questions began to be asked about the direction development should take and the way it should be done, the answers tended to have strong British overtones. How could they, under the circumstances, have been expected to be otherwise? As a result, at first, it was a British parliamentary system that was adopted, a British view of justice accepted and a British conception of administrational propriety that by and large became the norm. It was industrial Britain that served as the ideal type and nowhere, the army perhaps excepted, was the influence of that ideal type more strongly felt than in education.

As Ghana started out on its path to nationhood, whenever decisions had to be taken about education there was an understandable tendency to take an English point of view. There appeared to be good reason. It seemed on face value that there was a direct connection between economic advantage and education. When the English were in power they were certainly able to profit economically. The English also valued education. They were educated themselves, sought education for their children and favoured the children of indigenes who also were educated. Furthermore it seemed self-evident that development depended on there being an adequate supply of educated manpower to service the nation's needs. The only point at issue was, what sort of education?

In the first years of independence there was really little choice as to what kind of education that might be. Convinced by the conviction shown by the English, Ghana set out to do as many new nations did, to build a replica of their erstwhile colonizers' system. There is no need to provide much detail but it is necessary to make the point that in Ghana, as elsewhere in many British colonies, it was the upper end of the educational pyramid that at first tended to attract much attention and a perhaps disproportionate amount of investment. Seen as the acme of education, universities were thought to hold the golden key to success. The new universities were unquestioningly faithful to the English model – Oxbridge was reincarnate – until eventually the students revolted, literally burning caps and gowns to symbolize the beginning of the Africanization of education. Throughout the entire education system, however, the story was rather the same. There were to be found English-type structures, English-type procedures, English-type curricula and even genuine English examinations – O and A levels administered from Cambridge, no less. The idea of an indigenous education that took Ghana as its cultural departure point was yet to emerge. In the meantime, the English model flourished, but under circumstances that had a slightly ironical twist to them. The model being employed in Ghana, though English in origin, was one that itself was falling out of favour in its homeland. Classical and traditional in form, it was being found in Britain itself to be no longer appropriate for the second half of the 20th century. There, new forms were emerging. They included new curricula, new teaching styles, new organizational structures, new methods of assessment and new definitions of the scope, purpose and range of education. Open-plan schools, spiral curricula, integrated education, comprehensive schools, community schools, resource centres, the Schools Council and the Open University had blossomed or were about to. They arose, it was said, because education as it had been previously constituted was inappropriate to meet the needs of society.

It is no great wonder then, that Ghana came to a similar conclusion in a very short time, but a conclusion precipitated by the special circumstances that developed during Ghana's early years and that were all the more poignant given the earlier faith in education. Those circumstances contained events that were as dramatic as they were telling. They served not only to require a review of the role of education, but they also served to place severe limits on what might be done about it. In its first 20 years, Ghana was not only to be transformed from a colony to a nation state, but it was also to experience an amount and rate of social change that would pose a fearsome challenge to any country. Because the Continuation Schools Project comprises one component of that change, some attention has to be given to the circumstances prompting it. They were complex indeed.

Since Independence

Political circumstances
Properly we should start with the political scene, partly because it tends to be the point at which many issues crystallize and partly because it makes

dramatic reading. Conveniently, the periodical *Africa* has already produced a crisply succinct account.

'Ghana, formerly the Gold Coast, operating a Westminster type of parliamentary democracy, became independent on March 6, 1957, with Mr. Nkrumah's Convention People's Party (CPP) forming the government and the United Party led by Dr. Busia as the main opposition. On July 1, 1960, the country became a republic with Dr. Nkrumah as Executive President. It became a one-party state in February 1964. On February 24, 1966, the army and police in a combined operation seized power in a coup led by Colonel Kotoka and Mr. Harlley, Commander of the Police Force. Dr. Nkrumah was accused of concentrating power in his own hands and abusing individual rights. The Constitution was suspended and the CPP was banned. A National Liberation Council (NLC) was set up to administer the country under the chairmanship of General Ankrah, former head of the Army, who had been retired compulsorily by the Nkrumah administration.

'A counter coup on April 27, 1967, led by Lt. Sam Arthur was unsuccessful but General Kotoka was killed in the attempt. On April 3, 1966, General Ankrah was replaced as Chairman of the NCL by General Afrifa, after having been accused of corruption and violating the NLC's rule on political activities. On May 1, 1969, the ban on political activities was lifted. On August 22, 1969, the Constituent Assembly approved a new Constitution for the return to civilian rule. Following elections on August 26, 1969, Dr. Busia, as head of the victorious Progress Party, became Prime Minister. On September 30, 1969, the NLC was dissolved and power was formally transferred to the civilian administration.

'On January 13, 1972, Dr. Busia's government was overthrown in a military coup led by then Colonel Acheampong, who accused Dr. Busia of maladministration and economic mismanagement. The constitution was suspended and Parliament and political parties were dissolved. A National Redemption Council (NRC) was set up to run the country. Now, after six years of direct military rule, the Acheampong administration proposes to restore constitutional government. Because of its novelty and its exciting promises the next few months may well be another significant landmark in the country's tortuous itinerary in search of a stable political system. If the people of Ghana succeed, the result could be a guide for Africa, plagued as she is today with military coups and in need of a constitutional formula to satisfy the ever-growing political appetites of soldiers and civilians alike.'

The next few months were indeed telling. The referendum sought endorsement from the people for a new kind of military-civilian union that to its architects was thought to combine the best of both worlds. Although the results of the referendum were reported to favour the plan (56 per cent to 44 per cent), the outcome was to nobody's liking – a clear vote of confidence had certainly not been given. In the following months, with economic problems far from abating, and a strike of students adding to the Government's disarray, it became apparent that a full return to civilian government was almost inevitable. It was projected for June 1979.

As might be expected, coincidentally with this political flux in Ghana's early history, there occurred a number of economic developments that because of their influence need to be mentioned briefly too.

Economic circumstances

The policy adopted by the new Republic after Independence placed a strong emphasis on a drive for rapid industrialization and mechanization. A number of sizeable state enterprises were begun, including several large state farms – a matter not without significance for the continuation classes proposal that arose subsequently. But although great improvements were made in roads, harbours and the power supply system, the kind of financial benefits hoped for did not materialize. The mechanization of agriculture was not able to be accomplished and the state farm proved to be an idea ahead of its time. Unfortunately, the two hitherto secure areas of Ghana's agricultural industry, small family holdings and cocoa farming, had tended to fall into the background and output declined. Other factors played their part. Foreign exchange costs climbed, pushed by the substantial imbalance between escalating importation and a slower rate of exportation. Foreign and local investment became hesitant, presumably affected by the low rates of interest offered. By 1966 the situation was serious.

For the next two years a stabilizing policy was followed which did serve to result in economies in imports and in a slowing of the rate of inflation. But because these were not accompanied by a corresponding increase in exports, the situation by 1968 was still far from satisfactory. At that stage, some reassessment was made and the Government's attention turned more towards development, putting a high priority on agriculture. Had there not followed some dramatic fluctuations in the overseas cocoa market that saw Ghana first suffering from depressed prices and later (mysteriously) unable to profit from the boom, the economy might have picked up more rapidly. But by 1971, despite a number of government measures that tended to relieve some of the pressures for at least some of the time, the overall situation had not improved. In the next five years it became, in effect, worse. This was in spite of a considerable increase in agricultural production. The offsetting influence was the difficulty experienced in maintaining industrial development and investment because of the continuing foreign exchange shortage, together with an even more intractable problem. Inflation, despite two devaluations, had continued relentlessly, occasionally reaching imposing levels (an annual rate of 60 per cent in 1975/76, for example). Real incomes have suffered accordingly with the urban population feeling it most. Today, in 1978, the prospects for the future are at best for only a relatively modest improvement over all.

The educational scene

Against such a political and economic backdrop how did education fare? All things taken into account, remarkably well. The new nation had begun with a measure of primary and secondary education established by the British and with the foundations laid for the development of universities. Even before the British left there was talk of 'compulsory education for all children in the country' (Governor Burns, 1943, in McWilliam and Kwamena-Poh, 1975), and some headway had been made in that general direction. Legislation to this effect was introduced quite quickly by the new Government in 1961, four years after Independence. That action testified to the amount of faith the Government and the country placed in education. It also testified to a miscalculation (rectified at the next census) of the numbers likely to be involved.

> 'The immediate effects of the introduction of compulsory primary education were even more dramatic than had been foreseen. Instead of the expected 1,000 new schools...2,493 new primary schools were in fact opened in September 1961, and 219,480 children were enrolled in the first year classes. Just before this, in 1960-61, there had been 441,117 children in 3,514 public primary schools, but within two years both these figures had doubled: by the fall of the C.P.P. Government in 1966 the total had surged on to 1,137,494 children attending 8,144 schools.'
>
> *(McWilliam and Kwamena-Poh, 1975)*

McWilliam and Kwamena-Poh go on to point out that conditions at that time represented a 'high tide in the history of education in Ghana':

> 'for in 1966-67 the enrolment fell back to 1,116,843 and was below the one million mark at 975,629 by 1969-70. There was a corresponding decrease in the number of public primary schools: 7,913 in 1966-67 and 7,239 in 1969-79.'
>
> *(ibid)*

Over the same period (up to 1970) the middle schools also grew fast but, affected by increased primary enrolments, were able to sustain the growth rate throughout. In the first ten years, the number of schools and pupils both increased three-fold.

As McWilliam and Kwamena-Poh concluded, 'finance apart, the human and social implications of these events were among the most pressing problems facing the C.P.P. Government'. Those implications started to assert themselves in 1966 and that is where the story of the continuation schools has its real beginning.

Need for reform

The military leaders whose coup of 1966 had overthrown the Government had, understandably enough, the inclination and perhaps good reason to look at the policies and practices of the past governments with jaundiced eyes. Whether motivated by existing circumstances or not, they expressed particular concern over an alleged decline in educational standards. It was caused, they believed, by the degeneration of the teaching force which in turn had been brought about by the too-rapid expansion of the teaching service. They were also dismayed by the length of time children took from entry into school to qualification for the School Certificate or General Certificate of Education – 13 years in all. Both of these matters had also been of some concern to the previous CCP Government, but it was not until 1966 that anything was done about it. The National Liberation Council (the new military regime) set up a large (32-member) Education Review Committee to examine the status of education in Ghana and make recommendations accordingly. Their conclusions found the previous Government culpable, a finding that had its echo when civilian rule returned briefly in 1969 and the new Government claimed the then existing state of affairs to be no better and the causes to be just the same.

Structural reform

Interestingly enough, however, both the NLC and its CCP predecessor saw the remedy to lie mainly (but not exclusively) in organizational and structural reform. If the schooling period were too long, it could be shortened. In the original 1962 plan this was to be done gradually and in three parts. In the first place, the old six-year basic primary course would continue and would be followed by a four-year middle school. Successful pupils would then proceed to secondary schools. In the second place, a new eight-year elementary school would be introduced. Those who completed it successfully could then go directly to secondary school, missing the intervening middle school. Those who were *un*successful had a further two years of schooling in store for them, but *in continuation classes*. Thirdly, the Government was to start a few six-year primary schools from which children were to go to *either* secondary or middle schools. These new six-year primary schools were to be better staffed and were to serve as prototypes to which the whole system would convert once an adequate supply of trained teachers was available.

Now whether or not such a preference for structural reform sprang out of the conviction that the organizational frame within which education operated was the reason for whatever educational malaise existed is not clear. It certainly reflects a frame of mind that is to be found in many countries belonging to the British Commonwealth of Nations: Australia and New Zealand are both capable of providing numerous illustrations. Nor is it clear whether such a solution was preferred because the cost was likely to be relatively slight, in the meantime anyway, a reason that in the existing economic conditions would be readily justifiable. Whatever the motivation at that time, the reason that has come to be given greatest credence in recent years is nonetheless an educational one, the one that had its origin in joblessness and urban drift. But as a reason it evolved as circumstances changed.

While the array of problems, particularly economic ones, existing at the time was more than sufficient, one that did seem on face value less influenced by conditions outside the Government's control was the problem of unemployed school leavers. Perhaps the schools might be able to help set it right. After all, the problem surfaced for children *after* they had been through the schools. Without taking a *post hoc ergo propter hoc* position, one nonetheless might still argue that if the schools did their job differently, then the effect on the school leavers ought to be different too. It needed to be, because the problem was big enough. Approximately 80 per cent of the children who completed middle-level education did not continue to secondary school.

What then could the schools do in the face of this stark fact of life? The solution chosen was to try to look life in the face – and this entailed trying to relate the work of the schools to the conditions that the young school leavers faced. And what that meant was trying to do in school something that could be directly useful to Ghanaian youngsters in the Ghanaian community. Education had to become indigenous. The cry for 'relevance' was heard in Ghana too. But here the cry was not the bedfellow of affluence, expanded social awareness and a diminished sense of concern for economic security that characterized the Western 'relevance' phenomenon of the 1960-70s. Here relevance was a necessity. Society's survival depended on it. However, although the problem was insistent and although the kind of solution envisaged by the Review Committee had official support, the omens were not all in favour of the continuation classes idea. The community was 'not impressed' yet. For too long, education had been seen as the way to vocational advancement, and it still was. But it was the academic kind of education that was regarded as best because vocational success had always been defined in white-collar terms. The agricultural life was regarded as a last resort, something to move away from rather than to rely on. There was a widespread belief among farming parents that education should release the ties that would otherwise bind their children to a life of toil on the soil, as they themselves had been bound.

Continuation classes inaugurated

It was left to the 1966 Education Review Committee to give real impetus to the continuation classes idea. Taking up the CPP's proposition, they accepted the implicit intention to replace the existing middle schools with schools that would provide a more appropriate terminal educational for school leavers. 'Continuation' classes were to provide the means. The continuation classes were initially to occupy the two years at the end of the primary school period, but once the six-year primary school became a reality, continuation schools with four-year courses were to be set up. The courses in these schools were to have practical overtones and were, it was hoped, to become more relevant to the Ghanaian situation. But the Review Committee foresaw the development taking place slowly. They recommended that two schools in each region should be chosen as the first subjects for the new experiment. This was duly done in 1969.

A further year passed and with it the Government. The new Progress Party Government, however, as part of its 'One-Year Development Plan of 1970-71' expressed a wish that ten more continuation schools should be started in each region. They saw reason to believe that the 20 schools existing at the time were 'providing valuable experience on the best means of organizing suitable practical courses for young people'. Most significantly, they added:

'The development of these courses and the subsequent work experience of continuation school leavers will be watched particularly closely as a guide to the best way of developing and modifying the middle school course.'

Despite these encouraging words there was a long way to go. There were, in the total situation as Ghana faced it in the mid-1960s, many problems that because of their interaction with each other yielded great complexity. Because there was no easy way out, as time went by, need for a more and more workable solution became more and more insistent. The search for a workable solution had led the Government and some of the people to give attention to the recommendations of the 1962/63 Review of Education.

'1. There was need to plan towards the eventual solution of the unemployment problem.
2. There was need to plan towards effecting change in the attitudes of school leavers from white collar jobs to more profitable practical vocational occupations.
3. There was need to train children to acquire the necessary skills that will aid development in rural areas.'

(Anim and Bassa-Kwansa, 1978)

The continuation classes were to become the vehicle through which the aims might be realized.

Impending impediments
These broad aims were well in tune with the discernible needs of the country but at that stage they were expressions of hope. Whether or not the schools had the capability to achieve that hope was quite another question. In fact, the dice seemed loaded against the schools. Despite the fact that there was widespread national concern over the conditions obtaining in Ghana at the time and despite the national will to remedy them, there were countervailing forces. Some have already been mentioned, eg the time-honoured 'academic' character of the education system, the restraint that had to be exercised over the use of the limited resources available, and the general lack of popularity of farming as a future way of life. To these must be added the

formidable influence of institutional inertia. Reluctance to change is a very human condition. And in educational institutions, whose basic task involves conservation of knowledge and culture, there are strong inclinations to preserve and conserve rather than innovate and modify. Furthermore, it is characteristic of education systems that their cognitive content, like entropy, increases. Bits and pieces may be added to the curriculum, but seldom is anything discarded as redundant. The points being made are that (i) the inhabitants of an education system tend to want to preserve the status quo, and (ii) if change does become acceptable, it tends to be incremental change rather than substitutional. The consequence of the latter is that the total amount of work tends to increase. Sometimes institutions resenting the increase or unable to deal with it develop their own forms of resistance.

While such barriers to change are universal, in Ghana there were as well specific conditions that influenced the development of the continuation schools. Had an attempt been made to launch the Continuation School Project, say in 1960, there are good reasons for believing that if it had attempted to promote agricultural activities as the most relevant of relevant experience for children this predominantly agricultural emphasis would have resulted in failure. Failure would have occurred for the same reason that many such programmes failed in many developing and developed countries. Because progress at the time was perceived in terms of mechanization and industrialization, 'consumer resistance' would have been too powerful to overcome. But during the early sixties in Ghana a campaign called 'Feed yourself' had been introduced as one of a number of steps to encourage individual self-sufficiency and reduce national dependence on imported food. This campaign had been well timed, met a perceived national need and resulted in farming coming to be seen through new eyes. It was no longer regarded, as before, as a vocational trap for the educationally unfortunate but rather now as a means to a very necessary end. Furthermore, agricultural activities not only had quick, tangible and usable results, but also they now bore the stamp of official approval and national commendation.

Early events

Thus when the Ministry of Education made its move to initiate the continuation classes in line with the Review Committee's recommendation number 38, '... classes patterned on the industrial and farming needs of the country', the timing was right and the continuation classes came as the culmination of a series of events. They should be summarized in order to illustrate how two important ideas became established, viz: (i) that education should have a vocational orientation, (ii) that vocational education came eventually to mean more than agricultural education.

The first official indication is to be found in the 'Report of the Ministry of Education 1960-62' published in 1963. Under a section headed 'Development Policy', attention was drawn to the undue amount of time consumed from entry to primary school to graduation from secondary. As part of the Seven-Year Development Plan it was intended to:

(i) select pupils for secondary school after six years of primary school;
(ii) eliminate 'middle schools' as such; and
(iii) replace them with continuation schools.

In the latter '*the courses offered would be of a vocational nature, such as Agriculture, Shorthand and Typing and Office Practice, Simple Bookkeeping, Elementary Accountancy, Housecraft and Handicrafts*'.

The second followed several years later and appears in 'Report of the Education Review Committee appointed by the National Schools Council June 1966 to July 1967', published in 1967. Recommendation 37: 'Two year continuation classes patterned on the farming and industrial needs of the country should be established in two middle schools of each region as a pilot scheme; pre-vocational work patterned on the farming and industrial needs of the country should be done in these classes'.

In the meantime the old pattern was to be sustained – eight years' primary education followed by selection for secondary and, for the failures, a further two years in continuation classes where available, or alternatively in the still surviving middle schools.

The third came as the official sanctioning of the continuation schools idea. It occurred in the White Paper on the Report of the Education Review Committee (1968), under the heading 'Agricultural Education':

'Government intends to increase progressively the facilities for the continuation classes so that eventually all pupils who do not proceed to secondary or equivalent level schools may be able to attend the continuation classes and be predisposed thereby to suitable occupations.

'*The Government accepts the recommendation that the continuation classes should be patterned on the farming and other needs of the country.*'

The White Paper stated that pupils would start attending pre-vocational continuation classes in September 1968.

And so it came to pass.

The continuation classes concept

The basic idea behind the continuation classes was that pupils not destined to go to secondary schools would spend a proportion of their time learning skills and techniques that would be useful to them in everyday life. Those skills and techniques therefore had to relate to what was customarily done in the local community and, more specifically, in families – the economic unit to which the unemployable school leaver would have to resort. That served to narrow the field. What it meant in fact was that schools would introduce into the curriculum activities that were already generating a measure of financial return in the district. That in turn boiled down to farming practice and local handicrafts. However, that is not quite what happened at first.

Evolution

In 1969, 18 schools, two from each of the nine regions, were selected as trial schools. To support the programme, the Government had done two things. First, it had voted a sizeable sum of money and second, it had approached Unicef for assistance. The situation, as it was then, is nicely summed up in a Unesco Review.

'Current attitudes make the task of curriculum development and design of examinations difficult, and at the same time critically important. The basic and secondary courses in particular offer problems. Students want promotion to higher courses; yet most of them will not achieve it, and of those in the basic course in particular, there will be no further schooling for the majority. They need to be prepared for living in their current environment, but that is not what most of them or their parents *want*. This is a difficult problem to which there is probably no ideal answer. The Ministry of Education is experimenting with "continuation classes" in an attempt to tackle the problem, in the hope of influencing the attitudes of students in their last two years of middle school.

'In this climate of opinion Unicef agreed to play its part.'

Unicef's contribution was to take responsibility for the supply of 18 sets of equipment deemed necessary for the project. The sets of equipment were to consist of 'science teaching aids, agricultural equipment (including poultry), home science equipment, woodworking tools, masonry tools and some games and sports equipment' *(Occasional Report on Education and Training for Development).*

The equipment thus constituted a rather appetizing carrot, especially when those supplies were contrasted both in type and extent with supplies required and available for the normal academic courses. But even so, all was not quite plain sailing. At that stage the way in which the idea was to be translated into action had not yet crystallized. It was left to the schools to work out solutions best suited to their own needs. There was thus no prescribed curriculum – a situation in striking contrast with the conditions obtaining for the regular programme. There was no set allocation of time and teachers could not be given special advance training for their new tasks. The decision was taken to proceed immediately, partly out of necessity because there had not been time nor were there the resources to preplan the whole operation step by step. It was also done partly out of desperation because there was need for immediate action. But it was also done with a measure of deliberation in the belief that the situation was such that schools would and could use their own initiative to solve the problem.

The undertaking, then, was partly a gamble taken in good faith and, it must be admitted, with some measure of hope. The risk of failure was quite substantial. At other times and in other places reforms and innovations have failed for the lack of any one of the three factors above: a curriculum, a time allocation, and teacher preparation. With all three not provided and some degree of scepticism, if not opposition, displayed by sections of the public, the odds seemed hardly tilted in favour of success.

With the scheme underway and time thus gained to assess future prospects, the Ministry decided not to put all their eggs in the equipment basket. They turned the four VW Kombi buses (also supplied by Unicef) to good effect, using them to help in the organization of courses and programmes. Then the Ministry appointed regional organizers whose task was to visit the schools giving advice, guidance and help. This system of area organizers is not unknown in other parts of the British Commonwealth and it seems to have developed as an offshoot of the inspectorial system. In the inspectorial system, it is the role of ministry-appointed inspectors to visit schools to evaluate their effectiveness and more particularly to judge the competency of teachers. As promotion and appointments hinged on the inspector's judgement (often subjected to institutionalized checks and balances, however), the inspector's visits were not always regarded with eager anticipation. However, it has always been a presumption made by the inspectors themselves (and usually expressed in the rhetoric of the inspectorial system), that, as well as being judges, they provide guidance and help. By contrast, the area organizer system was meant to do the latter only and usually in a very specialized way. But because area organizers are also Ministry officials, sometimes the boundaries between advice and command and between guidance and prescription became blurred. At worst the organizer becomes innocuous because he has no 'teeth' and the inspector becomes intimidating because he has. However, one of the uses of the organizer is as a diffuser of information. As well as bringing his own new ideas, he becomes a carrier passing ideas gained at one school onto the next. This not only can serve to sustain a level of interest and motivation, but in a situation where the curriculum is unstructured it tends to help a common pattern emerge. This common pattern can then become a convention and sooner or later the convention can become articulated into curriculum prescriptions and thus legitimized and sanctified. Be that as it may, the schools survived the first year well. At that point, Unicef, having produced the first of the promised new sets of equipment, sufficient to the needs of 20 schools, considered that it was time to have a look to see how the project was faring. In 1971 the Resident Director of Unicef in Lagos, in the course of a 1000-mile trip, visited some 12 of the schools in five of the regions. His account, produced as an Occasional Report for the Manpower and Training Section of the Economic Commission for Africa, provides brief graphic and sometimes picturesque descriptions of conditions as he saw them at the schools.

Progress

If one takes the essence of the report rather than the detail of its substance, it seems obvious that the Unicef observer, though noting one or two problems, was impressed by what he saw. And the diversity was considerable. He visited boys' schools, girls' schools and coeducational schools; church and state schools. But the chief variety was to be seen in the range and array of activities undertaken in the name of continuation education. There were school farms of various kinds, including poultry, sheep, staples (crops, such as plaintain and cassava). There were school market gardens that grew red peppers, aubergines, corn, beans and green vegetables. There were specialized craft centres producing sandals, Kente cloth (long slim hand-woven bands which when joined together make the spectacular robes worn on ceremonial occasions, particularly by chiefs). There were home science activities, baking and cooking, needlework and sewing (on Unicef machines). On the coast were also to be found well developed fishing classes. The general impression that the report gives is that there was much activity, some well organized and developed and most accompanied by a considerable degree of enthusiasm. One conclusion reads:

> 'The introduction of continuation classes in middle schools meets a felt need and that the teachers and children respond favourably and eagerly wherever the continuation classes are introduced.'

Oddly enough, it is one of the 'problems' that was identified during the visit that makes the most telling (and slightly poignant) point about the continuation schools operation. Because of Unicef's role in providing equipment, one of the principal reasons for the visit was to assess whether the equipment was found to be appropriate for its intended purpose, although occasionally not everything was being used to its fullest capacity. (For example, the report noted that one poultry incubator was lying idle.) However, it was apparent that a number of schools did not have complete sets of equipment, in fact some inventories were noticeably short. And this is the poignant part. The reason was that the idea of continuation classes had, in such a short space of time, proved so popular that the demand for them had escalated far beyond anticipation. (In 1969-70 there were only 20. One year later the number was up to 123.) The Ministry, faced by such a demand and with no wish to be seen as discriminating in favour of a select few, had done the obvious thing – split the available sets so that the equipment could at least be spread (even though thinly) round more schools. This understandably was a matter of concern to the Unicef visitor, who felt that with a full complement of equipment a school could do a better job. This is hardly arguable, but the fact that more than 80 extra schools were undertaking continuation work (and relatively successfully and happily, too) suggests that whatever loss was due to dividing the equipment sets could be offset by some pretty powerful gains. Given that the specifications of the original sets were based not on experience gained in Ghana, but on an *a priori* hypothetical judgement of what would be likely to be needed, the fact that so much had been done with so little leads one to ask how much equipment constitutes a critical mass. How much is really needed to spark continuation schools?

Another problem perceived by Unicef has been softened by time. There were initially delivery delays that upset schedules and plans for some schools.

While these constituted an annoyance and sometimes a handicap, they had no major long-term effect on the project itself.

At first sight, then, there was every reason for all concerned to be gratified by the general state of affairs pertaining at the end of 1971. Even the Ministry of Education report permitted a little enthusiasm to creep into its paragraphs.

'The number of continuation schools has steadily increased from 20 in 1969-70 to 123 in 1970-71 and it is intended to involve more schools each year as equipment and staff become available. The programme has aroused considerable interest and excellent progress has been reported from a number of schools.'

The rate of adoption or diffusion of the continuation schools idea continued steadily over the next three years. In 1972-73 more than 200 middle schools became new continuation schools and by 1973-74 the total was up to 467. Four years had passed since the first 18 pilot schools were initiated. On face value progress was good, certainly above expectation. However, one salutary fact had to be taken into account – there was still a long way to go. For example, if the average growth over the three years immediately after the first were to continue, and if all middle schools were to be converted to continuation schools, and if the total number of middle schools were to remain the same (all very tenuous assumptions), then it would take until 1995-96 to convert the whole system. But 1995 was too far off, so some reassessment of the situation was needed. Before we consider what happened, however, it is necessary to give further attention to two issues: (i) the overall picture of the continuation school programme, and (ii) what was actually happening at the 'pit face', as it were, in the schools themselves.

The 1972 Report of the Ministry, in tallying the number of schools, also listed some of the activities that were being undertaken in them. Sixteen in all were selected for mention. They ranged from 'fish smoking' to 'tailoring', and from 'horticulture' to 'hair-dressing'. The Report of 1975-76 filled out the picture further. It indicated that in the over 600 continuation schools then existing, the

'course content had been systematically diversified to embrace some 32 different vocations, including vegetable gardening, crop and animal husbandry, poultry farming, cloth weaving, cane work, catering, extraction of vegetable oils, dress-making, hair-dressing, fishing, masonry, woodwork, vulcanising, charcoal burning, salt making, blacksmithing and welding'.

The Report went on to add: 'Whilst ensuring that the programme reflects the economic activity of the area, consideration is given to the availability of transportation and marketing facilities to ensure that the programme is self-supporting and attractive'.

Successes

Any visitor to a continuation school cannot fail to be impressed by the energy, application and apparent enthusiasm of both children and teachers. Levels of activity and motivation appear to be high. Even if the impression has to be discounted to some extent by a 'window-dressing' factor (a phenomenon only too familiar to education systems employing formal inspection), the degree of active involvement would still be high. How has this come about? What explains the fact that children work so hard at school and even then return after hours to continue working, *and* enjoy it? There are three main explanations that at least appear plausible.

In the first place, this 'pre-vocational' education component stands in stark contrast to the remainder of the curriculum. The latter is classically academic, arid and generates its own atmosphere of examination anxiety. It is also largely irrelevant for the majority of middle-school children, 80 per cent of whom are not destined to go to secondary school. To go to the pre-vocational classes, then, must almost have been seen as a reprieve.

In the second place, and this is where Skinnerian theory might have something to say, the schools have instituted another practice that is also fascinating in its simplicity. The pupils produce goods and services. The services yield economic returns. So the children get paid. A proportion of the money earned is given to the 'workers', and a proportion goes back to the school to provide capital for the next round of activity. It is not too difficult to imagine that such a 'reward' system is reinforcing and that the profit motive is accountable for at least part of the motivation shown – one matter which must be discussed in more detail later.

In the third place, there exists in Ghanaian society a set of social conventions that appear to play a particular role in generating and sustaining enthusiasm for the project. In a way that is rare, if not unknown in the Western world, the schools in Ghana are regarded by the community as theirs. They may be paid for by others, they may have been built by others, but to the people they are theirs. Thus it is the local chief's privilege and responsibility to protect and promote the interests of the school. His elders will give him close support and his people their backing. This involvement manifests itself in various ways. The chief and his elders usually constitute a Board of Management for the school and come and go as they please. Should a visitor appear, so will the tribal dignitaries. If he is influential, his aid will immediately be sought in the interests of the school. If he has some tribal or filial allegiance to the school or district, that pressure will be greater and more potent. As well, the chief and the people will mobilize their own resources in the interests of the school – often supplying materials and labour to further the school's development. When the community takes a school activity to heart, the aggregation of social power, social influence and social persuasion that results can be very imposing. And this is what often happened in the case of the continuation schools. The idea appealed and community support followed. The fact that craftsmen from the village were often invited in as (paid) specialist tutors also helped. So did the obvious fact that the money, goods and services that resulted were themselves generating further development. True, there were cases where community support was not forthcoming. Sometimes the introduction of pre-vocational agricultural courses was seen by farmer parents as a foreclosing of their children's vocational options. But even then, sometimes the momentum generated by the school activity was sufficient to counter such parental reticence.

In addition to these there was another factor that may well have been influential too. The fact that some communities were supporting the idea – and profiting from it – created its own contagion. This was felt not only across communities, but also within schools. Originally intended only for the ninth and tenth years of schooling, in some cases pre-vocational classes crept into the eighth and even the seventh.

With so many obviously good things resulting from the project, were there any problems? Relative to the circumstances obtaining in Ghana at the time and relative to the original intentions and to what reasonably might be expected – the answer is: very few in the continuation schools themselves. The fact that equipment was sometimes sparser than would have been liked had no great effect. The fact that some initial capital was required for materials (eg leather, cloth, etc) or agricultural 'starters' (eg seeds, seedlings, fertilizers, etc) had posed some problems, but the insolvency difficulties feared had not eventuated in the schools as most of the activities became self-supporting quite quickly.

The problems that did exist lay outside. The rate or diffusion of the innovation throughout the education system was one of two main ones. The other was the total cost involved in equipping and capitalizing many more schools than those already operating.

Developments

The project had had some by-products that themselves prompted further reconsideration. It had shown that practical activities were welcomed by children and teachers alike and that the resulting motivation was valuable. It had shown that the schools could engage in small economic ventures that in the long run yielded tangible advantages to them. But most importantly, it had shown that education, sensitive to the Ghanaian way of life and to local variations, was eminently acceptable. Education for life had become legitimate. This is not to say that the pristine image of academic education had faded – far from it – but it had lost a little of its lustre.

Towards a finale

However, by 1974 the Government was ready to make a new move for which the groundwork had been laid carefully. As early as 1972 the Ministry of Education had put forward some proposals for reorganizing the education system. These attracted much comment and led to the holding of a public meeting, the outcome of which was that a committee was set up to reassess the situation. The resulting Dzobo Committee report, together with the earlier Ministry proposals plus the public comments, were then used as a basis for a new plan that the Government formally approved in February 1974.

The basic rationale for the change is contained in a succinctly phrased paragraph on the first page of an explanatory booklet entitled 'The New Structure and Content of Education for Ghana' (1974):

'The Need for Reforms

The new proposals recognize that any system of education should aim at serving the needs of the individual, the society in which he lives and the country as a whole. In particular, that the system should, in a country like Ghana, aim at instilling in the individual, an appreciation of the need for change directed towards the development of the human and material resources of the country. Equally importantly, it must generate in the individual an awareness of the ability of man, using the power derived from science and technology, to transform his environment and improve the quality of his life.'

The new structure and content proposed did represent a change for Ghana, but not a radical one. In effect, it constituted another step in the rational evolution of an indigenous national system. As such it sought to capitalize on past experience as an aid in the adaptation-evolutionary process. The continuation schools, as part of the immediate history of Ghana's education, constituted a potential point of adaptation. The questions were, then, was anything to be learned from the continuation schools episode? Should the continuation schools continue? Was it possible to grow beyond them?

There are certain aspects of the restructuring proposals that give an indication of how the continuation schools might have exerted their influence – although the document itself, because it makes no reference to the continuation schools *per se*, does not make the 'wheels within wheels' explicit. The specific clauses that seem to provide a basis for discerning the influence of the continuation schools idea are printed below.

'Basic Principles Underlying the Proposals

5. (iii) The length of basic formal education should be 9 years (free and compulsory).
   (iv) Practical programmes which lead to the acquisition of skills should be an essential part of all formal education.
   (v) Throughout the entire pre-university course, emphasis should be laid on:
      (a) the development of practical activities and the acquisition of manual skills;
      (c) the study of indigenous language, science and mathematics.
   (vi) Teacher education should be relevant.

The Process of Educational Innovation

The New Structure of Education
6. (ii) Basic first cycle education – six years primary plus three years junior secondary.

Aims and Objectives of the System
9. Primary Education
   (iii) Socialization, i.e. the development of such skills and attitudes that will enable the individual to be an effective citizen.

Skills
   (b) Creative skills. – these shall include the development of
       (i) Manipulative skills: use of tools, etc.
       (iii) Aesthetic skills: drama, music, home economics, etc.

Attitudes
   (c) To help children to learn, appreciate and practise those things which are worthy of preservation and improvement in our culture.
   (h) (i) To provide opportunities that will pre-dispose our pupils to acquire the knowledge, skills and pre-vocational experiences that will enable them to discover their aptitudes and potentialities and to develop a longing for further improvement.
       (ii) To help our pupils appreciate the dignity of work...
11. Teacher Education – objectives
    (iv) (c) to integrate the school with the community.

Content
13. The study of Languages, Mathematics, Science, Agriculture and Practical and Vocational subjects shall be given the greatest emphasis...

Primary Course
15. ... *Practical Activities* – relating to crop and animal husbandry, Local Crafts and Vocations.
    Cultural Studies – ... Arts and Crafts and Home Science.'

These specific points from the 'New Structure' have been printed in their original published form because of the document's omission of any reference to the continuation schools themselves.

In a sense, then, the document constituted the official sentence of death for the continuation schools. Nor was that sentence of death commuted by a Ministry report that followed in 1976. Entitled 'The Development of Education in Ghana', it reiterated the plans, indicated that implementation had begun in 1974-75 and made no mention of the continuation schools. It did, however, make an additional point:

'The content of the new educational structure aims at a type of curriculum that will make education *both terminal and continuing* [emphasis added]. It will be terminal in the sense that it will orientate the pupil psychologically to his immediate environment and provide him with some basic knowledge and necessary skills to earn a living in this environment.'

('The Development of Education in Ghana', 1975 and 1976)

There the book on the continuation schools might be closed but for two things. The continuation schools still exist both in fact and, even more pervasively, in spirit. Because the new structure of education is to be implemented in phases, not until 1980-81 will the old continuation schools have been officially metamorphosed into junior schools. Consequently, they can still be seen in their original form in Ghana today. But although not officially acknowledged in this way, the essential idea of the continuation schools flourishes. In so far as the proposed new structure has accepted as its foundation a concept of an education that is environmentally based and is practical, useful and relevant, it embraces the idea at the heart of the continuation schools. Further, in adapting to the fact that primary education is terminal for many, it takes over from where the continuation schools had got to. It would be an exaggeration to say that the continuation schools had dominated the thinking of the reformers, but it is no exaggeration to say that they played an important and vital role.

The future

We come now to consider an issue that is central to the fundamental purpose of this book: the question 'What of the future?' In this case it is a somewhat redundant question. The continuation schools have no future if the restructuring process continues. The continuation of the restructuring process is perhaps not inevitable. A new civilian government is about to take over from a military one in June 1979. If history repeats itself the new regime, faced with a number of existing difficulties, will reverse some of the previous government's policies. Whether or not educational policy will be affected and whether or not this aspect of educational practice will be singled out is problematical. One of the factors in the situation is likely to be the degree of continuity between the old administration and the new – and at the moment the die is not yet cast. However, given the gradual evolution of the idea of the new structure (in effect starting in 1962); given the means by which it was debated, modified and crystallized, and given also the length of time people have had to become used to it, it perhaps runs fewer risks than other aspects.

As a final word on the Continuation Schools Project, the questions raised at the beginning should be raised again. They asked, fundamentally, did the continuation schools succeed? Clearly, in one particularly significant sense they did. Without them it is extremely unlikely that the new structure of education would have been arrived at in the way it was. It is also unlikely that it would have received the support it has received or that arguments about its feasibility would have been so convincing. In another sense again, those continuation schools that did come into existence were also successful. Many were economically successful. Many were educationally successful in that they encouraged a degree of motivation hitherto unknown at that level with terminal pupils. They also succeeded in gaining strong public support. What more might one reasonably ask for?

But on at least two counts the project cannot be said to have actually culminated in the way that was originally envisaged. In the first place not more than 700 continuation schools ever came into being – that means there were still 3000 middle schools unconverted. In the second place, the effects of continuation school education on school leavers is not known. It is not known, therefore, whether or not its graduates have become self-employed or gainfully employed and if so, to what extent. The ministry is considering undertaking follow-up studies to investigate this more thoroughly but at the moment few facts are available. There is, however, some evidence from casual observation that pupils from continuation schools seem to stand a better chance of gaining employment. However, in fact, whether or not one of the major aims of the project – providing occupational opportunities for the unemployable – was realized is uncertain.

On the other hand, there is another aim that was initially attributed to the project that has manifestly *not* been achieved – the reduction of unemployment. Since the inception of the continuation schools, unemployment has increased rather than decreased. This was unquestionably due to causes outside the control of the education system. Clearly in and of itself, the education system in general and the continuation schools in particular did not have the power to cope with the whole unemployment problem. Levin (1975) was, to that extent, right: education was not the cause, therefore it could not be the cure. Nonetheless, even though the national unemployment problem remains unsolved there are grounds for wondering whether the continuation schools did make a difference at the individual level? At the moment the case is unproven. It will therefore be most interesting to see if the Ministry's follow-up studies do yield employability and self-sufficiency rates higher among continuation school leavers than their peers from elsewhere in the system. If they did, however, it probably means that the continuation schools children merely replaced others in the job queue.

How, then, does the whole account balance up? It is not our place to act the auditor's role, but two observations are perhaps worth making.

The first observation is that it is very tempting to try to judge an innovation on the basis of its objectives. The reasoning is plausible. If a project sets out to achieve something, then the index of its success should be whether or not it did so. However, such a point of view begs two rather significant questions. The first is whether the original objectives were viable. The point here is that if subsequent events come to indicate that the objectives were inappropriate, why should the original aims be pursued regardless? The second question is related. Evaluation by objectives assumes that times will not change. In other words, while the innovation is being brought into being, environmental conditions will remain constant. In almost every instance of innovation, however, this last assumption is patently false – in Ghana it was overwhelmingly false. In Ghana the system adopted some of the ideas behind the continuation schools and incorporated them *in another guise* into its plans for reform. To this extent the system displayed adaptability – flexibility rather than inflexibility. It would seem that the circumstances justified such a step and that such adaptation was wise and beneficial. As a general principle it would also seem that such adaptability should be regarded as good rather than bad. Accordingly, the fact that the continuation schools as they were originally envisaged are not to be perpetuated throughout the system should not even be a matter for concern. One is thus tempted somewhat ironically to evaluate evaluation by objectives – and find it wanting.

The second observation grows out of the qualifications made in the preceding paragraphs. The Ghana innovation, because of its longer life, allowed us to look at this particular innovation on a more generous time scale. The interpretation that resulted allowed us to see not only the evolution of the innovation itself, but also its interface with the evolution of the larger educational and societal systems that embedded it. That all of these should have interactive effects on each other is not surprising. However, that fact raises a number of important and knotty issues about planning. In particular it raises the two issues:

(i) What do the conditions in society have to be in order for any innovation to have any chance of success?
(ii) What are the likely effects of the innovation on the society at large?

But these issues and others like them need special consideration. It will be in the next two chapters that they can get it.

Did our seven separate studies yield results that might have significance above and beyond the specific countries in which each occurred? We think so. And in the next two chapters an attempt will be made to surface some general issues and to develop an explanatory logic to fit them. In several senses the *dénouement* has to be rather tentative. In the first place none of the studies is yet complete and our seven reports are indeed interim reports. In the second place, the methodologies we used do not carry the kind of scientific pedigree that would endow the results with immediate legitimacy. Our methods were pragmatic, tailored to circumstances. To that extent they were realistic. In effect what comes out of the two final chapters is a kind of plausible theory about the processes of innovation and what some of the circumstances are that influence that process – for good or evil.

Chapter 9
Findings

This book started by accepting the general view that most innovations fail and by implying that such a state of affairs was undesirable. It then argued that if more were known about the process of innovation then the risk of failure could be reduced. Having thus encouraged itself, it set out to map seven innovations that were still in progress, hoping that, in providing a running account, some of the mystery might be reduced. Now, eight chapters later, comes the moment of truth when we must try to indicate what that mapping has revealed – what, in other words, the results are. To do so, it is necessary to set the stage a little.

Definitions

After many pages of script it is perhaps time to come to terms with terms. We have been using the words 'innovation' and 'reform' freely, frequently and, it must be admitted, sometimes loosely. The reasons are simple. In the first place, that is the way the words tend to be used in the real world. In the second, whether a definition is appropriate or not depends on the circumstances for which the definition is designed. Given our seven countries and their seven different innovations we are obliged to adopt a fairly pragmatic stance over the definition of innovation. For convenience, 'innovation' had to be seen primarily in sociological terms as whatever people regarded as an innovation. One of the consequences of taking this position is that any innovation is thus innovatory relative to its context and is, perhaps, *only* innovatory in its own context. It is an innovation there – though not necessarily elsewhere. For example, despite the variations built into their two approaches it could be argued that both the Indonesians and Israelis, in starting with the Mastery Learning idea that evolved in the United States of America, are not the 'real' innovators. The point is an academic one. The reality for the administrator and planner (and for that matter the sociologist) is that in both contexts – in Indonesia and Israel – the newly developed operation is *seen* as an innovation and does represent a (quite dramatic) deviation from existing practices. And here lies what appears to be a common feature of all our innovations – they represent departures from customary practice. They entail new activities on the part of some people.

They are more than transitory – they are new activities sustained for some time. In more precise terms then, to fit our situation:

An innovation is any persisting change in the patterns of behaviour of members of an identifiable social system.

The two most vulnerable aspects of the definition are (i) the definition of what constitutes *persisting* change – one week, one year, one decade, or what, and (ii) the identification of 'social systems'. Once again a sociologistic interpretation can provide a measure of help. Both definitions depend on what the indigenes themselves regard as being the case.

A second term that has tended to be used in an occasionally cavalier fashion throughout the book (and sometimes interchangeably with innovation) is 'reform'. Because it tends to carry overtones of 'improvement' and hence a value loading, its definition is a little more difficult. For our purposes, however, it seems satisfactory to regard reform as innovation writ large – innovation on a large scale. Any reform thus must be first an innovation but whether an innovation becomes a reform depends on the extent to which it pervades the relevent system. Thus the Ghanaian Continuation Schools project, when initially confined to the 20 'experimental' schools, was an innovation. Even when it spread to 400, because there were still many potential target schools untouched, it remained an innovation. Once, however, the idea becomes incorporated into the total structure of the system and *it becomes implemented*, reform status is warranted. Thus:

Reform is an innovation that is in widespread use throughout a specified target population.

Once again the definition of a target population is that which is acceptable in context.

This small exercise in definition was necessary primarily to set the limits within which our interpretations can themselves be interpreted, and thus allow their utility to be gauged. Our definitional stance is clearly different from that adopted by others. For example, our definitions of both innovation and reform are not based on the *intentions* that people might have to induce change (Dalin, 1978; Marklund *et al*, 1974). Again our definitions make no presumptions about whether the innovation or reform is good or bad. The definitions do not assume, as do the definitions from Miles (1964), Richland (1965) and Dalin (1978), that 'improvement' will necessarily follow. For us 'intentions', 'the value of the consequences', 'innovation' and 'reform' are all definitionally independent. It thus remains possible to test relationships empirically – to see, for example: (i) whether or not intention and actuality coincide and, more importantly, why (sometimes) they do not, (ii) the process by which innovations grow to become reforms, and (iii) given the reform, what the consequences are and whether they may then be judged good or bad.

A tentative framework

If the process of innovation is to be better understood there is some need at the outset for a set of descriptors that can be used to focus attention on its most important features. Such a conceptual framework was developed for the present study and, though a little battered by the realities of the seven innovations, it still appears to have some credibility. A description follows.

Initially we found it convenient to imagine that any innovation would have to go through a series of logical phases. First, there would be a problem – that might or might not be discerned fully, accurately or even at all. Second, there would have to be one or a number of prospective solutions advanced. Any solution accepted, we assumed, would be spelled out or specified in greater or lesser (or no) detail. Third, sooner or later would come an attempt to put a 'solution' into practice – into operation. Once in operation it might or might not be evaluated. Fourth, for the innovation to take hold, it would have to be spread or would have to spread itself throughout the target population for which it was relevant. Fifth and finally, thereafter it might undergo consolidation and be absorbed into the system or it might decline and die, unable to sustain itself as a viable part.

Implicit in this conceptual framework were several ideas that together constituted a kind of functional theory. Initially we saw the five phases as constituting logically sequenced stages. After the problem emerges, solutions surface, are trialled and evaluated, and then implemented on a wider scale prior to a final absorption into the system. However, struck with the thought that life might not be quite so orderly, the design of the study was not based on the assumption of logical sequence – and, as it turned out, just as well. The 'stages' did not emerge empirically as *de facto* stages at all. For example, sometimes solutions *preceded* the identification of problems, sometimes implementation *preceded* the development of a solution prototype and, sometimes, alternative solutions *followed* rather than preceded implementation. Nonetheless, our logical model led us to the formulation of a series of hypotheses, some of which may still seem to carry some authority. They are:

1. The success of an innovation depends on the degree of precision with which the original problem – which 'caused' the need for a solution – is identified.
2. The success of an innovation depends on the availability of alternative solutions and the appropriateness of the selection made among them.
3. The success of an innovation depends on the degree of precision with which the innovation is specified.
4. The success of an innovation depends on adequate trialling and evaluation.
5. The success of an innovation depends on the provision of conditions adequate for implementation.

The Process of Educational Innovation

Behind these hypotheses lie two very basic assumptions:

(i) For any of the five phases to come into being, certain conditions must necessarily *already exist* in the system.
(ii) For any given phase there are certain conditions that must be provided for that phase to be effectively completed.

Fairly clearly, everything that has been said so far fits in with the idea that innovations 'develop' and that in order for them to develop the initial circumstances must be right and that evolving circumstances must continue to be right. The problem is to specify both sets of circumstances. Shortly, we will indicate the extent to which the present study allows us to do so but first another and critical issue has to be discussed briefly.

In using the term 'success' of an innovation we have followed a convention well established in the innovation domain. Innovations, it seems, are supposed to succeed, though most are said not to. But the reason they fail is partly definitional. Success is usually taken to mean that the innovation has survived the one, two, three, five, ten years of its hazardous childhood and has emerged unscathed by the ravages of time and place. In other words, the innovation now exists exactly as was planned in the years before – the *objectives initially specified for it have been fully met*. Now as the chapter on the Ghanaian innovation went to some pains to point out, such a definition of success has an air of unreality about it. It presumes that at the stage objectives are set, wisdom is absolute. All that is needed to be known is known then, and between the time that the objectives are stated and the time that the innovation is put into practice nothing will occur that could cause the objectives to become inappropriate. In other words, the initial judgement is always right and no event occurring subsequently could justify a reconsideration of objectives. Consequently any modification, adaptation or even abandonment must always be wrong.

There will be occasion to return to a discussion of what might be regarded as a reasonable view of success later. At the moment we must admit, however, that at the beginning of our study we too accepted the conventional view uncritically. Thus our original concern was with the problem of having the innovation 'succeed' in its own original terms. Such a concern we still think is to some extent reasonable – but only as far as it goes, and that is not far enough.

However, if an innovation is to succeed (in whatever terms are adopted) and if one accepts the idea that certain pre-conditions and co-conditions have to exist for it to do so, the task still remains to specify what those conditions might be. Fundamentally that boils down to three questions about what is necessary to make an innovation work. These are: (i) What components or ingredients are necessary? (ii) What condition do they have to be in? and (iii) When do they have to be in place? For us the answer to the third question, the 'when' question, lies in the five phases outlined earlier. In other words, each phase requires the existence of specific components that at that point must also be in the necessary condition. The answer to the first question, 'What components are necessary?', is the same for all stages. To us there are 11 main components. The more difficult question on the appropriate state of those components will be considered after the 11 are outlined and discussed.

Essential elements

It is possible that somewhere in the research literature on innovation, or for that matter on educational administration, there exists a beautifully articulated, rational and convincing statement about the dimensions of innovations, but we were unable to find it. Consequently, we were forced back to a rather crude basis for arriving at our component categories. Our procedure was perhaps only one step better than intuition but it did have a kind of primitive logic to it. It was based on the idea that the kinds of questions that people ask limit (even determine) the way we think about things. By taking one linguistic definition of questions (*wh* questions – questions that ask 'who', 'what', 'which', 'where', 'when', 'why', and 'how' (in whatever manner) we were able to form a comprehensive, though rather quaint, composite question that we then applied to the innovation process. It went this way: 'Who does what, with what, to whom, where, when, in what manner and why and with what effect?'

Our attempt to respond to that composite question led us to generate 11 different kinds of answers that became initially our category system for the data-gathering method referred to in Chapter 1, and subsequently also became our innovation 'components' below. Thus at each stage of the innovation process, we consider that decisions have to be taken with respect to:

(i) the *personnel* to be employed,
(ii) the specification of what the actual *task* is,
(iii) the *method* (strategy or procedure to undertake the task),
(iv) the *equipment* needed,
(v) the *plant*, buildings or environment required,
(vi) the *cost* entailed,
(vii) other people or rather *other social contexts* on which the innovation *impinges*,
(viii) the *time* involved,
(ix) the *scheduling* or sequencing or coordinating of activities,
(x) the *rationale* for undertaking the innovation,
(xi) the evaluation of the *consequences* or *effects* resulting.

Predictably, there were a number of hypotheses buried in this selection of essential components that were based on assumptions made about the presence or absence of the ingredients. Initially all ingredients were thought to be essential if that elusive and illusory 'success' were to be achieved. In some cases this was plainly self-evident. For example, if to develop the innovation skilled people are necessary and skilled people are not available, then it cannot be done. Similarly, if money is essential, or equipment is, or buildings are, and none is available then again success is impossible. We also imagined, at that stage in our thinking, that if what had to be done remained unclear and unspecified, then the innovation could not come to pass. Finally, impressed by the arguments coming from the R & D school and from the various protagonists of evaluation, we also believed that without methodological precision and approved forms of evaluation, failure could be the only outcome. Now, at our present stage of thinking, half-way through the project, we have come to reconsider the situation and withdraw a little from our original dogmatic position. *Some* of the components are still useful, we think, in helping to *understand* or *explain* the process of innovation itself. Others have relevance for management too but *only if* certain purposes (to be discussed later) have to be accomplished. For the *planning* of innovations, however, we still regard all components as necessary, in that neglecting to take conscious decisions about each one is to increase sharply the vulnerability of the innovation process.

When planning or administration is involved, the decisions that have to be taken about each component, though, go beyond the mere issue of making sure that each of the components exists and is in place. Clearly, in each case, each component must also be appropriate for the purposes intended. This now brings us to the third matter on which discussion was raised earlier – the condition of the components. Basically what is at issue here is whether the components are or are not appropriate for the task in hand, that is, whether they are sufficient in quantity *and* quality. Discussion follows.

Ingredient adequacy

Table 5 provides a summary model of the conceptual map of the innovation process that has been presented so far. It is a two-dimensional map in which the phases appear across the top and the 11 components down the left-hand column.

The inference to be drawn from Table 5 for *planning* is that for *each* stage there have to be specifications drawn up for *every* component together with an overall design for the sequencing of provisions.

The inference to be drawn for *administration* is that at each stage the supply of components has to be managed so that they separately and collectively come to fulfil their appointed roles. The beguiling simplicity of those two statements should deceive no one. Both hide a series of assumptions about 'cause' and 'effect', about 'conditions' and their 'consequences', for which so far no justification has been provided. The attempt that follows represents a first tentative step towards providing that justification.

*   *   *

Table 5: *Dimensions of the innovation process*

Components	Phases				
	1 Problem identification	2 Specification of the solution	3 Initial use ('Trial')	4 Implementation Diffusion	5 Consolidation Rejection
Personnel	1.01	2.01	3.01	4.01	5.01
Task (specification)	1.02	2.02	3.02	4.02	5.02
Method – procedure	1.03	2.03	3.03	4.03	5.03
Equipment	1.04	2.04	3.04	4.04	5.04
Plant – buildings	1.05	2.05	3.05	4.05	5.05
Cost	1.06	2.06	3.06	4.06	5.06
Impinging contexts	1.07	2.07	3.07	4.07	5.07
Time	1.08	2.08	3.08	4.08	5.08
Scheduling	1.09	2.09	3.09	4.09	5.09
Rationale	1.10	2.10	3.10	4.10	5.10
Evaluation	1.11	2.11	3.11	4.11	5.11

In this section of the chapter which attempts to deal with an explanation of how innovation occurs, two strategic ploys are to be used.

First, the studies of the seven countries are to be used to provide illustrations of points serving to produce both verification and falsification. At this stage in our exercise, however, we have to proceed on the brave and perhaps rash assumption that all our innovations will succeed. Thus in our seven studies, when the conditions we originally thought necessary and sufficient are upset, we will make the interpretation that the original theorizing was wrong. We will also try to provide at least a plausible explanation of this unexpected state of affairs. Second, in our presentation we will initially have to approach explanation in a piecemeal fashion, taking each phase in turn and, as far as possible, each component in it.

It will be left to the final chapter to follow on from this fragmentary approach and relate phase to phase – to surface what we have discerned about the relationships between them. In that final chapter, too, we will attempt to draw conclusions at the most universal level we can, proceeding from what we imagine we have learned so far from our exercise.

Phase 1 – Identifying the problem

If it can be assumed that any innovation represents (at least to its supporters) a way of *improving* the situation, then the conditions that 'needed' improvement can be thought to constitute a 'problem'. If so, then a certain seductive quality attaches itself to the argument that in the interests of effective innovation, the underlying problem should be defined accurately and early. The argument is hardly contestable when the *planner* is commissioned to 'overcome a specific problem'. But is it equally uncontestable for an *administrator* given the task of managing an innovation (as a presumed solution to a problem)? And is it the case that the early and precise definition of the problem is a good indicator or predictor of the likely survival and adoption of an innovation?

On the basis of our studies, there appears to be no necessary connection between identifying the problem at the outset and the subsequent survival capacity of the innovation. We have examples where the problem was (i) defined early (Indonesia, Ghana, the Federal Republic of Germany and New Zealand); (ii) gradually but deliberately sought out and discovered (Israel); (iii) redefined, following a series of successive approximations (Malaysia); and (iv) seen more in terms of the feasibility, viability and usefulness of a proposed solution (Sierra Leone).

In fact, looking at our innovations, it seems as if an innovation may even become *less* vulnerable if the problem with which it is supposed to deal is *not* defined too early. Delayed definition not only prevents premature closure but also gives scope for the definition of the problem to be adaptable in the light of developing circumstances.

On the basis of our studies, it also seems as if the degree of *precision* with which the problem is defined does not necessarily offer any great advantage to an administrator or any great predictive power to the researcher seeking to explain the fate of an innovation. On reflection, there are several reasons that might account for this. For example, defining the problem precisely offers no necessary guarantee that the innovation (solution) will itself be designed to accord with it – although the probability that it might be presumably increases. Again, defining the problem precisely makes the administrator vulnerable to accusations of inconsistency, if unanticipated circumstances subsequently force a (desirable) deviation. It seems as if the precise definition of the problem would be of most value to (i) the planner who wishes to propose action that is likely to be effective in solving the problem, or (ii) to the evaluator who wishes to judge the innovation in terms of its problem-solving efficiency.

It also seems to be the case that the nature of the problem influences the amount of definitional precision that is possible. For example, the problem that gave rise to the innovations in both the Federal Republic of Germany and Ghana consisted of an undesired escalation of the number of unemployed youth – an increasing proportion of school leavers were unable to get jobs. At face value the problem seems clear and relatively straightforward. By contrast, the problem for Indonesia was an obviously complex one – to convert an inadequate old education system into a satisfactory new one. Again, the problem behind Sierra Leone's drive to improve rural living through education was presumably the conviction that rural living conditions were not adequate, coupled with the belief that the (complex) link between education and rural development could be established. New Zealand's problem presumably was that the existing prototype for secondary school buildings was inadequate for the future – a relatively simple issue, one might think. Malaysia and Israel in their turn viewed the existing organizational structure and practice of education in the first three years of school as inadequate but chose to regard the degree of complexity involved in very different ways. The Israelis have deliberately promoted a complicated approach; the Malaysians, on the other hand, have favoured one that starts from relatively simple and straightforward first steps.

The significance of the extent to which the problem is seen as a complex or simple matter clearly affects how fully the problem can be specified. It also has another effect – on prospective solutions. In all of the cases illustrated above there is an implicit acceptance of the idea of 'cause'. Something 'caused' the undesired circumstances and (therefore) something else could 'cause' them to be improved. Given that the underlying assumptions about cause are likely to have an influence on determining the direction in which a solution is sought, perhaps a *full* definition of the problem requires the making of those implicit ideas explicit. This appears to have particular bearing on whether or not the solution *can* indeed solve the problem and whether it will attempt to do so directly or indirectly. Ghana and the Federal Republic of Germany provide intriguing cases in point. In both cases education was not the cause of increased unemployment. In the Federal Republic of Germany's case it looks as if the educational solution adopted cannot (logically) solve the unemployment problem there (though it appears to be helping to solve others). In Ghana's case it looks as if the educational solution is working to some extent in that by increasing the proportion of the self-employed, a small structural change is being introduced into the labour market.

It follows from this line of argument that if the problem is to be defined fully (as well as precisely and early) and if some explanation of 'cause' is also required, then much more information is likely to be required – with the quantity of information no doubt proportional to the complexity of the problem – the more complex the problem is seen to be, the greater the amount of information that would be required. The nature of such information and the (delaying) effects of requiring it may be guessed at for the moment. They will need to be discussed later when we give attention to alternative strategies of planning and administration. Meantime, however, attention now turns to the specific components of the 'Problem Identification Phase'. In dealing with the components, our approach will be to select from our own studies points that seem to be of particular relevance and interest, although we are obliged to add that we do not pretend to have the last word to say on what would constitute an ideal condition for each or any of the components.

1.01 Personnel

Our studies reveal quite vast differences of approach. For example, in Nordrhein-Westfalen, because the unemployment 'problem' was a matter of widespread public and political concern, it was debated on many public occasions, featured repeatedly in the media, and was given attention by many interested parties and a number of ministries. By contrast, the New Zealand problem definers consisted of a selected and select group of some 30 people who, though having been drawn from a number of educational agencies, were not required to represent them. The education-consuming public – children or parents, or for that matter employers – were not party to the task. In Sierra Leone the main burden of problem definition fell first on the Ministry or, more properly, a segment of it, which then worked informally with the Principal of the Bunumbu Teachers College, prior to being closely involved with International Funding Agencies. In Israel a handful of interested people who possessed different and complementary kinds of educational expertise were the problem definers.

Can it therefore be said that one 'mix' of personnel constitutes a better mix than any other? Not surprisingly, the answer depends on the kind of purposes that are being accomplished by having the problem defined at all – and, it goes almost without saying, whose purposes are thus being served. Clearly, in our cases, the purposes were different and the ways in which the definitional task was attacked were different. Accordingly, the answer to the personnel question is to some extent bound up with the answer to the next question and successive ones.

1.02 The specifications of the problem

As the preceding section indicated, the countries varied in their selection of the people to be involved in the problem definition task. Predictably, too, they varied in the extent of definition called for. The Israelis, in setting out to first *find* what the problem was, worked off different premises than did most of the other countries who, having accepted the existence of a specific problem, were bent on clarifying that problem. Some did so quickly, delaying but a short time before putting their full effort into contemplating solutions (Sierra Leone and Ghana constitute cases in point). Probably the most systematic attempts at defining the problem were undertaken by Indonesia, Israel and New Zealand. The Indonesians started from a major statement of public policy, subsequently engaged in a series of successive refinements of problem after problem until they arrived at the specific problem of producing a curriculum 'delivery system' appropriate for existing conditions. Both the Israelis and the New Zealanders used select groups of educators who, perhaps inevitably, came to define the problem in educational terms. In both cases, in the light of subsequent political and economic conditions, it seems questionable that such a restricted (though no doubt meritorious) perspective was sufficient.

There will be occasion to return (often) to the issue of what kinds of purposes are being served at any particular time. For example, if the sole purpose to be served in Israel and New Zealand was to produce an *educational specification*, then both types of groups did their jobs well, it seems. On the other hand, the Sierra Leoneans and Malaysians and Indonesians, in collaborating with international funding agencies, succeeded admirably in accommodating another purpose – the economic one of ensuring financial support. Apparently, in the Federal Republic of Germany, the problem was of such widespread concern that, in contrast with all the other countries (Indonesia perhaps excepted) many, many people were involved in public discussion of it. This, no doubt, helped accommodate a political purpose.

On face value then, it seems that educational purposes call for one particular mix of personnel and result in a particular specification of the problem. Similarly, political purposes call for another mix and result again in a particular kind of specification. Similarly, it can be argued that social and economic purposes are served by alternative mixtures and are likely to yield different specifications again. All this raises fundamental questions about the purposes (and products) of innovation itself and indeed to what uses the competing 'models' of the innovation process themselves can be put – a matter to be considered in the final chapter.

1.03 Methods of problem definition

In this case one might reasonably assume that the procedures used for defining the problem are likely to be influenced by outside circumstances, particularly those that determine the resources available and conventions that are usually followed. For example, within the relatively centralized education systems of Malaysia, Indonesia, Ghana, Sierra Leone and New Zealand, it is not altogether surprising that the ministries all played prominent roles making use of consultations, committees and individuals in ways that were customary in their institutions.

Obviously the methods used by all countries were constrained by the amount of background data available on the kind of qualitative problems facing them. In this respect qualitative planning stands in marked contrast to what has been called quantitative planning where the need for hard data on, for example, the teaching force, pupil enrolments, school buildings, supplies and equipment etc has long been regarded as necessary for providing the data base essential for quantitative decision making. Qualitative planning, however, is faced with two major problems. First, it is not altogether clear what data bases would be most useful. Second, few systems have yet accumulated much data that might be thought to be relevant to qualitative planning. Under such circumstances it is not surprising that the main method used in problem defining tends to be informed (and sometimes misinformed) deliberation. At this stage in education's development, intelligent guesswork continues to play a significant part. This has particular significance when one has to ask who is likely to make the most intelligent guesses. Once again the answer to this question appears to be relative to the purposes to be served, the use to which the results are to be put and the people who have to use them.

1.04 and 1.05 Equipment and plant needed

None of the seven countries reported any difficulties associated with the availability of plant and equipment for their problem-defining task. Both New Zealand and Israel, at critical stages in the evolution of their task, did choose to isolate their planning groups for several days and thus give them uninterrupted time free from the demands of the outside world. On the other hand, none of the countries indicated whether or not the quality of their deliberations *at this stage* might have been enhanced by their gaining access to further relevant information that might have entailed the use of computers, videotaping and other 'equipment' resources. In contrast with other phases, where the cost and appropriateness of plant, equipment and resources appear very important, in this phase all of the countries regarded the material circumstances under which they had to operate as quite satisfactory.

1.06 Cost

In none of our countries did cost loom large during this phase either. Whatever cost was entailed over and above the ordinary labour and operational costs normally met by the system was, apparently, minimal. Obviously New Zealand had to meet the travel and accommodation expenses (but not remuneration) of their planning group's two sessions. But in a million-dollar project this was insignificant. Initial planning costs in the Israeli project were born partly by the two host organizations (the University of Tel Aviv and MATACH) and partly by the participants themselves. Some of the other countries were able to take advantage of aid programmes already in existence.

1.08 and 1.09 Time and scheduling

Five of the seven countries were inclined to consider that the amount of time made available during this phase was either insufficient or almost so. With apologies to Parkinson – work had apparently expanded to overflow the time available, or near enough to it. Curiously the two countries considering the allocation of time to be 'very sufficient' expressed reservations over whether or not the time available was scheduled appropriately enough. The other countries, though pressed for time, were more inclined to regard the way the limited time available was put to use as reasonably satisfactory.

Given the 'conversational' way in which the problem-defining task proceeded, the major difficulty appeared to be a familiar one – coordinating events so that whoever needed to be free to participate could do so.

1.10 Rationale

For this phase, a rationale should, in essence, indicate why the problem is perceived in the way that it is and why steps are being taken to deal with it in the way that they are. To a considerable extent, any rationale must be clearly tied up with how the *task* is specified, the *procedures* used to specify it and the *people* involved in doing it. In not all our cases was a rationale made explicit in advance although several countries have subsequently produced documents that provide fairly systematic explanations of previous events. In Indonesia the modular instruction problem was logically and rationally located within a broader problem of educational development. In Ghana and the Federal Republic of Germany the innovation owed its justification to socio-economic issues similar in kind. Sierra Leone had a social and economic frame of reference for its innovation but for the other countries an educational justification seemed to suffice.

However, some of the other surrounding events prompt conjecture. The four developing countries in the project all have received and continue to receive outside financial aid. This is seen as a means for improving the system and enhancing its capacity to develop. Without examining the success rates of aided projects – which seem little different from innovation projects in general – it is obvious that aid provides scope for systems to do things that they otherwise might not. However, the aid agencies, understandably enough, specify the terms and conditions under which aid would be forthcoming. Consequently, in order to gain project aid, countries have to design their activities to meet the approval of the donors. It follows then that sometimes the rationale for a project may be an economic one, with the obtaining of aid a principal objective. It is probably true to say that Indonesia, Malaysia and Sierra Leone, and to a lesser extent Ghana, were all sensitive to this aspect. So was Israel in a not too dissimilar fashion – although there the source of 'aid' was to be the Ministry of Education itself. Neither the Federal Republic of Germany nor New Zealand found it necessary to take such considerations into account because their financial support was not in question – it came from the Ministry.

1.07 Impinging contexts

We are led by the discussion on rationale to consider the extent to which other sections of the community were involved in this early phase. The issue under consideration here is not only whether or not additional inputs (of different kinds) would be useful but whether or not the *failure to involve* interested sectors might lead to difficulties afterwards. It is easy to be swayed by the copious literature on the importance of group interaction, territorial rights and power sharing to give particular emphasis to this aspect of innovation. Once again our seven countries displayed quite noteworthy differences in the extent to which they involved other interested parties in the phase of problem specification.

Given that the purpose of involving others is primarily to placate them, does trouble lie ahead for those countries that restricted participation and does success necessarily lie ahead for those that extended it widely? We think not, although when we come later to suggest that this aspect of innovation *is* the single most important one, we will have one or two qualifications to add.

1.11 Evaluation

The final word in this section has been kept, appropriately enough, for evaluation. Conventionally evaluation has tended to occur at the end – when there is something to evaluate. However, there is evidence from our study that often evaluation is not made at all and, in contrast, sometimes evaluatory statements are made before anything exists to be evaluated. Problem definition as such came in for no formal evaluation in any of our countries. Whatever evaluation occurred tended to be informal – merely the result of feedback. It also tended to be delayed until other events had occurred that encouraged a retrospective look – either in dismay or delight. Formative evaluation, apart from the way in which dialogue encouraged it, was not considered a prime essential at this point.

Summary

Sufficient diversity was demonstrated among the countries to indicate that if all the innovations do succeed, the formal and systematic definition of the problem is not a necessary condition for success. Further, the evidence almost seems to suggest that no single one of the components of this phase needs to be regarded as essential either. It does seem, however, that if the purposes being served at this early stage are made explicit, for example, if the undertaking is academic at heart, or political or educational, then the combination of components that would help that purpose might be more easily specified. If, as well, it were possible to have (i) the rationale spelled out, (ii) the undertaking justified and (iii) the ends in view appreciated, then again, the state of the components likely to yield such results could be specified. However, it must be admitted in passing that where the objective is to conceal rather than reveal, to achieve an oblique purpose rather than a direct one, to create a 'facade' of legitimacy, then the conditions of the various components would need to be in a somewhat different condition. Such a comment is no endorsement of a Machiavellian approach to administration and planning, merely the foreshadowing of another issue – the relationship between the rhetoric and reality – that will also surface in the final chapter.

Phase 2 – Specifications for a solution

Someone once put it, 'there are no such things as problems, only opportunities'. As far as innovations are concerned this would appear to be often a truism. The literature on innovation is full of accounts of 'good ideas' that are thought to be good in their own right. Those good ideas are often supported by earnest and energetic advocates who also often display a measure of charisma that leads others to invest faith and hope (and money) in the schemes they propose. Such innovations really constitute solutions. But whether or not any problem related to the solution exists in the system is quite another question. For example, throughout the world 'open plan' classrooms have been introduced, not in response to an identified problem but simply because they were considered to be inherently good. On face value, it would be reasonable to think that there is some merit in knowing, before a solution is tried, whether there *is* a problem for it to solve. However, after the somewhat equivocal conclusions we reached about phase 1, we have some hesitation over too readily supporting the sweet reasonableness of such obvious logic. After all, it may turn out that to specify a solution is more important than to have identified a problem.

Two of the countries, Ghana and the Federal Republic of Germany, in the early stages of their innovations chose, at the level of central authority, not to produce anything other than very general specifications. In both, the responsibility was left to the schools who themselves were given considerable scope to exercise their initiative. In New Zealand, the new architectural specifications were all thoroughly defined but only broad (and very optional) guidelines were provided as *educational* specifications. Indonesia's specifications were the most intricate and systematic and the detail they contained was very much in tune with, in particular, contemporary American theorizing on curriculum development. In Sierra Leone, again, the project document came complete with a detailed list of plans and equipment components, an indication of the kind of curriculum materials that would result, and an outline of some of the procedures to be used in producing and disseminating them. Malaysia, it will be recalled, started with a carefully thought-out project document but the project itself initially ran into a series of unexpected problems that were subsequently overcome because of the scope for flexible adaptation that the project permitted.

In the light of this variety among our countries it is again difficult to claim that specifying the solution, at least in the early stages, is absolutely essential. In fact, once again, premature closure on such specifications may result in a degree of inflexibility that could prejudice future events.

2.01 Personnel

Whether or not those countries that did not produce early 'specifications' of their solutions lacked the personnel necessary is unknown. Those that did attempt to do so, however, did use their personnel in various ways. The Indonesian procedure involved a considerable amount of consultation among senior officials of the Education Ministry, officials from other ministries, Government officers, influential citizens, the teaching profession, others likely to be interested and affected – mostly, however, within ready reach of Jakarta. In Malaysia the first steps were taken within the Ministry's Education Planning and Research Division and subsequently the Curriculum Development Unit. In Sierra Leone, the first efforts also came from the Planning Division, subsequently augmented by Bunumbu College and the Teachers Training Division of the Ministry. In New Zealand, various educational 'authorities' were involved in initial relatively free consultation but the final documentation was left in the hands of the Ministry. In the Federal Republic of Germany the legislation was, of course, passed in Parliament but the teachers' handbook which contained guidelines (*Richtlinien*) was drawn up by Ministry officials working with co-opted practitioners. The Ghanaian regulations similarly had their origin in the Education Ministry. Only in Israel was the activity undertaken beyond the fringe of ministerial skirts. There, the first specification consisted of a research proposal to 'identify the problem'. Once the problem had been identified there followed an operating definition of the solution. It is worth noting that everything achieved there was done without official commitment – financial support yes, commitment no.

The countries varied in what might be called the amount of pre-specification of the solution. For example, although the Indonesians had a very elaborate plan from the outset, the detailed specification of the modules of instruction themselves was itself part of an evolving process. In Malaysia, too, working specifications evolved as a response to existing contingencies but they did so almost in the face of the original plan.

2.02 Task specification

At issue here is the way in which the task of producing specifications for the solution was undertaken itself. In New Zealand, the Ministry of Education, having decided that it wanted to plan for the school of the future, set out to organize and do it as a consultative exercise. In Indonesia, the task of producing specifications for a new modular 'delivery' system followed on logically from other earlier educational and political decisions to reform the total system. The Ministry of Education and Science then gave the mandate for what was essentially a curriculum development task. In Malaysia, as in other countries, the decision to seek foreign aid was partly a political decision.

The fact that some of the conditions laid down by one funding agency appealed to some educational interests of the Ministry led, reasonably enough, to the production of a research proposal that in effect comprised the first set of prescriptions. The Sierra Leone situation shared much with the Indonesian one, but early action there saw also some involvement of the prospective funding agencies themselves. Ghana and the Federal Republic of Germany once again have much in common. In so far as any specifications were drawn up, the Ministries were responsible for producing them, more or less as a footnote to legislation.

Fundamentally, at this stage in the evolution of any innovation, the purpose of task specification is to provide a sufficient basis for getting into *action*. By definition then, any project proposal that succeeds in attracting the financial support needed has achieved its purpose. So, for that matter, has *anything* that serves to get action under way. But the differences in the mechanisms used – project proposals (Malaysia and Sierra Leone), legislation (Federal Republic of Germany), experiment (Ghana and Israel), routine development procedures (Indonesia and New Zealand), suggest that there are many possible roads to salvation. Of our alternative roads perhaps the Federal Republic of Germany's is the most uncertain. As a legislated action, depending on the acquiescence and the initiative of schools, and under conditions where little policing is likely, it will be interesting to see how many of the schools begin the journey and how they choose to travel.

Probably the most basic issue here is the extent to which the initial specifications, whatever their form, left scope for subsequent modification. Theoretically a perfect plan would anticipate the future perfectly. That few plans are perfect (moonshots excluded sometimes) is notorious. Presumably, then, a good plan would allow the imperfections that do occur to be remedied easily. This also presumably means that those people who are best able to produce remedies are free and available to do so. Here, once again, the issue of responsibility and autonomy seems central. And this issue was resolved differently by different countries. It is the case that the Indonesian plan foresaw problems being solved essentially at the centre of operations. That was the original intention too in Malaysia but force of circumstances resulted in the evolution of a much greater degree of feedback between the experimental teachers and the project leaders than expected. The Israeli plan had made provision for the use of such an interaction right from the start, but this time involving teachers, researchers and technology developers together. In New Zealand, although the Ministry of Education provided the material means (the building) and some 'suggestions', once the building was erected, the teachers and the school had complete control with, it must be admitted, some consequences not foreseen by the original planners. Ministry involvement in Ghana's case was relatively slight initially, although with the appointment of advisory officers it increased a little. In Germany, once the Ministry had laid the keel it kept its distance, giving schools and teachers almost complete freedom to do as they pleased.

2.04 and 2.05 Plant and equipment

It is predictable that plant and equipment specifications for this phase will be highly idiosyncratic to the particular innovation. Thus there are detailed specifications of the Whanau House *building* in the New Zealand project as there are also detailed listings of the equipment needed for the Bunumbu project and for the Ghana project too, etc. This idiosyncratic character makes any detailed description unnecessary.

With the exception of the New Zealand project which was, in part, designed expressly to evaluate the plant proposed, the other projects assumed that the equipment and plant specified would serve its intended purpose. Developments in two projects, however, encourage a closer look at that assumption. It will be remembered that the original specifications for the experimental sets of equipment to be used in the 20 experimental schools in Ghana were based on an informed estimate. It will also be remembered that, because of social pressure, that equipment became spread (of necessity more thinly) to a greater number of schools. This led us, in the Ghana chapter, to conjecture over what might really constitute a 'critical mass' – an adequate but unextravagant supply of equipment sufficient to enable the project to function. In a similar way, the cost of a relatively ideal set of plant and equipment initially specified in Sierra Leone has led to conjecture over how much would be really necessary if the replications of the Bunumbu project were thought to be desirable elsewhere in the country. There is apparently a nice and useful distinction to make between too little equipment, just enough and too much. Obviously too little prevents action. Also, as research in the USA shows, too much may stultify. The trick, then, is to determine how much is just enough. And that is a matter that seldom receives systematic attention.

2.06 Costing

It seems as if the fairly careful attention given by all countries to costing during this stage is to ensure that innovations are not entered into rashly. Almost invariably, though, it is the cost of the first (experimental) steps that attracts closest attention. In none of our countries was any attempt made to anticipate the costs of subsequent steps. By and large the future was expected to take care of itself, and facing up to the problem of expansion and implementation costs was one that could consequently be deferred. Some of the countries, notably Indonesia and Sierra Leone, acknowledged the necessity to consider such costs but not until later on. Other countries presumably preferred to wait and see.

2.08 and 2.09 Time and scheduling

When the countries were asked to indicate whether sufficient time had been available for drawing up specifications, Indonesia and Ghana both indicated that more time would have been desirable; much more in Ghana's case. Both apparently wished to have had better opportunity to sort out difficulties at the level of central authority. Other countries expressed themselves relatively satisfied with the time at their disposal. All of the countries reported that the time available was appropriately used. The idiosyncratic nature of each of the innovations again makes any generalization about how much time is enough out of the question.

2.07 Context links

To a large extent the comments made about phase 1 apply here. Contacts with various interested groups varied appreciably from country to country. If there is a clear pattern to be discerned it probably is that, at this stage in the operation, those groups or agencies that were thought likely to react unfavourably if excluded and who were powerful enough to make the reaction felt were, in fact, included.

The essential point at issue here appears to be a matter of territorial rights. Given that rights are defined by convention, what the pattern of involvement in each country reflects is presumably the way decision making occurs on matters like this and at this *particular stage*. Thus New Zealand saw no reason to go outside an educational fraternity, neither did Israel, Ghana or Malaysia. The Federal Republic of Germany and Indonesia both did, but presumably because of the widespread ramifications of the actions they were contemplating.

2.11 Evaluation

It is in the nature of fund-seeking projects that they must be evaluated. The five projects that sought money were all successful in obtaining it. It follows then that on one criterion, at least, those projects have been evaluated and found good.

It is also true that in the process of evolving their particular solutions all the countries considered alternatives (sometimes, as in Indonesia's case, in considerable depth), rejecting them in favour of the innovation selected. As exercises in the development of specifications, then, the countries have no reason to consider that the decisions taken were not appropriate for their purposes. Of course, the real test of that assumption lies in what happens when the plans are put into practice.

2.10 Rationale

When attention turns to the questions, 'what is the rationalization for the "solution" put forward?' and 'why that solution?', quite a measure of conjecture becomes inevitable. For example, how much was Indonesia under the influence of the 'planning' orientation that had been a feature of its approach to social, economic and political development? Again, to what extent were any of the countries who used their project to gain financial funding influenced by the prevailing climate in the funding market? To what extent did politics play its part? Obviously, the decision taken in Nordrhein-Westfalen was politically convenient – was it also in Ghana, or Sierra Leone? New Zealand and Israel appear to provide the most non-conventional examples – at least in their own contexts. The New Zealand 'solution' resulted from a new venture in liaison, not only between the building division of the Ministry and the professional divisions but also between the Central Ministry and other educational interest groups. Was the choice to involve the latter educationally advantageous, or perhaps politically too? The Israel research proposal broke a number of local conventions: it was bigger, much more ambitious and appreciably more expensive than was customary. Why did it get funded? Did the elegance of the scientific argument carry the day? If it did not, what did?

There might be no difficulty in gaining answers to such questions but it is likely that the answers would vary with the point of view of the informant. For example, in Israel, the staff from the University of Tel Aviv, the staff of the Institute of Technology, the original participating teachers and the Municipality authorities all see the early situation somewhat differently. Which perspective then provides the best indication of why the 'solution' came to be specified in the terms it was? Is it reasonable to ask whose rationale is best? Once again we find ourselves forced to consider that any answer is inextricably bound up with questions of purpose and power and control.

We turn next to the phase during which activity first began and when each innovation as an attempt to produce an improved form of education got under way.

Phase 3 – Operation: the solution under trial

This is the stage that six of our seven innovations have not yet grown beyond. The innovations, as yet incompletely formed, are under a variety of sorts of trial. Most of the trials have an evaluation component built in, although there are noteworthy variations to be found among the countries in their approach to evaluation.

For each of the innovations, then, a kind of moment of truth draws nigh. If, at this stage, they are shown to be inadequate then theoretically the activity should be aborted. However, in only one case is this an officially stated option. In all cases except the Malaysian one, there is a kind of tacit assumption that the innovation will work, and, by implication, thereafter its benefits will be felt on a wider scale. Malaysia, on the other hand, has stated unequivocally that on a certain date a decision will be made to proceed or *terminate*. Such a firm statement clearly establishes the Malaysian project as an experiment, and realistically acknowledges that results from an experiment can be found acceptable or not. By contrast, the other countries, though acknowledging to some extent the experimental nature of their innovations, have not chosen to state their options as explicitly as have the Malaysians.

None of the innovations has had a completely trouble-free run at this stage. All have experienced setbacks of one form or another. Interestingly, as the commentary below shows, they range over all of the components in our model, though predictably there is considerable overlap among them.

3.01 Personnel

When all the countries are lumped together the conclusion is warranted that somewhere, at some time, various kinds of personnel problems surfaced. In some cases the people needed to do the job were simply not available – nor, on balance, might one have expected them to be. The advanced nature of the project, coupled with the youth of the education system and the problem of providing qualified and competent indigenes to replace erstwhile colonial officials, all combined to limit the extent to which the system could produce diversely competent personnel. In a somewhat similar vein, too, there was evidence that the personnel who were available (either within the country or from without) were not always able to master the difficulties to be faced. Sometimes they simply did not appreciate the nature of the task – what the essential problem to be solved was. In the early days of the Malaysian project, it is probably true to say that the imported and no doubt talented experts in interpreting the situation in terms of their own understandings and experience were sometimes wide of the mark. The curriculum development knowledge and skills needed were not part of their armoury.

In fact the whole issue of foreign involvement in any of the projects is quite a vexed one. It is based, presumably, on the assumption that in order to carry out certain tasks efficiently, specific expertise is required. This position, basically technocratic, predictably comes under stress when local, indigenous, cultural factors exert an influence in transferring the (foreign) expertise to indigenes in such a way that the expertise becomes (a) acceptable, (b) internalized by them and (c) integrated into conventional practice.

In the countries of the IIEP studies, various expedients were used to encourage the inflow of what was considered to be technocratic expertise. Most countries sent some of their people overseas for training. Those that imported foreign experts used different devices. Some called them in for short periods when a particular problem or issue was about to surface. Some had them, as it were, permanently on tap.

Apparently the single most critical issue in all cases was who was to exercise 'control'. For what it is worth, the countries that made minimum use of 'outsiders' did in fact put the greatest amount of control closest to the grassroots – in the hands of the teachers – the 'workers'. As well, Malaysia, having decided to reduce the foreign element in its project, is tending to move more and more in the same direction. Obviously there are advantages in importing expertise, as there are in relying solely on local capabilities. But a little more is at stake than whether technical expertise can compensate for lack of involvement and commitment, or whether involvement and commitment can compensate for lack of technical expertise. What also is at issue is the currently popular sociological controversy over who controls knowledge – in whose *terms* does knowledge come to be defined? There is here, whenever expatriates are involved, the delicate and difficult issue of intellectual colonization to take into account.

3.02 Specifying the operational task

At this point we are concerned with what has to be done; what the innovation in action consists of. This obliges us to take both a narrow view and a wide one, to examine action at the workface, in the classroom, and at the level of the larger education system, too. In both cases we seek to comment on the extent to which specification occurred, what kind of specification it was and what some of the implications were.

Ghana and the Federal Republic of Germany perhaps make the simplest starting point. In fact, in Ghana there was no prior specification of what teachers had to do, there were just the regulations indicating that locally relevant, practical activities that had the possibility of encouraging gainful self-employment should be incorporated into the teaching programme. Subsequently, at the system level, 'adviser' posts were provided for. In both cases, what the 'workers' did became the *de facto* specifications for the operation. The Federal Republic of Germany gave a similar amount of autonomy to their teachers (and schools) with similar consequences. There the working specifications can only be discerned by examining what is done by the teachers themselves. In a similar way, the New Zealand teachers wrote their own educational specifications, as it were. The Central Ministry, apart from giving its blessing, kept its customary distance from the operation. It even contracted the evaluation task out to an independent agency that also drew up its own specifications. The *architectural* specifications for the new building, however, were formulated in the usual intricate detail by the school buildings section and their operation was strictly supervised by Ministry of Works officials according to firmly prescribed procedures. The way in which the Malaysian task specifications evolved makes perhaps the most interesting reading. In brief, an operation that was initially expected to be quite centrally controlled has evolved its own distinctive cooperative aspects that result in teachers and project officers working closely together. Distinctive of the strategy, too, has been a key decision to adopt what might be called a progressive developmental approach. It entailed (i) assessing the prevailing state of teaching in the experimental schools, (ii) diagnosing (with teacher help) what was therefore needed to move from existing chalk-and-talk teaching methods to an integrated activity-based curriculum, (iii) converting this diagnosis into a series of progressive (and progressively more complex) steps, and (iv) developing curricular and training programmes to help teachers master whatever steps were appropriate for them. In this case, again, the actual specifications *follow* from the action, not vice versa. Collaboration was also a feature of the Israeli innovation. The organization of the project was based on collaboration. The curricula materials that have come out of the project were also the result of practice, trial and error, and consultation too. But in the Israeli case the whole operation was specified in advance. The roles of teachers, researchers and technologists were to quite an extent pre-ordained and so was the organizational structure within which the entire undertaking proceeded. However, it was a largely self-contained exercise with, as yet, no official ramifications for the system as a whole. At the moment, the Education

Ministry bides its time. If a comparison were made between the New Zealand and Israeli projects, the *strategy and style of procedure* of Israel's would have more in common with the quantitative building aspect of New Zealand's than it would have with the qualitative educational one. By contrast, the Indonesians, faced with a task of awe-inspiring proportions, spelled out the whole complex strategy of the Development Schools project in considerable organizational detail. It is a highly systematic and rational specification that vests control and direction in the hands of (mainly indigenous) experts who in effect 'master-mind', from their positions of authority, the activities of their subordinates. The modular instruction method was developed within such a framework. Once the method had been selected, local and overseas experts were used to train module writers, oversee the production of modules and test and evaluate them. In this process the classroom teachers were mainly (but not exclusively) the field agents who put the modules into practice.

If the main difference between countries is the extent to which the task of operating the innovation in its initial (trial) stages was laid down in detail, are there any noteworthy consequences? In the first place it seems as if the looser the specification, the easier it is to make adjustments when contingencies force them. The Malaysian capacity to make adjustments constitutes a good case in point. In Indonesia, when the evaluation feedback from teachers proved to be less useful than anticipated, the adjustments needed created further (but admittedly not devastating) difficulties.

From the examples provided by our countries, it also seems as if the decision to provide detailed or open specifications is related to the capacity of those who have to perform the task. The Indonesians, entertaining considerable reservations about the present capability of the teaching force, deliberately took the decision to produce curriculum materials that were as 'teacher-proof' as possible. The New Zealanders and West Germans, in the face of the presumed competence (and political independence) of their teachers, took a different stance. But it must be admitted, in neither the Federal Republic of Germany nor New Zealand were the teachers expected to do anything substantially different from their customary work. In Indonesia and Israel, the opposite applied. There, dramatic and major change was foreseen. While the implications of attempting to achieve change of such magnitude are many, one of the main problems is to avoid having too many 'uncontrolled' variables exerting negative influences. In Indonesia it was considered necessary to regard the teacher variable as needing such control. To some extent it was so in Israel too and some control was exercised through the curricula materials. That control was supplemented, however, by also providing the teachers with a measure of autonomy (for which they had to be extensively trained) to make their own decisions.

3.03 Method
To some extent the information in the previous section touched on the issue

of method. Two of the projects very clearly have opted for a classical Research and Development approach. The Indonesians were committed to it right from the start. The Israelis, on the other hand, argued initially that strategies that were appropriate for research in science would prove to be equally appropriate in education. As a consequence the Israeli project took on a scale and scope considerably greater than has ever been seen there before.

By contrast, the Ghanaian and Federal Republic of Germany's 'method' was basically legislative – with some supporting guidance provided for good measure.

On an imaginary continuum between the R & D model and the legislative one, Sierra Leone probably falls closer to Indonesia and Israel than does Malaysia, but both projects in their original conception had R & D overtones with, perhaps, the evaluation component not elaborated in such detail. Both provided for adaptation during evolution – Malaysia employing it to a greater extent.

New Zealand, by comparison, makes a strange case. A considerable amount of effort went into the formulation of what might be regarded as educational guidelines for their innovation. But, once produced, the teachers were entirely free to use them or not. This latter-day *laissez-faire* aspect brings New Zealand into line with the Federal Republic of Germany and points up the dilemma that occurs whenever services are advisory rather than mandatory.

3.04 and 3.05 Plant and equipment

With the Federal Republic of Germany a notable exception, all the countries in the project have given considerable attention to plant and equipment as essential components in their projects. New Zealand's project, of course, revolved round the plant component. Up to the moment, as a piece of educational plant, the Whanau House school has passed with flying colours. In the Bunumbu project, too, plant and equipment were integral. Not only were new schools and college buildings specified but, in addition to curriculum materials, new (and, in context, radical) plans existed for using videotape recorders, a printing press, modern woodworking and other craft machines. The upgrading of electricity and water supplies and the provision and maintenance of a transport fleet were also essential provisions. Not everything is yet in place or operation – a state of affairs that has not been without its effects. Perhaps the most beneficial effect has been that the amount and degree of personnel and institutional change required has so far been less than originally anticipated. This has allowed (some) breathing space in what was anyway a complex and demanding revision of practices. Ghana's equipment component consisted of the 'packages' of practical equipment supplied to the experimental schools. Those packages were more than sufficient for their purposes, as the subsequent 'sharing' arrangement indicated.

If curriculum packages are regarded as equipment, then equipment is particularly important to the three remaining projects. In Indonesia the instruction modules might even be regarded as *the* critical components. It is anticipated that once these modules have been developed, trialled and stringently evaluated, they will become the means by which the major task of 'reforming' teacher behaviour will be carried out. They are required to be as self-sufficient as possible. In Israel, the individualized instruction packages also carry a major part of the burden of reform. They too are stringently trialled and tested. However, additional and extensive teacher re-training is regarded as an essential accompaniment, if the scheme is to be operated effectively. In a sense the academic justification for the Malaysian curriculum materials and equipment is less to the fore than in Israel and Indonesia. What has been produced, though, has sprung directly from the needs of the teachers. Thus the practical relevance is immediately discernible. In addition there is the added benefit that the materials produced are not necessarily tied to the new system exclusively.

It is probably true to say that in all six countries the careful attention given to equipment and plant has meant that few dissatisfactions have been expressed and disadvantages experienced, although the Ghanaians would have some reservations to make in their own case.

3.06 Cost

Given that the countries working off project funding had carefully estimated the likely costs of their 'operation' phases, it is not altogether surprising that none of them have reported that financial difficulties have arisen yet. Furthermore, because the other countries were working within established budget codes, they too have not had reason to express concern over financing.

3.08 and 3.09 Timing and scheduling

Financing of the innovations in this phase may have excited no anxiety – not so, however, timing and scheduling. Harrary's law is reputed to state 'No matter how long you think it will take, it will take twice as long'. This has not proved to be precisely the case in the seven projects but each has experienced something of an uncomfortable relationship between the original expectations and the time things took. Sierra Leone faced noteworthy delays in first having the project formally approved and then finding alternative sources of finance when the Unesco liquidity crisis struck. The net result was that certain components did not arrive in time (in fact some are still awaited). Malaysia right at the outset experienced and continues to experience delays in obtaining appropriate personnel. Israel ran into delays at the beginning in getting the proposal funded and it looks as if the Ministry's decision over implementation may also be delayed. New Zealand's delay affected the building completion date. The lack of some critical Australian building components, coupled with the Christmas summer vacation (when Australia and New Zealand are both said to 'close down' for a month!) conspired to move the opening date from the beginning of the academic year to the beginning of the second school term. During the operation phase, the delay in Ghana occurred in having the sets of equipment available for some of the experimental schools. Indonesia's timetable was to some extent affected when the feedback from teachers after the trial of the modules proved less useful than was hoped.

Did these delays matter? Apart from a certain annoyance value, maybe not. In fact, Sierra Leone *may* have profited from the space provided. It looks too as if Malaysia's approach may have become more effective and fitting because of the delay. What caused the delay for the Indonesians *may* also prove to be very pertinent when the problems of implementation come under consideration. The delay in Ghana certainly did not affect the project adversely. On the other hand, perhaps the Whanau House might have been less likely to meet with outside pressures or might have been more able to counter them had their operation started at the beginning of the school year – perhaps not.

If there is anything to take out of all this, it is the possibility that haste *can* be made too quickly. Often the procedures and priorities of funding agencies place a premium on quick results. But it is a characteristic of people and social systems that changes are seldom welcomed, are often regarded suspiciously and usually put into practice with caution. Providing more time rather than less would seem to be a policy worthy of careful consideration – even if it imposes costing difficulties.

3.10 Rationale

The question to be faced here is: What are the justifications for the particular approaches used in the operational phase? It invites, of course, a range of answers that could vary from 'because it was expedient' through to 'because it was desirable'. It is true though that the Federal Republic of Germany's approach was consistent with what we have earlier called a reactive planning stance. It is also true to say that the planned Indonesian approach was consistent with the proactive planning practice that at that time was being vigorously pursued at the national level of policy making as well. Those countries that sought project funding were also acting consistently with established practice in using external aid as a means for educational development. Israel's approach in seeking Government support for what was considered to be a 'worthwhile investigation' was also consistent with established practice – though the magnitude of the operation was not. New Zealand's exercise in its kind of consultative planning was relatively new, however. Admittedly other consultative devices had been in vogue for some time – government-promoted committees and commissions of inquiry notable among them – but in such cases the terms of reference are fairly firmly prescribed. In the Whanau House project, once the object of providing an educational blueprint for the school of the future was set, the consultants were given scope for intellectual free play. The architects, of course, had to work within their normal restraints.

In each case, then, the form of the operational phase can be seen following as a logical extension of the planning philosophy used. Thus the German and New Zealand teachers were left to their own devices. The Indonesians and Israelis had to develop and evaluate their materials within their R & D models. The Malaysians, Indonesians and the Ghanaians had to give evidence that the original project covenant had been fulfilled to a reasonable extent.

The particular point to take out of this interpretation is that innovations seem prone to reflect their environments. If so, there is reason to conjecture over whether or not a radical model (that is, a model that represented a substantial deviation from established practice) would or even could survive. For example, could a strictly R & D model have been used for the educational component in the New Zealand case? Given the structure of the system and the conventional autonomy of teachers, to carry an R & D model to its logical conclusion there would imply quite massive changes throughout the whole of the education system. Similarly, for those countries that are gaining many direct and, more importantly, indirect benefits from external project-based aid, to shift to an alternative procedure would have manifold implications and consequences.

3.11 Evaluation

All of the countries made provision for some kind of evaluation during their operational phase or subsequent to it. Some did both. Inevitably the development of curriculum materials entails a certain amount of evaluation. Thus Indonesia, Israel, Malaysia and Sierra Leone have employed evaluation procedures of greater or lesser academic sophistication. The Federal Republic of Germany has made provisions for some evaluation of the BVJ in the future. Ghana used the established evaluation conventions built into the school system to form its conclusions about the Continuation Schools. But it is only in this latter case that the key decision about future implementation has been taken. All the other projects await the 'thumbs up' or 'thumbs down' signal. Theoretically, which signal will be given *should* depend on the results of a terminal (summatory) evaluation but it is not at all clear that it will. In fact the Israeli authorities, in interpreting the realities with which they have to contend, indicated frankly that implementation decisions in general tend to depend on (i) the political climate, (ii) availability of 'energy' in the system to carry it out and (iii) priorities. Such criteria might well apply elsewhere. The future of the Whanau House design in New Zealand is, for example, more likely to turn on economic criteria than educational. Similarly there is reason at least to wonder about what will influence the decision in Indonesia, Sierra Leone and Malaysia. Given the desirability of external aid, will another new 'project' carrying promise of greater national economic benefit take precedence over an *educationally* legitimized old one?

Once again this kind of conjecture gives rise to the question: Whose purposes and what purposes are to be served by evaluation and, therefore, what type of evaluation is appropriate?

3.07 Impinging contexts

Several of the projects have given evidence of approaching the matter of inter-group relationships very carefully. In Indonesia, once the reorganization of the Development Schools Project was taken over by BP3K, detailed, even elaborate provision was made to keep all the interested authorities informed of, and involved in, developments. It is true that this has tended, at this stage, to be a matter largely for the upper echelons of the various hierarchies rather than the lower. In Sierra Leone the links between Ministry, the College and the community have been carefully nurtured and repeatedly reinforced. In Ghana, social norms already existing placed great importance on community-school interaction. Not surprisingly, this had flow-over effects and benefits throughout the system. In Malaysia, the 'Improved Curriculum' project is, it seems, pioneering a new kind of Ministry-schools association. Under usual circumstances, Ministry officers stand in a supervisory relationship to teachers. In this case, the relationship is a cooperative one that has already yielded identifiable pay-offs. It is in both the Federal Republic of Germany and New Zealand that least attention has been given to impinging contexts. In the Whanau House experiment the consequences became real and, from the point of view of the original Whanau House objectives, detrimental. The embedding school context did exert a considerable influence, virtually bringing about a major change in the operation. What the teachers will do in Germany is problematical. Some are already conforming to the legislation, and with enthusiasm. Will others do so too or will they turn to passive or even active resistance? All options seem possible.

We are inclined to interpret the evidence from the countries as implying that it is wise and perhaps essential, in one way or another, to gain the cooperation or at least acquiescence of interested parties who might otherwise regard their territory or prerogatives as having been violated.

Phase 4 – Implementation

In all of our countries but one (Ghana) the decision whether or not to implement on a wider scale lies in the future. We cannot therefore examine this phase in the same way that the other phases have been examined. Because they have not yet occurred, we cannot look at events and interpret their significance for either understanding the process of innovation, or managing it. This time we are forced to put on the planners' mantle and to try to *anticipate* what actions might prove beneficial. In going beyond our information base, as we must, we will be relying to some extent on implications drawn from the other phases and also on what seems to be a reasonable interpretation of contemporary viewpoints.

We should start with an assertion. Everything points to the conclusion that for effective planning and execution, implementation should be regarded as a discrete and distinguishable process. It is not merely an extension of the earlier 'development' phase. It is not merely a longer version of the try-out operations. It entails new and distinctive issues and problems that cannot be met without new and distinctive approaches. For example, spreading the Whanau House school building throughout New Zealand would entail production and distribution procedures vastly different from those used in the first one-off experimental situation. A critical element in the whole Whanau House experiment was the prospect of using modular construction methods to reduce costs. But for that to work, the construction operation has to be centralized, with provision made for supply and delivery networks. The 'one-off' experiment made no such provision. Similarly, if it were thought desirable to disseminate an *educational* aspect of the Whanau House school, then many activities, from letter writing to teacher training programmes, from travel to supervision, are implied. Attending to them requires an operation different from and additional to the earlier development activity. Some of the prospective complexity of such an operation may be gleaned by giving a moment's thought to what might be entailed in taking the Indonesian experimental mini-system, operating as it is with 20 schools, and then spreading it to Indonesia's 130 million people and throughout its 7000 (inhabited) islands.

Presumably any implementation process starts with a decision to implement – a decision that *can* be taken at several different places inside the education system or even outside it. Depending on that location, the decision will attract varying degrees of support, will activate varying amounts of effort and will be affected by outside pressures to a greater or lesser extent. Clearly a decision that has the sanction of the Head of State and the Government is likely to carry more force than one that does not, and presumably will do so, as long as it continues to have official support. But official support alone is not enough. Within the education system itself are varying (vested) interest groups whose expertise or good will or both may be essential for the effective development of the innovation process. As well, resources have to be (made) available, people will have to become embroiled and the whole operation will have to be organized so that its various parts dovetail neatly and in the right order.

In our necessarily cursory treatment of implementation below, the main thrust will be to raise issues that seem to be germane to achieving the kind of circumstances that will allow implementation to proceed smoothly.

4.10 Rationale

Given that the decision to implement has been taken and that the target group has been specified, is there some point in producing a rationale? The answer appears to be 'yes', provided rationale is taken to include both the reason for taking the decision *and* the consequences thought likely to follow.

Identifying the reason has the potential for indicating how appropriate that reason is for the various audiences involved. For example, the Federal Republic of Germany's BVJ carried a basically political rationale that, at the time, was well appreciated by most of the public audiences involved. What it did not do, however, was address the *educational* audiences (and maybe the consumer audiences) in terms that would be equally well appreciated. The *Richtlinien* (book of guidelines) went some distance towards accommodating teacher interests and needs, but whether or not *on its own* it will be sufficient to provide both initial motivation and continuing impetus is questionable. Again, the educational rationale produced for the Whanau House school failed to give due attention to the public domain with the result that the general public became misinformed and the local parents quite agitated.

4.02 Task definition

If a rationale consists of, in effect, a statement about the intended target and the intended effects (or 'objectives' if you prefer) and as well a statement of the reason for undertaking the task, then it follows that the size and scope of the job at hand should be able to be appreciated more readily. For example, it was estimated, in the case of the Ghana project, that to convert the relevant target schools into Continuation Schools would, at the rate achieved after three years, take until the 1990s. What then would it take to move the Israeli system, from its experimental condition in its two Municipalities, to a full implementation throughout Israel? Similarly, what would be required in terms of sequenced activities to take the Indonesian modular instruction project and distribute it (effectively) throughout that huge, geographically extended country? What is being called for here is first an identification of the actions that would be essential in order for implementation to occur, and second an assessment of what pre-conditions would have to exist for those essential actions to be able to be taken. Necessarily, both of those forms of system analysis depend in turn on what implementation and innovation methodology is to be chosen.

4.03 Methodology

There are two major and somewhat opposed models available to planners setting out to spread an innovation. The first entails a *laissez-faire* approach that assumes the new idea will gradually catch on and be spread throughout the target population, as it were, 'naturally'. The appropriate model in this case is a diffusion one and the planner using it presumably tries to find ways of accelerating the diffusion process by, for example, providing advisors, animateurs and community developers, and by advertising and educational programmes and the like. The second, entailing a directive, legislative approach, is designed to require individuals to act in accordance with (new) regulations. The appropriate model then becomes a formal, events-flow model in which the planner provides for the required events to take place in the appropriate order.

In between the two basic extremes lie the various alternatives possible. However, it seems apparent that the more the approach approximates to the diffusion model, the greater will be the amount of time consumed, the more diversified the interpretations will be. The formal model, on the other hand, though it has the potential to accelerate the rate of implementation because of its organizational tidiness, has nonetheless a particular disadvantage. Because it employs a basically 'controlled' approach, when contingencies occur (and in a 'controlled' exercise it is difficult to anticipate all possible circumstances) the implementation process is unlikely to adapt of itself. Control once again will have to be exerted – presumably from the centre. What is at stake here is the delicate relationship between groups of people in the system and the scope and capability they have to exercise their autonomy constructively. This in turn involves two other related aspects – the kinds of links existing between the various groups involved and the type and quality of personnel.

Each is taken in turn below.

4.07 Context links

Murphy's law states 'If anything can go wrong, it will'. According to the literature, nowhere in the innovation process is this more likely to occur than at the interface between 'interest' groups. The evidence from our study tends to lend support. In our countries, where care was taken to ensure close and reasonable links, things have gone smoothly. Where such links were not possible for one reason or another, progress slowed and sometimes considerable difficulty resulted. But our study also tended to indicate that it was not necessary 'to contact all of the people, all of the time'. It seems as if contacts need to be timed in accordance with the degree and kind of interest the contexts have. This in turn implies the need for what might be called a context analysis (to go hand-in-hand with task analysis) to identify what group interests are likely to be impinged on, when. For example, if an innovation is likely to affect promotion prospects for teachers, discussion with teachers' organizations would need to *precede* any declaration about the innovation that might lead teachers' organizations to jump to (perhaps false) conclusions. Similar PRO work might well be required elsewhere as might active, two-way consultation with a view to mutual accommodation. Fairly clearly then, the implementation system needs the capability to: (i) undertake the kind of analysis necessary to locate the interest groups, (ii) gain entry to them and (iii) employ the means to conduct mutually gratifying dialogues or negotiations.

4.01 Personnel

Whatever implementation strategy is employed, ideally everybody all along the line ought to be fully competent at their respective jobs. Such an ideal state of affairs seldom exists, although there are some countries in our study that operate on the (optimistic) assumption that it does – or if not, that the resulting difficulties will not be insurmountable. Equally, there are some countries that make the (pessimistic) assumption that very few people are really competent and therefore the exercise should be master-minded and programmed. We noted in the study that in those countries where teachers were the most highly trained and educated, there was a slightly greater tendency to accord them more scope for control over the innovation situation.

The Process of Educational Innovation

Even so, as far as the planning of the implementation phase is concerned, it is hard to imagine that some kind of systems analysis would not be useful. Whatever implementation model is in vogue, there appears to be considerable use in (i) anticipating what will happen when, (ii) what might be the consequences and (iii), therefore, what actions might be necessary. This in turn suggests that among the skills that the implementation personnel might require would be competency to undertake this kind of analysis.

4.05, 4.06 and 4.07 Plant, equipment and cost
If plant and equipment are part and parcel of any innovation then the means will be needed for producing and delivering them – a relatively obvious conclusion that the literature shows, however, has often been ignored during the implementation process. Ignored as well has sometimes been the necessity to recognize that the implementation process itself may entail plant and equipment. For example, if a new method of curriculum use is to be promoted, those who are undertaking the task of promotion may well themselves require equipment and plant appropriate for their purposes. For example, if the Israeli scheme with its important teacher-training component is implemented, provision will have to be made for providing the equipment and the locations necessary for such teacher training to be undertaken.

Cost is included under this heading although its influence is recognizably all-pervasive. Very little in the whole implementation phase is cost-free. The critical issue, though, becomes: What costs can be absorbed by the system (as normal operating costs), and what additional ones are involved? Presumably, when existing system procedures allow the redirection of 'work' from one part of the system to another, then there are least two key questions to be faced:

(i) What consequences follow from the reduction of the work previously done elsewhere?
(ii) Is the new work necessarily within the competency of the 'transferred' workers?

Cost, then, has several faces – not only a financial face but also a 'work efficiency' face, a 'psychological-stress' face, an 'organization-effectiveness' face, to name a few. A minimal exercise in implementation planning should at least recognize the various costs that potential strategies and tactics imply.

4.08 and 4.09 Time and scheduling
One of the lessons coming out of the literature on educational innovation appears to be that the time that change takes is usually much longer than innovators anticipate (or hope). Often the time scale originally provided for is quite unrealistic for the complexity of the task. If this is true then the implication for planners is that much more time needs to be allowed and, because of that, complementary actions are likely to be necessary. For example, a series of *in*-service training programmes in schools might be more effective than *pre*-service ones in training institutions.

But the trickiest task in the implementation process is the coordination one – especially, it seems, at the beginning. Until production times can be worked out, delivery dates and times estimated (whether for qualitative or quantitative aspects), the likelihood of disruption and disarray increases.

4.11 Evaluation

It seems reasonable to argue that if an ongoing monitoring of the implementation process can be called evaluation, then evaluation is necessary and valuable – that is, if it has the capacity to identify both prospective trouble spots and possible points of improvement. On the other hand, an evaluation that sets out without such a 'reformative' capability would appear to be more useful for political (in the broadest sense of the word) purposes. For example, to demonstrate what a given innovation has or has not accomplished (whether in relation to its objectives or not) enables credit and blame to be allocated. In so far as success increases power and failure undermines it, such evaluation may serve a regulatory function within the system – enhancing the successful or diminishing the unsuccessful. There are two particularly perplexing issues that arise here, however. On the one hand, in a complex social system like education, when a complex operation like implementation occurs, there are many reasons for 'failure' that are not legitimately attributable to a specific (and avoidable) cause. The second is that the criterion of success used may often be alien to or even antithetical to the more fundamental objectives of the education system. For example, the criteria cheapness, organizational neatness and administrational convenience do not necessarily yield educational benefit. The fact that they often come to prevail, however, is perhaps in part testimony to the difficulty of defining and demonstrating educational benefit and is partly due to the potency of the other political criteria – one of the matters to which the next chapter will give some attention.

Chapter 10

Conclusions

It is the purpose of this final chapter to attempt to tie together results that have so far come out of the seven studies, and to venture some tentative generalizations. The generalizations must necessarily be tentative because all of our innovations are still in full flight. Of none of them can it yet be written that they have either succeeded or failed. In every case the final word is far from being said. However, to delay interpretation until they have ended would be self-defeating. It would force the study into the retrospective mould which, though conventional enough, was rejected at the outset. The design adopted at that time committed the project to use a prospective stance, concerned not so much with after the event explanations as with before the (next) event forecasting. The reasoning was relatively simple and, mindful of the anticipated audience, was based on two related assumptions: (i) in essence, planning is an exercise in forecasting – an activity that attempts to provide for events to happen in the future and (ii) it is the task of any administrator not only to 'maintain' the system, not only to 'repair' it when it goes wrong but also to act in advance both to prevent trouble and to improve the operation.

It follows, then, that the planner and the administrator must work in a state of some ignorance. They cannot be expected to anticipate everything in the future. They cannot know in advance many of the events that will subsequently affect the fates of earlier decisions. On the other hand, take decisions they must. And they must do so as if they *did* know that unknown future. Under normal conditions, when mere maintenance of the system is the main concern, the risk of decision-making error is not great. An essentially conservative institution, education tends to plod well worn paths. Deviations tend to be few (and usually minor) and when they occur the stability of the remainder of the system can be taken pretty much for granted. Under non-normal conditions, however, whether socially, economically or politically induced, the risk factor tends to be high. The greater the degree of unpredictability in the system, the greater the risk of decision-making error. But whether conditions are in general normal or abnormal, *any* attempt at innovation, because, by definition, it introduces a measure of unexpectedness, puts strain on the system and tends to increase the risk factor – as the literature on innovation often asserts. Under such circumstances, to minimize the risk, the best that the planner can hope for is to be successful in anticipating as many future events as possible and being able to provide 'fail-safe' mechanisms to cover those events that were unforeseen. Similarly, the best that the administrator can hope for is to be able to employ successful monitoring and 'trouble-shooting' mechanisms that allow potential disasters to be nipped in the bud and 'improvements' to be adopted along the way.

In either case, however, it is unvoidable that both planner and administrator make a number of assumptions about the consequences of their (proposed) actions. They are forced to rely on a series of hypotheses or even theories of 'cause' and 'effect'. Both must fundamentally reason: 'if A is done X will follow'; eg 'if the size of classes is reduced, pupil learning will improve'; 'if more vocational training is provided, children will be better prepared for getting and keeping jobs', etc. Such reasoning can only be based on an assumed connection between A and X, between class size and performance, between training and job retention. But, and this is where the first risk materializes, that chain of reasoning may be partial or even flawed. To illustrate – the attempt made in the Nordrhein-Westfalen innovation to provide further education for the unemployed as a means of reducing unemployment can only achieve that purpose if jobs are available for the (further) educated. If this condition does not exist (and there are grounds for believing it does not, to any great extent), the objective of reducing unemployment *must* be vitiated – although, of course, other benefits might be obtained.

Other kinds of assumptions must also be made both by the planner when he starts to plan the *means* for achieving his objectives, and by the administrator when he sets about carrying them out. Invariably, assumptions have to be made about the capability of the system to support the action, for example: if costs can be covered; if the needed plant and equipment can be procured; if there exist people capable of doing the various jobs required; if competent administrative and managerial expertise is plentiful; if means for delivering the 'goods' are to hand, etc, etc. But these in turn imply other assumptions that, in the case of a novel event such as an innovation, can only be based on an (informed, it is to be hoped) estimation that conditions prevailing in similar events in the past will prevail in this case too. For example: if, as often occurs with many innovations, there exists no actual precedent for assessing the actual cost (as was so for all the innovations in our study); if the plant and equipment requirements can only be guessed at (as in the Ghanaian case); if the people available to do the job do not initially have the new skills needed (as in the Malaysian case); if the administrative-managerial task entails new and unfamiliar roles to be adopted (as in the New Zealand case), then under such circumstances the risk of dislocation increases. Again, and perhaps most importantly, assumptions have to be made about the *effects* of the undertaking as well. Presumably, if the innovation is supposed to be solving a problem, everyone hopes that it will do so and that, in the process, it will not create others. In actual fact our studies and studies elsewhere show that there is no necessary guarantee that any innovation will solve its parent problem in precisely the way hoped at the outset. Sometimes innovations do provide a bonus and solve other problems – for example as the Indonesian modular instruction materials did for the new 'open' schools. Sometimes, however, innovations create new problems. The impact of an alien building form on the social structure and organization of an established school in New Zealand represents a case in point. The possibility of unanticipated consequences suggests that 'guesstimates' ought to be made about side effects that might follow from the action taken. For example, consideration ought to be given to the effect that the innovation might have on particular interest groups in the system. Will the public react positively or negatively? Will the teachers accept it? Will the pupils like it? Will the Ministry officials find it attractive or threatening? Again, will there be repercussions on other parts of the system? Will expenditure here lead to expenditure there? Will a change in one part of the school programme produce other effects (good or bad) on another? Will a curriculum change carry implications for the levels above or below?

All of these questions, and, it must be admitted, many others, lead to further exercises in hope and faith in which both the administrator and planner are forced to engage. To cap it off, once the answers to such questions have been anticipated, the consequences of those answers ought to be considered too.

It follows from all this that in a very real sense a continuing major question for planners and administrators is 'so what?' Whether that question is asked often enough and answered perceptively enough will, in turn, strongly influence the degree of effectiveness achieved.

It becomes self-evident, then, why undertaking innovations results in an escalation of decision-making risk and why there are many points at which an innovation may come apart. It is also apparent that when the many assumptions which have to be made remain implicit rather than become explicit, when their validity is thus not subjected to question, when their mutual compatibility stays unexamined, 'unexpected' events can come to create havoc.

While all that may constitute a reasonable interpretation of the plight of the planner and administrator, it goes little distance towards producing solutions. But what might a solution consist of? Should it be a series of recipes for action? Should it comprise a catalogue of dos and don'ts? In what form might it best materialize? To us, one answer lies in amalgamating the perspectives of researcher and practitioner – in attempting to use research results to generate a kind of understanding that addresses the concerns of both planner and administrator. But 'understanding' is a global term, obviously virtuous but conveniently nebulous. To be useful, understanding itself has to be rendered down to become a coherent set of organizing principles, a rational argument that makes sense to those who would seek to use it. In other words, it has to become a kind of practically useful theory. The provision of such a practically useful theory we believe to be an essential step for the professionalization of planning and administration because we concur with Kurt Lewin: 'nothing is as practical as a good theory'. So we propose to present one. However, at this stage of the innovations and of our thinking we have to admit to a measure of hesitation – in several senses our theory is indeed embryonic.

Research method

Some of the hesitation we have in drawing conclusions stems from the methodology we used. On a number of counts it falls short of the ideal. We have gathered 'impressions' from each of the countries. Sometimes these impressions have been derived from official statistics (which vary in their comprehensiveness and relevance). Sometimes they have been derived from scholarly writings in the country. Sometimes they have come from an examination of more orthodox research studies undertaken locally. However, our two main sources of data have been: (i) the papers written by our administrator-researcher teams from each of the countries – papers which provided descriptions and critiques of the respective innovations and some background on the national situation and (ii) the lengthy innovation dossiers, again completed by members of the teams of others in the country who had specialized knowledge of the innovations. (For example, in the Federal Republic of Germany, the university research team examining the BVJ participated, and in Sierra Leone, Bunumbu College personnel were also involved.) These data, however, came fundamentally from the same source and to that extent represent a particular perspective, a particular perception of reality.

Though the composition of the teams, consisting as they did of an administrator and a researcher, gave a more varied perspective than usual, in order to enlarge it further we adopted two other devices. In the first place, every national contribution came up for scrutiny and discussion at working seminars involving all team members. The seminars served to make the IIEP project the *collective* responsibility of the group. This responsibility was exercised firstly through the sympathetic but searching examination each project was given by the entire group, and secondly by producing guidelines for each stage of operation. In a very real sense the seminars became occasions for cooperative decision making and participatory planning. In the second place, the IIEP member of the group was invited to all of the countries to both witness the innovations on the ground and discuss issues with a variety of interested parties in each case. He too was given the task of 'filtering' the various kinds of information from the various sources and submitting the resulting distillation for collective comment and criticism.

The methodology of the study, then, is something of a *mélange* with considerable reliance placed on several varieties of ethnographic method. The papers produced by the team members constitute one ethnographic record. The dossiers with their specific answers plus their (important) comments constitute another, perhaps more systematic than usual, ethnographic resource. The interviews conducted in the different countries constitute another while the meetings of the international group itself (all tape-recorded and reviewed) could be considered to constitute a kind of group-derived ethnography as well.

The advantages and disadvantages of ethnographic approaches are currently being argued vehemently among sociologists of education. The obvious weaknesses of the methodology – selectivity, possible bias, fortuitousness, subjectivity, etc – are supposedly counteracted by gaining directly the 'perceptions of reality' held by the people intimately involved. Whatever the outcome of the argument – and it will rage for some time to come – we, at least, found our approach manageable and, within the limits of our resources, possible. And this gives rise to an important point of general interest that concerns this project and others.

One of our purposes was to attempt to bring researchers and administrators at least into the same orbit, so that each, we hoped, would come to appreciate the other's perspective. That, we understand, occurred. However, more importantly perhaps, the dialogue between them led to some rather critical questions about the *use* and *worth* of research to the administrator and the extent to which investment in research is warranted. To the administrator-planners, the situation is quite clear. They want research results that will aid in the decision-making process. Such a point of view, however, puts severe limits on the operation of researchers. It puts constraints on them in particular over the time they have available and, accordingly, on what they can logistically accomplish in the time. In other words, in effect it prohibits researchers from strictly observing the canons of their craft. Their methods, procedures and analyses may thus have to be less (sometimes considerably less) than ideal. Because applied research is in this way subject to external constraints, before and during its life-time (like innovations are) *before* the research is undertaken, a decision has to be reached as to what kind of investment in research is worth while. In other words, given the nature of the planning or administrative decisions that will have to be made, the question is: What sort of research is *sufficient* for the purpose? What are the advantages of investment in ideal research or in less-than-ideal research, or even in no research at all, relative to costs and consequences? Perhaps the results from a 'crude' piece of research will be only marginally inferior to those from a 'sophisticated' one but they may be appreciably cheaper.

Such an argument is, of course, confined by the concerns of planners and administrators and their understandably pragmatic problems. It ignores completely the wider significance of non-applied research – an issue that will not be argued here. But the moral we were forced to acknowledge in our study was the need to consider the *relative* usefulness of research procedures. As a consequence, our research strategy set out to take advantage of (evaluation) studies whenever they existed in the countries and to supplement them with our (ethnographic) procedures which entailed only minor costs for the participants.

Towards a theory of innovation

The readers who have had the fortitude to travel with us through the seven case studies in the earlier chapters will no doubt have remarked on two features of the accounts. The first is the immense diversity to be found within and between the countries of our project. The second consists of the sometimes brave, sometimes desperate, attempts we have made to seek common ground between them. It must be patently obvious, from the tortuous paths we followed, that our countries are indeed individually unique and that what happens to their innovations is often a function of the uniqueness of their cultures. How any process of innovation evolves then is, to a marked degree, relative to the culture in which it is located. But notwithstanding that uniqueness, can some general principles be educed? We think so, but to explain them entails developing a theory that both recognizes and accommodates to cultural relativity. Such a theory too ought to be able to incorporate a number of features that have already come to be associated with the process of innovation. Notable among those are the propositions that: (i) innovations usually fail, (ii) barriers to innovations invariably emerge, (iii) resistance to change seems universal, (iv) change is usually transitory, (v) willingness to change appears related to conditions in society and (vi) change may or may not be rational. If, as a result of its attempt to discuss cause and effect relationships, the theory can to some extent 'explain' such matters, the means for subsequently controlling and influencing them should be that much closer.

Elements

Levels of analysis

(i) The individual In our interpretation of the process of innovation within education systems it is convenient to start with the smallest elements first. For our purposes, they are the individuals, the human beings who collectively make up the human part of the system. Each individual is regarded as a discrete unit with its own integrity – in two senses of the word. First, it has physical integrity in that it is observably separate from other units. Second, it has what might be called psychological integrity in a particular sense. In a manner similar to Havelock and Huberman's (1977) concept of an innovation as a boundary-maintaining system, we regard our human units as personal boundary-maintaining systems too. And it is convenient to regard them as maintaining three kinds of personal boundaries, viz: (i) their view of reality or the *meanings* they give to the world around them, (ii) the behaviour patterns or *norms* (their own and others') into which they have been socialized, and (iii) the *values*, the ideas of good and bad, right and wrong to which they have become accustomed. Under most circumstances individuals tend to protect, preserve and promote their own view of reality, their own norms and their own values. They also tend to resist (except under

circumstances to be discussed later) the intrusion of alien meanings, norms and values. This is presumably because it is from their own meanings, norms and values that individuals derive their identity and through the continuation of them that they sustain their integrity.

(ii) Groups or collectivities Obviously individuals cannot be entirely self-sufficient and, furthermore, the fact that meanings, norms and values are the result of socialization indicates that individuals cohere into groups. The import of such an obvious statement is not that they do so but that those groups may also be regarded as boundary-maintaining organisms that also have their own identity and integrity. Thus a school as an organization can be regarded as comprising a series of identifiable sub-groups that, having something in common, from time to time coalesce to protect or promote common interests. For example, Penrose High School with its teachers, pupils and parents constitutes a group or collectivity with its own form of identity and, accordingly, a particular view of its collective integrity. Again, within Penrose High School, the Whanau House staff and pupils constitute another sub-group with some things held in common with the larger school group but others clearly not in common.

Sometimes however, collectivities do not have this kind of concreteness. For example, in most countries, though representatives of teachers' unions may meet from time to time, all the teachers, as a collectivity, virtually never do. Yet it is reasonable to regard the teacher collectivity as a boundary-maintaining organism too – simply on the basis of the collective action taken from time to time. At a more abstract level, again, it is convenient and useful, though sometimes risky, to also talk of social classes as if they had a collective identity.

One implication of the discussion so far is that the whole education system can also be seen in the same way, as a collectivity with its own (generalized) view of reality, its own norms of behaviour and its own established values.

And by extrapolation it follows that not only can the whole nation be regarded in the same light, but that within the nation there will be other identifiable collectivities with similar self-seeking, self-protecting identities.

It is not very difficult to take out of our case studies illustrations of the points made above. It may be remembered that in the first chapter, attention was drawn to the concern *all* of our countries had to establish and clarify their *national* identities. Again it was quite apparent that some education systems, in answer to a national need, were attempting to establish, as part of their identity, their capacity to contribute to national development – Sierra Leone and Ghana constitute cases in point. It was also apparent too, in Israel, that identifiable sub-groups came together to create a new (expanded) amalgamated identity while by contrast, in New Zealand, existing sub-groups came into conflict in protection of their own interests.

There are two particular points that need to be taken up at this stage. We have produced a kind of crude picture of the structure of the system that can be envisaged as a cluster of circles (some concentric) with the smallest comprising individuals and the largest, the all-embracing one, the nation as a whole. The first point then is that such a picture implies that the whole structure can be regarded as static. This, however, is only possible if one regards time as frozen. But time, perhaps unfortunately, does not freeze. In a particular group, in the real world, individuals come and go, advance and retreat, protect and promote continuously. Any group (or for that matter any individual) is to a greater or lesser degree dynamic. The degree of dynamism varies, leading, of course, to some groups (and individuals) being regarded as stable and others unstable, and some regarded as conservative and others as radical, etc. The second point is that the membership of groups overlaps. Consequently a teacher in one of Indonesia's development schools may also be a father, a member of a political party, a badminton player, etc. He will have some measure of investment in the integrity of all the other collectivities to which he belongs. Consequently the concentric circles in our model have to have somewhat flexible boundaries that bulge and bend as different identities and integrities come into contact.

Interaction between elements

We come now to one of the more critical points of our analysis. Consistently with Havelock and Huberman (1977) we regard the individuals involved in an *innovation* as themselves constituting a boundary-maintaining group (very likely with internal sub-groups too). As a new group, in order to survive, it has to establish is own boundaries by manufacturing its own identity and establishing its own integrity. Once those boundaries are set up, however, they will have to be protected, preserved and, given the nature of innovations, probably promoted also. But because any innovation is new (by definition), to some extent the character of that new group will be new. Its definition of reality may well be different from that of existing groups, its patterns of behaviour may well be different and its values may well be different also. Accordingly, the innovation group, to the extent that it *is* new, will be *alien* to the existing system.

Perhaps this construction can be illustrated by regarding the national context as a gigantic multi-cell organism, with each of the cells comprising the various internal groups. They in turn are composed of lesser sub-groups with individuals (as the smallest unit of analysis) cohering to make up the various collectivities. Each individual might be pictorially represented as a kind of small amoeba which sits there pulsing (as it makes its internal boundary adjustments to its own meanings, values and norms). The sub-group and groups can also be seen in the same way, pulsing too, in response to internal forces. But all of these amoeba-like elements move in relation to their fellow amoebas, attracted by some, repelled by others. When two or more make contact, however, some kind of accommodation is necessary. That accommodation may lead to total amalgamation, part amalgamation, agreement to go separate ways or even destruction of one or the other. For the sake of the illustration let us imagine, then, a total (national) organism (system) with all its established elements (individuals, sub-groups and groups) existing in this kind of dynamic flux. Let them be coloured black. To these let us add *one* new sub-group to represent the innovation sub-group. To indicate its alien nature, let it be a different colour, say, red. For both the established black elements and the new red one, the problem is the same – to achieve accommodation to each other. Given that all the elements, red or black, are boundary-maintaining elements and given that the red elements are alien, how will accommodation occur? What will cause the black system to accept and proliferate the red elements? What will cause it to reject them and destroy them? Our answer requires us, perhaps fortunately, to dispense with the biological analogy further and come a little closer to everyday reality.

The substance

In recent years the contributions of Michael Young in England, Bowles and Gintis in the USA, Bourdieu in France, and others have highlighted the point that one of the major social issues of our time is: 'who defines what knowledge shall be regarded as legitimate, and who shall exercise control over access to it?' The issue becomes, in our terms, who has *control* over the meanings, values and norms that are regarded as appropriate for society to perpetuate and, *therefore*, who determines subsequently who the privileged and underprivileged will be? Some supporters of this point of view argue that the institutional forms of society – economic and educational forms in particular – determine reality. Those who have control over the economic and educational institutions act to preserve them and in this way protect their own interests and those of their children. Classic illustration of their theoretical position is to be found in the lingering effects of colonial influence once the colonial powers have left, although the argument is thought to apply equally well to all societies.

Now be that as it may, it is reasonable to argue that any economic, political or ideological innovation that surfaces in any existing society runs the risk of upsetting the existing forms of social control. It is also reasonable to anticipate that defences will be erected against it. But it has not been customary for promoters of educational innovations to see their beloved innovations as intrusions into an established system. Rather, innovations have usually been conceptualized as benign and potentially beneficial additions. They are rarely regarded as threats to the existing social fabric, as constituting alien perceptions of realities, alien norms of behaviour and alien values. Consequently much of the literature on innovation has tended to reflect bemusement and dismay that a 'myopic' 'reactionary' society should apparently reject something that promises to be so valuable.

Now the kinds of innovations with which this study has been concerned – qualitative innovations that attempt to improve (ie change) the educational performance of children by changing (ie improving) the teaching performance are to some extent ideological and political innovations.

Conclusions

They certainly represent a particular kind of social change – change in the definition and control of institutionalized school knowledge (in the largest sense of the word). They represent, to some extent, assaults on the established forms of meanings, and on established norms of behaviour. They may even represent assaults on established social values. Even if they are not, they may well come to be regarded as if they were.

To take the most dramatic of our illustrations: the complex mastery learning-based modular instruction system under development in Indonesia is vastly different from the practices that have come to be regarded as conventionally appropriate for teachers, pupils, administrators and parents alike. In the new approach, learning has a new definition. No longer does it consist of the accumulation, repetition and regurgitation of factual information. Teaching also has a new definition. The teacher now becomes a resource manager, a guide, a director – not an oracle, the unquestioned fountainhead of all knowledge. The routine patterns of teaching-learning interaction are vastly different too, as are the kinds of administrative procedures necessary to sustain the system, the kinds of resources needed and even the kinds of physical setting in which 'education' is carried out. Parents, to the extent that they can participate in their children's education, will find this new definition of educational reality, with its new norms, very different from the ones they knew earlier. They may even see, in the pronounced individualization of instruction that is part and parcel of the system, a deviation from some of the values they hold about interpersonal relationships, rights and responsibilities. It should in no way be concluded from this hypothetical analysis that this is actually the case. This overly dramatic (and oversimplified) illustration from Indonesia has been used to encourage a realistic view of the problems entailed in mounting innovations. A realistic view must, on the general weight of information, indicate that problems lie ahead. What we are trying to say is that to recognize them in advance *decreases* the likelihood of failure.

What is fundamentally under debate here is how an old system (the black amoebas) can accommodate to the new (red amoebas) and how that accommodation can be promoted.

We are thus led now to a consideration of the circumstances under which innovations gain first toe-holds in the system and subsequently come to consolidate their positions. The issues at stake, though complex themselves, can be stated quite simply. They are:

1. Under what conditions do innovations tend to become initially acceptable?
2. Under what conditions do innovations tend to persist beyond the stage of initial acceptance?
3. How long does it take for an innovation to permeate the system?
4. How extensive may an innovation be (how big an innovation can be tolerated at any time)?

Fairly clearly, these are issues that bear on the concerns of planners and administrators – and on scientists who are concerned with the process of social change. However, they do not address the issues that have to some extent been foci of interest to some scholars of innovations.

In the first place, the particular perspective adopted here clearly ignores the matter of the *origins of innovations*. This is partly an artefact of the study in that all of our innovations were *de facto* – they were in existence when we started and where they came from was not taken much into account. In retrospect this may have been unfortunate in that we have almost virtually ignored grass roots innovations that spring up spontaneously within systems, to struggle and strive, survive or die, as it were, in spite of the system. These may represent a condition of innovation for which a quite different perspective than ours might (or might not) be more appropriate.

In the second place, apart from differentiating qualitative innovations from quantitative ones, we have not sought to provide a classification of *types of innovation* but we also had no grounds, theoretical or *a priori*, for doing so. Our concern for the process of innovating obviated the necessity – or so we thought. It may be, however, that, for example, curriculum innovations *are* significantly different from teaching style innovations, and so on, but others will have to demonstrate it.

In the third place, we have not looked yet very closely at the specific *effects of innovations*. For example, we do not yet know the full details of the educational performances of children in Indonesia, Malaysia or Israel on their new curricula materials. We have not scrutinized evidence on the efficiency of Bunumbu College teachers in their community development roles. Nor have we other than touched on the effects of the specific innovations on the structure and functions of schools or the educational system. We cannot, then, venture any reasoned judgement on whether a Whanau House would be a good idea for someone else to try, or whether the *Richtlinien* were effective guidelines for the BVJ teachers in the Federal Republic of Germany. As we said in the introduction, our task was not to evaluate each innovation but to examine the process of innovating, with a view of understanding it better.

The understanding we have gained has crystallized as 12 propositions that address the four issues above. They will be presented in turn, together with brief elaborations.

Initial acceptability

It almost goes without saying that within society and within education systems power is distributed, and the kinds of distribution vary. For example, power may be concentrated at the centre (centralized), or distributed throughout (decentralized). But power is also particularized so that political, economic, industrial, educational, social, etc power, in so far as they refer to institutionalized forms of behaviour, can be regarded separately. When specific innovation issues are examined it often becomes apparent that there are political, economic, social, moral and other aspects that exert their own special influences.

The present studies provide examples, not only of centralized and decentralized systems and the points at which power is concentrated, but also some of the sources of power likely to exert an influence. For example: the Federal Republic of Germany's education and, for that matter, political systems were more decentralized than those of the other countries; in Sierra Leone, the eminence of the President meant that once he had declared in favour of the Bunumbu project, national support was assured; in New Zealand, the Whanau House decision, though ratified by Cabinet, was basically taken by educationists within the education system and on educational grounds, though whether or not implementation of the Whanau House will go any distance later on depends not on the educational authorities but, very likely, on the economic state of the country (and therefore government and treasury); in Israel, the decision to implement also hangs to some extent on matters outside the control of the education system – viz (i) political support, (ii) 'energy' in the system and (iii) priorities.

All this implies that for an innovation to have safe passage through the various sub-groups in the system, certain routes are likely to be better than others. But the routes do not seem to be identical from system to system. Clearly the President's endorsement was an 'open sesame' for the Bunumbu project but why, for example, is highest approval not always necessary or even useful in every case? The answer seems particularly sensitive to cultural differences and, in particular, to the extent to which different groups or subsystems are conceded to have the right (or authority) to exercise power over others. There is obviously need, within any general propositions dealing with power, to recognize that on some occasions the authoritarian exercise of power is expected (and works) and that on others it is not (and it will not work). It would seem then that innovations, to become acceptable, must gain *relevant* support, ie support from the quarter regarded as having legitimate jurisdiction. Thus Presidential endorsement *was not* necessary for the Continuation Schools project in Ghana (given the changes that followed in the political situation, it might subsequently have even proved disadvantageous) but support in the Ministry and at the local level clearly *was*. In both cases, these relevant power structures willingly provided support. Similarly, so long as the Federal Republic of Germany's innovation is school-based, its operation *in practice* depends primarily on support from the (separate) schools themselves. Thus:

Proposition 1
The initial acceptance of an innovation is a function of the relevant power that can be marshalled in its support. The greater the relevant power, the greater the likelihood of acceptability.

As a corollary of proposition 1 it follows that different levels and types of power need to be recognized and an appreciation needs to be gained of what is regarded as legitimized jurisdiction. This seems necessary if we are to understand why so many innovations have foundered at the workface – through the simple but subtle opposition of teachers, who at that point, because they exercise effective control over what is done, constitute the source of relevant power.

However, to recognize the configuration of (legitimized) power within a system is one thing, to ensure that it is exercised in the interests of the innovation is another. Whether or not the source of relevant power can be mobilized (or is willing to mobilize itself) in support of any innovation is problematical but on the basis of our studies seems to depend on the delicate interface between that power source and the innovation – the point at which territories overlap. Altogether we have four more propositions to address this issue. Most of them are quite consistent with positions that are commonly acceptable in social psychology and sociology.

Proposition 2
The initial acceptability of an innovation is a function of the extent to which, as a change, it is seen to threaten the power of existing groups. The less the perceived threat, the greater the acceptability.

If groups or sub-systems are taken to be boundary-maintaining organisms, then it is almost axiomatic that threats to their identity, integrity and territory will, in the first instance, invoke opposition.

It does not follow from this, however, that the absence of (perceived) threat is sufficient to ensure that safe passage of an innovation – far from it. In terms of our earlier analogy, for the red amoeba to be accepted by any black amoeba depends on what happens when the two come into contact.

It seems, on the basis of our evidence, that whenever any new sub-system comes into contact with the innovation, the negotiations that occur are of prime importance. For example, there were at least three occasions when important negotiations took place in Sierra Leone between the Ministry of Education, the Government and international funding agencies. Those negotiations were obviously important in that in each case the future of the project virtually hung in the balance.

In Sierra Leone, again, the formal negotiations of the Tripartite reviews were of considerable significance as were the (many) informal negotiations between the College authorities and the 'community'. It is unfortunate that the 'blow by blow' detail of these negotiations was never recorded. Within the fine detail of such key events may be locked some secrets about the manner, form and style of successful negotiation that, once discerned, might prove a veritable gold-mine of useful information for planners and administrators. In the other countries, potentially useful leads also lie undiscovered, as yet unrecorded. For example, in the Federal Republic of Germany, what was it that persuaded the Ministry of Education, *after discussion with other ministries*, to take up the youth-unemployment gauntlet? And what happens in Indonesia, when a consultant on, say, curriculum evaluation has to negotiate procedures with BP3K officials? In what way too do the Ghanaian elders represent their cases for support to the Director of Education when they visit him at his home at 5 o'clock in the morning? Behind all the many and various contacts between agents of the innovation and between other agents and agencies lie probably fascinating studies of human interaction and social dynamics. Clearly, much of the fine detail will be culturally particular – for example, being on time in Germany, sprinkling libation in Africa, preferring positive to negative responses in South-East Asia and so on.

Despite the lack of detailed information, we are still inclined to think that the negotiation process can be usefully regarded in generalized terms. The position we take is based on the assumption that negotiation involves essentially an interchange between parties that have the potential to help or harm each other. At the heart is a 'give and take' process during which the benefits to be gained are weighed against benefits to be lost or costs entailed. There is, in any negotiation, a range (sometimes large, sometimes small) within which the parties operate, just as there is a point at which the price can be too high or the returns too low. Thus:

Proposition 3
The initial acceptability of an innovation is a function of the extent to which the benefits expected to result are thought to be in excess of the costs entailed. The greater the benefits (relative to cost), the greater the likelihood of acceptance (and vice versa).

Our model, though basically economic, does not just entail economic benefits. In fact, it allows for three generalized kinds of cost benefits – one basically material, one basically social and one basically psychological. For convenience, we have labelled them utility, status and affect. Utility means essentially anything that can be regarded as a material cost or benefit, eg money, goods, services, etc (and in education's case, for pupils, 'learning' and 'knowledge'). Status means respect, deference and recognition – acknowledgement of social worth. Affect covers the feeling component and refers to such aspects as love, liking, friendship, loyalty and their opposites. At the heart of this formulation is the idea that in any social context or group these three kinds of exchangeables are all available to a lesser or greater extent *and, as well, expectations exist within a group over what an appropriate form and rate of exchange will be.*

Violations of these expectations which can be regarded as violations of (formal and informal) protocol can impair and even terminate negotiation. Thus:

Proposition 4
The initial acceptability of an innovation is a function of negotiation protocol. The greater the violation of protocol, the less the likelihood of acceptability.

Proposition 4 acknowledges the part played by convention in social interaction. Any interaction depends, among those involved, on some measure of agreement over what constitutes reasonable, acceptable and appropriate behaviour. In established social contexts there are codes to be observed and rules (written and unwritten) to be followed. Conformity to codes and rules is taken to indicate solidarity with the group. Violation, even unwitting, is often taken to indicate hostility or disassociation. Where two sub-systems with different codes and conventions impinge, those differences have to be negotiated if association is to continue. If the new innovation with its likely differences, then, is to prove acceptable to established groups, these differences will have to be demonstrated to be either benign or tolerable. Anything less puts the innovation's acceptability at risk. Diplomatic negotiation thus becomes critically important.

However, negotiation entails communication. Perhaps this is why the importance of communication is repeatedly stressed in the literature of innovation. The line of reasoning appears to be that if people are given information about the innovation they will understand it and if they understand the information they will accept the innovation. Unfortunately this line of reasoning only commands weak support in the innovation literature. Nonetheless we believe that a case can be made for inter-group communication as a significant factor in innovation, but not quite in the usual way.

On examination, many if not all innovation projects appear to be accompanied by what can only be regarded as an amount of 'promotion'. Usually couched in very positive and eulogistic terms, the promotion draws attention to the many virtues thought to be attendant on the innovation. While the amount of promotional rhetoric seems to vary from case to case, it hardly ever appears to be totally absent. If such rhetoric is so universal then presumably it serves some useful purpose. As we see it, rhetoric exists for two main reasons. In the first place it serves to weld the innovating group together, affirming a collective faith, stating shared meanings, norms and values. In the second, it testifies publicly to the group's identity and integrity, drawing the boundaries, as it were, for others to see. As a form of communication, then, the rhetoric serves to alert the outside world to the existence of this new entity. It may thus serve to both 'alarm' those groups that see their own boundaries threatened and 'sooth' those who do not. Thus:

Proposition 5
The initial acceptability of an innovation is a function of the rhetoric used. The more the rhetoric conveys the impression of difference between the innovation and the status quo, the greater the likelihood of rejection.

Collectively these five propositions cover some of the more major issues involved in the initial establishment of an innovation. Necessarily, no one proposition can be regarded as taking precedence over another. Depending on the situation, one may prove more critical than another. More than likely, however, they will interact with each other, thus proving to be mutually supportive or mutually destructive.

Persistence

Attention now shifts to five propositions that deal with the prospect an innovation has to persist. Here a distinction needs to be made between (i) the survival of the original prototype(s) and (ii) their widespread adoption throughout the system. The latter we see as an issue of implementation which, as such, is best distinguished conceptually and operationally from the process of establishment. The propositions that follow are directed at the problem of ensuring that an innovation once initiated can persist long enough to become regarded as established.

By definition the idea of persistence implies a period of time. This set of propositions, then, is based on the assumption that with more time will come the opportunity to view the innovation in ways that are to some extent different from the ways it can be viewed when initial acceptability is the matter of prime concern.

Invariably any innovation rhetoric includes promises of what the innovation will or will not do in the future. Often, as part of the promotion, much virtue is attributed to a prospective innovation – particularly in advance. As there is always the possibility that the promised benefits will not eventuate, the innovation, once it becomes a reality, may not live up to its advance propaganda. Reality may cancel out the rhetoric. There is a point at which the magnitude of this sort of 'failure' can be such that the credibility of the innovation can be destroyed by disillusionment – among the innovators themselves or the watching outsiders. Thus:

Proposition 6
Persistence of an innovation is a function of the innovation's credibility. The greater the gap between promise and performance, the less the credibility. The less the credibility, the less the likelihood of persistence.

However, for the discrepancy between promise and performance to be discovered, the reality of the innovation has to become known. As a case in point, it was many years before some of the Headstart programmes in the United States were discovered to have never even been put into practice. What is at issue here are the uses and abuses of evaluation – whether formal or informal.

Throughout the study we came time and time again to confront the problem of evaluation. In every case there were certain face value grounds for expecting that evaluation (or rather evaluations) should occur. After all, it is very plausible to argue that if an attempt is made to accomplish something, then one ought to find out whether it has in fact been accomplished. On the other hand, it is obvious that evaluation is a roomy word which covers not only a great number of alternative procedures (from the use of standardized achievement tests to opinion surveys, to cost analyses, to foreign inter-visitations), but also supposedly addresses a great variety of needs and interests.

We were led, by the complexity of evaluation practice, to ask several times: Whose interests were being served? and, by implication, to raise the question: What was the evaluation itself worth? In fact, the net outcome of our consideration of evaluation was that we have more questions than answers. Perhaps one or two semi-hypothetical illustrations might serve to point up the kind of dilemmas that result. In the development of the modular instruction materials in the Indonesian project, the materials themselves are being subjected to systematic evaluation primarily to determine that on the tests that are given to the 'experimental' children, the average performance level is high and the range of differences in performance is small. For good and understandable reasons this procedure largely misses out the teacher. There are thus grounds for wondering if the teachers, when they taught the relevant modules, actually did what was required in the way that was required and to the extent that was required, and consequently, whether, as the evaluations indicate, the curriculum materials themselves warrant adjustment.

However, there is a more imponderable issue that really bears on the concerns of all education systems. That is the issue surfaced earlier in the chapter, the control of knowledge. We have seen in our countries various influences at work. In many, especially since independence, there has been a manifested wish to 'indigenize' education, at least to the extent that matters of national and local relevance come to feature more prominently in the curriculum. Similarly, a wish to put education to service in the national interest often surfaces. As well, the international funding agencies, in return for providing support, often set out the terms under which aid will be forthcoming. Finally, there are contributions made to education systems by 'experts' from overseas and by the introduction of technologies (including, for example, curriculum development technologies), also from the outside. All of these constitute influences that serve to exercise control over what comes to be regarded as proper knowledge. And the 'control' they exert is influenced by the basic assumptions that lie behind *their* views of reality. And, it must be noted, those views may differ.

All this, of course, may be most valuable in that without such alternative views the opportunity for choice is limited. But, the fact that different perspectives of reality then come into competition with each other makes the question of evaluation all the more difficult. Perhaps the simplest illustration we had was the evaluation in Ghana that legitimately drew attention to the 'failure' to keep the sets of equipment intact and confined to the 20 experimental schools. The criterion was in fact the funding agency's criterion. What went unnoticed was that the 'screened off' equipment had been put to good use elsewhere, thus *expanding* the impact of the project, presumably in the interests of the country.

Although there is no scope to extend (and illustrate) the evaluation argument here, it must be patently obvious that political differences of interest (even conflicts of interest) make the question of evaluation a particularly vexed one. It is clear that different evaluations serve different purposes and address different audiences. It is also clear that some evaluations, though important to some audiences, are inconsequential to others. The literature shows that negative or neutral education evaluations do not necessarily result in the (political) rejection of innovations (innovation boundary maintenance is too strong). There are also illustrations of positive education evaluations being insufficient to 'save' innovations politically. The key to this apparent inconsistency, we think, tends to reside in (i) the *relevance* of the evaluation to those who exert power over the fate of the innovation and (ii) the terms of evaluation that the latter are prepared to find acceptable. Israel provides an example. As the Ministry officials saw their own situation there, the *educational* evaluation of the NILI project would be regarded with interest *but* decisions about implementation would be likely to be taken on quite different grounds.

Proposition 7
Given an evaluation, the persistence of an innovation is a function of the outcome of the evaluation and the relevance of the evaluation. The more positive the assessment and the more relevant the evaluation to the decision-making function, the greater the likelihood of persistence.

The link between this proposition and its predecessor, then, is to be found by recognizing that discerning any promise-performance gap entails at least some kind of evaluation and that whether or not discovering the gap is important depends on whether or not those in decision-making positions find that particular discovery relevant. There have been numerous academic exposés of such promise-performance inconsistencies in education systems that have gone unheeded because they have addressed the wrong audiences and in the wrong terms, ie terms irrelevant to the audiences' concerns and responsibilities.

At this point there remain for consideration two management functions that are to some extent self-evident but, we think, in ways that have not been customarily recognized. They concern (i) resources and (ii) personnel.

Our own study has not given us reason for minimizing the need for adequate provision of plant, equipment, supplies and personnel in order for innovations to survive. However, it has not led us to reason that the greater the supply, the greater the chances of survival or, for that matter, the higher the quality of performance. The quite appreciable thinning of the original equipment sets in Ghana led us in Chapter 8 to conjecture over what a 'critical mass' of equipment might comprise under various circumstances. Similarly, the part played by the Montessori-trained teacher in Malaysia again raises consideration of whether or not there might be circumstances when the presence of one or two personnel of quality might be more important than a greater number of less well suited personnel. However, the absence of definitive principles forces us to a rather weak generalization.

Proposition 8
The persistence of an innovation is a function of the availability of a critical

mass of resources (plant, personnel and people). A critical mass deficiency results in failure.

Although it is a far from profound statement to make about resources – 'enough is (it seems) enough'.

Personnel, on the other hand, cannot be regarded in quite the same way. The literature on the desirable qualities of innovators is more characterized by the enthusiasm of the advocacy than the presence of evidence. Certainly, little has been done on the mix of qualities needed within an organization if innovations are to both surface and persist. We suspect the human qualities needed *in combination* within any sub-system will defy ready identification for a long time yet.

Nonetheless if the road to educational development is strewn with the debris of shattered innovations, as it appears to be, then one of the continuing problems is to find out to what extent personnel factors contribute to the breakdown. One factor that seems to crop up repeatedly is the extent to which the people involved with an innovation can continue to work at it. The research on experimental schools tends to show a rapid turnover of key personnel. The very adventurous Kensington School experiment (Smith and Keith, 1971) is a case in point. Within two years, none of the original innovative school teachers remained. The Whanau House school in our study has an almost identical record. Now, two years after the beginning, only one of the original team of teachers survives. The Kensington School reverted to conventional type. The Whanau House gives indications of going the same route. On the other hand, the very adventurous and ambitious Bunumbu project has had, for an innovation, an unusual measure of indigenous staff stability in the top positions. And that innovation continues to persist – spectacularly. Proposition 9 addresses the point.

Proposition 9
The persistence of an innovation is a function of personnel stability – the greater the stability, the longer the persistence.

The final proposition in this set is a particularly important one because it calls into question a basic position taken regularly in the research literature. Explanation follows.

Innovation, success or failure At the beginning of this book attention was drawn to the lamentable record of innovations. Innovations usually fail, we said. We said that in good faith, believing the evidence from the literature. Now we have reason to revise that position. It is not that the evidence is wrong – it is not. It is just that we think the way that success and failure have been regarded is wrong.

If, as we assert, the education system (and even the country) is full of groups who (legitimately) have different interests and different perspectives, and if a number of these interest groups are together involved in an innovation then, predictably, the interests of some will take precedence over the interests of others. Predictably too, as the innovation evolves, these different interest groups will exert their pressures differently, now pulling, now pushing, but continuously affecting the passage of the innovation. All the events likely to influence the future of an innovation (from oil crises to military coups to the non-arrival of consultants and the 'promotion' of key personnel, for example) could not be expected to be anticipated before the innovation began. Consequently it seems reasonable to assume that any innovation worth its salt should be able (within reason) to adapt to the pressures that from time to time are brought to bear on it.

Proposition 10
Persistence of an innovation is a function of its adaptability. The greater the adaptability, the greater the likelihood of persistence.

However, it would be wrong to assume that it is only the innovation that needs to be adaptable. There may well be stronger justification for the system to change from time to time; thus any *education system* worth *its* salt should demonstrate a degree of adaptability and flexibility, showing itself able to exploit to advantage the situations that occur.

It follows from this line of argument that rather than taking 'failure to achieve stated objectives' as the criterion for evaluating an innovation, as has traditionally been the case, there would be good grounds for shifting to an *effects* criterion – one that focuses on what happened as a result of beginning and carrying on the innovation process. Fairly clearly, such an approach would have to be culturally sensitive – recognizing that no innovation (as a boundary-maintaining system) has complete control over events. It would also have to be broad visioned, looking not only for anticipated effects but unanticipated effects also. The thalidomide syndrome could apply in education too. The damage that some side effects may cause could, in theory, far outweigh the benefits of some desirable but less important direct effects (and thalidomide *was* a very efficient sleeping pill!). Consequently, a significant feature of effects analysis would have to be the recognition of extenuating circumstances, conditions both within the evolving innovation and outside it, that had to be taken into account. To this end it may become necessary to assess both the innovation's capability to be adaptable (as, in our study, the Continuation Schools in Ghana were) and the education system's capacity to be (reasonably) adaptable too (as the Malaysian system was in the early years of the Improved Curriculum Project).

Admittedly, such an orientation shifts the emphasis away from 'success' or 'failure' to relative usefulness, placing an emphasis on what happens because of the innovation. Paradoxically this leads to the theoretical possibility that, by being terminated, an innovation may become successful – that is, if conditions in the system no longer warrant continuation and if the effects of stopping would be more beneficial than the effects of carrying on. However, this is no more paradoxical than the circumstances existing at the moment that admit of the possibility that an innovation that has met its objectives has succeeded, even though its effects may be totally disadvantageous all round. Evaluation in the sense we are considering now would thus become a means for determining both the system's and the innovation's capacity for 'creative' adaptation, in particular, to each other.

The last two remaining propositions refer to two matters with which planners and administrators have to contend repeatedly – the questions 'how long will it take?' and 'how much can be accomplished?'

Given the paucity of definitive evidence on the duration of innovations it is tempting to invoke Harrary's flippant law, 'No matter how long you think it will take it will take twice as long!' Any number of events can conspire to delay the operation. In our studies, the Whanau House was 'delayed' by the lack of a critical building component. The Bunumbu project was 'delayed' by Unesco's liquidity crisis. In some Indonesian schools, conversion to modular instruction was 'delayed' by an interruption in the supply of modules. In Malaysia, the 'delay' was caused by the lack of available expertise initially – and so on.

Unfortunately our study is also equivocal about the effects of the delays. In some cases they seemed to be even advantageous, in others quite detrimental. We are led thus to another weak generalization that is concerned rather with the conditions under which 'interruptions' may be avoided. Presumably the avoidance of interruptions depends on the appropriate sequence of events, so that no event precedes another on which it is dependent. What is at stake here is logistical efficiency – coordination.

Proposition 11
The amount of time taken in the innovation process is a function of the sequencing and coordinating of events: the more precise the coordination, the faster the process.

Whether speed is desirable or beneficial is quite another question. So too is whether investment in planning is worth the benefit of avoiding delays.

The final proposition that deals with the magnitude of change that is tolerable is also not without its enigmatic characteristics. Explanation follows.

We have found it useful to regard the interface between the innovation and the established system as a problem in the *negotiation of social control –* in our cases control of school knowledge. The fundamental questions that follow then are: Under what terms may control be negotiated? What mechanisms seem useful? How will negoitiation affect events? If we start with an established education system it is reasonable to expect that the various tasks performed and offices provided for can be seen as a structure – the kind of structure that features in the inevitable organizational chart. Further examination of the system is likely to reveal that there are a variety of mechanisms, from committees to consultations to inspections to auditings, etc, which enable the functions of the system to be carried out (to greater or lesser effect) and which sustain the structure in its appointed shape. Further scrutiny should show, however, that there are many informal mechanisms as well that aid in this process by providing both access (where official procedures do not) and ways round those bureaucratic procedures that might otherwise be restricting. It is not hard to imagine, and not completely impossible to produce, a map of such interacting elements, the paths that link them and the kind of functions entailed. If this were done, it would then be possible to see each component part of the education system as a boundary-maintaining entity with, of course, its definition of its relevant reality, its norms of behaviour and its values. What might also become apparent is the degree to which the whole system was in a relatively stable state – in equilibrium, if you like. Equilibrium presumably exists when the various elements, having established their own integrity, respect the integrity of others and have their own integrity respected in turn. In a stable system there are, in fact, few intrusions on 'territory' and threats to the integrities of the various sub-groups.

As our study showed, education systems seem to vary in the extent to which they have established equilibrium. It was obvious that Ghana, in the early years of the Development Schools project, was beset by all kinds of economic and political problems that resulted in a great state of political and economic flux in the country. Some of that flux obviously flowed over into education. It seemed apparent too that Malaysia and Indonesia, while making rapid strides since independence, were still not satisfied that their educational infrastructure was yet developed or staffed with the diversity of skills to the level thought desirable. By contrast, the older systems in New Zealand and the Federal Republic of Germany had reached a relative degree of stability – perhaps even rigidity.

In our study we discerned two strategies of planning that seemed to be associated with the extent to which education systems were still in a condition of flux. Those countries whose systems had had time to 'shake down' or consolidate (or ossify!) tended towards *reactive planning*, that is they relied on their capacity to respond to problems as they arose rather than going so far as to develop a set of procedures to anticipate them in advance. The other, younger systems, depending on the extent to which they envisaged change as imperative, tended to adopt a *proactive planning stance*, attempting to devise and work towards quite distant solutions. In a sense the reactive planners were only engaged in 'fine-tuning' action. The proactive planners, on the other hand, were concerned with major changes, even substantial 'reconstruction' of their systems.

It is our contention that in both cases these strategies represent not only a response to what was thought to be needed by the system but also a recognition of what was and was not possible. Given our earlier amoebic model, in a system that is already in a state of considerable flux, boundaries, by definition, are being redrawn regularly. There is thus in the system an expectation that boundary changes are likely and may even be advantageous. In other words, territories and benefits are still negotiable. In long-established systems, the territorial lines are much clearer: territorial rights and responsibilities are known. 'Protection' thus becomes the *modus operandi*. In other words, in a 'settled' system the sub-systems are ready to repel intrusions –

and that, of course, includes innovations and innovators. This leads us to the final proposition.

Proposition 12
The amount and size of educational change possible is a function of the degree of flux existing within both the education system and the embedding society. The greater the flux, the greater the potential for change.

It follows then that in established systems even small changes may invoke strenuous opposition. Systems still in a state of rapid growth are likely to accommodate to small changes easily and it will tend to be only at larger ones that opposition will be directed.

Stock taking

It is perhaps not altogether surprising that in focusing on the process of innovation as we have, we have come to the conclusion that giving more attention to the process will be likely to pay dividends for planners and administrators. This, in a sense, is little more than a reaffirmation of our earlier expressed belief in the usefulness of 'monitoring' and 'troubleshooting' procedures. To this extent we have come full circle. What is perhaps a little surprising – to ourselves even – is that we have been led by our study to place such an emphasis on the interfaces between the 'innovation' and the 'system' and accordingly, to regard the adaptive capacities of both as being perhaps the most critical aspect. That we have finished up there, however, is to some extent proper because it raises the essential question of the very purpose of innovation. Two alternative stances appear to be available. The first tends to regard each innovation in isolation. The second adopts a more global view. Studies of *individual* innovations usually tend to make the assumption that the particular innovation, once incorporated into the system, will upgrade it. Thus a replacement curriculum for arithmetic will upgrade the arithmetic performance of the target population. The prime concern then becomes to ensure that the specific innovation comes to function – is put into operation efficiently. In the light of our analysis of the process of innovation such a position (though legitimate) is quite myopic because it fails to take into account the plethora of direct and side effects such an action might have on the system right from the time it begins until (perhaps long) after it has finished. Such 'one-shot' views of innovation can ignore the ramifications of 'innovating'. Presumably, however, the planner and administrator cannot. To them, immediate, short-term and long-term consequences on the system are of prime concern. Consequently if innovations have 'ripple' effects (Kounin and Gump, 1958) throughout the system, it becomes the job of the administrator and planner to comprehend the speed, direction and magnitude of those effects and, where necessary, control them – again throughout the whole innovation process. Given that all innovations have the capacity to produce multiple effects, some of which may have been anticipated and some of which may not have been, and given that some of these effects may be beneficial and some may not be, how does the register of accounts balance up over all? What is at issue here is not just whether individual innovations have separate effects but whether the total quantum of innovation in a system has general effects. The prime concern in this case is not with the efficient operation of the specific innovation but its manifold effects – its effectiveness if you like. Can the level of intensity of innovating be too low, serving to encourage stagnation? Is there an optimum level where the amount is just right? The present study at the moment cannot supply an answer. Admittedly some of our countries were more 'innovation prone' than others but then their local circumstances were notably different. It did seem as if the more established systems tended to be less ambitious in their conception of innovation, preferring small adjustments rather than major ones.

Also we have to admit that in following the approach we did, we have confined our attention to officially sanctioned innovations, some admittedly having stronger support than others. This means that an important class of innovations is largely absent from these pages. Grass roots innovations that have developed spontaneously as the result of local initiatives *outside* the framework of official approval are not included. Even the Israeli innovation, which had a kind of grass roots origin, soon received a measure of official blessing. It may be the case then that had grass roots innovations been included we would have benefited from an enlarged awareness and there would have been a better basis for seeing to what extent the evolving processes of 'top-down' innovation and 'bottom-up' innovation are similar or different. We think that the principles implicit in the two processes are fundamentally the same but we do not have the means to substantiate such an assertion. Presumably also, the inclusion of grass roots innovations might have led to some conclusions about the effects of innovating as such. For example, do grass roots innovations that spread by diffusion, gradually (and relatively painlessly), have benefits that ordained innovations do not? Do they engender greater acceptance of change? Do they encourage greater initiative? Do they result in distributed (rather than delegated or centralized) responsibility? Or do they not?

There are several other features of the study of innovation that have necessarily been neglected. In these pages we have not undertaken an analysis of different types of innovation, classifying them and attempting to draw conclusions relevant to their differences. We were confined by our concern for a certain kind of innovation – qualitative innovation attempting to induce changes in teacher behaviour and (it is hoped) consequential improvements in pupils' performance. Thus we swiftly passed over one of the most favoured innovatory devices of administrators and planners – structural innovation. Our reason for doing so is that we find considerable difficulty in seeing how changes in the structure of a system – even its allocation of personnel to tasks – will make much difference to the function of teaching. The lesson from history largely appears to be that teachers rarely change what they do *because* the system has been reorganized structurally.

In a similar way we have not made any value judgements of the worth or desirability of each innovation. There are several reasons for this that even transcend political and diplomatic necessity. Our concern has been with the planning and administering of innovations. In the present study, that has led us to be preoccupied with the way in which innovations develop and evolve. Whether an innovation is good or bad not only depends on the eye of the beholder but is also rather incidental to the problem of drawing 'general' conclusions about the process of innovating. This, of course, is not to deny the importance of judging and pre-judging innovations – of justifying the social appropriateness of any innovation in its context. But that is a problem for a different type of study. In our case, given the existence of the innovation, it was for us a matter of tracking it: monitoring, as it were, its progress. It was not our role to endorse (or condemn) any of the innovations *per se* – we had neither the mandate nor the need to do so.

This has led us into a politically neutral stance which has, in effect, left us not taking a specific ideological side although it has left us tacitly taking the side of the existing status quo. To this extent we have studied the process of innovation as it has occurred within the existing political and power structures of our seven countries. To the extent that those political structures serve to preserve the ideological status quo and to the extent that any innovation is constrained and contained by the prevailing ideology and power structure, so possibly are the findings of our study similarly constrained and contained. Without a broader and more diversified selection of countries we are simply in no position to draw conclusions about the effects of ideological differences. Neither are we in a position to attribute ideological cause to our findings.

At this moment in the study there is an amount of unfinished business left. Of course, all of the seven innovations continue to continue, but each approaches a critical stage. In Israel, the decision to implement or not is less than a year away. Under normal circumstances, that decision would be taken by the Ministry (to be followed by government authorization). But will the growth of grass roots support influence the Government or the Ministry? Might the decision even be taken out of the hands of the Ministry, at one stroke perpetuating NILI and gaining the municipalities new power and authority? In Ghana, at the exact moment of writing, a new military coup has occurred and the plans for a return to civilian government are, at least temporarily, in question. Will new developments affect the new educational restructuring proposed? Will the Continuation Schools after all continue, *de facto*, as they are doing at the moment? In New Zealand, a full Whanau House school is being built and will open in 1980. But national school roll projections show a continuing decline (accelerated by an increasing rate of emigration). Will there be any great need for more schools and will the worsening economic situation see a return to the old S68 prototype favoured, as a climate of conservatism and caution comes to prevail generally? In Malaysia, the Improved Curriculum Project makes steady progress and is due shortly to move into an expanded phase. During it, the main burden of teacher training is to be carried by the principals of the schools. Will this (theoretically very astute) strategy work? Alternatively, will some of the more spectacular of the numerous other projects being mounted in Malaysia capture the limelight at the expense of this particular project? In Sierra Leone, the Bunumbu project is about to come up to full strength as the College buildings are completed and the additional new students arrive. To what extent will the new scale of operation affect the smooth running of the project? And what will happen later to the graduates? Will they go to country schools or will they follow the bright lights to town? How will the campaign to involve other areas than those round Bunumbu fare – given the road, the transport service and power and water supplies? In Indonesia, the modules are gradually finding their way into schools outside the experimental set and, as well, are destined to be used extensively in the new open schools. Will they work? Will the results of tests on this new population require the rewriting of curriculum materials? And how will 'individualized instruction' be received in the teaching profession? In the Federal Republic of Germany another moment of truth approaches for the BVJ. As a follow-up to legislation, a project to discern and assess what is happening to BVJ pupils is getting under way. What will it reveal about what the schools are actually doing? What will the results turn out to be? What will be the consequences if unemployment continues to rise?

Beyond the separate studies, however, the IIEP has its own unfinished business. So far, in its project an embryo theory has been produced. It needs to grow, to be fleshed out, expanded to cover more of the many aspects of the process of innovation still uncovered. Further it needs to be tested. And this entails a more direct attack on the issues it raises. For example if, as the theory asserts, the acceptability of an innovation hinges both on the extent to which and the way in which power is brought to its aid, what constitutes an optimum extent and what ways are effective? In other words, the theory merely supplies an orientation. It says, look in these general directions – or rather 'look out' for difficulties from these general directions. There are as yet a number of unanswered questions about how best to 'look' or 'look out'. For example, we talked of 'routes of passage' through the system. What kind of system mapping is implied (and is possible)? What sort of information is likely to be considered useful? In other words, if monitoring is important, and we think it is, what procedures might be employed? If trouble-sensing is important, and we think it is, what are the indicators of potential trouble? If trouble-shooting is important, and we think that is too, what methods are likely to be effective?

We spoke, too, with airy ease about 'effects monitoring', emphasizing in particular unintended, unanticipated or side effects. What effects need to be mapped? We implied that the view had to be much broader than a narrow educational one, broad enough, in fact, to cover not only minor matters of local politics but presumably, on occasion, major national matters too. Clearly, cost and plant and equipment issues cannot be left out of the equation. Tied up with the general monitoring issue too is the question of context links. What contexts ought to be taken into account, and when? Implied here is the development of a kind of context network analysis, a kind of sociometric mapping of the various interest groups on which any innovation might impinge. Even a limited catalogue like this only raises a number of questions about the kind of monitoring procedures that would be most useful.

Such general questions about the process of innovation seem to apply with particular force to the implementation phase. In the present study we have had to opt out of consideration of implementation primarily because six of our seven innovations have not yet arrived there. Whether or not the seventh (Ghana) produced a rare and atypical form of implementation is an open question. Certainly the decision was made deliberately to expand the Continuation Schools scheme and the expansion was begun. But the surface of the target group was barely scratched before the idea behind the Continuation Schools became incorporated into the general educational development plan. Whether or not such an evolution is typical or not is unknown. But if it is a common variation of the implementation theme, then clearly the implications are quite different from those commonly believed to go hand-in-hand with systematic, step-by-step implementations.

At this stage in the study, then, there are still many unknowns and desiderata. It would be desirable, for instance, to know more about trends in innovations, indicators of effective innovation practice, circumstances that facilitate survival and growth of innovations, and the conditions necessary and sufficient for effective innovation. It would be also desirable to know more of what strategies are suitable under what circumstances. What, for instance, are the relative merits of Havelock and Huberman's (1977) four strategies, and for what purpose is each best suited? What, too, are the organizational conditions most appropriate for one strategy or another?

The questions, it seems, are endless. And to finish the book on such a note of uncertainty is distressingly unimaginative. Like so many other research studies we have arrived triumphantly at the conclusion that what is needed is...more research! The one point we would make in defence, though, is that this time to the researcher's (not altogether disinterested) voice has been added that of the administrator-planner. And if they *both* think so, it *must* be true!

Bibliography

Abdul Hamid bin Ayob and Syed Omar bin Syed Ahmad (1978) *The development of the improved primary project for the first three years in primary school in Malaysia.* Unpublished seminar paper. Paris: IIEP.

Adams, Raymond S (1975) *Educational planning: towards a qualitative perspective.* Paris: IIEP.

Anim, N O and Bassa-Kwansa, K (1978) *The continuation education system in Ghana.* Unpublished seminar paper. Paris: IIEP.

Awang, H Salleh (1977) *Sustainability of change in education.* Unpublished paper, Seminar on early childhood. Brussels: Bernard van Leer Foundation.

Beeby, C E (1966) *The quality of education in developing countries.* Cambridge, Massachusetts: Harvard University Press.

Berufsvorbereitungsjahr Richtlinien (1976) *Die Schule in Nordrhein-Westfalen. Eine Schriftenreihe des Kultusministers.* Dortmund.

Chen, David (1977) *The individualized learning instruction strategy project – NILI.* Seminar paper number 34. Paris: IIEP.

Dalin, P (1978) *Limits to educational change.* London: Macmillan.

Ghana Ministry of Education (1974) *The new structure and content of education for Ghana.* Accra.

Government of Malaysia (1976) *Third Malaysian Plan 1976-1980.* Kuala Lumpur: Jabatan Cetak Kerajaan.

Havelock, R G and Huberman, A M (1977) *Solving educational problems: the planning and reality of innovation in developing countries.* Paris: Unesco.

House, Ernest R (1979) Technology and craft: a ten-year perspective on innovation, London, *Journal of Curriculum Studies*, **II**, 1, January-March.

Howarth, T (1977) Schools and people, *Education*, **26**, 7 (NZ).

Hunter, G (1966) *South East Asia: race, culture and nation.* London: Oxford University Press.

Kounin, J S and Gump, P V (1958) The ripple effect in discipline, *Elementary School Journal*, **35**.

Labor, A, N'geba, F, Pessima, J, Hedd, G and Lucan, T Arie (1978) *The Bunumbu project: a case study.* Freetown: Institute of Education, University of Sierra Leone.

Levin, H M (1975) Qualitative planning: a broad view, Chapter IV *in* Raymond S Adams, *op cit.*

Malaysia Ministry of Education (1957) Education Committee Report (Malaysia RAZAK Committee). Kuala Lumpur.

Malaysia Ministry of Education (1960) *Education Review Committee Report (Abdul Rahman Tahlib Committee)*. Kuala Lumpur.

Marklund, Sixten *et al* (1974) *New patterns of teacher education and tasks; country experience, Sweden*. Paris: OECD.

McWilliam, H O A and Kwamena-Poh, M A (1975) *Development of education in Ghana*. London: Longman.

Miles, M B (ed) (1964) *Innovation in education*. New York: Bureau of Publications, Teachers College, Columbia University.

Miller, T W G (ed) (1968) *Education in South East Asia*. Sydney: Novak.

Munro, R G (1977) *The Hillary Whanau unit*. Case Study VIII. The Auckland Project on Classroom Monitoring. Unpublished document. Secondary Teachers College. Auckland, New Zealand.

Murad Bin Mohd Noor (1973) *Lapuran; Jawatankuasa di atas kajian pendapat mengenai pelajaran dan masyarakat (Lapuran keciciran)*. Bahagian Perancang dan Penyelidikan Pelajaran Kementerian Pelajaran dan Jabatan Perangkaan.

New Zealand Department of Education (1975) *Secondary schools for tomorrow: a new approach to design and construction*. Wellington.

Nordin, Megat M (1972) Public bureaucracy as a change agent in a plural society: a case study of the Malaysian civil service as an agent of change. Unpublished thesis. Pittsburgh: University of Pittsburgh.

Richland, M (1965) *Final report: Travelling seminar and conference for the implementation of educational innovations*. Santa Monica, California: Systems Analysis Corp.

Roff, W R (1967) *The origins of Malay nationals*. Kuala Lumpur: University of Malaya Press and Yale University Press.

Schacham, Igal (1978) *The Israel education system as a changing system*. Unpublished paper. Jerusalem: Ministry of Finance.

Schacham, Igal and Chen, David (1978) *The educational system in Israel: a suggestion for change*. Unpublished seminar paper. Paris: IIEP.

Smith, Louis M and Keith, P M (1971) *Anatomy of educational innovation*. New York: Wiley.

Soedijarto (1977) *The modular instructional system as a teaching-learning strategy in the Indonesian development school*. Seminar paper number 31. Paris: IIEP.

Spies, W (1978) *Behaviour modification in prevocational training in schools*. Unpublished seminar paper. Paris: IIEP.

Soeprapto, Benny and Ibrahim, R (1978) *Modular instruction project in the Indonesian development schools*. Unpublished seminar paper. Paris: IIEP.